THE CHARTERED INSTITUTE OF MARKETING

Professional Diploma in Marketing

STUDY TEXT

Managing Marketing

Valid for assessments up to September 2013

The Chartered
Institute of Marketing

BPP
LEARNING MEDIA

First edition July 2012

ISBN 9781 4453 9147 2

e-ISBN 9781 4453 7620 2

British Library Cataloguing-in-Publication Data
A catalogue record for this book
is available from the British Library

Published by

BPP Learning Media Ltd
Aldine House, Aldine Place
142-144 Uxbridge Road
London W12 8AA

www.bpp.com/learningmedia

Printed in the United Kingdom by Polestar Wheatons

Hennock Road
Marsh Barton Industrial Estate
Exeter, Devon
EX2 8RP

Your learning materials, published by BPP Learning
Media Ltd, are printed on paper obtained from
traceable sustainable sources.

The Chartered
Institute of Marketing

Contents

1 Studying for The Chartered Institute of Marketing (CIM) qualifications

There are a few key points to remember as you study for your CIM qualification:

(a) You are studying for a **professional** qualification. This means that you are required to use professional language and adopt a business approach in your work.

(b) You are expected to show that you have 'read widely'. Make sure that you read the quality press (and don't skip the business pages), *Marketing*, *The Marketer*, *Research* and *Marketing Week* avidly.

(c) Become aware of the marketing initiatives you come across on a daily basis, for example, when you go shopping look around and think about why the store layout is as it is; consider the messages, channel choice and timings of ads when you are watching TV. It is surprising how much you will learn just by taking an interest in the marketing world around you.

(d) Get to know the way CIM write their exam papers and assignments. They use a specific approach (the Magic Formula) which is to ensure a consistent approach when designing assessment materials. Make sure you are fully aware of this as it will help you interpret what the examiner is looking for (a full description of the Magic Formula appears later).

(e) Learn how to use Harvard referencing. This is explained in detail in our CIM Professional Diploma Assessment Workbook.

(f) Ensure that you read very carefully all assessment details sent to you from CIM. There are strict deadlines to meet, as well as paperwork to complete for any assignment or project you do. Failing to meet any assessment entry deadlines or completing written work on time will mean that you will have to wait for the next round of assessment dates and will need to pay the relevant assessment fees again.

2 The Professional Diploma Syllabus

The Professional Diploma in Marketing is aimed at anyone who is employed in a marketing management role such as Brand Manager, Account Manager or Marketing Executive. If you are a graduate, you will be expected to have covered a minimum of a third of your credits in marketing subjects. You are therefore expected at this level of the qualification to be aware of the key marketing theories and be able to apply them to different organisational contexts.

The aim of the qualification is to provide the knowledge and skills for you to develop an 'ability to do' in relation to marketing planning. CIM qualifications concentrate on applied marketing within real workplaces.

The complete qualification is made from four units:

- Unit 1 The Marketing Planning Process
- Unit 2 Delivering Customer Value through Marketing
- Unit 3 Managing Marketing
- Unit 4 Project Management in Marketing

CIM stipulates that each module should take 50 guided learning hours to complete. Guided learning hours refer to time in class, using distance learning materials and completing any work set by your tutor. Guided learning hours do not include the time it will take you to complete the necessary reading for your studies.

The syllabus as provided by CIM can be found below with reference to our coverage within this Study Text.

Unit characteristics – Managing Marketing

The focus of this unit is about developing the marketer as a manager, including giving them the knowledge and understanding required to develop and manage the marketing infrastructure and the organisation's talent development, capability and capacity. This includes developing effective quality systems and processes to support compliance and approaches to measuring and monitoring marketing activities.

The unit also includes developing and managing marketing teams, which includes co-ordinating the human, financial and physical resources within the team effectively.

Finally, the unit includes developing a detailed understanding of managing the financial aspects of the marketing function and its associated activities in order to ensure that the financial performance of the function is consistent, reliable and effective.

By the end of this unit, students should be able to demonstrate how they would approach the management of the marketing function and its associated marketing teams, including effective resource and financial management.

Overarching learning outcomes

By the end of this unit students should be able to:

- Recommend how a marketing function should be structured to deliver competitive advantage, marketing and organisational success

- Assess a range of approaches that can be used to manage the marketing function on a day-to-day basis

- Prepare plans for showing how a team should be structured, selected, formed, managed and developed to demonstrate effective performance against objectives

- Critically assess the organisation's resource needs and capabilities for the marketing team and manage its marketing activities effectively and efficiently

- Prepare appropriate budgets and accounting documentation to support the financial management of the marketing function and associated marketing activities

- Critically assess the ongoing financial situation including manageability of the budget, financial stability and success of the marketing function.

SECTION 1 – The marketing infrastructure (weighting 30%)

		Covered in chapter(s)
1.1	Critically evaluate the importance of organisational structures in delivering marketing value, focus and creativity including consideration of how the work of the marketing operations is going to be undertaken: ■ Functional structure ■ Product/market structure ■ Brand structure ■ Territory structure ■ Matrix structure ■ International and multinational organisational structures	1
1.2	Critically assess the requirements of developing effective and efficient quality systems and processes to support compliance including evaluating and assessing the relevance of key quality concepts: ■ The importance of quality systems to the organisation ■ A range of quality models eg Total Quality Management, European Foundation of Quality Management, ISO 9001, Six Sigma, ISO 14001, PAS2050, benchmarking ■ PDCA Cycle – Plan, Do, Check, Act ■ Deming 14 steps for improving quality	2
1.3	Determine innovative and effective methods of measuring and monitoring marketing performance for marketing operation, marketing activities and effective resource management: ■ Accounting measures of performance – profit and loss, balance sheets, cash flow and budgetary control ■ Productivity measures of performance – inputs versus outputs ■ Relationship marketing and customer related measures – retention, satisfaction and communication ■ Internal measures of performance – recruitment, retention, attitude, performance, communications ■ Innovation and learning measures of performance	3
1.4	Critically analyse monitoring information and recommend ways in which to improve marketing performance: ■ Productivity analysis – inputs versus outputs ■ Comparative analysis – measuring changes over time ■ Segmental analysis – analysis of markets ■ Innovation audit – organisational climate, current performance, policies, practices and cognitive styles ■ Competitor comparisons and benchmarking	3

SECTION 2 – Managing marketing teams (weighting 40%)

		Covered in chapter(s)
2.1	Critically evaluate the differences between management and leadership and identify the role of an 'operational marketing manager':	4
	▪ Leadership traits, skills and attitude	
	▪ Leadership and management styles eg Action-Centred Leadership, Transactional Leadership, Transformational Leadership, Situational Leadership, the management styles continuum	
	▪ The scope of leadership – providing strategic direction	
	▪ The manager's role – planning, organising, co-ordinating, controlling, communication, team-building, coaching, networking, developing the functions of the marketing manager – information, value creation, communications	
	▪ Reflect on personal approach to management and leadership and produce a personal development plan	
2.2	Determine the needs for and show how to establish and build synergistic and harmonious marketing teams including preparing a plan to show how teams should be structured to deliver organisational and marketing objectives:	4
	▪ Structuring the team – the team audit, functional roles, team roles	
	▪ Team development and talent management – stages in team development, team cohesiveness, high performance teams, the manager's role	
	▪ Job analysis, job design, job enlargement, job enrichment	
	▪ Competency development requirements	
	▪ Flexible working practices	
	▪ Assess and apply a range of team theories eg Belbin's team roles, Tuckman's stages of team development	
2.3	Propose a range of approaches for the sourcing of a team, including consideration of recruitment, training and development to provide the right balance of competency and skills:	4
	▪ Recruitment channels – internally and externally	
	▪ Selection tools – job description, person specification	
	▪ Selection techniques – assessment centres, interviews	
	▪ On-boarding – induction	
	▪ Training and development	
	▪ Outsourcing of jobs/projects	
	▪ Recruitment evaluation – determining recruitment effectiveness	
	▪ Legal considerations when recruiting	
2.4	Plan how the work of the team will be undertaken establishing priorities and critical activities required to meet marketing and organisational objectives and with customers in mind:	5
	▪ Performance management and measurement – marketing strategy and individual objectives, communicating standards, techniques to measure performance against objectives and standards	
	▪ Internal marketing – aligning internal communications with external communications, managing knowledge	

The Chartered Institute of Marketing

		Covered in chapter(s)
2.5	Propose approaches to manage and co-ordinate the work of teams and individuals to create effective working relations including appropriate levels of consultation, taking into account the balance of skills and activities available: ■ Characteristics of effective teamwork/high performing teams ■ Management skills and techniques – communication, motivation, empowerment, involvement, delegation, task allocation, feedback, running effective meetings, listening, assertiveness, group decision making ■ Assess and apply a range of management theories eg McGregor's Theory X/Y, Maslow's Hierarchy of Needs, Herzberg's Motivation-Hygiene Theory, McClelland's Motivation Needs Theory, Vroom's Expectancy Theory ■ Job enrichment/enlargement ■ Preventing discrimination and valuing diversity – equal opportunities and employment law ■ Reflect on personal approach to team management and produce a personal development plan ■ Flexible working practices	5
2.6	Propose approaches to manage and co-ordinate the work of remote teams to create effective working relations: ■ Managing international teams, cultural considerations eg Hofstede's Cultural Dimensions, Trompenaar's Cross Cultural Communication ■ Managing virtual teams – benefits and constraints	5
2.7	Identify potential areas of team conflict, identifying causes and making recommendations for ways in which to overcome it: ■ Sources of conflict – interpersonal, change, organisational, external environment ■ Cultural differences ■ Assess the impact of conflict both positively and negatively ■ Conflict resolution and management ■ Change management strategies	6
2.8	Critically assess levels of performance in order to identify poor performance and reasons for it and recommendations of how to overcome it including consideration of loyalty and motivation programmes: ■ Performance management – measuring performance against objectives and standards and providing feedback ■ Appraisal and peer review including 360 degree feedback ■ Internal marketing – employee motivation and satisfaction, customer orientation and satisfaction, inter-functional co-ordination ■ Competency assessment and achievement	6

SECTION 3 – Operational finances for marketing (weighting 30%)

		Covered in chapter(s)
3.1	Assess the different requirements of managing the finances of the marketing function and associated marketing activities: ■ The manager's role – control, managing information, cross-functional communication ■ The purpose of budgeting – planning, co-ordination of activities, motivation, control, relationship to management of the marketing team ■ Budget considerations – fixed, semi-fixed, variable and semi-variable costs	7
3.2	Critically evaluate the different approaches to setting the marketing and communications budget and associated marketing activities: ■ Top-down budgets, bottom-up budgets ■ The financial approach to setting budget – the budgeting process, percentage of sales/profit, competitive parity, affordable method ■ The marketing approach – the planning and control process, objective and task approach, Share of Voice, cost-volume-profit ■ Forecasting, financial analysis, balanced scorecard, resourcing	7
3.3	Evaluate the different information sources required to determine the marketing budget for marketing operations and activities: ■ Data, information, intelligence and knowledge ■ Internal data sources – sales figures, headcount, outsourcing costs, consultant costs, electronic point of sales (EPOS) system, MkIS external data sources including exchange rates variances arising from international trading	7
3.4	Negotiate delegated budgets with colleagues and agree provisional budgets: ■ Preparing a budget bid/business case to obtain priority budget for marketing activities ■ Negotiation tactics for bidding internally for budget to senior management	8
3.5	Undertake cost benefit analysis of marketing activities establishing priorities and best value approaches to operations: ■ The balanced scorecard – learning and growth perspective, business process perspective, customer perspective, financial perspective ■ Value chain analysis ■ Cost control, cost improvement ■ Cost-volume-profit analysis ■ Break-even analysis ■ Sensitivity analysis	8
3.6	Establish effective cost management processes for marketing operations to ensure that costs are managed effectively to achieve viability in the long-term: ■ Variance analysis – sales variance, cost variance ■ Cost control ■ Activity-based costing ■ Business process re-engineering	8

3.7	Assess budget variances, identify causes and recommend corrective actions where appropriate:	9
	■ Internal variance – organisational, impact of marketing strategy, internal constraints, product portfolio, international exchange rates	
	■ External variance – the macro environment, customers, competitors, partners, suppliers, external stakeholders	
	■ Reconciling variances	
3.8	Establish systems to monitor, evaluate and report on the financial performance of marketing operations and associated activities against the delegated budget:	9
	■ Stated standards of performance, KPIs, qualitative and quantitative standards	
	■ Internal sources of data – operating statements, expenditure, profit forecasts, cash flow statements, MIS, MkIS	
	■ Actual versus forecast	
	■ Plans to improve performance – cost reduction, marketing activities	

3 Assessment

The Managing Marketing unit is assessed by a choice of assignment (one from two) each with a number of set tasks to complete.

In order to help you to prepare for the assessment we have also written a Professional Diploma in Marketing Assessment Workbook which is available either through your usual book retailer or our website www.bpp.com/learningmedia.

4 The Magic Formula

The Magic Formula is a tool used by CIM to help both examiners write exam and assignment questions, and you, to more easily interpret what you are being asked to write about. It is useful for helping you to check that you are using an appropriate balance between theory and practice for your particular level of qualification.

Contrary to the title, there is nothing mystical about the Magic Formula and simply by knowing it (or even mentioning it in an assessment) will not automatically secure a pass. What it does do, however, is to help you to check that you are presenting your answers in an appropriate format, including enough marketing theory and applying it to a real marketing context or issue.

The Magic Formula for the Professional Diploma in Marketing is shown below:

Figure A   The Magic Formula for the Professional Diploma in Marketing

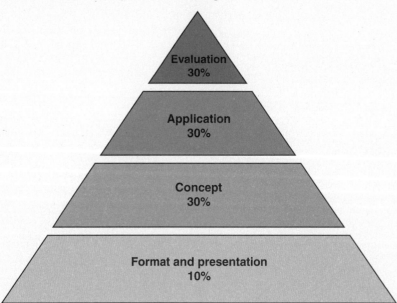

You can see from the pyramid that for the Professional Diploma marks are awarded in the following proportions:

- **Presentation and format – 10%**

    You are expected to present your work professionally which means that assignments and projects should **always** be typed. Even in an exam situation attention should be paid to making your work look as visually appealing as possible. CIM will also stipulate the format that you should present your work in. The assessment formats you will be given will be varied and can include things like reports to write,

The Chartered
Institute of Marketing

slides to prepare, emails, memos, formal letters, press releases, discussion documents, briefing papers, agendas and newsletters.

- **Concept – 30%**

  Concept refers to your ability to state, recall and describe marketing theory. The definition of marketing is a core CIM syllabus topic. If we take this as an example, you would be expected to recognise, recall and write this definition to a word perfect standard to gain the full marks for concept.

- **Application – 30%**

  Application based marks are given for your ability to apply marketing theories to real life marketing situations. For example, a question may ask you to discuss the definition of marketing and how it is applied within your own organisation. Here you are not only using the definition but are applying it in order to consider the market orientation of the company.

- **Evaluation – 30%**

  Evaluation is the ability to asses the value or worth of something, sometimes through careful consideration of related advantages and disadvantages, or weighing up of alternatives. Results from your evaluation should enable you to discuss the importance of an issue using evidence to support your opinions.

  For example, if you were asked to evaluate whether or not your organisation adopts a marketing approach you should provide reasons and specific examples of why you think they might take this approach, as well as considering why they may not take this approach, before coming to a final conclusion.

  You should have noticed that for the Professional Diploma, you are expected to consider the equal weightings of concept, application and evaluation in order to gain maximum marks in assessments.

5 A guide to the features of the Study Text

Each of the chapter features (see below) will help you to break down the content into manageable chunks and ensure that you are developing the skills required for a professional qualification.

Chapter feature	Relevance and how you should use it
Introduction	Shows why topics need to be studied and is a route guide through the chapter
Syllabus reference	Outlines the syllabus learning outcomes covered in the chapter
Chapter topic list	Study the list, each numbered topic denotes a numbered section in the chapter
Key term	Highlights the core vocabulary you need to learn
Activity	An application-based activity for you to complete
The Real World	A short case study to illustrate marketing practice
Exam tip/Assessment tip	Key advice based on the assessment
Chapter roundups	Use this to review what you have learnt
Quick quiz	Use this to check your learning
Further reading	Further reading will give you a wider perspective on the subjects you're covering

6 Additional resources

To help you pass the Professional Diploma in Marketing we have created a complete study package. The **Professional Diploma Assessment Workbook** covers all four units of the Professional Diploma level. Practice questions and answers, tips on tackling assignments and work-based projects are included to help you succeed in your assessments.

Our A6 set of spiral bound **Passcards** are handy revision cards and are ideal to reinforce key topics for the Managing Marketing assignment.

7 Your personal study plan

Preparing a Study Plan (and sticking to it) is one of the key elements to learning success.

CIM has stipulated that there should be a minimum of 50 guided learning hours spent on each unit. Guided learning hours will include time spent in lessons, working on distance learning materials, formal workshops and work set by your tutor. We also know that to be successful, students should spend **approximately 100 hours** conducting self study. This means that for the entire qualification with four units you should spend 200 hours working in a tutor-guided manner and approximately 400 hours completing recommended reading, working on assignments, and revising for exams. This Study Text will help you to organise this 100-hour portion of self study time.

Now think about the exact amount of time you have (don't forget you will still need some leisure time!) and complete the following tables to help you keep to a schedule.

	Date	Duration in weeks
Course start		
Course finish		Total weeks of course:

Assignment received	Submission date	Total weeks to complete

 The Chartered Institute of Marketing

Content chapter coverage plan

Chapter	To be completed by	Considered in relation to the assignment?
1 Organisational structures		
2 Quality systems and processes		
3 Measuring, monitoring and improving marketing performance		
4 Management, leadership and establishing teams		
5 Managing teams		
6 Improving team performance		
7 Budgeting for marketing		
8 Justifying and managing marketing finances		
9 Variance and monitoring		

Managing Marketing

The Chartered
Institute of Marketing

Section 1: The marketing infrastructure

Section 1 is concerned with establishing effective systems and processes to measure and improve marketing performance. It will describe how the marketing infrastructure impacts on the management activities that are explored in Section 2 (Managing Marketing Teams). Organisational structures are examined in detail along with the impact of the structure on work organisation, authority, relationships and job roles. It explores quality systems and processes, demonstrating how quality systems can be used to improve marketing performance.

Application of a range of methods for measuring marketing performance in different organisational contexts is dealt with, and you will therefore need to understand the models, concepts and theories in some detail to apply them to your studies.

Finally, this section will help you to determine which measures should be used in relation to organisational and marketing objectives, analysing the monitoring information resulting from those measures and make recommendations to improve marketing performance.

CHAPTER 1

Organisational structures

Introduction

Marketing infrastructure (the subject of Section 1 of your syllabus) refers to all the resources and structures that are needed in order for marketing activity to take place. This includes but is not limited to:

- Staff
- Transportation
- Administration
- Marketing intelligence systems
- Communication
- Planning
- Quality assurance
- Budgets

Organisations require systems and processes for all of their operations, such as gathering and analysing marketing intelligence, developing the product mix, communicating value propositions, capturing potentially valuable leads through feedback (solicited or otherwise), increasing brand equity and building customer loyalty.

How the work of marketing operations is going to be undertaken may be determined by organisational structure. This is the basis in which its operations and routines are based and determines how individuals interact within it.

Topic list

1.1	Critically evaluate the importance of organisational structures in delivering marketing value, focus and creativity including consideration of how the work of the marketing operations is going to be undertaken:
	  ■ Functional structure
	  ■ Product/market structure
	  ■ Brand structure
	  ■ Territory structure
	  ■ Matrix structure
	  ■ International and multinational organisational structures

1 The importance of organisational structures

> ▶ **Key term**
>
> **Organisation structure** may be defined as 'the pattern of relationships among positions in the organisation and among members of the organisation. Structure makes possible the application of the process of management and creates a framework of order and command through which the activities of the organisation can be planned, organised, directed and controlled.' (Mullins, 1999).

Mintzberg (1983) defines an **organisation's structure** as: 'The sum total of the ways in which it divides its labour into distinct tasks and then achieves co-ordination among them'.

There are a number of different types of organisational structures commonly used, and the choice is an important one and therefore the most effective ways of organising marketing infrastructure need to be considered.

Structures fundamentally affect:

- The ways in which resources are controlled
- How authority is wielded and accountability distributed
- Where the sources of power lie
- How an organisation delivers its mission.

Often the structures have been adopted through a slow accumulation of change and development, but occasionally they are reviewed and may be redesigned to suit the emergent challenges of the external environment and the priorities of the organisation more effectively. In this section we will explore a number of different models.

The form of organisational structure favoured will depend on many factors, such as size and age of organisation, market conditions, external environment, product mix, relationships with suppliers and buyers, skills of staff, technological innovation, competitor behaviour, organisational culture, and the preferred styles for decision-making and authority. Our focus will be on how differences in structures affect the ability of marketing to achieve its core purposes.

Organisation structure therefore implies a framework intended to:

- Define **work roles and relationships**, so that areas and flows of authority and responsibility are clearly established.

- Define **work tasks and responsibilities**, grouping and allocating them to suitable individuals and groups.

- Channel **information flows** (communication) efficiently through the organisation.

- **Co-ordinate** the objectives and activities of different units, so that overall aims are achieved without gaps or overlaps in the flow of work.

- Control the **flow of work**, information and resources, through the organisation.

- Support **flexibility** and **adaptability** to changing internal and external demands.

- Support the **commitment, involvement and satisfaction** of the people who work for the organisation, by offering opportunities for participation, responsibility, team working and so on.

- Support **value-adding, customer-focused business processes**.

- Support and improve **organisational performance** through all of the above.

2 Dimensions of organisational structure

Many organisations develop organically as they grow, responding to internal ambition and external conditions. Their structures often reflect this, having been built up over time, sometimes expanding, sometimes contracting. Occasionally – following the appointment of a new CEO, or as a result of a merger, or in response to adverse economic conditions, for example, but also through a deliberate desire to improve the arrangements that have arisen in an *ad hoc* fashion – organisations may undergo partial or wholesale restructuring.

There are many variations to choose from, and senior managers must identify an appropriate form that best meets the priorities of their own particular organisation.

Organisational structures describe and determine the way work is arranged, how authority is exercised and the channels of communication that prevail, up, down and across the various divisions. The structures vary in a number of key dimensions and these will help us understand different organisational forms. These are shown in Table 1.1, reflecting Max Weber's *The Theory of Social and Economic Organization* (1997) and the work of many of those who followed his modernist conception.

Table 1.1   Dimensions of organisations

Dimension	Description
Size	In this context, size is a measure of headcount (although size of organisations may also be given by volume of sales, turnover or capital).
Differentiation	The amount of vertical differentiation is an indication of the number of levels of hierarchy (the more differentiation there is, the greater the number of levels), while the amount of horizontal differentiation or departmentalisation reflects the number of divisions.
Integration	The amount of vertical integration is the degree to which the different levels of hierarchy operate in isolation or in unison, while horizontal integration is a similar measure for collaboration between divisions, reflecting the structures for accountability, communication and reporting.
Spans of control	The span of control is the number of staff that report directly to a given manager. In general, the greater the amount of vertical differentiation, the higher the number of levels of hierarchy and the narrower the spans of control.
Specialisation	Specialisation is the uniqueness or similarity of job and team roles arising from the division of labour.
Formalisation	Formalisation refers to the level of bureaucracy and the extent to which processes are prescribed in order to regulate activity.
Centralisation and decentralisation	In a highly centralised organisation, the authority is held among a small group of senior managers with limited autonomy for teams and divisions. In a decentralised organisation, power is more evenly distributed, allowing those lower down or further out from the centre to exercise a degree of power and control.

For Weber, a German sociologist, complex operations were best handled by a "rational bureaucracy", based on clearly defined rules and authority.

We tend to view bureaucracy in a negative fashion, but for Weber it was the desirable cohesive force that led to authority, control, order and efficiency. Generally, organisational activity is co-ordinated through hierarchy, structure and communication as well as the formal standardisation of processes.

Later theorists, like Elton Mayo, recognised the importance of the human dimension as well. Managers should bear in mind that there are also informal structures that are equally important to understanding employee behaviour and for effecting change.

The informal organisation accounts for the ways in which staff engage with each other, how messages are commonly communicated, and the lines of loyalty and dependency that exist through work-related social networks. Prior experience, cultural background, social conditioning and personal expectations all shape the organisation as it is understood by the individual. In some sense, the organisation does not exist beyond the ways in which it is encountered.

It is important that organisations as a whole and the divisions within them find the right structure to match their needs. An inappropriate structure may lead to difficulties in communication, unresponsiveness to external change, slow product or service development rates, unsatisfactory service to customers, unclear lines of authority and accountability, a lack of control, and ultimately in total failure.

Structures play such an important role in determining operational effectiveness and efficiency that the marketing manager needs to take account of the dynamics of their own function as well as the organisation as a whole in order to take active and successful control.

3 Aspects of organisation structure

Some of the decisions that will have to be made in designing (or evaluating) an organisation structure (Huczyinski and Buchanan, 2001) include:

- **Specialisation**: How should the work of the organisation be divided up? Should tasks be grouped to allow units to specialise (allowing efficient focusing of training, equipment and management) – or should specialisation be minimised (to simplify communication and allow units and individuals to be versatile and flexible)?

- **Hierarchy**: Should the overall structure be 'tall' (with many levels or tiers of management) or 'flat' (fewer tiers – meaning that each manager has to control more people: a wider 'span of control')? Tall organisations allow closer managerial control (due to narrower spans of control), while flat organisations save on managerial costs and empower and satisfy workers (who are given more authority and discretion).

- **Grouping**: How should jobs and departments be grouped together? Options include departmentation by the specialist expertise and resources required (function), or the services/products offered (product/market/brand), or the geographical area being targeted (territory).

- **Co-ordination**: How can the organisation foster integration between its different units, in order to maximise the 'horizontal' flow of business processes from one to the other? This will involve mechanisms such as rules and policies, carefully aligned goals and plans, liaison/co-ordinator roles, cross-functional team-working and so on.

- **Control**: Should decisions be mainly 'centralised' (taken at the top) or 'decentralised' (delegated to lower levels) – or a mixture of both? Centralisation allows swift, decisive control and co-ordination, while decentralisation empowers and satisfies workers, and can support organisational responsiveness by having decisions taken closer to the customer or local market.

3.1 Power and authority

One of the most important aspects of formal organisation structure is the allocation of formal authority to perform tasks and make decisions.

French & Raven (1958) identified five types or sources of power in organisations.

- **Coercive power**: the power of physical or psychological force or intimidation. (This should be rare in business organisations, for ethical reasons.)

- **Reward (or resource) power** based on access to or control over valued resources. Marketing managers, for example, have access to information, contacts and financial rewards for team members. The amount of resource power a person has depends on the scarcity of the resource, how much the resource is valued by others, and how far the resource is perceived as being under the manager's control.

- **Legitimate (or position) power**: formally conferred by the organisation, by virtue of the individual's position in the organisation structure. For example, a marketing manager has the authority to make certain decisions, and to command his or her team.

- **Expert power**: based on knowledge and expertise. For example, marketers have expert power because of their knowledge of the market and marketing techniques. Expert power depends on others recognising the expertise in an area which they need or value.

- **Referent (personal) power**: based on force of personality, 'charisma' or being a role model, which can attract, influence and inspire other people.

The organisation structure confers authority (legitimate or positional power) on individuals and teams. Note, however, that it need not directly convey other sorts of power, which may be wielded by people with no designated authority position: think about the most knowledgeable or experienced people in your team, for example, or individuals that other team members look up to.

3.2 Line, staff and functional authority

Expert power may be acknowledged in an organisation structure in various ways, in the concept of line, staff and functional authority:

- **Line authority** is the authority a manager has over a subordinate, flowing done the vertical chain (or line) of command in the organisation hierarchy.

- **Staff authority** is the influence one manager or unit may have in giving specialist advice or assistance to another manager or unit, over which they have no direct line authority. Staff authority does not entail the right to make or influence decisions or procedures: line managers may (or may not) accept the advice or assistance purely because of the perceived value of the staff unit's expertise. An example would be the HR department advising the marketing manager on selection interviewing techniques.

- **Functional authority** is the formalisation of staff authority, where a staff department management is given the authority, in certain circumstances, to direct, design or control the decisions or procedures of another unit. An example is where the finance manager has authority to enforce budgetary control disciplines in the marketing function.

These distinctions are a frequent cause of organisational problems, due to the ambiguity of the authority exercised in practice by staff/functional units such as HR, finance, market research and so on.

Table 1.2   Possible solutions to power/authority problems

Power/authority issue	Possible solution
Staff units attempt to build influence in line units. This can be resented as 'interference' by line managers, especially if staff experts are perceived as 'ivory tower' theorists, distanced from the operational realities of line functions – and not being accountable for the success of their advice.	Ensure that staff units are fully aware of operational issues. Improve two-way communication. Encourage staff units to position themselves as internal consultants, with line units as internal clients.
Unclear boundaries of authority for line and functional managers.	Clarify areas in which functional managers have authority.
Functional managers 'empire building' to enforce their authority in line departments: eg causing the proliferation of rules, policies and red tape.	Encourage communication and collaboration between line/functional managers in the pursuit of shared objectives.

3.3 Centralisation

Another key power and authority issue, expressed in the organisation structure, is the extent of centralisation or decentralisation. We can look at centralisation in two ways:

- **Geography**: Some functions may be centralised rather than dispersed in different offices, departments or locations. So, for example, secretarial support, IT support and human resources may be centralised in specialist departments (whose services are shared by other functions) rather than carried out by staff/equipment duplicated in each departmental office.

- **Authority**: Centralisation also refers to the extent to which people have to refer decisions upwards to their superiors. Decentralisation therefore implies increased delegation, empowerment and autonomy at lower levels of the organisation.

The following table summarises some of the arguments in favour of centralisation and decentralisation.

Table 1.3   Arguments for centralisation and decentralisation

Arguments for centralisation	Arguments for decentralisation
Decisions flow down from a central point, and so co-ordinate lower levels of activity more efficiently.	Avoids overburdening top managers, in terms of workload and stress.
Senior managers can take a wider view of problems and consequences, for better 'big picture' decisions.	Improves motivation of lower levels of management and staff, who are given more challenge and responsibility.
Senior managers can balance the interests of different functions (eg in resource allocations).	Greater awareness of local and front-line problems by decision makers (as opposed to top management 'distant' from the market and customers).
Quality of decisions is potentially higher due to senior managers' skill and experience.	Greater speed of decision making, and response to changing events, without the need to refer decisions upwards: particularly important in fast-change markets.
Crisis decisions are taken more quickly at the centre.	Separate spheres of responsibility can be identified: controls, performance measurement and accountability are better.
Policies, procedures and documentation can be standardised organisation-wide.	ICT supports decentralised decision-making, with the sharing of central decision-support data and tools.

Extended Knowledge

This is obviously a very brief overview of some of the issues in organisation structure, power and authority. If you need to follow this unit up in more detail for an assignment, see Cole and Kelly: 'Management: theory and practice', from the core reading list for this unit.

4 Organisation structure – roles and relationships

4.1 Job roles

The division of labour and specialisation of work activities is an inevitable feature of large, complex organisations. The organisation's tasks are broken down into sub-tasks which can be allocated to individuals and teams in the form of 'jobs'. The organisation structure defines:

- How the organisation's work is divided up – and therefore what the appropriate content of each team's and person's job should be.

- Whether skills and specialisms are gathered together (eg in specialised or centralised departments) or dispersed and duplicated throughout the organisation.

- Where there are flows or overlaps in tasks from one organisational unit to another – and therefore how this flow of work should be co-ordinated or integrated.

There are a number of related issues here. We will look at the topic of **departmentation** (dividing up the tasks of the organisation in various ways) below, and at **job design** in Chapter 4 (in the context of designing a marketing team).

4.2 Relationships

The formal organisation expresses the inter-relationship between job roles and organisational units, in terms of:

- The nature and structure of the **authority** they wield in relation to each other: line, staff and functional relationships, as discussed in Paragraph 3.2 above.

- The lines of **communication** between them, by which information flows downwards (in the form of plans, briefings and instructions), side-ways (in the form of co-ordinating information) and upwards (in the form of feedback, reports and perhaps suggestions).

- The **flow of work** between them through 'horizontal' business processes and internal supply and value chains.

5 Elements of organisation structure

Henry Mintzberg (1983) provided a framework and language for discussing organisation structure, by categorising the building blocks of organisation. He suggested that all organisations can be analysed into five components, according to how they relate to the work of the organisation.

Figure 1.1   Mintzberg's organisational components

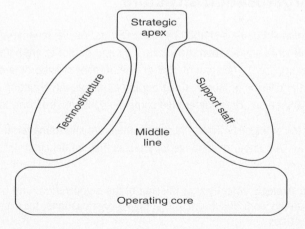

The components can be explained as follows.

Table 1.4

Component	Function
Strategic apex	Ensures the organisation follows its mission and services the needs of its key stakeholders. Manages the organisation's relationship with the environment (boundary management). Acts as a force for **direction** (shared vision and goals).
Operating core	People *directly* involved in the process of obtaining inputs, and converting them into outputs (goods and services). Acts as a force for **proficiency** (competence).
Middle line	Conveys the goals set by the strategic apex and controls the work of the operating core in pursuit of those goals: ie middle management. Acts as a force for **concentration** (technical or product specialisation and accountability).
Technostructure	Analyses, determines and standardises work processes, techniques, skills and outputs. (Examples include strategic planners, quality controllers, human resource management: specialist advice and analysis.) Acts as a force for **efficiency**.
Support staff	Ancillary and administrative services such as PR, legal counsel, building maintenance and security. Support staff do not plan or standardise production, but function independently of the operating core. Acts as a force for **learning**.

These various components serve to **co-ordinate** the activities of the organisation in different ways:

- **Direct supervision**: favoured by the strategic apex and middle line. Power is directly applied to control and co-ordinate activity.

- **Mutual adjustment**: the integration of goals by communication and negotiation, favoured by the operating core and support staff.

- **Standardisation** of work processes, outputs and/or skills and knowledge, favoured by the technostructure.

The organisation also has a sixth component, which Mintzberg calls **ideology**: its paradigm or set of guiding assumptions and beliefs. This is identified with organisation **culture**, that is in simple terms 'the way we do things around here' (Charles Handy). Organisational culture is the subject of Section 9 in Chapter 5.

> ▶ **Assessment tip**
>
> Mintzberg's components are particularly useful when discussing issues of organisational structure. The vocabulary is precise and well-established.

6 Influences on organisation structure

Organisational structure is shaped by many factors. As we saw earlier, there are certain internal principles and dynamics of work organisation: how far power and authority are held at the top (centralised) or given to lower levels (decentralised); the span of control (the number of subordinates that can be supervised by any one superior); the division of labour; the grouping of people into working units; the need for communication channels, and so on. These determine some elements of structure, to an extent, according to internal logic.

According to contingency theory, however, there are still **managerial choices** to be made in order to optimise the structure. A number of contingent variables may influence structural choices and organisational development.

- The **strategic objectives** or **mission** of the organisation, and how these are broken down to define and guide the work of sub-units. Diversified organisations, for example, may require more decentralised structures.

The Chartered Institute of Marketing

- The **task** or 'business' of the organisation, which will determine which line or task functions are required (development, production, marketing, finance) and which support or staff functions (HR, planning, quality control, maintenance).

- The **technology** of the task may necessitate certain forms of organisation to maximise its efficiency (eg assembly line organisation of mass production) and the needs of people (eg team working to enhance human involvement in highly automated tasks).

- The **size** of the organisation. As it gets larger, its structure will get more complex: specialisation, subdivision and formalisation are required in order to control and co-ordinate performance (typically leading to the bureaucratisation of large organisations).

- **Geographical dispersion** may require federalised structures to take into account relevant factors at local, regional, national, international or global levels of operation.

- The **environment** of the organisation. Factors (and especially changes) in the legal, commercial, technical and social environment represent demands and constraints on organisational activity, and opportunities and threats to which organisation structure must adapt. As one example, information and communication technology (ICT) has enabled organisations to adopt looser, more network-style units or 'virtual teams'.

- The **culture and management** style of the organisation: eg the willingness of management to delegate authority and adopt more fluid facilitate-and-empower roles; organisational values about team working, formality, flexibility and so on.

6.1 Supporting marketing value and focus

> ▶ **Key term**
>
> **Marketing focus** - Kotler *et al* (1999) suggests that as a business grows, it will adopt an increasingly evolved and integrated view of marketing which supports the delivery of marketing value, and the development of marketing focus: that is, an extension of marketing influence throughout the organisation, so that all units cultivate a customer-focused marketing orientation.

Kotler *et al* (1999) note that there has been both an absolute and a relative rise in the importance of marketing in the organisation. The responsibility of marketing has increased due to the increasingly complex environment, the slowing of demand in existing product fields and the rise in global competition. Meanwhile, companies have been forced to move from a product or production orientation (in which the priority was product quality or production efficiency) to a marketing orientation (in which the priority is anticipating and satisfying customer needs and wants), making marketing one of the critical management functions.

Figure 1.2   The evolution of marketing organisation

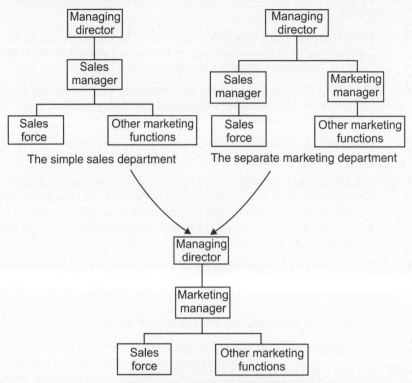

The simple sales department   The separate marketing department

The modern marketing company

Marketing value and focus can be supported in an organisation structure by:

- **Positioning** the marketing function centrally, at a strategic level, so that strategy flows down from a marketing-oriented strategic apex.

- **Business process alignment** (or realignment): taking a horizontal process view of the organisation (facilitating the flow of work, information and value towards the customer) and aligning all business processes (research and development; purchasing, supply and distribution; production; sales and marketing) so that they service the same objectives of customer satisfaction.

- Establishing **communication mechanisms** for internal marketing: supporting the sharing of marketing values and information throughout the organisation.

- Establishing mechanisms for **cross-functional collaboration**: supporting the involvement and influence of marketing personnel in areas (such as product development and quality management) which potentially impact on customer satisfaction, and therefore benefit from marketing's understanding of customer needs.

7 Structure types

7.1 Functional structure

Functional organisational structures are arranged around the roles undertaken by individuals and teams. For example, a large manufacturing organisation may have the following major divisions:

- Research and development
- Production
- Distribution
- Human resources
- Finance
- Marketing and communications

These may be further subdivided. Marketing and communications, for example, may be arranged to include:

- Sales
- Advertising
- Market research and intelligence
- Public relations
- Customer relations
- Website management
- Marketing administration

This is extended further into specific and individual job roles.

Figure 1.3   Functional departmentation

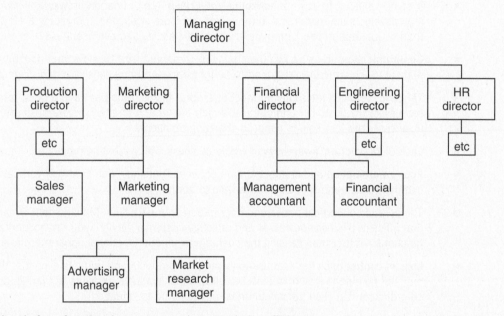

The rationale for a functional arrangement is to maximise efficiency.

- The tasks needed by the organisation to deliver its mission are first identified and then grouped according to specialism.

- The skills needed to undertake the tasks determine the labour requirements of each division.

- There is a high degree of horizontal differentiation between teams, and probably high levels of specialisation as well.

- Managers and supervisors have authority over teams of staff undertaking similar or related roles, often leading to hierarchical and bureaucratic structures through the need to exercise control and to standardise activity.

The larger the organisation, the greater these tendencies to formalisation and vertical differentiation. This may be regarded as the basis for the more traditional organisational form.

Functional structures are most ideally suited to organisations with a single product or service or with a portfolio of very similar items, and there are many advantages to such structures. They make efficient use of specialised skills through a highly evolved division of labour with minimal overlap and duplication.

There are several advantages to such a structure.

- There is a high degree of **accountability** for staff and managers since roles are clearly defined and highly ordered.

- **Reporting and communication** lines follow the chain of command up and down the levels of authority.

- There are opportunities to **specialise** and to **progress** within the hierarchy. Individuals are likely to feel comfortable in the structure with a clear sense of their place in it.

- **Specialist expertise** is pooled and focused. Individuals and units can develop their specialisms, while the marketing director co-ordinates their plans and budgets to ensure the development of a coherent and consistent (integrated) marketing mix.

- It **avoids duplication** (eg having a marketing manager for each geographic area or product group).

- It enables **economies of scale** and **efficient sharing** of equipment and facilities.

- It facilitates the **recruitment, management and development** of functional specialists.

There are also a number of disadvantages, including the following:

- It can be difficult to achieve **horizontal integration** (co-ordination between divisions). A silo mentality may develop such that staff and managers are more interested in pursuing their divisional objectives than supporting broader corporate goals. Inefficiencies and even conflicts may ensue.

- **Communication** up and down the chains of command may be slow, and horizontally may be very difficult. Such structures also tend to be inflexible and unresponsive to a changing external environment.

- Tendency to **focus internally on** functional specialisms, processes and inputs, rather than on business processes, the customer and outputs, which are what ultimately drive a business. Inward-looking businesses are less able to adapt to changing demands.

- Lack of **'big picture' awareness** of whole-business, value-creating processes.

- **Poor co-ordination** and communication between functions, due to formal vertical channels of communication and specialist focus (and jargon).

- The creation of **vertical barriers** to information and work flow. Management writer Tom Peters suggests that efficient business processes and effective customer service requires 'horizontal' flow between functions – rather than passing the customer from one functional department to another.

- **Loss of control** once the organisation's range of products and markets expands: the functional manager may not be able to stay on top of the full range of products, markets or brands, and the burden of co-ordination between functional units may become too great.

Application to marketing:

For the marketing manager it may be advantageous to have all of the resources (staff and others) pooled together rather than dispersed between a number of different divisions. This should result in a more efficient use of budgets as it enables marketing activity to be tightly planned and closely monitored.

The manager is more likely to be able to respond flexibly to changes in the external environment by moving resources between different campaigns and initiatives. In addition, some marketing activity needs to be focused on high-level corporate image, public relations and brand awareness, and so it is much more suited to a centralised function.

However, with the marketing function separated from other departments, difficulties may arise in trying to achieve co-ordination and co-operation.

If marketing is seen as the responsibility of a separate team, then production units and service providers may feel less inclined to support marketing activity.

Horizontal communication between the marketing function and other divisions may be slow and ineffective, making it more difficult to respond to adverse variances and other problems as they arise. It may also create unrealistic expectations borne out of a misunderstanding of marketing, so that when sales are disappointing, for example, the production manager may ask for some more advertising as a quick fix.

The Chartered Institute of Marketing

7.2 Product/Market Structure

Another way of arranging staff and resources is around the various products or services that the organisation provides, or alternatively around particular markets by creating semi-autonomous units and profit centres acting as mini-businesses. A clothing manufacturer, for example, may organise its activities on the basis of menswear, ladies' wear and children's wear, while a large local authority is likely to have such departments as:

- Housing
- Education
- Children's services
- Health and social care
- Highways
- Town planning

An organisation providing goods and services both on a business-to-business (B2B) and a business-to-customer (B2C) basis may divide its operations on these lines. Each of these divisions will need a functional team that may include administration, customer services, accounting, human resources, sales and marketing.

Figure 1.4   Product/brand organisation

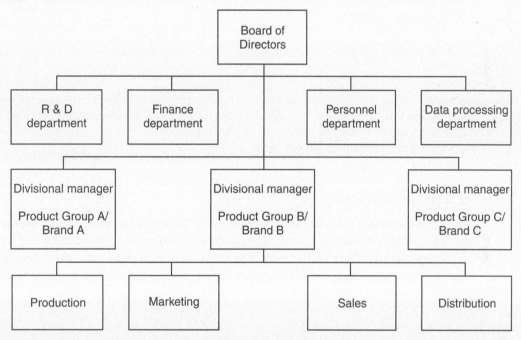

This type of approach may be particularly appropriate for organisations with a very diverse or very large range of products – especially if some of them are direct or indirect competitors with each other. Advantages include:

- Marketing is more fully **integrated** with operations. The function is closer to the action, better informed and better understood by staff. It will be easier to integrate operational and marketing plans, to set collective targets and performance indicators, and to respond more rapidly should variances arise.

- The total marketing resource will be divided between the products or markets, enabling marketing activity to reflect the particular needs of customers, based on appropriate characteristics and market factors.

- **Accountability**. Individual managers can be held accountable for the profitability of individual products or lines.

- **Specialisation**. Product managers can build up considerable experience and understanding of their product groups and markets, which is valuable in a rapidly changing competitive environment. Salespeople may be trained to sell a specific product in which they may develop technical expertise, for example, and thereby offer a better sales service to customers.

- **Co-ordination**. The different functional activities and efforts required to make and sell each product can be co-ordinated and integrated by the divisional/product manager.

Disadvantages include:

- It may prove harder to ensure that marketing activity on an organisation-wide basis is sufficiently focused and integrated.

- **Duplication** of effort and overlaps in areas of responsibility may occur.

- Circumstances may change where resource needs to be reallocated to a particular area which often proves more difficult within such a structure.

- **Increased overhead costs** and managerial complexity.

- The risk that different product divisions may become competitive, **fragmenting objectives, markets and resources** in a way that is sub-optimal for the organisation as a whole.

A product or market structure may make expansion easier since the organisation can add new divisions to support new products or markets without radically altering the underlying structure. Autonomy may be high, with the product or market experts being empowered to make the decisions within their division. At the same time, accountability can be readily enforced as performance of individual products or markets should be relatively easy to identify.

THE REAL WORLD

Many organisations which sell to both consumer markets and business markets include market structures within the organisation. For example, mobile phone network providers have specific areas which look after organisations who have requirements for phones for many users, generally having different elements in the marketing mix for these customers to those which are provided to individual consumers by different teams in the structure.

7.3 Brand structure

Smaller organisations may offer a single brand, while larger more established ones are likely to have a more complex profile with multiple brands, sub-brands, endorsed or joint brands, and a number of partnerships with other organisations. These organisations may choose to organise their activity and resources around their brands. This is illustrated in The 'Real World' feature opposite based on food retailer Nestlé.

THE REAL WORLD

Nestlé is a very large, multi-product and multi-brand organisation which is set up with a brand structure. Despite operating in a variety of different regions around the world the brand structure is the key form under which the organisation operates, with the brands having regional representation. The structure of Nestlé can be seen in this organisation chart:

The Chartered Institute of Marketing

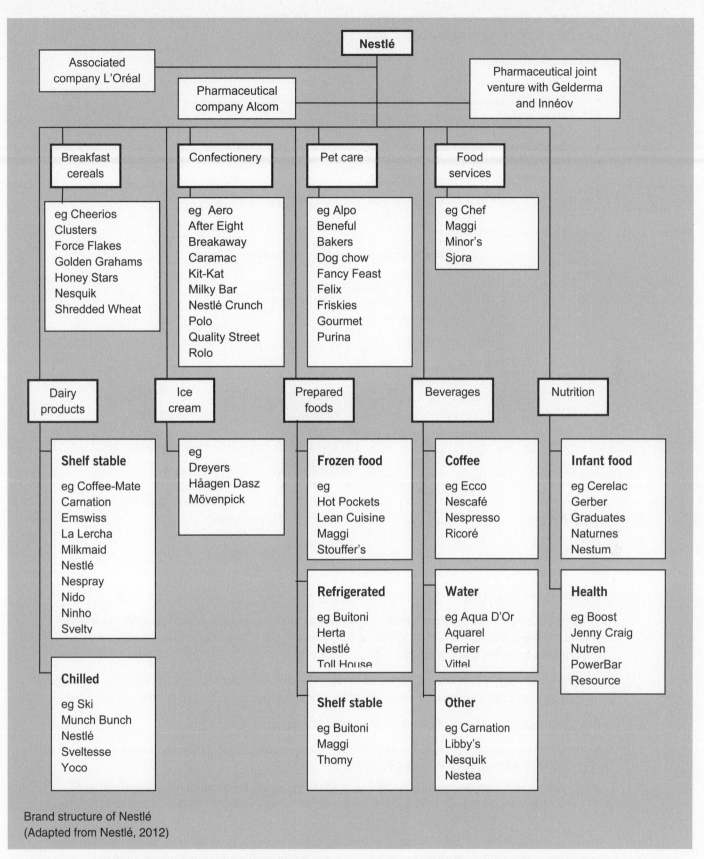

Brand structure of Nestlé
(Adapted from Nestlé, 2012)

Brand management is of particular interest to organisations selling fast-moving consumer goods. A brand may be treated as a mini-business, requiring the full range of resources and services needed to support it that you would find in an organisation. By focusing the planning and decision-making processes around the brand, it is possible to achieve a coherence of vision with clear accountability.

For example, the brand will require:

- Market research
- Product development
- Production
- Supply chain management
- Logistics and distribution
- Marketing communications
- Customer service

This focusing of marketing infrastructure around the brand is illustrated below.

Figure 1.5   Focusing resources on the brand

Brand Management Focus (The Brand Wheel)

(Marketing Minds, 2012)

In an organisation whose structure reflects the brand structure, the operations and resources are focused around the major brands in a fashion similar to that shown above. There will be brand managers with responsibility for building brand equity.

Budgets would also be built around the brands so that monthly management accounts reflect progress against budget, and other Key Performance Indicators (KPIs) are all centred on individual brands and groups of brands.

Brand management may be particularly effective, because:

- Brands are packaged, promoted and sold in distinctive ways: arguably there is a need for specialisation of customer research and marketing effort.

- Brands may compete with each other, so it will be helpful to focus performance measurement (profitability, contribution) on a brand-by-brand basis – and to focus managerial accountability for performance accordingly.

While such models can be highly effective in building brands, care must be taken to ensure that the organisation does not lose its customer focus. Customer equity is ultimately more important than brand equity. While brands may continue to reflect the needs of customers, customer equity helps to reinforce the importance of relationships.

The Chartered
Institute of Marketing

7.4 Territory structure

Where the organisation is structured according to geographic area, some authority is retained at Head Office but day-to-day operations are handled on a **territorial** basis (eg Southern region, Western region).

Territorial structure

A simple geographical organisation for a marketing department is an extension of the functional organisation in which responsibility for some or all functional activities is devolved to a regional level.

Figure 1.6   Territorial marketing structure

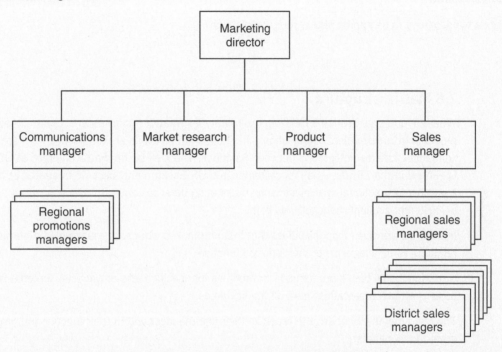

This type of organisation would be suitable for firms operating **internationally**, where the various functional activities would be required for *each* national market or group of national markets, in order to remain close to local customers, suppliers and contacts. The structure also tends to be adopted by larger companies where there are strong **regional differences**, for the same reason. **Sales departments** are often organised territorially, so that salesforces can focus travel time and resources, and build relationships, within defined areas.

There are advantages to geographic departmentation:

■   There is **local decision-making** at the interface between the organisation and its customers, suppliers and other stakeholders (who may have distinctive needs).

■   It is cost-effective because of shorter lines of supply, travel and communication to local markets, plants or offices.

But there are disadvantages to:

■   **Duplication** and possible loss of economies of scale might arise. For example, a national organisation divided into ten regions might have a customer liaison department in each regional office. If the organisation did all customer liaison work from head office (centralised) it might need fewer managerial staff.

■   **Inconsistency** in methods or standards may develop across different areas.

7.5 Hybrid structures

'Hybrid' simply means 'mixed'. As you may have noticed from the various organisation charts shown above, business generally combined a variety of organisational forms. Hybrid structures allow the advantages of each form of organisation to be leveraged in appropriate ways: brand identity to be reinforced by a brand division, for example, with regional knowledge to be capitalised on by territorial sales departments, and economics of scale to be gained by specialised marketing or purchasing functions.

ACTIVITY 1.1

How might a hybrid structure be appropriate in your organisation?

7.6 Matrix structure

Where hybrid organisation 'mixes' organisation types, **matrix** organisation actually *crosses* functional and product/customer/project organisation – the horizontal divisions are diminished or in some cases removed completely to allow integration between functions. The idea of the matrix emerged at US aerospace company Lockheed in the 1950s, when its customer (the US Government) became frustrated at dealing separately with a number of functional specialists when negotiating defence contracts. The concept of the 'project co-ordinator' or 'customer account manager' was born.

Individuals are given responsibilities that require them to work with members of other functions while still retaining some allegiance to their primary function.

Cross-functional teams are formed – sometimes for specific tasks or projects, sometimes on a semi-permanent basis – with representatives from all the key areas.

The team members continue to report to their line manager within their function but also to the leader of the cross-functional team.

It is these horizontal and vertical relationships that form the matrix:

Figure 1.7   A matrix structure

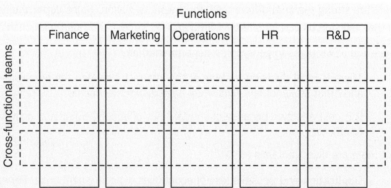

As with all organisational structures, a matrix is not simply a form but also a way of approaching the challenges of business. Complex tasks can be tackled in a highly collaborative fashion, ensuring cross-fertilisation of ideas and a high degree of co-ordination. The structure breaks down the tendency of other structures for individuals to work in silos, with allegiances up and down the hierarchy rather than across or to the organisation as a whole.

The Chartered
Institute of Marketing

One of the first organisations to be associated with the matrix structure was NASA which depended upon close co-operation of functions focused on specific, complex projects. NASA found traditional, functional structures too bureaucratic, inflexible, politically charged and slow.

THE REAL WORLD

An early adopter of matrix structures was Chrysler. In 1992, faced with a loss of $795 million Chrysler faced a requirement to reinvent the corporation and the way they developed vehicles. The introduced a matrix structure with involvement of many different skills in cross functional platform teams to develop vehicles with those in the team working together to solve issues with their platform increasing efficiency of the process through reduced development time and better solutions to manufacture issues. These teams included engineers with many specialisations and also marketing and finance staff. This structure of team working is still largely in existence within Chrysler despite mergers, de-mergers and takeovers demonstrating the success of the concept.

The focus for the cross-functional teams may vary considerably. In some organisations, it is on a product or market basis. In other words, a matrix structure may act as a combination of an organisation divided on functional grounds with a product/market structure laid over the top. Alternatively, the cross-functional teams may join forces in order to address a fixed term project, such as product development or change implementation.

Three different kinds of matrix structures have been identified and described (Knight, 1977):

- **Co-ordination** where staff remain within their main function or department and cross-functional activity is achieved through integrated planning.

- **Overlay** where staff are more formally part of two different teams, within their function and within a cross-functional unit, having two managers.

- **Secondment** where staff will sometimes work within their functional divisions and sometimes within cross-functional teams but not simultaneously.

Advantages of matrix organisation include:

- Greater **flexibility** of:

    - **People**. Employees develop an attitude geared to accepting change, and departmental monopolies are broken down.

    - **Workflow and decision-making**. Direct contact between staff encourages problem solving and big picture thinking.

    - **Tasks and structure**. The matrix structure may be readily amended, once projects are completed.

- **Inter-disciplinary co-operation** and a mixing of skills and expertise, along with **improved communication** and **co-ordination**.

- **Motivation and employee development**: providing employees with greater participation in planning and control decisions.

- **Market awareness**: the organisation tends to become more customer/quality focused.

- **Horizontal workflow**: bureaucratic obstacles are removed, and departmental specialisms become less powerful.

Again, there are disadvantages, however:

- **Dual authority** threatens a **conflict** between functional managers and project (or other co-ordinating) managers.

- An individual with two or more bosses may suffer stress from **conflicting demands** or **ambiguous roles**.

- **Cost**: management posts are added, meetings have to be held, and so on.

- **Slower decision making** due to the added complexity.

7.7 International and multinational organisational structures

'The search for an appropriate organisational structure must balance the forces for local responsiveness against the forces for global integration.'

Hennessey and Jeannet (2001)

It is estimated that there are over 35,000 multinational organisations (source: UN data). The revenues earned by the top 100 in 2011 topped $12 trillion, the largest earner being Wal-Mart with revenue of $421 billion (CNN, 2012). Most structures evolve as organisations grow and this is especially pertinent to international and multinational operations.

Four different kinds of multinational organisations may be distinguished:

1   **Multinational**: a decentralised organisation operating in several countries while retaining a significant level of activity in its domestic market

2   **Global**: a centralised organisation spreading its activities on a world scale chiefly to derive cost advantages

3   **International**: an organisation that builds upon its parent firm's technology or research and development

4   **Transnational**: organisations with a mix of the above models

The significance of this is not so much the precise definitions but the recognition that there are different models for operating in more than one country and these relate to organisational structures. The specific ways in which multinationals tend to grow are:

- **Organic growth** – year on year increases in revenues and profits and an expansion of operations

- **Diversification** – expanding operations into new areas of activity (often through mergers and acquisitions)

- **Horizontal integration** – mergers and acquisitions with firms engaged in similar activities at the same level in the supply chain

- **Vertical integration** – mergers and acquisitions with firms engaged in operations at earlier or later stages in the supply chain

Given the various ways in which organisations grow, there is no single model that describes the development of multinational and international organisational structures. However, some studies have identified some common characteristics and patterns. For example, the findings of Hollensen (2004) are illustrated below:

Figure 1.8 The evolution of international organisational structures

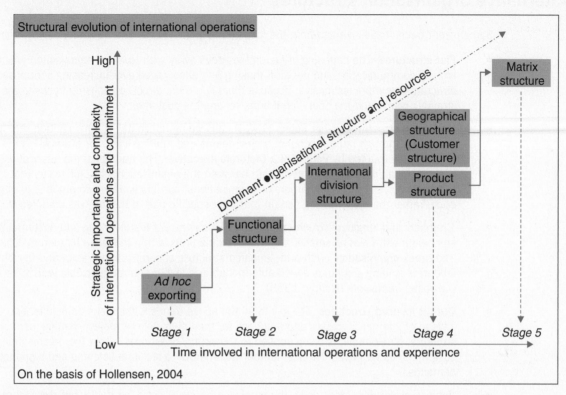

On the basis of Hollensen, 2004

(Busch, 2012)

As the organisation gains more experience in international activity and commits more resources overseas, it is likely to develop from *ad hoc* arrangements (stage 1) to a more highly structured functional structure (stage 2).

Progressing further, as it extends its reach into multiple regions, a multinational typically forms divisions on a geographical basis (stage 3) with managers having responsibility over single or groups of countries.

With further advances in the scale and complexity of international operations, this develops even further into a focus on products and markets (stage 4), enabling the business to reflect more precisely local variations in preferences and needs and so build valuable long-term relationships with its customers.

At its most advanced, a multinational typically reaches a matrix structure (stage 5) in an attempt to increase its flexibility and responsiveness to changing market conditions by sharing expertise and maximising the speed of communications and decision-making.

Sometimes international matrix structures are described as '3D' as the cross-divisional activity spans multiple functions, products or markets, and countries. There are many different ways of arranging activities and resources. For example, products may be developed and managed globally, while functions (human resources, marketing, finance, etc) are duplicated for each significant geographical region, mindful of culture, legislation, custom, economic conditions and so on. Overlaying this structure, a regional manager may have responsibility for the local market.

For the marketing manager operating in an international environment, there is the need to complement their skills in strategy, planning, budgetary control, communication, information management and so on with additional expertise in such matters as multi-cultural understanding, geographical knowledge, global economics, international politics and legislation.

The structures of large multinationals can be incredibly complex and potentially very expensive to maintain. Individuals are likely to require strong interpersonal skills to thrive and prosper.

8 Alternative organisation structures

Some recent trends have emerged from the focus on **responsiveness and flexibility** as key organisational values.

- **Flat structures.** The flattening of hierarchies does away with levels of organisation which lengthened lines of communication and decision-making and encouraged ever-increasing specialisation. Flat structures are more responsive, because there is a more direct relationship between the organisation's strategic centre and the operational units serving the customer.

- **Horizontal structures**. What Peters (1994) calls 'going horizontal' is a recognition that functional versatility (through multi-functional project teams and multi-skilling, for example) is the key to flexibility. In the words (quoted by Peters) of a Motorola executive: 'The traditional job descriptions were barriers. We needed an organisation soft enough between the organisational disciplines so that ... people would run freely across functional barriers or organisational barriers with the common goal of getting the job done, rather than just making certain that their specific part of the job was completed'.

- **'Chunked' and 'unglued' structures**. So far, this has meant teamworking and decentralisation, or empowerment, creating smaller and more flexible units within the overall structure. Charles Handy's **'shamrock organisation'** (with a three-leafed structure of core, subcontractor and flexible part-time labour) is gaining ground as a workable model for a leaner and more flexible workforce, within a controlled framework (Handy, 1989).

- **Output-focused structures**. The key to all the above trends is the focus on results, and on the customer, instead of internal processes and functions for their own sake. A project management orientation and structure, for example, is being applied to the supply of services within the organisation (to internal customers) as well as to the external market, in order to facilitate listening and responding to customer demands.

- **'Jobless' structures**. Meanwhile, the employee becomes not a job-holder but the vendor of a portfolio of demonstrated outputs and competencies (Bridges, 1994). However daunting, this is a concrete expression of the concept of employability, which says that a person needs to have a portfolio of skills which are valuable on the open labour market: employees need to be mobile, moving between organisations rather than settling in to a particular job.

- **Boundaryless structures** (Milkovitch & Boudreau, 1996; Welch, 2005). Horizontal (status) barriers are removed or softened by delayering and participative decision-making, and vertical (functional) barriers by empowered cross-functional team working – in order to align business processes. The boundaries of the organisation are also softened, by co-opting suppliers, distributors, business allies and customers as collaborators in the value-adding process, creating an 'extended' or 'networked' enterprise.

- **Ad hocracy** (Huczynski & Buchanan, 2001) is 'a type of organisation design which is temporary, adaptive, creative – in contrast to bureaucracy, which tends to be permanent, rule-driven and inflexible'. It is associated with creative thinking, innovation and organisational learning. It would typically involve the use of a loose network of flexible, temporary, cross-functional project teams or networks of specialists, banding together and disbanding as required to seize business opportunities. While ideally suited to turbulent, innovative markets, it presents a challenge for managers and employees, since it means living with disorder, ambiguity and uncertainty on an on-going basis.

ACTIVITY 1.2

You might like to consider how elements of such structures could beneficially be built into your marketing organisation.

The Chartered
Institute of Marketing

9 The flexible firm

Attention has focused on both functional and numerical flexibility, in order to help organisations to respond to changes and fluctuations in demand.

9.1 Functional flexibility

Functional flexibility or versatility may be achieved by methods such as:

- **Multidisciplinary teamworking** (eg multifunctional project or procurement strategy teams, bringing together individuals with different skills and specialisms, across functional boundaries, so that their competencies and resources can be pooled or exchanged).

- **Multi-skilling** (where each individual within a team is functionally versatile, and able to perform a number of different tasks as required).

We will look at these aspects further in Chapter 5 on structuring teams.

9.2 Numerical flexibility

Numerical flexibility: the ability to shrink or enlarge the labour force in response to fluctuations in demand. This may be done by: using non-standard-contract and subcontracted labour (temporary, short-contract or freelance workers); outsourcing functions to other organisations; or introducing flexible working hours schemes. In practice, an organisation may adopt a 'core-periphery' model.

Handy (1989) proposes a '**Shamrock**' (four-leaf clover) configuration, with various 'leaves'.

- A small, stable **professional core** of full-time permanent labour, who represent the distinctive knowledge and competences of the firm: qualified professionals, technicians and managers, whose commitment is focused on their work and career within the organisation.

- A **periphery** of part-time and temporary labour (the 'flexible labour force') which can be deployed flexibly according to work flow peaks and troughs. Their commitment is typically focused on the immediate job and work group, rather than career or the organisation. However, they are crucial in maintaining standards of service – so it is important for the firm not to treat them 'casually': they should receive fair and equitable treatment (now enshrined in employment law), adequate training and status.

- The **option of contracting out** areas of work to a 'contractual fringe': external providers (freelancers, consultants and sub-contractors) who are able to undertake non-core activities and/or provide specialist services, more economically than the firm could manage internally. Their commitment is typically to achieving specified results in return for fees.

These represent three distinct labour forces, each with its own type of psychological (and legal) contract with the firm.

Figure 1.9   The Shamrock organisation

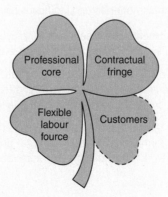

(Handy, 1989)

In addition, Handy (1989) notes the 'lucky' fourth leaf of the clover: the organisation may be able to 'sub-contract' some sales, service and supply tasks – for free – to **customers**. Information and communication technology (ICT) has supported a wide range of 'self service' applications such as: internet/phone banking and automated teller machines (ATMs); internet/telephone reservations and ticketing, in entertainment and travel; on-line information services and so on – in addition to traditional self-service retail and catering outlets, self-assembly products and so on. This should allow labour savings in other 'leaves' of the organisation.

9.3 Whole-organisation marketing

Can a flexible firm deliver better customer service than a more traditional structure?

Egan (2004, p158) argues that one of the key causes of customer service problems is poor teamwork. Different functions in the organisation often operate as isolated towers or 'silos': unconnected to each other, acting independently and with little co-ordination or sense of shared goals. This causes problems because activities in the value chain are interrelated.

Customers experience the organisation '**horizontally**': that is, they deal in sequence with marketing, sales, order processing, accounts, deliveries, after-sales service – being passed from one department to another. Customers want this experience to be seamless: they don't want to come up against 'vertical' barriers or gaps between the units and functions of the organisation, where one department isn't talking to another, or has different systems and policies, or gives completely different messages.

Effective marketing and customer service therefore depends on cross-functional sharing of goals, values and information. It also requires all employees to see themselves as 'part time marketers': as direct or indirect contributors to customer relations, customer satisfaction and customer value.

10 The informal organisation

An **informal organisation** exists side by side with the formal one. When people work together, they establish social relationships and customary ways of doing things. Unlike the formal organisation, the informal organisation is loosely structured, flexible and spontaneous. It embraces such mechanisms as:

- **Social relationships** and groupings (eg cliques) within – or across – formal structures.
- The '**grapevine**', 'bush telegraph', or informal communication which by-passes the formal reporting channels and routes.
- **Behavioural norms** and ways of doing things, both social and work-related, which may circumvent formal procedures and systems (for good or ill). New members must 'learn the ropes' and get used to 'the way we do things here'.
- **Power/influence structures**, irrespective of organisational authority: informal leaders are those who are trusted and looked to for advice.

The informal organisation can offer some significant benefits for management.

- **Employee commitment**. The meeting of employees' social needs may contribute to morale and job satisfaction, with benefits in reduced absenteeism and labour turnover.
- **Knowledge sharing**. The availability of information through informal networks can give employees a wider perspective on their role in the task and the organisation, potentially stimulating 'big picture' problem-solving, cross-boundary co-operation and innovation.
- **Speed**. Informal networks and methods may sometimes be more efficient in achieving organisational goals, where the formal organisation has rigid procedures or lengthy communication channels, enabling decisions to be taken and implemented more rapidly.

The Chartered
Institute of Marketing

- **Responsiveness**. The directness, information-richness and flexibility of the informal organisation may be particularly helpful in conditions of rapid environmental change, facilitating both the mechanisms and culture of anti-bureaucratic responsiveness.

- **Co-operation**. The formation and strengthening of interpersonal networks can facilitate teamworking and co-ordination across organisational boundaries. It may reduce organisational politics – or utilise it positively by mobilising effective decision-making coalitions and by-passing communication blocks.

Each of the positive attributes of informal organisation could as easily be detrimental if the power of the informal organisation is directed towards goals unrelated to, or at odds with, those of the formal organisation.

- Social groupings may act collectively against organisational interests, strengthened by collective power and information networks. Even if they are aligned with organisational goals, group/network maintenance may take a lot of time and energy away from tasks.

- The grapevine is notoriously inaccurate and can carry morale-damaging rumours.

- The informal organisation can become too important in fulfilling employees' needs: individuals can suffer acutely when excluded from cliques and networks.

- Informal work practices may 'cut corners', violating safety or quality assurance measures.

Managers can **minimise problems** by:

- Meeting employees' **needs** as far as possible via the *formal* organisation: providing information, encouragement, social interaction and so on.

- Harnessing the **dynamics** of the informal organisation – for example, by using informal leaders to secure employee commitment to goals or changes.

- **Involving themselves** in the informal structure, so that they support information sharing, the breaking down of unhelpful rules and so on.

ACTIVITY 1.3

Referring to your own organisation, or one with which you are familiar, describe the organisational structure. You should refer to size, differentiation, integration, formalisation, spans of control and centralisation/decentralisation.

What benefits does this structure provide for the effective operation of the marketing function? What barriers or hindrances does the structure also give to marketing?

- The importance of organisation structures

    – It is important that organisations as a whole and the divisions within them find the right structure to match their needs.

- Aspects of organisation structure

    – Allocation of power and authority with appropriate solutions
    – Whether activities should be centralised or decentralised

- Structure – roles and relationships

    – Structure defines the way work is divided (creating jobs)
    – Inter-relationships exist between roles and organisational units

- Elements of organisation structure

    – Components of the organisation serve to co-ordinate activities

- Influences on organisation structure

    – Managerial choices can be made to optimise the structure
    – Increasing importance of the value of marketing in organisations

- Structure types

    – Organisations can be structured around functions, products or markets, brands, territories or be hybrid structures

    – Matrix structures are becoming increasingly important

    – Structures need to be considered carefully for multi-national organisations

- New organisation structures

    – Provide responsiveness and flexibility
    – Organisations and jobs are flexible

- The flexible firm

    – An organisation can be a flexible firm either through functional or numerical flexibility, members being flexible about job roles or the numbers of people employed changing

- The informal organisation

    – Informal organisations do not have structured methods for internal communication

FURTHER READING

The integration of marketing and sales functions is discussed in the CIM paper 'Marketing and sales fusion' published in 2011.

Boddy, D. (2008) *Management: An Introduction*. Europe, Prentice Hall.

Hatch, M.J. (2006) *Organization Theory*. 2nd edition. Oxford, Oxford University Press.

The Chartered
Institute of Marketing

Boddy, D. (2005) *Management: An Introduction*. 3rd edition. Harlow, FT Prentice Hall.

Bridges, W. (1994) *Jobshift: How to prosper in a workplace without jobs*. London, Allen & Unwin.

Burns, T. and Stalker, G.M. (1961) *The Management of Innovation*. London, Tavistock.

Busch, R. (2012) Structural Evolution Internal Operations. Busch, R. http://www.rainerbusch.de/mo_13_1-imorg.htm [Accessed on 20 April 2012]

CNN Money (2012) Global 500. CNN Money, http://www.money.cnn.com/magazines/fortune/global500/2011/full_list/index.html [Accessed on 30 May 2012]

Cole, G.A. and Kelly, P (2011) *Management: theory and practice*. 7th edition. London, Cengage Learning.

Deal, T.E. and Kennedy, A.A. (1982) *Organisation Cultures: The Rites and Rituals of Organisation Life*. Reading , MA Addison-Wesley.

Drucker, P. (1955) *The Practice of Management*. London, Heinemann.

Egan, J. (2004) *Relationship Marketing: Exploring Relational Strategies in Marketing*. 2nd edition. Harlow, Pearson Education.

French, J. and Raven, B. (1958) The bases of social power. *In:* Cartright D (ed) *Studies in Social Power*. Institute for Social Research, Ann Arbor, MI.

George, W.R. and Grönroos, C. (1989) Developing customer-conscious employees at every level – internal marketing. *In:* Congram & Friedman (eds) *Handbook of Services Marketing*. New York, AMACOM.

Handy, C. (1989) *The Age of Unreason*. Harmondsworth, Penguin.

Handy, C. (1995) *Gods of Management: The Changing Work of Organisations*. London, Random House Business.

Hennessey, D. and Jeannet J.P. (2001) *Global Marketing: Strategy and Cases*. 5th edition. Boston MA, Houghton Mifflin Company.

Hollensen, S. (2004) *Global Marketing: A Decision-Oriented Approach*. Harlow, Prentice Hall.

Huczynski, A. and Buchanan, D. (2001) *Organizational Behaviour: An Introductory Text*. 4th edition. Harlow, FT Prentice Hall.

Jobber, D. (2007) *Principles and Practice of Marketing*. 5th edition. Maidenhead, McGraw Hill Education.

Johnson, G. *et al* (2005) *Exploring Corporate Strategy: Text and Cases*. 7th edition. Harlow, Pearson Education.

Knight, K. (ed) (1977) *Matrix Management: A Cross-Functional Approach to Organization*. New York, PBI-Petrocelli Books.

Kotler, P. (2002) *Marketing Management*. 11th edition. US Imports and PHIPES.

Kotler, P. *et al* (1999) *Marketing: An Introduction*. Sydney, Prentice Hall.

Lancaster, G. and Withey, F. (2005) *Marketing Fundamentals*. Oxford, Butterworth-Heinemann.

Marketing Minds (2012) Brand Management and Organizational Structure. Marketing Minds, http://www.marketingminds.com.au/branding/brand_and_management.html [Accessed on 18 April 2012]

Milkovitch, G.T. and Boudreau, J.W. (1996) *Human Resource Management*. 8th edition. New York, McGraw Hill.

Mintzberg, H. (1983) *Structure in Fives: Designing Effective Organisations*. New Jersey, Prentice Hall.

Mullins, L. (1999) *Management and Organisation Behaviour*. 5th edition. Harlow, FT Prentice Hall.

Nestlé (2012) Brands. Nestlé, http://www.nestle.com/Brands/Pages/Brands.aspx [Accessed on 12 June 2012]

Peck, H.L. *et al* (2004) *Relationship Marketing: Strategy and Implementation*. Oxford, Elsevier Butterworth-Heinemann.

Pedler, M. *et al* (1991) *The Learning Company*. Maidenhead, McGraw Hill.

Peters, T.J. (1994) *Liberation Management*. New York, Pan.

Peters, T.J. and Waterman, R.H. (1981) *In Search of Excellence*. New York, Harper Collins.

Schein, E.H. (1985) *Organisational Culture and Leadership*. San Francisco, Jossey-Bass.

Schwartz, H. and Davies, S.M. (1981) Matching Corporate Culture and Business Strategy. *Organisational Dynamics*, Vol 9, pp30 – 48.

Trompenaars, F. (1993) *Riding the Waves of Culture*. London, Nicholas Brealey.

Weber, M. (1997) *The Theory of Social and Economic Organization*. London, The Free Press.

Welch, J. (2005) *Winning*. New York, Harper Business.

QUICK QUIZ

1   To what does organisational structure refer?

2   What are the components of Mintzberg's organisational structure?

3   ICT has enabled organisations to outsource and decentralise. What else has been possible?

4   Matrix structures offer more flexibility. True or false?

5   What are the three labour forces represented in the Shamrock organisation?

6   What is represented by the cultural web?

ACTIVITY DEBRIEFS

Activity 1.1

This will depend upon the context of the organisation chosen. As an example, imagine an international food producer who specialises in both branded and own label chilled ready meals. It may be more appropriate for the product/brand structure or territorial structure to be adopted, so that the organisation has different territory groups each with their own branded and own label departments to deal with their respective markets.

Activity 1.2

This will depend on the context of your own organisation.

Activity 1.3

This will depend on the context of your own organisation.

1   Ways to divide labour into distinct co-ordinated tasks.

2   Operating core, technostructure, support staff, strategic apex, middle line and operating core.

3   Centralise shared functions, create virtual teams, delayer and flatten.

4   True.

5   Professional core, flexible labour force, contractual fringe.

6   The taken for granted assumptions or paradigms of an organisation, and how they are manifest in an organisation's culture.

CHAPTER 2

Quality systems and processes

Introduction

Definitions of quality have focused on dimensions such as:

- **Quality of design**: the potential customer satisfactions built into a product.
- **Fitness for use or fitness for purpose**: that is, the extent to which a product does what it is intended and expected to do, or meets the customer's needs. (This is sometimes called the 'user-based' approach to quality.)
- **Conformance to requirement** (or **meeting specification**): that is, the product complies with the features, attributes, performance and other aspects set out as a requirement in the product specification. (This is the 'product-based' approach.)
- **Acceptable quality and value for money**: customers may be willing to sacrifice some performance and features for a lower price, as long as fitness for use is still acceptable. (This is the 'value-based' approach.)

Topic list

Dimensions of quality	1
Quality systems	2
Costs of quality	3
The importance of quality systems	4
Quality management system models	5
Quality Management standards	6
Quality improvement processes	7
Quality and relationship marketing	8

1.2	Critically assess the requirements of developing effective and efficient quality systems and processes to support compliance including evaluating and assessing the relevance of key quality concepts:
	■ The importance of quality systems to the organisation
	■ A range of quality models eg Total Quality Management, European Foundation of Quality Management, ISO 9001, Six Sigma, ISO 14001, PAS2050, benchmarking
	■ PDCA cycle – Plan, Do, Check, Ask
	■ Deming 14 steps for improving quality

1 Dimensions of quality

> ▶ **Key term**
>
> '**Quality** is the totality of features and characteristics of a product or service that bear on its ability to satisfy stated or implied needs.'
>
> Kotler and Armstrong (2001)

Quality is a measure of the features and characteristics of a product or service which affects their ability to meet stated or implied needs.

Garvin (1987) identifies eight generic dimensions of product quality.

- **Performance**: the operating characteristics of the product
- **Features**: value-adding characteristics and service elements (eg warranties, after-sales service)
- **Reliability**: the ability of the product to perform consistently over time
- **Durability**: the length of time a product will last without deterioration
- **Conformance**: whether agreed specifications and standards are met
- **Serviceability**: the ease and availability of service support
- **Aesthetics**: customer perceptions of how pleasing the product looks, sounds, tastes etc
- **Perceived quality**: the subjective expectations and perceptions developed by customers, as a result of marketing, brand identity, price and so on.

Essentially and inevitably, however, quality means different things to different operations. For example, think what it might mean for a toy manufacturer, a medical practice and a professional body like The Chartered Institute of Marketing.

It is also important to note that customers may perceive quality in different ways – and that quality must always be understood from the customer's perspective! Marketers need to identify 'quality gaps': shortfalls between what customers expect or perceive, and what the organisation provides.

Slack *et al* (2004) suggest that there may be a gap between the customer's specification and the organisation's specification; between the concept and the specification; between quality specification and actual quality; or between actual quality and the quality promised to the customer. Different strategies may be necessary to reduce or eliminate gaps, embracing product specification and development, materials and production quality – *and* marketing.

2 Quality systems

Quality is a natural aim of organisations but it can be elusive. To describe products or services as being high quality is common but what does it really mean?

High performance, durable materials, elegant design, attention to detail, attentive and responsive staff, fitness for purpose and value for money may all form part of a conception of quality.

In order to be confident of delivering quality, most organisations adopt systems and processes that reduce failure rates, ensure consistency of output, focus activity towards the customer and provide a means of gauging the quality of the service delivered.

There are many similarities in such schemes and they are not without critics. There is always a danger that by committing time and resources to meeting the demands of a particular model, the attention of staff and managers is taken away from more important operational and strategic matters.

The interest of quality systems and processes to marketing managers should be high, given the importance of brand value and organisational reputation in building long-term relationships, securing loyalty and maximising lifetime customer values.

3 Costs of quality

It is important for management to assess the true costs of quality, in order to make a compelling case for quality management and improvement.

The **costs of ensuring and assuring quality** include:

- **Prevention costs**: costs incurred prior to producing the product or delivering the service – to prevent or reduce defects or failures produced by the process.

  Examples include: the time and cost of building quality into the product/service design, implementing quality circles, preparing detailed specifications, training staff, maintaining equipment, setting up processes and systems, designing or purchasing prevention devices (eg fail-safe features) and so on.

- **Appraisal costs**: costs incurred *after* the product has been made or service delivered, to evaluate its conformance to quality requirements or agreed service levels.

  Examples include: inspection and testing costs, supplier vetting and monitoring, designing and using customer feedback forms and so on.

Losses incurred when quality is not achieved include:

- **Internal failure costs**: costs arising from quality failure, where the problems is identified *before* the product or service reaches the customer.

  Examples include: costs of materials scrapped due to obsolescence or damage; cost of materials and components lost during production/delivery; cost of output rejected during inspection; cost of re-working faulty output; losses due to having to sell faulty output at lower prices; and so on.

- **External failure costs**: costs arising from quality failure discovered *after* the product/services has been delivered to the customer.

  Examples include: cost of product liability and warranty claims; cost of repairing or replacing products returned by customers; other costs of complaint adjustment (eg cost of the customer complaints unit);

loss of customer loyalty and future sales; reputational damage arising from word-of-mouth about poor quality or product recalls (especially on safety grounds); and so on.

The costs and risks incurred as a result of poor quality are generally perceived to be higher than the costs of securing quality, and this is the rationale behind quality management systems and approaches.

ACTIVITY 2.1

The UK Government Department for Trade and Industry promotes the adoption of a quality management approach by British companies. To compete successfully, British companies must start by eliminating the following weaknesses.

1   Doing what has always been done.

2   Not understanding competitive positioning.

3   Compartmentalising of functions.

4   Trying to control people through systems.

5   Confusing quality with grade, or grade with quality.

6   Having an acceptable quality level (AQL).

7   Fire fighting is regarded as macho.

8   The 'not my problem' syndrome.

Explain each of these weaknesses and briefly state how a quality management approach would attempt to address each one.

4 The importance of quality systems

Quality systems may be applied to specific functions or activities, or to a whole organisation. Their importance is to maximise effectiveness which is essential for competitive or organisational advantage and delivering value for money.

Quality systems may be applied to:

- Individual teams and divisions

- Targeted processes and systems in administration, production, finance, distribution, communications, etc

- Products, brands or services

- One-off projects and initiatives

- The whole organisation

All of the above are applicable both to the organisation overall and the marketing department specifically.

Given the elusive nature of quality, it is helpful to have historical data, targets and benchmarks with which to compare actual performance. Most models emphasise the need for a co-ordinated, embedded and holistic approach.

Quality is not something that you add to a product or service like packaging or a separate feature, rather it often arises from the approaches taken to delivering it at all stages, starting with the initial design – designed in quality.

It is not something that remains static either, and managers need to keep attuned to new challenges and changing demands from inside and outside of the organisation. Technology may contribute but it also needs an inbuilt set of quality processes for managing the inputs it makes to the value chain.

Another common feature of most quality models is the need to take a systematic and sustained approach. Quality is not achieved quickly and requires the support of managers at all levels for the long term.

The desire of management to control is one of the major drivers for quality metrics, but caution should always be exercised to ensure that the data measures what is required and can be collected without undue time and expense.

Managers need metrics that are representative of the current state of things, indicating trends and allowing forecasts to be made so as to underpin effective decision making and control.

The business case for quality management in marketing can be summarised as follows.

- **Cost**: as we mentioned above, the potential costs and risks of quality failure are more extensive, and higher, than the controllable costs of managing quality.

- **Competitive advantage**: quality is a key dimension on which products can be meaningfully differentiated from their competitors. The ability to offer consistently high quality may be a core distinguishing competence for an organisation. At the micro-level, quality comparison is likely to be a key decision factor for a customer choosing between competing products, and quality failures may be sufficient to cause brand switching.

- **Brand positioning**: quality is one of the main dimensions on which a marketing organisation may seek to position a brand in the perception of the market. High quality, premium or luxury brands deliberate engage customers on a brand platform focused on quality attributes. Quality failures may significantly damage the identity and positioning of such brands.

- **Relationship marketing**: quality is a tool of customer acquisition, but the consistent quality of goods and service encounters is also extremely important in customer retention, the building and maintenance of trust, and the engagement of customer loyalty – the main focus of relationship marketing. (We will discuss this aspect in a little more detail in Section 8 of this chapter.) Repeated disappointments (however well managed) will ultimately be fatal to the maintenance of on-going customer relationships – and reduce customer lifetime profitability.

- **Price**: quality is related to customer perceptions of value for money. The market will often bear higher or premium pricing for products and services perceived to be (or marketed as) of high quality.

- **Compliance**: in some areas, quality is an issue of legal compliance. If goods are not of satisfactory quality or are not fit for their purpose, or are actually or potentially unsafe, the supplier may be liable:

    - For breach of contract under the Sale of Goods Act 1979

    - For negligence, or a breach of the common law duty of reasonable care owed by a manufacturer or supplier to a consumer

    - For breach of consumer protection law (eg in the UK, the Consumer Protection Act, Food Safety Act, Enterprise Act 2002 and so on).

- **Reputation management**: quality – and more particularly, safety – failures can be highly damaging to the organisation's corporate reputation and standing, if goods are exposed as 'shoddy' or are forced to be recalled for safety reasons. (You might think of examples such as the mass recall of Mattel toys manufactured in China, which were found to include toxic lead paint.)

- **Culture and morale**: a culture built on values such as customer satisfaction, excellence and quality (whether 'premium/prestige' or 'value for money') is more compelling and positive than a culture of indifference, customer exploitation and 'corner cutting'. Pride in the organisation and brand can be a strong source of employee morale and team spirit.

- **Employee satisfaction and loyalty**: employee satisfaction and loyalty are linked to product and service quality in complex ways. The **loyalty-based cycle of growth** (Reichheld, 1996) suggests that superior quality and service creates satisfied and loyal customers – but, at the same time:

- Satisfied and loyal customers generate revenue which can be invested in employees (eg through superior rewards)

- Consistent delivery of superior value to customers gives employees pride and satisfaction in their work (and avoids the stress and frustration of complaint handling etc).

A simplified version of this virtuous cycle can be depicted as follows.

Figure 2.1   Reichheld's loyalty-based cycle of growth (simplified)

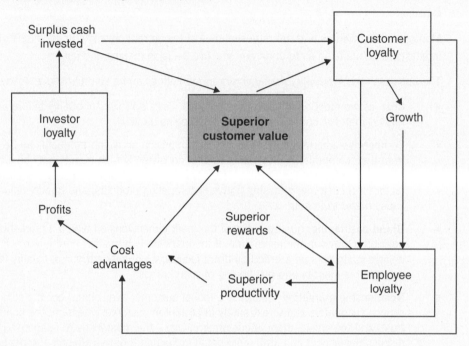

5 Quality management system models

The main thrust of a QMS is defining and managing the **processes** which will result in the production of quality products and services (a quality assurance strategy) – rather than in detecting defective products or services (a quality control strategy).

A fully documented, systematic QMS is designed to ensure that:

- Customers' requirements are met, and they have confidence in the ability of the organisation consistently to deliver products and services which meet their needs and expectations.

- Organisational performance objectives are consistently achieved, through improved process control and reduced wastage, with the efficient use of available resources (materials, human, technology and information).

- Staff competence, training and morale are enhanced, through clear expectations and process requirements.

- Quality gains are maintained once achieved: learning and good practices do not 'slip' for lack of documentation, adoption and consistency.

The Chartered
Institute of Marketing

5.1 Total Quality Management

Total quality management (TQM) was very popular in the 1970s and 1980s and while it may have since peaked in popularity, it is still a very persuasive model and holds sway in many organisations even today.

The influence of the TQM philosophy can be seen in much of the subsequent thinking in quality systems and processes.

TQM, as the name suggests, strives for quality in all processes. Indeed, its philosophy maintains that anything less than this is inefficient as it results in higher levels of waste, rejected items, failures and customer dissatisfaction. It requires the buy-in by all levels of the organisation led by the senior team and a suitable set of metrics by which to gauge success or otherwise.

Some of the key principles and values of TQM can be summarised as follows.

- **Get it right first time**. Quality should be **designed** into products, services and **processes**, with the aim of achieving **zero defects**. The traditional approach to quality management argued that there is an optimal level of quality effort which minimises total quality costs: there is a point beyond which spending more on quality yields a benefit that is less than the additional cost incurred. TQM, however, argues that:

    - Failure and poor quality are simply unacceptable: the inevitability of error is not something that an organisation should accept, as a cultural value. The target should be zero defects.

    - Taking into account the 'wider' costs of poor quality – the potential to lose customers, the taking up of managerial time on non-value adding problem-solving, the loss of morale and trust among staff – *no* amount of defects can be considered 'optimal'.

    - Quality can and should be continually improved, and this need not incur high costs or diminishing returns.

- **Quality chains**. The quality chain extends from suppliers through to consumers, via the 'internal supply chain' (supplier and customer units representing the flow of work within the organisation). The work of each link in this chain impacts on the next one, and will eventually affect the quality provided to the consumer. The chain may be broken at any point where people or processes fail to fulfil the quality requirements of their immediate (internal or external) customer. Clear customer relationships and accountabilities (including service level agreements, where required) need to be established throughout the chain.

- **Quality culture and total involvement**. Quality is a 'way of life': a key cultural value in the organisation. Every person within an organisation potentially has an impact on quality, and it is the responsibility of everyone to get quality right. This needs to be consistently and compellingly expressed and modelled by senior management, and supported and reinforced by recruitment, training, team building, appraisal and reward systems.

- **Quality through people**. Commitment, communication, awareness and problem-solving are more important in securing quality than mere systems. Team-based management and empowerment are key elements of TQM. Teams must be empowered and equipped to take action necessary to correct problems, propose and implement improvements, and respond flexibly and fast to customer needs (particularly in service contexts). There must be high-quality, multi-directional communication. Strict control systems (and associated 'blaming') should be replaced by a culture of learning, in which people are not afraid to try new things or take the initiative to make small improvements.

- **Process alignment**. Business processes should be deliberately designed and modified so that every activity is geared to the same end: meeting the customer's wants and needs. Where this is not the case, there may be the need for radical change programmes such as Business Process Re-engineering (BPR).

- **Quality management**. All processes and operations are monitored and controlled according to clear, specific, measurable performance criteria. Attention is focused on getting the process right – and only secondarily on outputs. Refusal to focus on short-term effects ensures a more proactive commitment to long-term improvement. Quality systems should be thoroughly documented is the following forms:

- A company quality manual, summarising the quality management policy and system

- A procedures manual setting out the functions, structures and responsibilities for quality in each department

- Detailed work instructions and specifications for how work should be carried out in order to achieve the desired quality standards. These will have to be continually updated as improvements and adjustments are made.

- **Continuous improvement**. Quality is not a 'one-off' exercise. By seeking to improve continually, organisations remain sensitive to new opportunities and approaches, and encourage learning and flexibility at all levels. In contrast to radical, 'discontinuous' or 'blank slate' change approaches such as BPR, continuous improvement may operate by small-step or incremental changes. Such evolutionary change is less traumatic, less risky, less costly, and can be driven from the bottom up by empowered employees.

Within a marketing context TQM can be related both for the internal marketing process and the process element of the seven P marketing mix, ensuring total quality in the process of supporting customer purchases.

5.1.1 Continuous improvement

Quality management involves the on-going and continual examination and improvement of existing processes: 'getting it more right, next time'. This process is sometimes referred by its Japanese name of 'kaizen': 'a Japanese concept of a total quality approach based on continual evolutionary change with considerable responsibility given to employees within certain fixed boundaries' (Mullins, 1999).

Kaizen looks for uninterrupted, ongoing incremental change: there is always room for improvement and continuously trying to become better, for example through:

- Elimination of wastes (non value-adding activities)
- Immediately accessible improvements to equipment, materials or team behaviour.

It is essentially a **cyclical approach to change**, because it incorporates reflection or evaluation for future learning and improvement. It is also essentially a **bottom-up or empowerment-based** approach to quality, because it utilises the feedback, ideas and initiatives of those closest to quality issues: operational staff and customers.

A basic cyclical approach to kaizen involves:

- Identifying potential areas for improvement, by monitoring performance and gathering feedback from employees and other stakeholders

- Analysing the data to identify possible causes of performance shortfalls common factors or 'hidden messages' in the results

- Plan and implement action to improve performance in the identified area

- Assess the effects of the action, and identify any further problems (in a continuous cycle).

5.1.2 Quality circles

> ▶ **Key term**
>
> A **quality circle** is a team of workers from different levels and functions of an organisation which meets regularly to discuss issues relating to quality, and to recommend improvements.

Japanese quality guru Ishikawa (1991) stressed the importance of people and participation in the process of solving quality problems. He devised the idea of **quality circle** to achieve participation, harness the expertise and commitment of staff, share best practice, and overcome resistance to quality management.

A quality circle typically consists of a **voluntary-participation group** of about eight employees, from different functions, which meets regularly (during working hours) to discuss problems of **quality and quality control** in their areas of work, and to suggest quality improvements. The circle is facilitated by a leader who directs the

discussion and helps to orient and develop members of the circle (if required) in quality management and problem-solving techniques.

Management should not impose agendas on the meetings, in order to permit openness about problems and conflicts, and to encourage thinking 'outside the box'. Feedback on suggestions offered and problems raised should, however, be swift and constructive, in order to demonstrate that the quality circle is taken seriously as a participation and quality tool.

6 Quality Management standards

6.1 European Foundation of Quality Management

The European Foundation of Quality Management (EFQM) created a quality model in 1992 as the basis for European Quality Awards, and these are still awarded to organisations deemed to have demonstrated high levels of quality of their systems and processes. However, the application of the model has gained more widespread usage as a framework for benchmarking, self-assessment and improvement.

The EFQM model recognises five enablers for quality.

Table 2.1   EFQM five enablers for quality

Enabler criteria	What is the approach in this area and is it appropriate? Does the approach support the organisation's overall aims? How widely used is the approach? How is the approach reviewed? What improvements are undertaken following review?
Leadership How the behaviour and actions of leaders support a culture of excellence	■ Leaders develop the mission, vision and values and are role models of a culture of excellence ■ Leaders are personally involved in ensuring the organisation's management system is developed, implemented and continuously improved ■ Leaders are involved with customers, partners and representatives of society (stakeholders) ■ Leaders motivate, support and recognise the organisation's people
Policy and strategy How effectively these are formulated and deployed into plans and action	■ Policy and strategy are based on the present and future needs and expectations of stakeholders ■ Policy and strategy are based on information from performance measurement, research, learning and creativity related activities ■ Policy and strategy area developed, reviewed and updated ■ Policy and strategy are deployed through a framework of key processes ■ Policy and strategy are communicated and implemented
People How the organisation develops and realises the potential of its human resources	■ People resources are planned, managed and improved ■ People's knowledge and competencies are identified, developed and sustained ■ People are involved and empowered ■ People and the organisation have a dialogue ■ People are rewarded, recognised and cared for
Partnerships and resources How effectively and efficiently the organisation manages its resources	■ External partnerships are managed ■ Finances are managed ■ Buildings, equipment and materials are managed ■ Technology is managed ■ Information and knowledge are managed

Enabler criteria	What is the approach in this area and is it appropriate?
	Does the approach support the organisation's overall aims?
	How widely used is the approach?
	How is the approach reviewed?
	What improvements are undertaken following review?
Processes How the organisation manages and improves its processes	▪ Processes are systematically designed and managed
	▪ Processes are improved, as needed, using innovation in order to fully satisfy and generate increasing value for customers and other stakeholders
	▪ Products and services are designed and developed based on customer needs and expectations
	▪ Products and services are produced, delivered and serviced
	▪ Customer relationships are managed and enhanced

In addition, there are four areas for quality results criteria within EFQM.

Table 2.2   EFQM quality results criteria

Results criteria	What has the performance been over a period of time?
	How does performance compare against internal targets and other organisations?
	Were the results caused by the approaches described in the enabler criteria?
	To what extent do the measures cover the range of the organisation's or business area's activities?
Customer results	▪ Perception measures: what is the customer's perception of the organisation?
	▪ Performance indicators: how good are the drivers of (key factors in bringing about) customer satisfaction?
People results	▪ Perception measures: what are employees' perceptions of the organisation?
	▪ Performance indicators: how good are the drivers of employee satisfaction?
Society results	▪ Perception measures: how does society and the local community perceive the organisation?
	▪ Performance indicators: what results have been achieved relating to community and environmental concerns?
Key performance results	▪ What is the organisation achieving in relation to its planned performance?

THE REAL WORLD

British Telecommunications (BT) is a founding member of the European Foundation for Quality Management (EFQM) and the British Quality Foundation (BQF). It is committed to the principles of Total Quality, has been the winner of many excellence awards and is certified under ISO 9001 (Quality Management Systems) and ISO 14001 (Environmental Management Systems).

For more information, and to access some useful tools: check out http://www.bt.com/quality

Visit http://www.efqm.org to learn more about EFQM and its members.

The Chartered Institute of Marketing

Make a very general informal assessment of your work organisation using some of the criteria listed in the EFQM tables above.

- What immediate areas for improvement (if any) might you highlight for later follow-up?

- What areas strike you as most relevant to, or dependent upon, marketing input and activity?

6.2 ISO 9001

ISO 9000 was launched in 1987 and comprises a group of quality management standards laid down by the International Organisation for Standardisation (ISO): a worldwide federation of national standards bodies. ISO 9000 standards are 'built around business processes, with a strong emphasis on improvement and focus on meeting the needs of customers': they are intended to be generic and adaptable to all kinds of organisations. The ISO series includes:

- ISO 9000   Quality Management Systems: Fundamentals and vocabulary
- ISO 9001   Quality Management Systems: Requirements
- ISO 9004   Guidelines for Performance Improvements

Organisations may use the standards framework as a benchmark for planning and improving their own quality management systems, or they may seek certification to demonstrate compliance to customers and clients.

There are over 17,000 sets of standards relating to everything from agriculture to wood technology. The advantage of universally accepted statements is that they standardise:

- Language and terminology, including documentation, symbols and labelling
- Requirements for safety and pollution
- Compatibility of components, including dimensions, weights and measures, and performance

ISO 9001 is the standard for quality management. It covers the processes relating to production and service delivery together with the controls that need to be in place to ensure that customer satisfaction is maximised.

The benefit of adopting the standards is that it helps organisations identify and define the key roles and responsibilities in quality management.

By following the quality processes described in the standards, an organisation should be rewarded by achieving cost savings from improved productivity and reduced wastage and defects.

The benefits to customers will be in the form of high levels of correct order fulfilments within time.

In addition, once an organisation has been accredited, it is able to declare its adherence to ISO 9001 which signals to customers, suppliers and other stakeholders that its quality management processes meet recognised international standards.

In order to apply for accreditation, an organisation should first familiarise itself with the requirements of the standards and how they impact on routine operations and activities. The standards need to be adopted, integrated into stated policies and procedures, and embedded in operation manuals.

There also needs to be a process for confirming achievement of the standards. Compliance with the standards must to be confirmed by the work of compliance assessors or internal auditors. The organisation may apply for accreditation through an audit by a third party. If successful, the organisation is then issued a certificate of registration in acknowledgement.

The standard identifies quality management systems as comprising four processes. Note the importance of the customer in the model. Customer requirements determine product/service design and production, and monitoring of customer satisfaction (by the marketing function) is key to evaluate and validate whether customer requirements have been met.

Figure 2.2   The ISO 9001 conceptual model

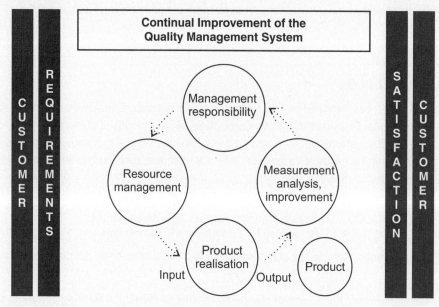

(Adapted from ISO, 2012)

- **Management responsibility** includes aspects such as: management commitment, customer focus, quality policy-setting, planning, responsibility/accountability, communication, and management review

- **Resource management** includes aspects such as: provision of resources, human resources, infrastructure and work environment to support quality

- **Product realisation** includes aspects such as: customer research, product design and/or development, purchasing, production and service operations, and control of measuring and monitoring devices

- **Measurement, analysis and improvement** includes aspects such as: monitoring and measurement of performance, control of non-conforming product, analysis of data, and improvement planning

Periodic audits are used to determine ongoing compliance.

ISO 9000 contains eight **quality management principles** designed to support an efficient, effective and adaptable QMS. (You should recognise some of these from our earlier discussion of TQM.)

- **Customer focus**. Product and service requirements must be based on customer needs and expectations.

- **Leadership**. Quality management requires direction and unity of purpose. Leaders must formulate quality policy and ensure that clear, measurable objectives are set.

- **Involvement of people**. Management must act as enablers for employee involvement in quality, which both harnesses their abilities in the interests of the organisation – and enhances their role and satisfaction.

- **Process approach**. Quality management systems must be seen as a business process, transforming one or more inputs to create an output of value to the customer. This is an efficient approach to managing resources and activities.

- **Systems approach to management**. Quality is a complex system of inter-related processes, which need to by identified, understood and managed.

- **Continual improvement**, as a permanent and on-going objective, requiring proactive customer research and feedback monitoring, as well as measuring and monitoring of performance.

- **Factual approach to decision-making**, requiring systems in place to provide timely, relevant data and information to managers.

- **Mutually beneficial supplier relationships**, enhancing the ability of both partners to create value, as links in the quality chain.

All of the above can be applied directly to the activities of the marketing function in an organisation.

ISO standards are not without their critics.

First, the philosophy rests of the assumption that it is possible to improve quality through the adoption of a generic set of standard processes. Given the richness and diversity of activity, it seems unlikely that a single approach to documentation, control, corrective action, audit and continuous improvement could be effective.

There are a number of industry-specific variations for IT, telecommunications and car manufacturers among others to help overcome this.

The process of documentation, and seeking and maintaining accreditation can be time consuming and expensive, and some have argued that it may act as a distraction from genuine quality management by focusing the attention on the wording rather than the principle of the standards. It may reduce the sense of responsibility for quality if managers believe that it has been 'taken care of'.

Slavishly following the standards may make them blind to genuine problems in their own organisation.

It is not clear how much stakeholders are impressed by a certification like ISO 9001. What often happens is that there is a trend towards gaining accreditation for new initiatives – like the Charter Mark, Investors in People and so on – but their very success creates a diminution in the perceived value. If everyone has the certificate, it no longer provides a mean of distinguishing between competing organisations.

6.3 ISO 14001

ISO 14001 is a set of environmental management standards first introduced in 1996, specifically focusing on Environmental Management Systems (EMS). The EMS gives a systematic approach to assessing and managing the impact of an organisation on the environment, considering the consequences of the operations.

The comments made earlier in relation to ISO 9001 are equally relevant here. The rationale and process for implementation are the same. So too, are the potential advantages and pitfalls. The standards cover:

- Management systems for environmental control
- Auditing processes for environmental management
- Methods for measuring performance
- Labelling
- Life-cycle assessment
- Environmental factors in production[1]

The major **requirement for an EMS** under ISO 14001 include:

- An **environmental policy statement** which includes commitments to:

    - Prevention of pollution

    - Continual improvement of the EMS leading to improvements in overall environmental performance

    - Compliance with all relevant legal and regulatory requirements

- **Identification** of all aspects of the organisation's activities, products and services that could have a significant impact on the environment (whether or not regulated): focusing on environmental aspects that are within the organisation's control or ability to influence

- Establishing **performance objectives and targets** for the EMS, taking into account legal requirements and organisational policy commitments and information about significant environmental protection issues

- **Implementing** an EMS to meet these objectives and targets, including: training of employees, establishing work instructions and practices, establishing performance metrics and so on

- Establishing a programme for **periodic auditing and review** of environmental performance against the environmental policy and legal/regulatory framework

- Taking **corrective and preventive actions** when deviations from the EMS are identified

- Undertaking periodic **reviews of the EMS** by top management to ensure its continuing performance and adequacy in the face of changing environmental information

An organisation can make a self-assessment and self-declaration, or, if it wishes, it can be audited and certified by a third party, to demonstrate compliance to customers, clients and regulatory bodies.

THE REAL WORLD

In December 2010 full service marketing agency Ogilvy announced that they had been awarded ISO14001 accreditation. In a statement announcing this Ogilvy stated the following:

'Ogilvy has become one of the very few agencies in the world to achieve the internationally recognised Environmental Management Systems Standard, ISO 14001 (modelled above). This also means Ogilvy Group UK is now the only agency from across the entire Ogilvy global network to hold all three international accreditations : ISO 9001 (Quality Management), ISO 27001 (Information Security Management) and now ISO 14001.'

Some of the changes which Ogilvy introduced to gain ISO14001 (which was awarded by SGS) involved axing unnecessary newspapers, using zoned lighting to cut electricity and scrapping bins under individual desks, replacing them with segregated recycling bins.

The certification also ensures that the way Ogilvy works is as sustainable and environmentally aware as possible, with supply chain partners at multiple levels.

Examples of this include production companies working with the agency on TV commercial shoots having to comply with Ogilvy's Environmental Policy through respect for neighbours when on location, not damaging flora and fauna, polluting water courses, or disturbing protected species.

Ogilvy will now only partner fellow suppliers who are ISO 14001 accredited to ensure their supply chain is sustainable.

(Adapted from Ogilvy, 2012)

6.4 PAS 2050

BSI Standards Solutions produced Publicly Available Standards (PAS) 2050 *Assessing the life cycle greenhouse gas emissions of goods and services* in 2008 at the joint request of DEFRA and the Carbon Trust.

Unlike the ISO standards, PAS standards, as the name implies, are available for free.

The philosophy is very similar to that of ISO standards. The standards contain benchmarks for emissions and help organisations find means to reduce them. They enable the user to make an assessment of the total greenhouse gas emissions that are released in the natural life cycle of their goods and services and to compare this with other available materials, means of production and delivery[2].

You can download a free copy of PAS 2050 from the Carbon Trust, DEFRA or the BIS:
http://shop.bsigroup.com/en/ProductDetail/?pid=000000000030256750

The Chartered Institute of Marketing

7 Quality improvement processes

7.1 Six sigma

Motorola developed the principle of the six sigma method. It aims to remove processes that cause defects and damage customer satisfaction on the basis that it is cheaper to prevent failures than to fix them or discard rejects.

The model takes its name from a mathematical symbol used in statistics for standard deviation, that is, a measure of spread around the mean in a normal distribution.

When the spread of performance between the average and the minimum required standard is six times the standard deviation, then the number of items falling outside of acceptable tolerance is negligible (in fact, less than 3.4 in a million). The quality of output is so high and so consistent that the incidence of failure is tiny (Figure 2.3).

Figure 2.3   The falling costs of the six sigma model (based on a diagram by Johnson, Chvala and Voehl, 1997)

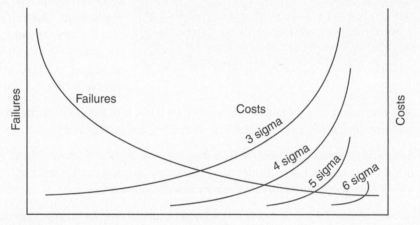

Six sigma uses the '**DMAIC**' model for **process improvement.**

- **Define** an opportunity or need for improvement: a project team is formed and given the responsibility and resources for solving the problem

- **Measure** current performance: gather data that describes accurately how the process is currently working and analyse it to produce some initial ideas about what may be causing the problem

- **Analyse** the opportunity for improvement: generate and test theories as to what might be causing the problem, to identify root causes

- **Improve** performance: remove root causes by designing and implementing changes to the 'offending' process

- **Control** performance by designing and implementing new controls to prevent the original problem from returning

In common with other models, like TQM, six sigma requires full commitment from the whole organisation with support from the highest level to be successful. It is a scientific model with a heavy focus on quantitative data.

It is particularly suited to production and financial outcomes. Champions are needed to generate and sustain enthusiasm for the model.

Motorola claim to have saved $17 billion as a direct result of the six sigma model since they adopted it in 2006[3].

Apple computers have adopted six sigma, applying the principles across the organisation. Ratings from the American Consumer Satisfaction Index (ACSI) report indicates that within the Personal Computers category, customers perceived Apple as the best company in terms of customer service. Apple's baseline score was 77 (on a 100-point scale), and since 2004 they have topped the charts in their category, with a score of 87 in 2011 against an industry average of 78.

The focus within Apple Computers on product innovation and quality along with customer service through the application of six sigma principles is almost certainly a major contributory factor to these ratings.

(Adapted from ACSI, 2012)

7.2 Benchmarking

> **Key term**
>
> **Benchmarking** is the establishment, through data gathering, of targets and comparators, through who use relative levels of performance (and particularly areas of underperformance) can be identified.

There are a large number of agencies who can provide external marketing benchmarks appropriate for any organisation, enabling you to compare performance with industry standards or norms. External benchmarks are potentially very powerful in helping an organisation set targets for improvement. However, they must be used with care.

A comparison is only valuable if one is comparing like with like and it is hard to find two identical organisations with matching goals, product portfolios, tactics, market profiles and so on.

Even when a reasonable comparison is possible, one might still wonder at the value of it. Pursuit of performance to match a particular benchmark may be inappropriate and may result in undue focus on a given aspect of activity at the expense of other more pressing matters.

At best, benchmarks should only be part of an overall model for quality. Historical performance and an organisation's own internal targets are equally important.

Bendell, Boulter & Kelly (1993) distinguish four types of benchmarking.

- **Internal benchmarking**: comparison with high-performing units or functions in the same organisation. One division's marketing function might be benchmarked against another, for example, to lift standards and consistency within the organisation.

- **Functional benchmarking**: comparison with a best-practice external example of a function, regardless of industry. This is also known as operational or process benchmarking. An IT company might benchmark its marketing function against that of Apple Computers or Coca Cola, say, as a way of lifting its processes to best-practice level.

- **Competitor benchmarking**: comparison with a high-performing competitor in key areas which impact on performance: for example, Dell comparing its product reliability, time-to-market for innovation or B2B marketing with Hewlett Packard.

- **Generic benchmarking**: comparison of business processes across functional boundaries and industries. The organisation can benchmark itself against 'excellent' companies or an excellence framework (such as the EFQM), or an organisation with a reputation for learning, innovation, relationship marketing – or whatever the organisation is interested in pursuing.

Benchmarks for marketing exist for every metric that the marketing manager may choose to use to guide them towards making improvements. For example, this might include benchmarks for the staffing of marketing including:

- **Headcount** – how big are marketing functions in organisations of comparable size and similar profiles?
- **Staff turnover** – how long, on average, do members of staff stay within marketing functions?

The Chartered Institute of Marketing

- **Salaries and wages** – what are the average rates of pay within marketing departments in the sector?
- **Staff satisfaction** – how well do members of marketing teams rate their employer?
- **Staff development** – what is the typical spend on training and upskilling?

Similar benchmarks may also be used for project appraisal, responsiveness to media campaigns, average lifetime customer value, average customer purchase, gross ratings points, rate of new product acceptance, conversion rates from enquiry to sale and so on.

There are also **limitations and drawbacks** to benchmarking as an approach to performance measurement and improvement.

- It may suggest that there is **one best way** of doing business. However, the organisation needs to take a contingency approach to problem-solving, suitable to its own resources, strengths, weaknesses and environment – rather than an 'off-the-shelf' approach drawn from other organisations' experience.

- The benchmark may be **'yesterday's solution to tomorrow's problem'**. For example, a cross-channel ferry company might have benchmarked its activities against airlines and other ferry companies – however, the Channel Tunnel emerged as the main competitor for cross-channel ferry services.

- It is a reactive, **'catch-up' or 'me too' exercise**, which may not result in the seeking and development of unique, distinctive and hard-to-imitate core competences.

- It depends on **accurate and detailed information** about competitors (which may pose research and ethical challenges), and on appropriate analogies/comparisons in other industries (because of the need to compare like with like).

Table 2.3   Oakland (2003) puts forward a 15-step benchmarking process.

Plan	1	Select the function, unit or process to be benchmarked
	2	Identify the exemplar of best practice, key competitor or successful partner (using industry analysis, customer feedback or a benchmarking consultant)
	3	Identify the criteria to be benchmarked (based on critical success factors)
	4	Establish a benchmarking project team (clear roles, authority and resources)
	5	Plan methods for data collection (surveys, interviews, documents, visits)
	6	Conduct research
	7	Manage direct contacts with the target organisation (interviews, visits etc)
Analyse	8	Collate and analyse benchmark data to compare performance: identify performance 'gaps'
	9	Create a 'competence centre' and knowledge bank: document information
	10	Analyse underlying cultural, structural and managerial factors that enable performance to benchmark standard (ie not just performance measures)
Develop	11	Develop new performance standards, targets and measures to reflect desired improvements
	12	Develop systematic action plans (change management programmes, resource plans etc with time-scales, accountabilities and monitoring/review processes)
Improve	13	Implement the action plans
Review	14	Continuously monitor and/or periodically review progress and results
	15	Review the benchmark process for future learning

7.3 PDCA cycle

The PDCA cycle (plan, do, check, act) was made popular by Deming and is implicitly or explicitly part of many other quality systems. For example, the six sigma model incorporates a cycle of define, measure, analyse, improve and control, which is just a variation of PDCA.

It can also be found in other similar cycles such as the standard scientific approach and Kolb's (1985) learning cycle which we will look at in Chapter 4 when we study the development and effectiveness of teams. A key to such cycles is that they form an iterative process such that the outcome informs the next cycle on a continuous basis, each time perfecting the process a little more. It is deceptively simple and incredibly powerful.

When applied to business processes the PDCA cycle allows managers to analyse activity in order to identify the causes of defects and failures of customer satisfaction. If adopted as a cyclical approach, it then allows feedback to be used to ascertain the success of changes made in reducing the number of defects (Figure 2.4).

Figure 2.4   PDCA cycle

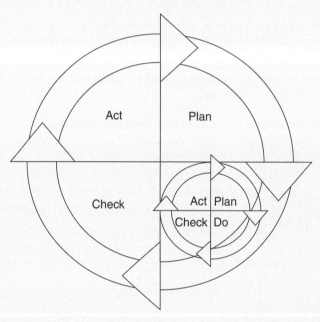

At the *plan* stage, the aim is to develop business processes so that they lead to improvements in outputs. At the *do* stage, the new or revised processes are implemented and performance is measured. At the *check* stage, the performance is analysed to help inform any future changes. At the act stage, further revisions are identified and agreed.

Deming's principal interest was in production. It is possible to refine the PDCA cycle using a secondary loop within the *do* segment to illustrate the relationship of operational activity as a sub-process within a larger cycle of strategic development (Figure 2.4).

Quality assurance within marketing may be viewed as a PDCA cycle. The performance indicators described elsewhere in this chapter are vital if a systematic approach is to be taken to raising the effectiveness of marketing activity. Being able to demonstrate the value that marketing adds to the strategic PDCA cycle is a further desirable outcome of using such a model.

Deming's approach to quality may be given as follows:

- Quality may be defined as the result of work efforts divided by costs.
- Where the focus is on quality, quality tends to increase over time and costs fall.
- Where the focus is on costs, the costs tend to rise over time and quality falls.

 The Chartered Institute of Marketing

7.4 Deming 14 steps

In addition to popularising the PDCA model for quality improvement, Deming has given his name to an annual award in the United States for quality and productivity. He has also been hugely influential in Japan where he taught for many years, and his name is used for prizes awarded in that country. In his book *Out of the Crisis*, Deming set out 14 steps that led to improved management. In doing so, he set out the framework for what become TQM and other similar models of quality. The following steps are paraphrased from his original work.

Step 1	Create a 'constancy of purpose' for improvement, focusing on long-term excellence, competitiveness and survival rather than short-term profits.
Step 2	Adopt a new approach ('a new philosophy') that embraces change.
Step 3	Stop relying on inspections to achieve quality, rather ensure that quality is built in.
Step 4	Choose suppliers based on price and quality, and establish long-term, trusting relationships.
Step 5	Keep on improving every process, and in this way reduce costs.
Step 6	Make training on the job a standard part of everyone's daily routine.
Step 7	Adopt and institute leadership.
Step 8	'Drive out fear' so that individuals are motivated by a desire to succeed rather than through threats and coercions.
Step 9	'Break down barriers' between individuals and departments to facilitate cross-functional working.
Step 10	Get rid of slogans, targets and 'exhortations', as they do not help to improve quality because quality is usually the result of processes not individuals.
Step 11	Remove numerical quotas for staff and managers, and use leadership instead.
Step 12	Encourage pride in workmanship and remove performance management systems that rate individuals.
Step 13	Foster a lively self-improvement programme for all staff and managers.
Step 14	Put everyone in charge of achieving the desired transformation of the workplace.

> ▶ **Assessment tip**
>
> When considering quality tools, whether management or improvement tools, they should be specifically applied to the context of the marketing function within the organisation, in conjunction with the wider organisation.

8 Quality and relationship marketing

It is one of the key principles of relationship marketing that customer retention and loyalty is built on the **creation and delivery of superior customer value** (that is, greater than that offered by competitors) on a sustained basis. The shift from transactional marketing to relationship marketing (as you may already be aware from your studies of *Stakeholder Marketing* for the Professional Certificate) reflects a shift in focus (Egan, 2004, p130) from what you can do *to* customers (persuade, capture, exploit) to what you can do *for* customers (added benefits) and *with* customers (dialogue and co-operation) to ensure customer satisfaction.

Value is effectively 'in the eye of the customer', and organisations must seek to understand exactly on what aspects of their offering customers will place value. However, quality of products/services and customer service (at all touch points, in all activities and throughout the relationship with the customer) is regarded as an essential element of value.

Customers give loyalty in exchange for their expectation that value will flow to them from a relationship with a supplier. Customers are more likely to become repeat customers, loyalty customers and perhaps even active advocates.

> 'Marketing is concerned with 'exchange relationships' between the organisation and its customers, and quality and customer service are key linkages in these relationships. At its simplest, the exchange relationship is the customer paying for the benefits they receive. But the relationship marketing view is that the customer gives loyalty in exchange for their expectation that value will flow to them from the relationship. This flow of value includes not just project benefits but a number of less tangible benefits relating to the quality of the experience within a wider customer service context. So the challenge to the organisation is to align marketing, quality and customer service strategies more closely. In the past organisations have tended to treat these as separate and unrelated. Consequently, decisions affecting customer service may have been taken by diverse functions such as distribution, manufacturing or sales. Likewise, quality was seen as the preserve of a specific quality control or assurance function. Under the relationship marketing paradigm, these three areas are merged and given a sharper focus..'.

(Christopher *et al*, 2002, p9-10)

Christopher *et al* (2002) argue that:

- **Customer satisfaction** is critical in maintaining relationships and fostering customer loyalty. Traditionally, marketing has focused on customer acquisition, but *retaining* **customers** involves delivering value through fulfilling promises and adding customer value through quality and customer service.

- Quality and customer service are not 'departmental' responsibilities: the ways in which they are delivered and maintained **across functional boundaries**. Marketers must build supportive relationships with 'part-time' marketers working in customer-facing roles: providing them with appropriate skills, processes and operational back-up to meet customer requirements. Quality thinking and know-how has to be **aligned** across all departments – and extend beyond the organisation to embrace the total value network.

- The traditional concept of quality as 'conformance to specifications' (internal quality) must be superseded by concepts of **quality defined by customers** ('customer perceived quality'). 'Because the manufacturing and operations functions have largely led the advances in quality management thinking and practice, the emphasis is on systems and processes, performance reliability and continuous improvement... But without collaborative marketing involvement, quality will never achieve its goals and will fall short of customer defined requirements.' (*ibid*, p152)

- Quality assurance alone does not guarantee that customers receive quality as they perceive it. It is marketing's key responsibility to **monitor and interpret customers' perceptions of quality**, providing rigorous market research to support collaborative quality management.

The Chartered
Institute of Marketing

Consider a marketing function with which you are familiar. Select one of the quality models described earlier assuming you are the marketing manager. Describe the steps you would take, to introduce the quality model into the marketing function.

What difficulties might you encounter in trying to introduce and implement the quality model?

What benefits would accrue from introducing the quality model?

- Dimensions of quality
    - Quality takes on different dimensions in relation to different organisations and the products or services they provide
    - Customers may perceive quality differently to the organisation providing it
- Quality systems
    - Quality systems assist with brand value and building long-term relationships
- Costs of quality
    - There are costs incurred for ensuring quality – prevention and appraisal costs
    - Losses can be incurred through not achieving quality – internal failure and external failure costs
- The importance of quality systems
    - Quality systems should be applied across the complete organisation
    - Business cases can be built for quality management
- Quality management system models
    - Managing the process of produce the products and services
    - Quality should be applied to all processes in the organisation (TQM)
    - Continuous improvement (Kaizen) recognises that there is always room for improvement
- Quality management standards
    - A variety of internationally recognised quality management systems exist – ISO and EFQM as examples
- Quality improvement processes
    - Many organisations have seen large improvements based on adoption of quality improvement processes such as six sigma and benchmarking
- Quality and relationship marketing
    - Quality and customer service are delivered across functional boundaries

FURTHER READING

[1] For more information see Anon (2012) ISO14001 Standard. BSi, http://www.bsigroup.com/en/Assessment-and-certification-services/management-systems/Standards-and-Schemes/ISO-14001/ [Accessed on 18 March 2012]

[2] For more information see Anon (2012) PAS 2050 Standard. BSi, http://www.bsigroup.com/en/Standards-and-Publications/How-we-can-help-you/Professional-Standards-Service/PAS-2050 [Accessed on 18 March 2012]

[3] For more information see Anon (2012) iSixSigma Cost Savings. iSixSigma, http://www.isixsigma.com/implementation/financial-analysis/Six-Sigma-Costs-and-Savings [Accessed on 18 March, 2012]

Boddy, D. (2008) *Management: An Introduction*. Europe, Prentice Hall.

Christopher M.G. *et al* (2002) *Relationship Marketing: Creating Stakeholder Value*. Oxford, Elsevier Butterworth-Heinemann.

Hatch, Mary Jo. (2006) *Organization Theory*. 2nd edition. Oxford, Oxford University Press.

Johnson, W.C. *et al* (1997) *Total Quality in Marketing*. CRC Press LLC.

REFERENCES

ACSI (2012) Scores By Company. ACSI, http://www.theacsi.org/index.php?option=com_content&view=article&id=149&Itemid=214&c=Apple+&i=Personal+Computers [Accessed on 20 April 2012]

Anon (2012) Ogilvy's Canary Wharf offices achieve international environmental management certification, ISO 14001. Ogilvy, http://www.ogilvy.co.uk/blog/environment/dummy-environment-blog-post/ [Accessed on 13 March 2012]

Bendell T. *et al* (1993) *Benchmarking for Competitive Advantage*. London, Pitman.

Boddy, D. (2005) *Management: An Introduction*. 3rd edition. Harlow, FT Prentice Hall.

Brue, G. (2005) *Six Sigma for Managers*. Maidenhead, McGraw Hill Professional Education.

Carlzon, J. (1989) *Moments of Truth*. London, Collins Business.

Christopher M.G. *et al* (2002) *Relationship Marketing: Creating Stakeholder Value*. Oxford, Elsevier Butterworth-Heinemann.

Crosby, P.B. (1979) *Quality is Free*. London, Mentor.

Deming, W.E. (1986) *Out of the Crisis*. Boston, Massachusetts Institute of Technology.

Egan, J. (2004) *Relationship Marketing: Exploring Relational Strategies in Marketing*. 2nd edition. Harlow, Pearson Education.

Garvin, D.A. (1987) Competing in eight dimensions of quality. *Harvard Business Review*, November – December.

Grönroos, C. (2000) *Service Management & Marketing*. 2nd edition. London, John Wiley.

Huczynski, A. and Buchanan, D. (2001) *Organizational Behaviour: An Introductory Text*. 4th edition. Harlow, FT Prentice Hall.

Ishikawa, K. (1991) *What is Total Quality Control? (The Japanese Way)*. Harlow, Prentice Hall.

ISO (2012) Conceptual Model from the ISO9001 Standard. ISO, http://www.iso.org/iso/home.htm [Accessed on 20 April 2012]

Jobber, D. (2009) *Principles and Practice of Marketing*. 6th edition. Maidenhead, McGraw Hill Higher Education.

Johnson, G. *et al* (2005) *Exploring Corporate Strategy*. 7th edition. Harlow, Pearson Education.

Juran, J.M. (ed) (1988) *Juran's Quality Control Handbook*. 4th edition. Maidenhead, McGraw Hill.

Kolb, D.A. (1983) *Experience as the source of Learning and Development*. Financial Times, Prentice Hall.

Kotler, P. and Armstrong, G. (2001) *Principles of Marketing*. 9th edition. Upper Saddle River, Prentice Hall.

Mullins, L. (1999) *Management & Organisational Behaviour*. 5th edition. Harlow, FT Prentice Hall.

Oakland, J.S. (2003) *Total Quality Management: the Route to Improving Performance*. Oxford, Butterworth-Heinemann.

Parasuraman, A. *et al* (1988) 'SERVQUAL: A multiple-item scale for measuring customer perceptions of service quality'. *Journal of Retailing*, Spring, pp12–40.

Peters, T. (1989) *Thriving on Chaos*. London, Macmillan.

Reichheld, F.F. (1996) *The Loyalty Effect*. Boston, Harvard Business School.

Slack, N. *et al* (2004) *Operations Management*. 4th edition. New Jersey, Prentice Hall.

Taguchi, G. (1986) *Introduction to Quality Engineering: Designing Quality into Products and Processes*. Quality Resources.

Zeithaml, V. *et al* (1990) *Delivering Quality Services*. New York, Free Press.

QUICK QUIZ

1   Quality control is based on the concept of zero tolerance in defects. True or false?

2   Total quality managements aims for zero defects. True or false?

3   What is the term used to refer to continuous improvement?

4   What are quality circles?

5   What are the four types of benchmarking as described by Bendell, Boulter and Kelly (1993)?

6   Six sigma is a qualitative approach to process improvement. True or false?

7   What are the implications of an episode of a negative service experience?

ACTIVITY DEBRIEFS

Activity 2.1

There is a tendency, when something doesn't work properly, to try doing it again. However, if something hasn't worked properly in the past, there is no reason to suppose that it will work in the future. Quality management encourages an attitude that seeks to change how things are done.

Understanding competitive positioning is largely a strategic issue for management, but the Government argues that without a proper understanding of competitive positioning, and the need to have a competitive position in its markets, companies will not survive – particularly in weak or declining industries. A quality management approach includes working out ways of achieving customer satisfaction in order to compete effectively.

In many companies, each department or function in an organisation thinks only about its own needs and doesn't think about the needs and expectations of other departments (that might be its 'internal customers' or 'internal suppliers'). This can create problems for the other department to resolve. For example, a hospital consultant might schedule a number of surgical operations requiring varied and sophisticated nursing support for the patients, without first consulting the ward sister or matron about what support would be required and whether it could be made available. The problem would then be one for the ward sister or matron to try to sort out.

Management have a tendency to treat people like robots. Employees who are treated in this way will tend to act accordingly – with little concern for the work they are doing.

Gold-plated taps in a bath represent a high grade of materials, but if the taps have faulty washers and leak, the quality will be poor. High grade does not ensure good quality. Equally, a low grade product can provide better

The Chartered
Institute of Marketing

quality than a high-grade item. For example, uniforms worn by workers might be of a better quality ('fit for the purpose') if they are made from a cheaper, hard-wearing material, than if they are made from more expensive material that is more easily torn or more difficult to clean.

Having an acceptable level of quality implies that some errors are tolerable. A quality management approach is that everything should be done right the first time.

Managers often enjoy dealing with problems (fire-fighting) as it gives them the sense of being 'in charge'. A quality management approach is that managers waste their time if they have to deal with problems that should not have arisen in the first place.

There is a tendency for individuals to be unconcerned about errors they make, so long as the problem does not affect them, but someone else. With a quality management approach, employees are encouraged to think of other departments as internal customers, and accept responsibility for poor service to their customers.

Activity 2.2

This will depend on the context of the organisation chosen.

Activity 2.3

This will depend on the context of the marketing function chosen.

QUICK QUIZ ANSWERS

1   False. Tolerance levels are determined (these are not always set to zero) and quality control detects defects within these tolerance limits.

2   True. The key principle is to 'get it right the first time'.

3   Kaizen

4   Teams of workers from different levels and functions within the organisation working together to solve specified problems.

5   Internal benchmarking, functional benchmarking, competitor benchmarking, generic benchmarking.

6   False. It is a quantitative approach using statistical problem solving tools to identify and quantify waste and improve processes.

7   Moments of truth– or service encounters are critical to building strong service relationships with customers. Negative critical incidents will only be tolerated in the short term or in exceptional circumstances.

CHAPTER 3

Measuring, monitoring and improving marketing performance

Introduction

Marketing has a fundamental role to play in any organisation by helping it realise its strategic objectives. It is also a **boundary spanning activity**, meaning that it projects messages about the organisation, its products and services to the external environment, as well as drawing information and intelligence from that environment in order to understand what is going on. It is natural that managers are keen to see the impact made by marketing as it is so closely associated with its core purposes – delivering goods and services, maximising returns on assets and investments, securing long-term financial viability and rewarding investors and shareholders.

As well providing a means by which an organisation may gauge its successes, marketing is also a mechanism for identifying changes in trading conditions, monitoring competitor actions, observing patterns of customer behaviour and forecasting future outturns. Potential problems or the crystallising of risks can be detected promptly to enable remedial action to be taken.

In driving the market and informing the organisation about prevailing conditions, marketing performance is a central concern. In this chapter, we will examine ways in which performance can be measured.

Topic list

Why measure? (1)

Accounting measures (2)

Productivity measures (3)

Relationship marketing and customer-related measures (4)

Customer lifetime value (5)

Internal measures of performance (6)

Competitor comparisons and benchmarking (7)

1.3	Determine innovative and effective methods of measuring and monitoring marketing performance for marketing operation, marketing activities and effective resource management: ■ Accounting measures of performance – profit and loss, balance sheets, cash flow, and budgetary control ■ Productivity measures of performance – inputs versus outputs ■ Relationship marketing and customer-related measures – retention, satisfaction, and communication ■ Internal measures of performance – recruitment, retention, attitude, performance, communications ■ Innovation and learning measures of performance
1.4	Critically analyse monitoring information and recommend ways to improve marketing performance: ■ Productivity analysis – inputs versus outputs ■ Comparative analysis – measuring changes over time ■ Segmental analysis – analysis of markets ■ Innovation audit – organisational climate, current performance, policies, practices and cognitive styles ■ Competitor comparisons and benchmarking

1 Why measure?

> ▶ **Key term**
>
> 'A **metric** is a measuring system that quantifies a trend, dynamic, or characteristic'.
>
> (Farris *et al* 2006, p1)

Data-based marketing where success is assessed through measurable performance and accountability is now a 'given' in business (Farris *et al*, 2006). The use of 'marketing metrics' is vital for any healthy business as Harvard Business School Associate Dean John Quelch (*op cit* Farris *et al*, 2006) discussed in the *Wall Street Journal*:

'Today's boards want chief marketing officers who can speak the language of productivity and return on investment and are willing to be held accountable. In recent years, manufacturing, procurement, and logistics have all tightened their belts in the cause of improved productivity. As a result, marketing expenditures account for a larger percentage of many corporate cost structures than ever before. Today's boards don't need chief marketing officers who have creative flair but no financial discipline. They need ambidextrous marketers who offer both'.

Generally the prime reasons for measurement and analysis within marketing are:

■ To evaluate success (or failure) of marketing plans

■ To rectify and implement corrective actions if an unsuccessful plan is underway and it is possible to change

■ To assist future decision making and planning

■ To provide a convincing and strong rationale for a marketing plan for the board

■ To demonstrate the value which is provided by marketing

Measuring marketing is an essential part of the control system as depicted in the following diagram.

Figure 3.1   Control system

Control System

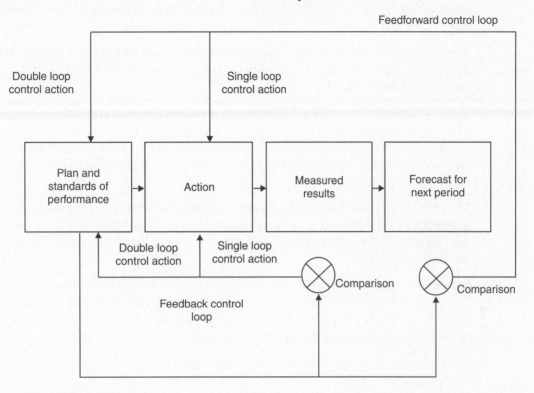

2 Accounting measures

Accounting measures of marketing performance reflect the financial impact that its activities have. They can be analysed according to:

- **Profit and loss** – the impact on incomes earned and costs incurred

- **Balance sheets** – the impact on assets and liabilities

- **Cash flows** – the impact on money moving into and out of the organisation

- **Budgetary controls** – the impact on the monitoring and management of income and expenditure

We shall later explore each of these accounting measures in turn.

Financial comparisons can aid decision-making by:

- **Past comparisons and trends**. Looking back at the organisation's financial history and records can identify similar situations and help draw conclusions and trends from the information.

- **Competitor analysis**. Examining published information of other organisations, such as competitors, for financial indicators may aid decision-making.

- **Forecasting** the future is based in part on financial assumptions.

- **Modelling**. Financial data may be used to model the effect of decisions.

2.1 Profit and loss

Organisations can measure a wide range of marketing metrics such as loyalty, brand awareness, customer satisfaction and so on (as we shall see below), but the reason why these measures are important is that they lead to sales and income.

Sales are possible only, of course, if customers are aware of an organisation's products and services, are able to differentiate them from those of its competitors and are willing and able to pay for them, and so marketing is hugely important in this area.

In accounting terms, the profit and loss account (sometimes referred to as the income statement, statement of profit or loss and other comprehensive income, trading and profit and loss account or the operating statement) is a record of the incomes earned and the expenses incurred for a given period. It is common to record incomes and expenditure on a monthly and a cumulative basis during the year, culminating in a statement, generally covering a 12-month period.

The profit or loss made is simply the difference between the incomes and the expenses. Where incomes are greater the excess is referred to as a profit, where expenses are greater the deficit is referred to as a loss. (Many not-for-profit activities refer to 'surplus' and 'deficit' in place of 'profit' and 'loss' but for our purposes the terms are interchangeable.)

It should be noted that incomes earned are not the same as monies received from sales, as much business is conducted on a credit basis (buy now and pay later). For the purpose of profit and loss, we record sales income at the point the sale is made, not when the money is received. The same is true of expenses. They are included at the point they arise rather than when they are paid.

As an example, let us look at the accounts of ARC Ltd.

ARC Limited
Profit and loss accounts for the years ended 31 December

	20X0	20X1
	£'000	£'000
Turnover (Revenue)	53,470	98,455
Cost of sales	(40,653)	(70,728)
Gross profit	12,817	27,727
Distribution costs	(2,317)	(4,911)
Administrative expenses	(1,100)	(2,176)
Profit on ordinary activities before interest	9,400	20,640
Interest receivable	100	40
Interest payable	–	(280)
Profit for the financial year	9,500	20,400
Taxation for the year	(3,200)	(5,200)
Profit	6,300	15,200

> **Key terms**
>
> A **profit and loss account** measures the operational performance of the company over a period of time.
>
> - **Gross profit** is the profit shown after the purchase or production cost of the goods sold is deducted from the value of sales.
>
> - **Net profit** is the gross profit, plus any other income from sources other than the sale of goods, minus other expenses of the business which are not included in the cost of goods sold.

Marketing costs (promotions, advertising, PR events, salaries and wages, agency costs, website development, etc) will appear as expenses in the profit and loss statement.

It is common to express the marketing cost as a percentage of turnover or of the total costs, enabling managers to make comparisons with other functions, with previous years, with budgets, with benchmark data and with external organisations and competitors.

This single measure is useful as a high-level indicator but it is a very simple indicator of marketing performance. The marketing manager will be interested in how activity impacts on sales and what return is achieved for particular expenditure.

Metrics relating to profit and loss may be focused internally as well as in comparison with the market (Table 3.1).

Information can be broken down to reflect the contribution made by products, brands, regions, retail outlets, sales representative, market segment, and so on. If an organisation wishes to measure the impact and effectiveness of particular campaigns, it needs to identify which sales have occurred as a result.

It cannot be assumed that all increases are due to advertising. The use of coded order forms, sales promotion reference numbers, surveys asking customers where they heard about the organisation and other techniques are used to help marketing managers assess the value of a given event or campaign.

The information derived from the profit and loss data can be used to inform strategies for competitive positioning, product development, pricing, promotion and so on, which themselves will require suitable metrics to measure their impact. The relationships between price, profits and volumes of sales may be described by using cost–volume–profit diagrams covered in Chapter 8.

Return on (marketing) investment is measured by:

$$\text{ROI (or ROMI)} = \text{profit or surplus/investment} \times 100\%$$

Table 3.1   Marketing metrics linked to profit and loss

Profit and loss items	Internal measures	External measures
Sales	Number of units Value of sales Percentage changes in sales Comparison with budgets	Percentage market share Comparison with competitor performance Comparison with sector averages Share of wallet
Expenses	Cost of marketing (by activity and by campaign) Marketing as a proportion of total costs	Comparison with competitors Comparison with sector averages Share of voice
Profits	Value of profit Movements in profit Comparison with budgets	Benchmark data for profit margins relevant to sector Trends in market performance
Ratios	Profit as a percentage of sales Expenses as a percentage of sales Marketing as a proportion of sales Return on Investment (ROI) Return on Marketing Investment (ROMI) Marketing spend per lead Sales acquisition cost	Benchmark data and competitor performance

For example, we may be interested in evaluating the ROI of an email or direct mail campaign. Suppose the following data were available:

- Number of mailouts 10,000
- Response rate 5%
- Conversion rate of responses 25%
- Cost of initiative (staff time, design, postage, etc) £1,000
- Average profit or surplus made on each sale £12

We can analyse this data and calculate a return on investment.

- 5% of 10,000 = 500 of the contacts who responded and of these 25% = 125 made a purchase.

- The average cost of each response is £1,000 divided by 500 responses, £2.

- The average cost per purchase is £1,000 divided by 125, £8.

- The 125 sales generate £12 profit each or a total of £1,500.

- Therefore, an investment of £1,000 has generated a £1,500 profit and an overall surplus (after deducting the cost of the campaign) of £500.

- This return of £500 is 50% of the investment of £1,000, so ROI = 50%.

This figure could be used to compare other campaigns and other options to determine whether it represents the most effective way of spending £1,000.

If an organisation aims to increase its incomes, it should do so on the basis of a planned growth strategy. It is possible to gain additional sales in a way that actually reduces profitability, and while this might be sustainable in the short term it cannot be continued indefinitely. Penetration pricing and loss leaders may help to raise awareness and secure larger market share but this must ultimately lead to new, profitable income streams. Even in the public and not-for-profit sectors, where the aims are principally around value for money and organisational advantage and where it may be acceptable for one profitable activity to subsidise a loss-making one, survival depends upon at least balancing income and expenditure in the long term.

Growth, therefore, should follow a number of key considerations:

- What is the level of penetration in existing markets?

- Is growth possible from existing markets by increasing customer loyalty and lifetime values?

- Is growth possible by attracting new customers for existing products and services by making adjustments to the marketing mix?

- Is it possible to take market share away from the competition by identifying and exploiting competitor's loyalty gaps?

- Are there any potential new markets large enough to make the necessary investment worthwhile?

- Are those markets likely to grow, stay the same or shrink in the long term?

In fact, using the Ansoff matrix, growth in sales and revenues may occur through four main strategies.

- **Market penetration** – increasing the sales value of existing products to existing customers or customers within the existing market by selling more of the same and so gaining a greater share of the market and wallet and increasing the lifetime value of customers.

- **Product development** – modifying existing products or introducing new ones to existing markets.

- **Market development** – selling existing products or services to new customers, such as new geographical regions or new population segments.

- **Diversification** – introducing new products to new markets.

The high-level strategy for growing the customer base together with the associated risks and costs needs to be determined before a revenue improvement plan could be devised. Whilst finding new customers, maintaining existing customer loyalty must remain a priority. Both are sources of revenue, but generally (depending on the

sector) it is easier (and cheaper) to secure repeat custom from the customer base than to sell to new ones. Table 3.2 illustrates some of the risks and potential revenue improvement tactics that may be deployed when seeking growth.

Table 3.2 Potential risks and revenue improvement tactics for growth strategies

Strategy	Risks to consider	Potential revenue improvement tactics
Market penetration	▪ A price war with competitors ▪ An inability to match demand ▪ Market becomes saturated	▪ Competitive pricing to shift the break even point while increasing volume of sales to improve profit ▪ Use of customer loyalty and reward schemes to encourage repeat purchase and improve lifetime values ▪ High profile promotion leading to increased and sustained sales activity ▪ Targeting high growth markets to benefit from rising sales ▪ Squeezing out competitors through aggressive marketing and secure the loyalty of their customers
Product development	▪ Insufficient demand for the new product ▪ Other suppliers introduce similar products ▪ Demand for new product substitutes existing demand for existing products	▪ Using technology to introduce new product features and charging a premium price (price skimming)
Market development	▪ Disaffecting as many existing customers as new ones generated	▪ Utilising (or developing) new channels of distribution to access other customers ▪ Introducing multiple pricing strategies to appeal to different potential market segments
Diversification	▪ Over-stretching resources ▪ Uncertainty about new products and new customers	▪ Entering into a strategic alliance to share risks (and revenues) until viability is confirmed

2.2 Balance sheets

> ▸ **Key term**
>
> A **balance sheet** (also known as a **statement of financial position**) is a snapshot of the financial position of a business at a point in time.

Balance sheets provide a schedule of the assets held and the liabilities owing by the organisation at a given moment in time. They are typically drawn up at the end of the year but may also be produced at any point.

Asset refers to all items of positive value held by the organisation.

▪ Long-term (or fixed) assets include tangible items such as premises, motor vehicles, machinery, computer equipment and investments, as well as intangible ones such as copyright, patents, goodwill and reputation, although this latter group may not always be listed on the balance sheet.

▪ Short-term (or current) assets are those subject to frequent change as part of normal activity and are not normally held for more than one year, such as stocks of finished goods, raw materials and work in progress, money in the bank and the till (cash in hand), and amounts owed to the organisation by customers who made purchases on credit (known as debtor or receivables).

Liabilities are amounts owed by the organisation to other parties, including suppliers (known as creditor or payables) and investors (shareholders, banks and others).

The balance sheet is so-called because it balances, showing that the value of the organisation (its total net assets) is equal to the investment in it by the owners (sole trader, partners, members or shareholders). The profits generated are added to the shareholders' funds as this is owed by the organisation back to the owners.

The accounting equation explains why the 'net assets' and the total of 'capital and reserves' are both equal to £16,100,000 in 20X1 in the following balance sheet.

ARC Limited
Balance sheet as at 31 December 20X1

	20X0		20X1	
Fixed assets (Non-current assets)	£'000	£'000	£'000	£'000
Intangible assets	100		100	
Tangible assets	7,900		12,950	
Investments	100		100	
		8,100		13,150
Current assets				
Stocks (Inventory)	5,000		15,000	
Debtors (Receivables)	8,900		27,100	
Cash at bank and in hand	600		–	
	14,500		42,100	
Creditors: amounts falling due within one year (Current liabilities)				
Bank loans and overdrafts	–		16,200	
Trade creditors (Payables)	6,000		10,000	
Accruals and deferred income	800		1,000	
Other creditors including taxation	6,200		11,200	
	13,000		38,400	
Net current assets		1,500		3,700
Creditors: amounts falling due after more than one year (non-current liabilities)				
15% debenture stock		600		750
Net assets		9,000		16,100

	20X0	20X1
Capital and reserves		
Called up share capital		
Ordinary shares of £1 each	6,000	6,000
Profit and loss account reserve	3,000	10,100
	9,000	16,100

The marketing function may have its share of assets (vehicles, equipment, furniture, stocks of collateral, etc) and the most effective way of gauging its performance using the balance sheet is by the Return on Assets (ROA).

$$\text{ROA} = \text{profit or surplus made/value of assets deployed} \times 100 \text{ \%}$$

This calculation can be made for the organisation as a whole, or for the marketing function or for specific initiatives. It looks at how well the assets have been used. For example, if the financial statements above relate to the same organisation, we can see that £16,100,000 of assets have been used to generate £15,200,000 of profit. This is a ROA of 94%. To answer the question whether this is any good, it is necessary to compare this result with other opportunities in which the assets could have been put to use, targeted performance, previous results and benchmarks for the sector.

Particular aspects to note about the balance sheets shown above are as follows.

(a)   **Date**. The balance sheet is headed up 'as at 31 December 20X1'. This is telling the user that it is a picture of the affairs of the company **at a point in time**. Over time this picture will change.

(b)   **Comparative figures** (figures for the previous period) are always given to indicate movement. They should be prepared on a consistent basis and usually refer to the balance sheet one year ago.

(c)   **Equation balances**. In the example, capital and reserves (or shareholders' funds) equal net assets.

We will now briefly discuss each heading.

2.2.1 Fixed assets (non-current assets)

A **fixed asset** is any asset, tangible or intangible, acquired for retention by a **business** to give continuing economic benefits (that is, it must be in use for over one year) by **the business**, and not held for resale in the normal course of trading.

(a)   A **tangible** fixed asset is a **physical** asset. A sales manager's car is a tangible fixed asset.

(b)   An **intangible** fixed asset does not have a physical existence. The expense of acquiring **patent rights** and some new product development costs on occasions would be classified as an intangible fixed asset. The value of a **brand name** also comes under this category although this is a matter of considerable dispute. (We deal with this later in this section.)

(c)   **Investments** held for the long term would be classified as fixed assets.

Fixed assets, except freehold land, **wear out or lose their usefulness in the course of time**. The accounts of a business try to recognise this by gradually writing off the asset's cost in the **profit and loss account** (income statement) over several accounting periods to reflect the loss in value in the balance sheet. This is called **depreciation**.

2.2.2 Current assets

Current assets fall into two categories.

(a)   **Items owned** by the business (or owed to the business) which will be turned into cash within one year
(b)   **Cash**, including money in the bank, owned by the business

These assets are **current** as they are **continually flowing** through the business.

Stock (inventory)

Stock comprises **goods for use or resale**. They can exist either in their original form (for example, as the component parts which when assembled make up the product), or as **work in progress** or as **finished goods** awaiting resale.

Debtors (receivables)

A debtor is a person, business or company who **owes money to the business**. When the debt is finally paid, the debtor disappears as an asset, to be replaced by cash at bank and in hand, another asset. **Most debtors are customers who have bought on credit but have not yet paid**.

2.2.3 Current liabilities

A **liability** is owed **by** a business **to** another person or organisation (eg to the bank or government). Here are some examples.

■   Loans repayable within one year
■   A bank overdraft is normally payable on demand
■   A **trade creditor** (owed money for debts incurred in the course of trading)
■   Taxation payable
■   Accrued charges (expenses incurred, for which no bill has yet been received)

2.2.4 Creditors (payables)

Creditors are owed money by the business. They represent the **liabilities** part of the accounting equation. It is important to know when their debts fall due for payment. **Trade creditors**, who have supplied goods and services, are usually payable after a very short period. Tax amounts due to the government are usually payable within a few months. Loans to finance the business usually have a **maturity date** which may be imminent or several years away. It is worth noting that bank overdrafts (which many businesses use as a source of working capital) are usually repayable **on demand**, so the bank manager wields a great deal of power.

The arbitrary division on the balance sheet of creditors into those payable within one year and those not payable until at least a year has passed provides a rough division for comparison with fixed and current assets.

This is why many firms have **credit control departments**. They assess the creditworthiness of new customers, and monitor their payments record. They chase any late-payers and employ debt collectors. The purpose of any sale is to make a profit, and offering credit has a cost and a risk.

2.2.5 Long-term liabilities (non-current liabilities)

Long-term liabilities include:

- Loans which are repayable after one year, such as a bank loan
- A mortgage, which is a loan specifically secured against a freehold property
- Debentures (borrowings at a fixed rate of interest usually repayable by a specified date)

2.2.6 Capital and reserves

The **capital and reserves** figure in the balance sheet represents the **shareholders' funds**.

(a) The original **capital** contributed by the ordinary shareholders (the cost of the shares).

(b) The **profits** the business has **retained** over the years **which** are accumulated in the profit and loss account balance.

ACTIVITY 3.1

Obtain some company reports which contain published accounts. These can be obtained from many UK public limited companies via their websites, generally through 'investor relations' sections (or similar).

Examine the content of the accounts. Look at the way they are laid out, typical content and consider their role as a piece of communication about the financial health of the organisation.

2.3 Cash flow

As opposed to profit and loss which measures incomes when they are earned and expenses when they arise, a cash flow shows money flowing in and out of an organisation.

This is an alternative and equally important view of performance and highlights the crucial dimension of timing.

Many organisations experience cyclical patterns of activity due to public holidays, religious festivals, changes in the weather and school calendars. While it may be possible to rely on large sales earned over a relatively short period to generate a profit for the year as a whole, it is desirable to spread cash inflows more evenly, at least so that they match outflows a little better.

Generally, organisations find that they are committed to fixed monthly costs (salaries, rent and rates, light and heat, leasing, hire purchase, etc) regardless of sales. If money does not flow in, they will need to draw upon reserves or may even need to borrow, adding to costs. Ideally, the cash flowing into the business each month should be enough to cover the necessary outgoings. This is what keeps an organisation solvent.

To illustrate this, suppose a business has the following earnings and expenditure for the months from November to June (Table 3.3).

The Chartered Institute of Marketing

Table 3.3   Income and cost items

	November	December	January	February	March	April	May	June
Sales								
Cash	1,800	3,000	1,300	1,000	1,800	2,500	4,000	5,500
Credit	3,000	6,100	3,000	2,600	3,200	5,400	8,900	15,000
Costs								
Purchases	2,200	5,200	2,600	1,500	2,700	3,900	6,500	11,600
Fixed costs	3,800	3,800	3,800	3,800	3,800	3,800	3,800	3,800

Let us also suppose that credit customers are given two months in which to pay while all supplies are made on credit which must be settled within one month. Assume the cash balance at the start of January is £6,000. The following table shows the cash flow for the six months from January to June (Table 3.4).

For the purposes of the cash flow, the receipts and payments have been put in the month in which they occur. For example, the receipt of £3,000 from debtors in January relates to sales made (on two months' credit) in November. Also, the payment of £5,200 to creditors in January relates to the purchases made in December (on one month's credit).

Table 3.4 Cash flow statement

	January	February	March	April	May	June
Cash inflows						
Cash sales	1,300	1,000	1,800	2,500	4,000	5,500
Debtors	3,000	6,100	3,000	2,600	3,200	5,400
Total inflows	4,300	7,100	4,800	5,100	7,200	10,900
Cash outflows						
Creditors	5,200	2,600	1,500	2,700	3,900	6,500
Fixed costs	3,800	3,800	3,800	3,800	3,800	3,800
Total outflows	9,000	6,400	5,300	6,500	7,700	10,300
Cash flow						
Opening balance	6,000	1,300	2,000	1,500	100	(400)
Inflows	4,300	7,100	4,800	5,100	7,200	10,900
Outflows	9,000	6,400	5,300	6,500	7,700	10,300
Closing balance	1,300	2,000	1,500	100	(400)	200

The closing balance of cash at the end of each month is equal to the opening balance plus the inflows minus the outflows. This then becomes the opening balance for the next month. The closing balance is initially positive but is declining until it becomes negative in May, becoming positive once more in June. In this case, the organisation deals with seasonal variations.

There have been higher sales over the winter holidays, followed by a decline and then an increase again up to summer.

Fixed costs remain the same each month, and although purchases vary with the level of sales, the timing of inflows and outflows does not prevent the reserves of cash dropping. Some form of borrowing is required for May (such as an overdraft), incurring additional costs as a result.

Marketing activity should understand the importance of cash flows. Marketing itself is a cost-and cash-outflow but more importantly it is responsible for attempting to create the most beneficial patterns of sales and sale

income. In our example, the organisation may decide that a price promotion is required to stimulate extra demand in Spring to compensate for falling sales.

2.4 Budgetary control

Much is said about budgetary control in Chapters 7 and 9 and its relationship to marketing performance. The main purpose of budgeting is to enable managers to exercise control over financial resources through monitoring and variance analysis. Marketing managers need to focus on their expenditure against plan but also respond to variances elsewhere in the budget, especially in sales. The degree of analysis should be appropriate to the organisation and might include a breakdown by product, brand, region or market segment. Control implies effective and timely decision-making which requires speedy information of the right kind.

3 Productivity measures

Historically, productivity was used as one of the earliest measures for marketing performance. The approach took manufacturing as a model and examined how much output could be achieved from a given unit of input. Marketing Productivity Analysis is typical of this approach (Sevin, 1965) in which products and activities are analysed for profitability.

As the discipline developed, other non-financial measures were included among inputs and outputs, increasing both the value of and the difficulties inherent in the analysis.

THE REAL WORLD

Coca-Cola

The importance of performance measures to Coca-Cola can be seen through specific areas which they have considered over recent decades. Coca-Cola enjoyed volume growth of 7 to 8% pa in the 15 years to 1998, with profits rising 18% pa. However, in 1999 it revealed a 13% fall in profits, and a return to shareholders of only 1.4%. The share price fell. Most worrying, unit-case volumes of syrup (the firm's preferred underlying measure of growth) fell by 1% Jan to March 1999, the first fall for a long time. Coca-Cola blamed the world economy.

Coke's previous growth had been due to a unique set of circumstances. It had rationalised its bottling operations and Pepsi had not performed well. But in the late 1990s there was market resistance to price increases. Selling expenses were $6.6bn, compared to net profit of $3.5bn. In 1997, a 4% rise in selling expenses produced a 10% rise in sales volumes. In 1998 a similar rise only increased volumes by 6%.

Since 1999, Coca-Cola has faced a public relations crisis in Belgium and two changes of chief executive. It is still successful, but is facing yet more changes in direction, and is investing in more brands. In May 2007, Coca-Cola announced its intention to buy *Glaceau*, a maker of energy and vitamin-enhanced drinks for $4.1 billion.

Dasani, Coca-Cola's bottled water brand, was launched in 1993. Dasani had to be withdrawn in the UK due to contamination and the fact that it turned out to be tap water from the mains. In 2010 Coca Cola announced they would be distributing Dasani water in new packaging comprised of 30% plant based materials. These bottles represent up to a 25% reduction in carbon emissions when compared to standard water bottles (though this still represents 2,000 times the energy usage of tap water!).

3.1 Inputs versus outputs

Productivity is a measure of the ability to transform inputs into outputs. The greater the productivity, the greater the outputs in proportion to the inputs. Marketing is interested in the productivity of the organisation as a whole, especially the areas of production or service delivery.

The Chartered Institute of Marketing

We can also measure the productivity of marketing activity itself. In simple terms, the value that marketing adds is calculated by working out the additional sales made as a result. It may not always be easy to determine, but in principle there should be a direct and positive relationship between marketing inputs and outputs in sales.

The inputs include investment, knowledge, skills, understanding, information and time, as well as the easier costed dimensions of design, materials, printing, postage, agency fees, IT support, and so on. The outputs may range from cash flow, profit, number and value of sales, and market share. There may be complications in determining the value of some of these.

For sales of specific products and services, it is reasonably straightforward (provided, there is a sophisticated cost accounting process that attaches direct and indirect costs to products). Where the output is about developing customer relationships, building brand value, raising awareness and increasing loyalty, it becomes less clear.

To measure inputs, we need to find a way of counting the cost of the work done. Resources and materials can be calculated readily.

The most common way of calculating the value of the time taken to make plans, generate ideas, produce copy, monitor, report and so on is by using a standard fee per hour, depending on the grade of staff involved.

A major proportion is simply salary. We can decide how many hours of productive time an employee should use per year and divide this into their salary, resulting in a rate of so much per hour.

We can add a percentage on top of this to account for overheads (light, heat, depreciation, rent, etc). In such matters, utility supersedes accuracy.

There is no point adding to the costs by spending hours calculating what that cost is. An approximation based on sound estimates and a good working model should suffice.

To measure outputs, it is necessary to have metrics that we can count, such as the:

- Growth in sales
- Number of leads generated
- Number of new names and contact details added to the database
- Number of times the organisation's name has been mentioned in the media
- Number of column inches in the trade press
- Number of positive responses to customer surveys
- Number of new customer loyalty cards issued
- Number of people who can recognise the organisation or the product name after it has appeared in adverts

To improve, productivity implies that more outputs are produced for fewer inputs, but several caveats must be taken into account.

- **Quality**: Not every hour of input is as effective (or as valuable) as any other. Not all publicity is good publicity. Marketing activity depends on being structured in its development, targeted, sophisticated and tailored.
- **Risk**: There are no guarantees that the inputs will deliver the planned outputs. What may be seen as short cuts of increasing productivity may also carry higher risk. Those risks include the risk of productivity actually falling and risks to damaging reputation. For example, greater press coverage may be achievable through shock tactics and high-profile stunts in advertising, press releases and PR events. However, such things can easily backfire and end up having the opposite effect from the one intended.
- **Focus**: It is possible to spread a marketing budget very thinly across multiple products, campaigns, launches, communications, promotions and events until it is not enough to make an impact anywhere. It is often more effective to limit oneself to fewer but better resourced activities, concentrating on those of greatest strategic relevance and potential for return.

- **Diminishing returns**: Doing more of the same will not necessarily generate more of the same outputs. Attention spans are short, demands made on people's time are immense, familiarity breeds contempt and boredom quickly sets in. Sometimes less is more. Change, innovation and progression command more attention.

Productivity is important because improvements lead to reduced unit costs and greater profit margins.

4 Relationship marketing and customer-related measures

One of the key influences of relationship marketing theory is the notion of the being able to measure the value of different customer groups. There are a number of commonly used customer measures including:

- **Customer acquisition** – how many new customers attracted; their value and the cost of attracting these customers (eg promotional campaigns, referrals, word of mouth etc)

- **Customer repeat purchase** – repeat purchase behaviour, frequency and value

- **Customer profitability** – net profit of a customer

- **Customer experience satisfaction** – perceptions, service, compare with other organisation

- **Customer retention** – longevity, lifetime value, costs

- **Customer loyalty status** – passive or active, good referral, value of loyalty and referral markets

- **Customer segment** – most profitable segments to target and encourage loyalty

One approach to measuring performance is to commence with a self-assessment of current activity. Many agencies, publications and websites offer surveys that can be used for this purpose. They usually allow some form of scoring or ranking a series of criteria or questions. A common way of scoring answers is by using a Likert scale, such as:

5 Strongly agree

4 Agree

3 Neither agree nor disagree

2 Disagree

1 Strongly disagree

The outcome of such a survey can then be used to formulate a plan for improvement.

An example of marketing performance self-assessment questions could be:

4.1 Marketing performance self-assessment

Purpose

1   I have a clear purpose and vision for my business.

2   I have business objectives that are specific, measurable, achievable, relevant and timely.

3   My company is structured and organised to carry out effective marketing.

4   I have strong marketing expertise within the company (or its key advisers).

5   I have an effective marketing planning process that maximises profits by identifying, attracting and keeping valuable customers.

 The Chartered Institute of Marketing

Market segment or niche

1   I have identified a valuable market opportunity that I could 'own'.

2   I clearly understand my market size and its future potential.

3   I monitor my key competitors.

4   I have a definition that effectively describes my target customer groups, especially the high value ones.

5   My strong understanding of my target customer groups needs, desires and requirements has driven the development of my solutions, benefits and features.

Core message

1   I have developed a simple and powerful core message that is focused on solving the customer's problem.

2   It is as clear and concise as it could be.

3   It is distinctive from the competition.

4   The benefits and features are compelling for my target customer groups, especially the high value ones.

5   It works equally well to attract new customers, get existing customers to buy more and to keep customers for longer period.

Marketing communications

1   My core message effectively reaches my target customer groups.

2   My communications have real impact and attract customers to come to me.

3   They generate high repeat sales.

4   They encourage high levels of referrals.

5   I am making the best use of the marketing communication options available (eg advertising, direct marketing, publicity marketing, networking, seminars, public speaking, newsletters, customer magazines, web marketing).

Sales conversion system

1   I have a marketing and sales system that converts a high percentage of sales prospects to customers.

2   I use new technology systems to automate the process and to capture vital data.

3   My system enables me to evaluate the performance of each step or activity and for different customer groups or channels.

4   I can accurately forecast future sales and profits.

5   I can determine which marketing activities give me the best results (highest profits) for each pound spent.

In this case, the lower scoring statements indicate areas that require attention. Such assessments can be useful as they focus on areas that need development. It is not a precise science and can only be effective if the assessment is made objectively and with a good understanding of the dimensions that are included.

Another related model describes marketing performance at a number of different levels, such as low, medium and high or poor, good and excellent, and then invites the user to identify the one that most closely matches their own organisation (Table 3.5).

4.2 Retention

Tactics for maintaining the loyalty of existing customers while aiming for growth might include building customer relationships, offering loyalty schemes, and providing other perks and benefits. Organisations may offer regular customers targeted (but not intrusive) contact, preferential access to information, advance notice of special offers and promotions, and the privileged provision of additional services, such as insurance, lines of credit and saving schemes.

When assessing their marketing performance, organisations should look at five aspects of performance:

- Level of product innovation
- Quality of product/service offered
- Driver of strategy
- Market segmentation
- Pricing policy.

For each aspect of performance, organisation should assess the performance on a continuum, as shown in Table 3.5 below.

Table 3.5

Aspect	Weak Performance Characteristics		Strong Performance Characteristics
Level of product innovation	Is a follower rather than an innovator	-------------------------------------	Leads the market
Quality of product/service offered	Minimum standard to meet customer needs	-------------------------------------	Exceed customer expectations
Driver of strategy	Product-led strategy	-------------------------------------	Market-led strategy; Identifies what customers want and then satisfies that want
Market segmentation	Mass marketing: no segmentation	-------------------------------------	Niche marketing: targeting individual customer
Pricing policy	Low prices	-------------------------------------	Delivering value for customers

In implementing measures to improve performance, we can take advantage of the brand value cycle. This model is usually described as having five or six stages (Figure 3.2).

The steps may be explained as follows:

- **Assessment** – research the market to identify the customers' attitudes with existing brands, what they are communicating, how they could be improved and so on

- **Development** – develop brands and devise appropriate strategies for product positioning

- **Marketing infrastructure** – arrange marketing infrastructure in a way that supports and reinforces brands through planning, processes, structure, distribution, communication and so on

- **Delivery** – apply the brands consistently in the market

- **Monitoring and evaluation** – maintain a continuous review of customer responses to brands

The Chartered Institute of Marketing

Figure 3.2   Brand value cycle

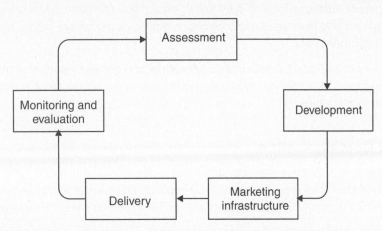

Brands and branding are of great importance to organisations and their customers. For the customer, brands make it easy to identify products and services through recognisable logos, packaging, presentation, communication and delivery, speeding up the process of decision making and purchasing.

This is true for B2B and B2C transactions.

Trusted brands reduce the risk involved in procurement. Brand loyalty also adds to a customer's satisfaction with the product or service as it adds to the perceived value. For the supplier, the brand has real value because it can be reflected in the price the buyer is prepared to pay. The brand also serves as a short cut to communicate a proposition requiring lower levels of promotion and generating faster recognition and adoption rates.

These benefits can be carried over into new but related brands which are subsequently cheaper to launch.

Brands, then, add directly to revenues by being part of the commodity sold and also have a favourable impact on costs. Understandably, organisations work hard to increase and protect brand value.

4.3 Satisfaction

Customer and consumer satisfaction can be classed as demand-side metrics for gauging marketing performance. In studies consumer satisfaction was found to be used as a measure by 68% of UK companies as a marketing metric while customer satisfaction featured for 45%[1]. Satisfaction is important because it is related to retention, sales and lifetime values. It is also true that happy customers promote products, brands, services and organisations to others by word of mouth and personal endorsement, leading to customer acquisition and further sales.

Typically satisfaction can be measured by asking customers to respond to the following kinds of questions:

- Are you completely satisfied with your purchase?
- How likely are you to make a similar purchase again in future?
- Would you recommend the product, service or organisation to friends?

There are a number of customer satisfaction indices used around the world, such as the UK Customer Satisfaction Index (UKCSI),[2] derived from asking questions such as these and then enabling organisations to be ranked and changes to be measured. The score is calculated between 0 and 100. The American Customer Satisfaction Index (ACSI)[3] is very similar, linking:

- Customer loyalty
- Customer complaints
- Perceived value
- Perceived quality
- Customer expectations

A series of three questions on satisfaction, expectation and performance are each graded 1 to 10 by sample consumers and then results are compiled to produce a percentage rating. Table 3.6 illustrates an extract from ACSI published data.

The extract in Table 3.6 shows customer satisfaction ratings for sectors of the US economy based on over 200 companies. It also shows how ratings have moved in the last 12 months and in comparison with readings first taken in the 1990s.

4.4 Communication

Engaging with customers is a key dimension to the activity of marketing and so one of importance for marketing performance. Customers engage with the product, brand, organisation and with each other in various different ways, but a communications strategy will deliver a planned series of messages and interactions.

This may be done with the assistance of technology. Interactive communication such as blogs, discussion forums, online user panels, online accounts, personal greetings, reminders and buying suggestions, emails and SMS texting may all be used to ensure the customer continues to engage with the organisation.

Table 3.6   Extract of ACSI statistics

Sector	2011	% change in year	% change since first year
Airlines	65	–1.5	-9.7
Automobiles and light vehicles	83	1.2	5.1
Supermarkets	73	1.3	0

(The ACSI, 2011. Reproduced with permission)

In addition, static web pages, such as product information, contact details and FAQs are also common. Mailouts may also be used, keeping customers updated on the details of their personal account, advising them of forthcoming promotions, seeking feedback and in general staying connected.

Clearly, the purpose of communication is to foster loyalty, encourage sales and maximise lifetime values. Encouraging customers to engage with others is a way of gaining word of mouth advocacy at no real cost.

In order to set metrics, an organisation needs to be able to measure an appropriate dimension:

- Number of recorded visits to a website
- Number of clicks on a certain web item
- Number of repeat visits as well as the number of first-time visitors
- Number of communication made (letters, brochures, emails, texts, etc)
- Contributions to an online survey
- Number of readers of a blog

Engagement has been proposed as a marketing metric with four components:

1   **Involvement** – measuring communication links an individual has with the organisation
2   **Interaction** – measuring the depth of involvement
3   **Intimacy** – measuring the affection the individual has for the brand
4   **Influence** – measuring the likelihood that the individual may persuade others to buy the brand[4]

In other words, engagement can be measured on four different levels, depending upon the sophistication of the metrics used, moving from purely quantitative to more qualitative and evaluative (Table 3.7).

Table 3.7 Suitable metrics for different levels of customer engagement

Level of engagement	Suitable metrics
Involvement	Number of website visits
	Duration of visits
	Number of pages viewed
	Key words used for searches
	Navigation routes taken through site
Interaction	Contribution to blogs and discussion forums (frequency, quantity, topics)
Intimacy	References made to products, brands and organisation on organisation's own or third party sites. Opinions expressed in customer service calls
Influence	Information forwarded to friends
	Encouragement made to others
	Product advocacy

(Based on Haven, 2007)

Capturing such information becomes harder the deeper the level of engagement one is trying to measure. While web analytics will provide the necessary data on *involvement*, a combination of market intelligence, surveys and direct contact with customers is necessary to measure *influence*.

5 Customer lifetime value

> ▶ **Key term**
>
> **Customer lifetime value** measures the worth of a customer to the firm either as an individual or as part of a segment. (Kumar, 2008).

Customer lifetime value is an important concept because it indicates long-term health of the customer relationship along with an upper limit on spending to acquire new customers (Farris *et al*, 2006).

Customer lifetime value can be calculated using the following formula

$$\text{CLV (£)} = \text{Margin (£)} \times \frac{\text{Retention (\%)}}{1 + \text{Discount (\%)} - \text{Retention (\%)}}$$

The components of the formula are:

- CLV = Customer lifetime value – expressed in £

- Margin = **Constant margin** (contribution after deducting variable costs including retention spending)

- Retention = **Retention rate expressed as a %**. When retention equals 0, the customer will never be retained, when it equals 1, the customer will always be retained.

- Discount = **Discount rate expressed as a %**. A discount rate is used because there is a time and a cost associated with money (eg everyone would rather be paid sooner rather than later). The exact *discount* factors depend on the discount rate chosen and the number of periods until cash is received. Money received in ten years will therefore be discounted (eg 50%) more than money received in five years' time (eg 25%).

An example CLV calculation:

A gym charges £19.95 per month for unlimited swimming in its pool.

Variable costs are £1.50 per member per month

Marketing spend (retention spending) equates to £6 per year

Constant margin is therefore (£19.95 − £1.50 − £6/12) = £17.95

Retention is high so a figure of 0.995 is given.

A monthly discount rate is 1% (expressed as 0.01)

CLV = margin × (retention/ (1 + discount − retention))

CLV = £17.95 × (0.995/(1 + 0.01 − 0.995)

CLV − £17.95 × 66.33

CLV = £1,191

(Example adapted from Farris *et al*, 2006)

6 Internal measures of performance

Collecting data in order to measure marketing performance does not need to be an expensive and time-consuming business. It quickly becomes counter-productive if vast amounts of time and resources are diverted to research, analysis, monitoring and reporting.

Organisations often overlook the potential of readily available information from internal sources. In many cases, it is the internal measures that are the most important.

It is interesting and sometimes useful to know how individual performance compares with sector averages and with particular competitor organisations. Indeed, such measures provide a necessary reality check on strategic thinking.

However, once the vision, mission, objectives and tactics are set, the focus should be on how well marketing is performing against the measures the organisation has set for itself. Every organisation is sufficiently unique for it to be necessary to treat external comparisons with a certain amount of qualification.

What matters ultimately – to customers, shareholders, suppliers, staff, managers and other stakeholders – is how well it is doing to deliver its value propositions.

The key to collecting data is to incorporate it within routine activity rather than having to run additional processes for capture. Marketing Information Systems (MkIS – covered in detail in Chapter 7), customer databases, web analytics and technology generally make this easier. Care and attention are required when planning data capture in order to ensure that the required information is clearly defined and recorded at the most appropriate time.

The secret with all data capture is getting it right first time. It is inefficient to go back to source materials to extract useful details that could – and should – have been recorded initially.

A series of metrics can be used based on internal sources. Table 3.8 illustrates some examples.

Table 3.8 Measuring marketing performance from internal sources

Dimension	Appropriate metrics	Comments
Recruitment	■ Number of new customers ■ Cost of customer acquisition ■ Lead conversion rate	The marketing funnel as a concept illustrates the move of potential customers through to becoming leads and then finally customers. Knowing the dynamics of this process including the number of customers gained in any particular period is fundamental to implementing effective marketing strategies. Measuring the cost of conversion and comparing with previous results also shows whether it is becoming easier or harder to secure new custom.
Retention	■ Customer retention rate ■ Customer loyalty ■ Churn rates (customer defection) ■ Lifetime customer values	The frequently repeated maxim that it is cheaper and easier to secure new sales from existing customers than it is to attract new customers is almost certainly true in most markets. One of the present trends is for a general decrease in loyalty. The internet makes it easier for customers to be informed of other available suppliers and prices, and switching costs have been minimised. Organisations have to work harder to keep their customers by providing value, by understanding their customers, by engaging with them and by rewarding loyalty.
Attitude	■ Customer satisfaction	Customer satisfaction levels are an indicator of likely loyalty. Satisfied customers will return for repeat purchases, thus increasing lifetime value and reducing the ratio of marketing costs to sales. Happy customers also promote goods and services to other potential customers, ensuring the organisation benefits from cost-free word of mouth promotion. Knowing how highly customers regard the organisation helps the organisation to make adjustments to the promotional mix or even just to provide information to answer questions and resolve misunderstandings.
Performance	■ Lifetime values ■ Average spend per customer ■ Average spend per visit ■ Profit ■ Value of sales	In the end, the aim of all marketing activity is to secure improved financial performance and long-term survival of the organisation. The ultimate criteria for measuring the effectiveness of marketing is a return in the form of increased sales and profitability.
Communications	■ Website analytics ■ Number of mailouts and emails ■ Analysis of customer service enquiries	Metrics for communications and customer engagement were discussed in Table 3.7.

▶ **Assessment tip**

When considering measures of marketing performance it is essential that those used relate specifically to the context of the organisation and marketing activities undertaken which are being discussed in the assessment. Rather than discussing theoretically what could be measured, knowledge of the actual use of the measures through application of appropriate areas of theory to the activity is required, with numerical measures included.

6.1 Innovation and learning measures of performance

One of the four quadrants of the balanced scorecard is learning and growth (see Chapter 8). This highlights the importance of focusing on development, innovation and change as part of the overall monitoring of performance.

Learning is not just staff development and training (although this is important). It is also a matter of the organisation learning, responding more effectively to customer needs by changing its manner of engagement. Metrics may include targets for staff satisfaction, appraisal, and personal and professional development, but should also reflect a more holistic dimension.

Table 3.9   Organisational goals and possible innovation and learning targets

Organisational goal	Possible innovation and learning targets
To raise the level of skills of staff	▪ Total spend on training and development ▪ Number of days of on-the-job and off-the-job training ▪ Investment per member of staff
To be recognised as an equal opportunities employer	Equal opportunity measures (gender, ethnicity, age, etc)
To raise staff loyalty and morale	▪ Staff satisfaction surveys ▪ Staff turnover ▪ Average number of days taken as sick leave
To retain the knowledge and experience of the best staff members	▪ Number of internal promotions ▪ Amount of cross-functional activity
To improve staff performance	▪ Number of staff achieving performance-related bonuses ▪ Revenue per employee
To remain at the forefront of innovation	▪ Spend on research and development (compared with competitors) ▪ Number of new products introduced

In describing the quadrant, Kaplan and Nolan described three distinct areas of focus:

- Information capital
- Organisation capital
- Human capital

As always, measures of performance should link to the strategic objectives, to what is important to the organisation and its stakeholders, and this is exactly what the balanced scorecard model (which you will study later) promotes. We should be interested in how the organisation must change and innovate in order to deliver its core purpose and satisfy its objectives. Table 3.9 illustrates some organisational goals with possible innovation and learning targets.

ACTIVITY 3.2

Consider a large marketing initiative with which you are involved or with which you are familiar. Select a range of suitable metrics for measuring its performance. Make sure you cover a range of different measures, such as productivity, accounting measures, and learning and growth. For each of the chosen metrics, state from where and how you would draw the required data and any difficulties that might arise from doing so. How might you respond to disappointing results if the performance measures revealed lower outcomes than expected?

The Chartered Institute of Marketing

6.2 Performance measures

In this section, we examine how information collected from various performance measures may be analysed to enable managers to take decisions resulting in positive change.

6.3 Productivity analysis (inputs versus outputs)

We have already noted above that productivity may be measured fairly easily when an organisation or function is engaged in the process of converting tangible inputs into tangible outputs (see Section 3.1). Productivity can be expressed very simply as a ratio of outputs to inputs. Productivity improves when more outputs are generated per unit of input.

$$Productivity = outputs/inputs$$

Sophisticated cost accounting techniques are required to enable the organisation to allocate and apportion direct and indirect costs to the unit of input. As an organisation moves from single to multiple inputs and outputs, it becomes more difficult to gather the data, and when delivering services rather than products, one must account for time, skill and knowledge as well.

It should always be remembered that such productivity measures are only intelligible when we make comparisons – with previous years, budgets, competitors and sector benchmarks. The trends in productivity are probably more important than the absolute value.

We can usually find some measurable unit even when analysing a service provider, public sector or not-for-profit organisation, such as bed occupancy, room utilisation or professional time. The analysis may be conducted for individual processes, divisions or functions, whole organisations or a sector of the economy, provided it is possible to identify a recognisable unit of input and output.

Natural efficiencies (known as economies of scale) may be gained through larger scale activity but not always, and sometime diseconomies occur that serve to reduce productivity.

Figure 3.3 illustrates a typical pattern.

Where the graph becomes steeper in the middle section, the ratio of outputs to inputs is higher, showing greater productivity. Productivity then peaks as diseconomies begin to emerge and more units of input are required to generate output. Optimum efficiency is achieved at or close to point X.

Figure 3.3   Relationship between inputs and outputs

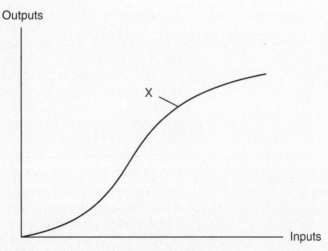

There are two alternative approaches to improving productivity (although they are not exclusive): reducing the costs of inputs or increasing the volume or value of outputs. This is not as easy as it sounds, since scaling back on the costs associated with production or service delivery is liable to have a negative qualitative impact on outputs.

Within the marketing function, various techniques may be tried to get greater return on marketing investment (Table 3.10).

Improving productivity, then, is about finding the best return on the investment, that is marketing. It requires a search to lower costs as well as maximise returns. The process for customer acquisition needs to be highly targeted while the process for customer retention can be tailored and personal.

Those customers (new and existing) with the greatest potential for lifetime values need to be prioritised. It is common in customer relationship management to categorise customers in such a way that high value ones are afforded extra careful attention, for good reason. The focus on retention and loyalty allows for cross-selling as well as word of mouth advocacy.

Table 3.10   Strategies for improving marketing productivity

Productivity improvement method	Explanation
Quality management	Earlier in this Study Text, we noted that it is often cheaper to reduce the number of defects occurring than to reject them. The implementation of quality models should improve productivity by identifying and eliminating inefficiencies. The whole process of setting goals and targets, monitoring performance and identifying scope for improvement is designed to increase efficiency (doing something cheaper) and effectiveness (doing something better).
Moving from customer acquisition to customer retention	In a general sense, shifting the primary focus from customer acquisition to customer retention is designed to capitalise on the lower costs associated with increasing lifetime values rather than attracting new leads and converting them. This is not to suggest that customer acquisition is not important but rather to prioritise keeping existing customers ahead of any growth strategy.
Moving from mass marketing to segmented and niche marketing, to individual customer and account marketing	Target marketing enables organisations to focus on the most likely prospects, reducing wasteful activity on those groups with the highest conversion costs. Blanket coverage and an unstructured approach are almost certainly less efficient, both because it will hit people with limited interest and those on the receiving end will feel less attracted by generalised messages.
Cycle time reduction	An analysis of processes and operations can reveal the incidence of idle time which may be shortened or eliminated. The gaps between the end of one activity and the start of the next can be the cause of inefficiencies. It may require a more holistic approach to planning with overlapping cycles or it may be a question of deploying staff skills in a different arrangement.
Management accounting techniques	To improve productivity, it is important to be able to measure it and to have an appreciation of costing. Understandably the Chief Finance Officer (or equivalent) is keen to know what contribution marketing makes to the bottom line. Hard financial targets – including return on investment, return on assets and the contributions to cash flow, profitability and share value – provide a much more convincing argument for not cutting the budget than more rarefied discussions of brand awareness and public profile. To achieve this, the marketing function needs to be able to identify and apportion its costs to units of activity. Overheads (staff time, rent and rates, light and heat, depreciation, etc) need to be included through a suitable basis (usually time). Armed with a reasonably sophisticated model, the marketing manager is much more able to gauge productivity and any changes to it over time.
Benchmarking	There are many sources of benchmarking data that the marketing function can use to help it set appropriate targets. When used with proper discernment they can add real value to performance management. Comparison with sector averages may highlight that an area of activity requires careful analysis if it is widely divergent. Benchmarks help to answer the question 'what should our productivity be?'

The Chartered Institute of Marketing

Productivity improvement method	Explanation
Staff training and development	It is always important to involve staff in sharing goals for improving productivity rather be seen to be imposing a potentially threatening system for measuring and assessing their work. Ideally, the marketing team should be involved in agreeing targets and suggesting opportunities for improvement. If linked to appraisal and professional development, this should lead to higher levels of commitment and motivation towards achieving those goals.
Research and development	R&D does not need to be solely about product innovation and manufacturing techniques. We have seen that in virtually all quality models there is a need to review existing practice and to test new approaches before implementing them on a wider scale. Most models take a cyclical approach so that innovation is a continuous process. R&D (either internal or an outsourced service) can provide a consultancy resource to the marketing function, exploring ergonomics, integrated operations, productivity trends, technology, skill requirements and processes, and bring their knowledge and experience of other systems to bear.
Technology	Technology – especially information technology – can be used both in the delivery of marketing and in gauging its productivity. Developing models for efficiency, building up a database of historical performance, monitoring and analysing activity, linking operations that may be isolated bureaucratically or geographically, carrying out continuous auditing and producing timely reports are all made easier through the use of technology. Analytical tools, databases and marketing intelligence all come together in the Marketing Intelligence System (MkIS) and if used properly this can be a considerable benefit to monitoring and improving productivity.

6.4 Comparative analysis (changes over time)

In all our considerations of targets, benchmarks and actual performance so far, we have stressed the need to consider trends and variations over time rather than just absolute values. In order to understand and interpret variations, it is necessary to use time series analysis to distinguish between:

- Random variations
- Seasonal variations
- Underlying trends

Sales, profitability, productivity and other measures are likely to be subject to change over time. Some of these may be purely random and need to be eliminated.

- Random (or stochastic) effects are more likely to be apparent with smaller samples or over shorter time periods. Using comparative data, it is possible to identify positive and negative movements that are purely random and to smooth out the data.

- Seasonal variations occur in a repeated cycle, often annually, due to patterns of weather, public and school holidays, festivals and religious observance as well as longer economic or political cycles. From previous records such variations should be predictable and should be included in forecasts and planning.

- After random and seasonal variations have been identified, the remaining pattern is the underlying trend – upwards, downwards or no change.

6.5 Segmental analysis (analysis of markets)

Market segmentation is a common approach taken to achieve target marketing. The total market population is divided according to certain characteristics that can be associated with a likely appetite for a particular variation of the marketing mix. The assumption is made that, although distinct from the rest of the market, the segment itself is undifferentiated, at least in respect of the relevant characteristic, and as such it can be targeted by a common marketing strategy. The marketing mix suitable for a given segment may only vary in

respect of one aspect, such as price, compared with other segments. It is the analysis of the market segments that allows the organisation to develop the right mix in order to maximise sales.

Segmental analysis may be made according to a number of broad categories of characteristics, such as:

- Lifestyle
- Economic status
- Geographical
- Demographic
- Psychographic

Narrow distinctions – or niche markets – can also be defined. A highly sophisticated form of segmentation is used by political parties to identify likely voting behaviour and susceptibility to canvassing so that they can target their resources in areas where it is likely to have the greatest impact. Segmentation is used to improve performance. It moves the organisation away from mass marketing and allows a more carefully targeted approach. It is conducted through a top-down approach – by which the total market is divided and subdivided according to appropriate distinguishing features – or a bottom-up approach – where market segments are constructed from recognisable types of customers. Segmentation may also be made on the basis of groups of products or services.

Having designed activity around segments it is then possible to monitor performance of those same divisions of the market. Many organisations report their earnings by segment in the annual accounting statements.

THE REAL WORLD

As an example, when Kcom plc published its accounts for 2011/12 it included the segmental analysis as shown below. Each of KC & Eclipse, Kcom and Smart 421 and PLC represent different segments.

	Revenue		EBITDA	
	2011 £'000	2010 £'000	2011 £'000	2010 £'000
Before exceptional items				
KC & Eclipse	**122,893**	123,536	**57,862**	57,277
Kcom & Smart421	**276,861**	290,973	**25,751**	22,693
PLC[1]	**(4,342)**	(1,709)	**(7,650)**	(10,175)
Activities before exceptional items	395,412	412,800	75,963	69,795

PLC includes Public Company central and share scheme expenses, inter-segment eliminations and the costs, excluding current and past service costs, associated with the Group's defined benefit pension schemes and the related assets and liabilities.

(Kcom PLC annual report, 2010-2011)

EBITDA is the profit before other items have been deducted (EBITDA stands for earnings before interest, taxes, depreciation and amortisation). In this case, the segmentation has been made on the basis of products and services.

6.6 Innovation audit

Innovation is important to an organisation, especially in competitive markets, because maintaining advantage very often depends upon responding to change rapidly and flexibly. The opportunities for innovation occur at every point. This includes, among many possibilities:

- New products
- New processes
- New approaches
- New ideas
- New channels

The Chartered Institute of Marketing

- New suppliers
- New quality models
- New partners
- New working arrangements
- New layouts
- New markets

The purpose of an innovation audit is to help organisations improve their creative and entrepreneurial skills. It follows a structured process of identifying strengths and weaknesses through analysis, interviews, surveys and other techniques.

Some audits also include self-assessment questionnaires to take an initial indication of present activity. The audit should show how innovation is currently being fostered within the organisation and what the inhibitors are.

It should help the organisation benchmark its approach to innovation against recognised best practice. The outcome of the audit is usually in the form of a report of the findings together with recommendations for developing innovative capabilities further.

The main components for innovation – and hence for innovation audits to focus on – are:

- The current **organisational climate**
- Measures of the organisation's **current performance** with regard to innovation
- Review of **policies and practices** supporting innovation and facilitating it
- The balance of **styles** of the management team

The organisational climate determines the degree of encouragement for innovation. The 'tone at the top' sets the vision for the rest of the organisation. To succeed, innovation requires its own strategy that is linked to the organisation's business goals.

An audit would need to identify from staff at all levels the extent to which innovation is encouraged.

Traditional, hierarchical organisations tend to have a high degree of formalisation and bureaucracy, requiring that operations follow strict procedures with little scope for innovation. This climate may also apply to the ways in which senior managers tackle strategic planning and problem solving.

While such an approach may be low in risk and avoid the possibility of being blamed for deviating from protocol, it may also lead to stagnation. This in turn may erode the organisation's ability to compete or deliver its primary aims.

To some extent, the licence to innovate is also a licence to make mistakes. Certain management styles may resist allowing such a possibility but that is how organisations, as well as people, learn and develop.

The growth and learning quadrant of the balanced scorecard reflects the importance of positive change. There is nothing wrong with taking risks, provided they are understood and that appropriate measures have been taken to mitigate them.

The innovation audit will attempt to measure the current performance in respect of new approaches. To do this, it will need to consider questions like:

- How are ideas generated?
- Who is involved in the problem solving process?
- Does the organisation follow structured techniques for stimulating innovative responses?
- What is the ratio of new ideas to ones implemented or of prototypes to launch?

There are a number of techniques for generating new ideas and stimulating innovative approaches. Common ones include:

- Brainstorming
- Synectics (what if)
- Mind mapping
- Role play

- Analogy and metaphor
- Six thinking hats
- Horizon scanning
- Six questions (who, why, where, what, when, how)
- Lateral thinking

Formal policies highlight the ways in which innovative approaches have been enshrined in the organisation and its operations. It is one thing for the CEO to declare that novel and creative thinking is encouraged if in practice the policies of the organisation make this difficult. Policies cover all aspects of organisational activity. They may reveal implicit or explicit support for innovative approaches, either by creating a more relaxed environment where staff feel that is okay to try new approaches or by a proactive support of innovation. The policies will impact on key aspects such as:

- Communication
- Planning
- Group work
- Accountability
- Allocation of resources
- Authorisation

Successful innovative organisations need frameworks in which progressive and alternative ideas may be proposed and implemented. This does not mean that accountability is removed, rather that senior managers (the ultimate risk owners) have delegated some of their responsibilities for creativity to others further down the chain. At all levels, there needs to be a balance between structured activity and greater openness to change.

Practices under scrutiny through the innovation audit include the processes for evaluating new proposals. Creativity is often stifled because proposals do not conform to expectation.

Innovation as an approach fits better with certain cognitive styles of personality and behaviour. It is more effective when an individual or team regards innovation as a natural and continuous process. Someone with an active desire to search for new ways of approaching situations should be one of the people to consider for being an innovation champion. They also need the courage to be different, to be tenacious and to learn to accept that sometimes new approaches will fail.

Some of the cognitive styles can be learnt, and innovative organisations provide training and development opportunities for their staff to develop the good habits and techniques. It is also important to ensure that problem solving teams have the right balance of personalities. There are a number of techniques and models used to profile team roles, one of the most popular and well-known being Belbin. Belbin's team roles include a plant, the name given to a creative problem-solver. However, a team of plants is unlikely to succeed since they tend to be too preoccupied in new ideas and may not be any good at developing or communicating them. Sometimes people need someone else to be asking searching questions in order to stimulate their creativity. Plants need co-ordinators, shapers, teamworkers, completer-finishers and others to complement their cognitive style and turn the innovative idea into a workable solution.[5] Team building is covered in more detail in Section 2 of this book.

7 Competitor comparisons and benchmarking

We have already touched on the use of benchmarks and the value of comparisons with competitors. These are of value if taken as part of a wider perspective and must be treated with an appropriate degree of circumspection.

While interesting the comparisons may not of themselves be very revealing. Organisations are unique in their size, shape, aims, history, culture, skills, ambitions, appetite for risk, performance, etc, and so at best we may look at similar firms with similar profiles.

This can be helpful in setting targets or judging how well the organisation is performing. However, there is a danger that it can become a distraction. Trends over time and comparisons with internal targets may be more important and more useful.

Guidelines for competitor comparisons and benchmarking may be summarised as follows.

- The use of competitor data and benchmarks needs to be part of a planned and systematic approach to performance management, based on a genuine need for making external comparisons rather than relying on internal targets and historical results. Specific high-priority areas of activity should be selected for making such comparisons where there is an accepted urgency for driving improvements.

- The competitors selected need to match the organisation as closely as possible, with consideration given to the sector, size, vision, strategic priorities and product portfolio. More than one competitor should be used for comparison purposes to reduce bias.

- Comparisons should be made and assessed over a period of time in order to establish trends.

THE REAL WORLD

Land Rover

Land Rover vehicles came last in J D Power's 2007 US Initial Quality Survey. Land Rover is now benchmarking the quality levels of Jaguar, its sister brand, and climbing its way back up the league tables. Ford announced the sale of Jaguar and Land Rover to Tata Motors in March 2008, so presumably the internal benchmarking programme can continue. However, the company undertakes a variety of internal and external benchmarking exercises, market testing and internal comparative analysis across its own vehicles, which help it to identify cost improvement opportunities for components, systems and sub-systems.

(Jaguar Land Rover, 2012)

A hair and beauty chain may be benchmarked against a lawn mower manufacturer because they are located in the same town and so have similar local external environment conditions.

ACTIVITY 3.3

Construct a survey that might be used with (a) staff and (b) senior managers as part of an innovation audit within an organisation with which you are familiar. What other indicators would you use to help you analyse the extent to which new ways of thinking are encouraged by the organisational climate, by its policies and practice and by the cognitive skills of the staff involved?

- Why measure:
    - Measurements prove the value of marketing activity

- Accounting measures
    - Financial comparisons aid decision making
    - Published financial accounts – demonstrate financial strengths and weaknesses
    - Cash flows aid marketing planning, determining when to carry out activities

- Productivity measures
    - Demonstrate marketing productivity – return on inputs

- Relationship marketing measures
    - Help to demonstrate areas needing improvement for customer retention and satisfaction

- Quality and relationship marketing
    - Quality has to cross functional boundaries to assist with building relationships

- Internal measures of performance
    - Essential to understand internal issues of performance
    - Understanding performance in different areas and segments
    - Auditing the innovation levels within the organisation to determine areas for improvement

- Competitor comparisons
    - Helpful for setting targets and judging performance

FURTHER READING

Clark, B. (1998) Measuring performance: the marketing perspective. *In*: N. Andy, and W. Daniel (eds.) *Business Performance Measurement: Theory and Practice*. Cambridge, Cambridge University Press.

REFERENCES

[1] Ambler, T. *et al* (2004) *Assess Marketing Performance: The Current State of Metrics*. Centre for Marketing, 01-903.

[2] See Institute of Customer Service (2012) http://www.instituteofcustomerservice.com [Accessed on 14 June 2012]

[3] See ACSI (2012) http://www.theacsi.org [Accessed on 14 June 2012]

[4] Haven, B. (2007) *Marketing's New Key Metric: Engagement*. Forrester Research Inc.

[5] For more on Belbin's team roles refer to Belbin (2012) http://www.belbin.com [Accessed on 14 June 2012]

Aaker, D. and McLoughlin, D. (2007) *Strategic Market Management*. European Edition. Chichester, John Wiley & Sons.

ACSI (2011) Extract of ACSI statistics. ACSI, http://www.theacsi.org [Accessed on 23 April 2012]

The Chartered Institute of Marketing

Anon (2010-2011) Kcom PLC annual report. Kcom PLC, http://www.kcomplc.com/docs/news-pdf/annual-reports/annual-report-2010-2011.pdf [Accessed on 3 March 2012]

Christopher *et al* (2002) *Relationship Marketing: Creating Stakeholder Value.* Oxford, Elsevier Butterworth Heinemann.

de Bono, E. and Heller, R. (2012) *'Employees and customers: In the quest for customer satisfaction the link between employees and customers is key'*. Thinking Managers, http://www.thinkingmanagers.com/management/employees-customers.php [Accessed on 6 March 2012].

Drummond G. *et al* (2001) *Strategic Marketing: Planning and control*. 2nd edition. Oxford, Butterworth Heinemann.

Egan, J. (2004) *Relationship Marketing: Exploring Relational Strategies in Marketing*. 2nd edition. Harlow, Pearson Education.

Farris, P. *et al* (2006), *Key Marketing Metrics: The 50+ metrics every manager needs to know*. Harlow, Wharton School Publishing.

Jaguar Land Rover (2012) 2010/11 Annual Report. Jaguar Land Rover, http://jaguarlandrover.com/pdf/2010-2011_annual_report.pdf [Accessed on 20 April 2012]

Kumar, V. (2008) *Customer Lifetime Value: The Path to Profitability*. New York, Now Publishers Inc.

Sevin, C. (1965) *Marketing Productivity Analysis*. New York, McGraw Hill.

Varey, R. and Lewis, B. (2000) *Internal Marketing: Directions for Management*. London, Routledge.

Walsh, C. (2008) *Key Management Ratios: The 100+ ratios every manager needs to know*. Harlow, Prentice Hall.

Watkis N.C. (2005) Do you believe the hype? *Accountancy Age*, 12th May, London.

QUICK QUIZ

1   What is customer lifetime value?

2   Why is loyalty difficult to measure?

3   Fill in the blank. _____: an external target of performance against which a firm measures its activities.

4   What is the alternative name for a profit and loss account?

5   The Chartered Institute of Marketing require you to reach the standard of an accountant when evaluating marketing using accountancy measures. True of false?

6   What are the three objectives that customer communications are designed to achieve?

7   Internal measures only refer to marketing procedures. True or false?

8   What measures can be used within comparative analysis?

ACTIVITY DEBRIEFS

Activity 3.1

This will depend upon the company reports obtained.

Activity 3.2

This will depend upon the initiative and metrics selected. Responses to disappointing results are covered in later chapters, 4 and 5 in particular.

Activity 3.3

This will depend upon the current innovation level of the selected organisation.

QUICK QUIZ ANSWERS

1   The financial value of a customer relationship over the time of the relationship.

2   Customers have repertoire of brands, different products may be useful at different stages of their lifetime and so on.

3   Benchmarking: an external target of performance against which a firm measures its activities.

4   Income statement.

5   False. You are to be aware and able to understand the figures but not to the level of detail expected of an accountant who will have trained for many years.

6   Increasing awareness, stimulating trial purchase, and reinforcing loyalty

7   False. Innovation and staff attitude, behaviour and performance are also important.

8   Time series (eg trends, seasonal variations etc), benchmarking.

The Chartered Institute of Marketing

Section 1:

Senior Examiner's comments

For Section 1, the assessment will require you to analyse the structure of the marketing function of an organisation to demonstrate the understanding of how it fits within the larger context of the organisation. You will need to include critical evaluation of the current organisation and marketing structure in order to generate value through marketing activity. Consideration may have to be given to the analysis of current processes for marketing and development of these to ensure compliance with best practice, emphasis should be paid to how the marketing function should use quality systems and ensure compliance with these along with the benefits gained.

The expectation of the assessment for this section is that you will consider the objectives of the marketing operation and how the structure and processes currently used enable or hinder the fulfilment of the objectives, recommending ways to improve, measure and monitor performance. The recommendation of appropriate improvements is of key importance throughout the assessment. You will be expected to evaluate measures, while also needing to develop your own measures, demonstrating how to be creative and innovative in terms of ensuring that marketing provides value for money (VFM) for the organisation.

It is expected that you will take a holistic view of the situation and tasks, producing an integrated piece of work that clearly demonstrates links between the tasks described in the assessment brief. These tasks are to be considered as a whole rather than as separate parts, with each task having implications for the others.

Section 2: Managing marketing teams

Section 2 is the highest weighting section with a clear focus on how to improve marketing performance through people. This section examines the role of the marketing manager as a manager of people and teams. It helps you to demonstrate an understanding of management and leadership approaches, tools, techniques and theories. It also assists in application of them practically within an organisational context. A key feature is encouragement to reflect on your personal approach to managing and leading others, and determine actions to improve both your own and your team's performance.

This section explores the whole spectrum of building high performing teams from team design and recruitment to operational management and performance management – the focus being on how to improve marketing performance through people.

The organisational context may vary, but the section places particular importance on consideration of the issues of working in virtual and international cross-functional teams and the complexities of diversity and culture, that many managers deal with on a day-to-day basis.

This section also examines how to build a high-performing team through effective team design and recruitment processes. It does not provide a detailed knowledge of employment law as this is not required of the marketing manager, but it does consider the impact of legislation throughout the recruitment process. When considering this element of the unit, it is important to take into account that this is leading towards building the organisations capacity and capability. Thus, it is essential to ensure that the right level of competency, combined with the right balance of individual talent is achieved to maximise the organisations potential to achieve competitive advantage. It explores aspects of performance management and sets objectives for individuals that are designed to meet with marketing and organisational objectives. Methods to measure individual performance and recommendations on how to improve individual performance are discussed together with the impact of the manager's approach on team member performance.

CHAPTER 4

Management, leadership and establishing teams

Introduction

An **organisation** has been defined as '*a social arrangement for the controlled performance of collective goals*' (Huczynski & Buchanan, 2001). This immediately suggests the need for management, because:

- The activity of the organisation, and its roles and relationships, have to be structured and co-ordinated (as we saw in Chapter 1).

- Goals or objectives have to be set for the organisation, at all levels.

- Progress and results have to be monitored to ensure that objectives are met.

- Corporate values, ethics and operating principles have to be communicated and sustained.

- Somebody has to look after the interests of the organisation's owners (shareholders) and other stakeholders.

For hundreds of years, people have been doing management in organisations. Yet every year there is new research and new ideas about why management is necessary; what managers actually do; and how they can do it better.

There are many different definitions of management. For example:

- The key purpose of management (and leadership) is to 'provide direction, facilitate change and achieve results through the efficient, creative and responsible use of resources' (Management Standards Centre).

- Management is 'a social process entailing responsibility for the effective and economic planning and regulation of the operations of an enterprise, in fulfilment of given purposes or tasks, such responsibility entailing: (a) judgement and decision in determining plans and in using data to control performance and progress against plans; and (b) the guidance, integration, motivation and supervision of the personnel composing the enterprise and carrying out its operations.' (Brech, 1965).

Topic list

What is management?	(1)	Sourcing and training teams	(7)
Leadership and management of teams	(2)	Legal considerations when recruiting	(8)
Personal development planning	(3)	Evaluating recruitment	(9)
Teams	(4)	Induction and training	(10)
Planning teams for effective performance	(5)	Talent management	(11)
Job analysis	(6)	Outsourcing jobs and projects	(12)

2.1	Critically evaluate the differences between management and leadership and identify the role of an 'operational marketing manager':
	▪ Leadership traits, skills and attitude
	▪ Leadership and management styles, eg, Action-Centred Leadership, Transactional Leadership, Transformational Leadership, Situational Leadership, the management styles continuum
	▪ The scope of leadership – providing strategic direction
	▪ The manager's role – planning, organising, co-ordinating, controlling, communication, teambuilding, coaching, networking, developing the functions of the marketing manager – information, value creation, communications
	▪ Reflect on personal approach to management and leadership and produce a personal development plan
2.2	Determine the needs for and show how to establish and build synergistic and harmonious marketing teams including preparing a plan to show how teams should be structured to deliver organisational and marketing objectives:
	▪ Structuring the team – the team audit, functional roles, team roles
	▪ Team development and talent management – stages in team development, team cohesiveness, high-performance teams, the manager's role
	▪ Job analysis, job design, job enlargement, job enrichment
	▪ Competency development requirements
	▪ Flexible working practices
	▪ Assess and apply a range of team theories, eg, Belbin's team roles, Tuckman's stages of team development
2.3	Propose a range of approaches for the sourcing of a team, including consideration of recruitment, training and development to provide the right balance of competency and skills:
	▪ Recruitment channels – internally and externally
	▪ Selection tools – job description, person specification
	▪ Selection techniques – assessment centres, interviews
	▪ On-boarding – induction
	▪ Training and development
	▪ Outsourcing of jobs/projects
	▪ Recruitment evaluation – determining recruitment effectiveness
	▪ Legal considerations when recruiting

1 What is management?

1.1 Management roles

▶ **Key term**

Management may be defined, most simply, as 'getting things done through other people'.

As management is such a commonly used word people think they share a common view of its meaning. Mintzberg (1973), based on researching the work of managers (confined to chief executives), concluded that managers adopt a variety of roles during the working day (Figure 4.1), essentially this consists of a mass of fragmented activities, constant interruption, pressure for immediate answers and reliance on word-of-mouth messages.

Managers value 'soft' information, often acquired through gossip, hearsay and speculation. Consequently, important information for the organisation is held, not necessarily in the memory of its computers but, in the minds of its managers.

Mintzberg offered a view of management based on 'roles'.

Each of the ten roles covers a different aspect of managerial work. The ten roles form an integrated whole but different managers are likely to give greater prominence to different roles as well as relative emphasis depending on work aspects considered.

For example, sales managers tend to spend relatively more time in their interpersonal roles, while production managers tend to devote more attention to the decisional roles. Any single manager is likely to emphasise different roles depending on the aspect of their work considered.

Figure 4.1 Mintzberg's managerial roles

Role category	Role	Indicative behaviour
Interpersonal	Figurehead	Performs ceremonial and symbolic duties such as greeting visitors, signing legal documents
	Leader	Sets the strategic direction of the organisation, motivates managers and other staff
	Liaison	Maintains information links both inside and outside the organisation
Informational	Monitor	Seeks and receives information, scans periodicals and reports, maintains personal contacts
	Disseminator	Forwards information to other organisation members, sends memos and reports
	Spokesperson	Transmits information to outsiders through speeches, reports and memos
	Entrepreneur	Initiates improvement projects, identifies new ideas, delegates responsibility to others
Decisional	Disturbance Handler	Takes corrective action during disputes or crises, resolves conflicts among subordinates, adapts to environmental crises
	Resource Allocator	Decides who gets resources, scheduling, budgeting, sets priorities
	Negotiator	Represents department during negotiation of contracts, sales, purchases, budgets

(Mintzberg, 1973)

Mintzberg found that the amount of time spent in each of the three main categories of roles varied with the level of the manager. For example,

- First-line supervisory positions are likely to have more decisional roles (at a day-to-day operational level).
- Senior managers spend more time on interpersonal roles.
- Middle managers tend to be more occupied with informational roles.
- Roles will also change with culture and organisational size.

Fayol (1841 – 1925) was a French industrialist who put forward and popularised the concept of the 'universality of management principles': in other words, the idea that all organisations could be structured and managed according to the same rational principles. Fayol himself recognised that applying such principles in practice was not simple: 'Seldom do we have to apply the same principles twice in identical conditions; allowance must be made for different and changing circumstances.'

However, Fayol classified five **functions of management** which apply to any organisation and can be related to the roles identified by Minzberg.

Table 4.1   Fayol's five functions of management

Function	Comment
Planning	Determining priorities and objectives, and strategies, policies, programmes and procedures for achieving those objectives, for the organisation and its sub-units.
Organising	Establishing a structure of tasks which need to be performed to achieve the goals of the organisation; grouping these tasks into jobs for individuals or teams; allocating jobs to sections and departments; delegating authority to carry out the jobs; and providing systems of information and communication, for the co-ordination of activities.
Commanding	Giving instructions to subordinates to carry out tasks, for which the manager has authority (to make decisions) and responsibility (for performance).
Co-ordinating	Harmonising the goals and activities of individuals and groups within the organisation. Management must reconcile differences in approach, effort, interest and timing, in favour of overall (or 'super-ordinate') shared goals.
Controlling	Measuring and correcting the activities of individuals and groups, to ensure that their performance is in accordance with plans. Deviations from plans are identified and corrected.

Mintzberg and other management researchers (eg Kotter) found that managers in fact spent relatively little time working on the classical perspective of marketing management, analysis, planning, implementation and control.

They came to this conclusion quite simply by following them around all day. Gaining information from the world around, for example, becomes a more important role, the more senior the manager. Informal discussions with other senior managers and experts are the best way of building a view of the longer term environment in which the business must compete.

Without this input it is really difficult for senior managers to build a future view beyond the time frame of standard research reports. The phrase 'management by walking about has been adopted to reflect this.

1.2 Management tasks and processes

Drucker (1955) described the basic function of management as comprising five processes.

- **Setting objectives for the organisation.** Managers decide what the objectives of the organisation should be and quantify the targets of achievement for each objective. They must then communicate these targets to other people in the organisation.

- **Organising the work.** The work to be done in the organisation must be divided into manageable activities and manageable jobs. The jobs must be integrated into a formal organisation structure, and people must be selected to do the jobs.

- **Motivating** employees and communicating information to them to enable them to do their work.

- **The job of measurement.** Management must:

  - Establish **objectives** or yardsticks of performance for all personnel

  - Analyse **actual performance**, appraise it against the objectives or yardsticks which have been set, and analyse the comparison

  - **Communicate** the findings and explain their significance both to subordinate employees and also to superiors.

- **Developing people.** The manager 'brings out what is in them or he stifles them. He strengthens their integrity or he corrupts them'.

The Chartered Institute of Marketing

1.3 Challenges of management

Management involves many challenges and trade-offs: between trust and control; between quality, speed and cost; between stability, order, consistency and risk management on one hand and creativity, flexibility, responsiveness and innovation on the other.

Rosabeth Moss Kanter (1992) highlighted some of the incompatible demands placed on managers when seeking improved performance and excellence in flexible, innovative environments – and these may strike a particular chord for marketing managers.

Table 4.2   Kanter's managerial dilemmas

Demands made on managers		
Be entrepreneurial and risk taking	*but*	Don't lose money
Invest in the future	*but*	Keep profitable now
Do everything you're doing now but even better	*but*	Spend more time communicating, on teams and new projects
Lead and direct	*but*	Participate, listen, co-operate
Know everything about your business	*but*	Delegate more
Work all hours	*but*	Keep fit
Be single-minded in your commitment to ideas	*but*	Be flexible and responsive
Demands made on organisations		
Be 'lean and mean'	*but*	Be a good employer
Be creative and innovative	*but*	'Stick to the knitting'
Decentralise to small, simple autonomous units	*but*	Centralise to be efficient and integrative
Have a sense of urgency	*but*	Deliberately plan for the future

ACTIVITY 4.1

Reflect on each of the dilemmas raised by Kanter, in your own experience, or informally interview a manager in your organisation about them.

- Which side of the scale do the culture and approaches of your organisation come down on, in each case?

- Which side of each dilemma supports innovation, flexibility and creativity, and which restricts it?

- What suggestions can you come up with for how a manager might resolve these dilemmas, and be supported in doing so by his or her organisation?

1.4 The role of the operational marketing manager

In addition to all of the above 'standard' functions of a manager, the marketing manager (at an operational level) has three distinct functions identified by the syllabus:

- Information
- Value creation
- Communication

The following is a job description for a marketing manager from CIM (2012)

Description

Responsible for the strategic direction of all marketing activity on specific products/services.

Personal profile

- 5-7 experience in marketing or product management
- Able to think strategically and deliver project goals
- Ability to work well in multi-disciplined/cross-functional teams
- Good interpersonal skills and ability to build close-knit relationships with outside agencies
- Strong leadership and influencing skills

Suggested CIM professional qualification

Professional Diploma in Marketing

Responsibilities

- Report to Marketing Director/Controller
- Ensure that a product or service matches brand positioning
- Identify target markets and work with the research teams exploring consumer insights
- Plan communication strategy and liaise with all members of the campaign team to ensure effective and efficient delivery
- Analyse the results of all marketing activity and presents findings and recommendations to senior management and product management
- Build both your own and cross-departmental teams
- Liaise with external agencies to ensure they have a clear understanding of the marketing strategy
- A good understanding of the importance of legal and regulatory frameworks

(CIM, 2012)

1.4.1 An interface role

The marketing manager also acts as the bridge between the company and its external stakeholder audiences, particularly customers.

- The marketing manager represents and champions the **customer's** needs and interests within the organisation, through customer research, complaint handling, service quality management – and generally seeking to embed customer focus (a marketing orientation) within the organisation, through internal marketing.

- The marketing function generally creates relationships with customers, and controls the firm's **communications** and **interactions** with them (especially through the disciplines of relationship marketing).

Figure 4.2   The marketing manager as interface

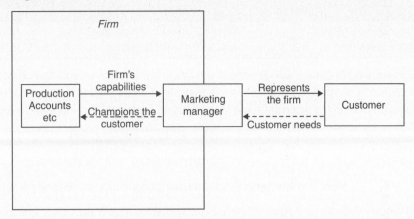

2 Leadership and management of teams

▶ **Key terms**

John Kotter (2001) makes a distinction between **leadership and management**. Management is about coping with complexity by planning and budgeting (usually for one month/year ahead) while he states that leadership, by contrast, is about coping with change by setting a direction though visions and strategy.

Peter Drucker (1955) defined the difference more simply as 'Management is doing things right; leadership is doing the right things'.

Not all leaders are managers and not all managers are leaders. However, managers can be leaders and *vice versa*. Managers and leaders both have some activity in common.

However, what distinguishes a leader from a manager is more a question of the balance of activities that comprise a job. There is an expectation that leaders engage in activities that support their central function of focusing on the strategic direction of the organisation.

The distinction is brought out in the present era of rapid technological change, changing demographics, economic turbulence and increasing levels of competition. Kotter brings this distinction home by using an example of a peacetime army which works well with sound administration and management throughout but with leadership concentrated at the top of the hierarchy.

In contrast, a wartime army requires competent leadership throughout as he states (p 86) that no one has worked out how to manage people into battle, they have to be led.

Kotter discusses more differences between leadership and managers and some more of these ideas are summarised in Table 4.3.

Table 4.3   Based on the ideas from Kotter (2001, p86)

	Managing – coping with complexity	*Leading/leadership* – coping with change
Complexity	Managed through planning and budgeting Establishing detailed approaches to achieving the plan	Setting direction through visions and strategies
Developing the capacity to achieve the plan or vision	Organising Staffing Creating organisation structure and job roles Suitable recruitment Communicating the plan Delegation	– Communicating the vision/ new direction – Selecting the appropriate people to whom the vision should be communicated who can create the groups of likeminded people to commit to its achievement

	Managing – coping with complexity	*Leading/leadership* – coping with change
Ensuring that the plan or vision is achieved	Controlling, problem solving, monitoring formal and informal targets	Motivating and inspiring people to achieve success

Gosling and Mintzberg (2003) provide a refreshingly different perspective on what management is. Rather than a collection of attributes in which one management writer's list is fairly similar to any other, they consider the problem of trying to reconcile some long standing, seemingly incompatible, management mantras. For example:

Be local and be global.

Change perpetually and maintain order.

Make the numbers (ie achieve your performance targets) while nurturing your people.

Their conclusion is that some of these objectives are mutually exclusive. The answer lies in how the manager should think in trying to address these and many other seemingly irreconcilable problems that they must resolve as managers. To do this requires the manager to have various mindsets. These are the tools which she or he must learn to be great managers. The five mindsets they came up with are termed:

1   **The Reflective MindSet**

Make time for digesting (ie processing and learning from) your experiences.

2   **The Analytical MindSet**

Analysis is all around us from industry analysis (ie the context in which we compete) to relationship analysis (eg 360 degree feedback). The main problem here is too much analysis. To use Gosling and Mintzberg's example – the marketer can be so busy studying consumers that they miss the sale.

The focus with this mindset is to move beyond the analysis of the obvious, to test the assumptions on which the analysis is based. This can lead you to questioning, for example, why the organisation has decided to launch a new product or the basis of resourcing a new marketing campaign based on the assumptions behind an optimistic forecast which no one thought to question.

Forecasts often become a perceived reality only disproved when a different outcome is realised.

3   **The Worldly MindSet**

This is in contrast to the global perspective that sees the world as a homogeneous landscape and ignores difference. A worldly mindset sensitises managers to look out for local differences and issues.

This ranges from consumers in the market and how they consume, to the supply chain and manufacturing operations.

4   **The Collaborative MindSet**

Leaders do not necessarily do, or command to be done, 'things' that the organisation does. However, they do set up structures and processes to enable things to be 'done'. To do this successfully requires an understanding about how people collaborate to work effectively.

Gosling and Mintzberg (2003) explain this effectively when they ask who manages self managing teams (p60). People in teams must collaborate within the team and between teams: successful leaders setting up these teams must understand how this collaboration works.

5   **The Action MindSet**

This is perhaps most curiously named as it is more about a call to sensitivity than a call to action. In other words, be sensitive to change and that which requires changing for the benefit of the organisation and to ensure that the unchanged continues to prosper.

In other words, do not simply focus on that which needs to be changed but also apply leadership to the unchanged organisation. It too needs leadership.

Is the distinction between management and leadership useful?

Whetten and Cameron (2002) note that management has come to be equated with values such as stability, hierarchy, equilibrium, control and 'doing the right things': leadership has come to be equated with values such as change, dynamism, vibrancy, charisma and 'doing things right'. They argue, however, that such distinctions are no longer useful.

> 'Managers cannot be successful without being good leaders, and leaders cannot be successful without being good managers. No longer do organisations and individuals have the luxury of holding on to the status quo; worrying about doing things right but failing to do the right things; keeping the system stable instead of leading change and improvement; monitoring current performance instead of formulating a vision of the future; concentrating on equilibrium and control instead of vibrancy and charisma. Effective management and leadership are inseparable. The skills required to do one are also required of the other. No organisation in a post-industrial, hyperturbulent, twenty-first century environment will survive without executives capable of providing both management and leadership.'

> (Whetten & Cameron, 2002, p16)

2.1 Why seek to develop managers as leaders?

Whether or not we make the distinction between management and leadership, attempts to define what makes leadership 'special' (such as those outlined above) have suggested some key points about the benefits effective leadership can bring in a marketing context, and why it is valuable.

- Leaders energise and support **change**, which is essential for survival in highly competitive and fast-changing business environments. By setting visionary goals, and encouraging contribution from teams, leaders create environments that:
    - Seek out new information and ideas
    - Allow challenges to existing procedures and ways of thinking
    - Invite innovation and creativity in finding better ways to achieve goals
    - Support and empower people to cope with the turbulence.

- Leaders secure **commitment**, mobilising the ideas, experience and motivation of employees – which contributes to innovation and improved quality and customer service. This is all the more essential in a competitive, customer-focused, knowledge-based business environment and culture such as marketing.

- Leaders set **direction**, helping teams and organisations to understand their purpose, goals and value to the organisation. This facilitates team-working and empowerment (allowing discretion and creativity about how to achieve the desired outcomes) without loss of co-ordination or direction. This may be particularly valuable in a marketing culture, which tends to attract creative, extraverted (and professionally qualified) types.

- Leaders support, challenge and develop **people**, maximising their contribution to the function and organisation. Leaders use an influence-based, facilitate-and-empower style rather than a command-and-control style, and this is better suited to the expectations of empowered, professional teams and the need for information-sharing in modern business environments.

Extending knowledge

Kotter's writing on the distinction between leaders and managers is well worth reading. He takes an applied approach and writes this in an easy to read style.

Kotter, J.P. (2001) What leaders really do. *Harvard Business Review – BEST OF HBR Breakthrough Leadership.*

(a)   Think about Kotter's war example and provide your own example that contrasts a situation in which you 'managed' with one in which you 'led'.

(b)   Obtain a copy of Kotter's *Harvard Business Review* paper and provide an example of how you already apply these ideas to your work. Where you do not already do this, consider how you *could* apply these ideas. Are there any experiences that you need to have at work to help you to complete this activity effectively? Discuss with you manager.

2.2 Leadership characteristics

Five characteristics of leadership:

- **Challenging the process** – encouraging others to develop new ideas and judicious risk taking.

- Inspiring a shared vision about the future.

- **Enabling others to act** – encouraging collaboration, co-operation, building teams and empowering others.

- **Modelling the way** – planning and reviewing progress and taking corrective action in a way that gains the respect of others; being clear about values and acting in a manner consistent with them.

- Recognising and celebrating others' achievements.

(Kouzes and Posner, 2002)

2.3 Understanding leadership and management styles

Various perspectives of leadership styles exist. A selection is presented below and these include so-called *situational perspectives* (often termed contingent models) in which managers adapt their approach to influencing others dependent on the context in which they do this and will change their approach accordingly.

Models of this type include 'action-centred leadership and Tannenbaum's management styles continuum'. Another general approach considers leadership from the perspective of the **characteristics** and **traits** of leaders. This includes the five (big) traits identified by McCrae and John (1992) and the contrasting transactional–transformational leadership perspective.

2.4 Situational perspectives models

2.4.1 Action-centred leadership

John Adair's (2002) action-centred leadership model is based on three parts:

1   Defining the task
2   Managing the team or group
3   Managing individuals

People need to be briefed properly about the objectives that need to be achieved, what needs to be done, why, how and when. The extent to which all of this needs to be spelled out by the leader or manager will depend on the people involved, the work context and the nature of any particular task. In a situation where there is an expectation that tasks will be delegated, there is no need to go into great detail about how something should be done because this will be the responsibility of the person carrying out the task. The purpose of the business is to deliver something of value to people. The leader is responsible for ensuring that the marketing task determines what that value is, and then organises work in the most effective and efficient way to deliver it.

The Chartered
Institute of Marketing

2.5 Core Functions of Leadership

Adair sets out the core functions of leadership that are central to the action-centred leadership model (see Figure 4.3):

Figure 4.3   Action-centred leadership roles

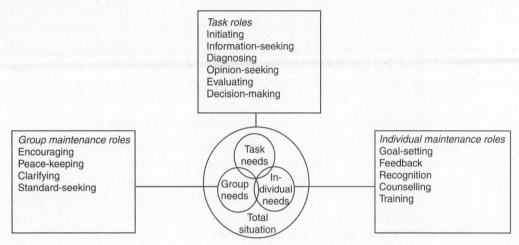

Table 4.4

Planning	Seeking information, defining and allocating tasks, setting aims, initiating, briefing, setting standards.
Controlling	Maintaining standards, ensuring progress, ongoing decision-making.
Supporting	Individuals' contributions, encouraging team spirit, reconciling, morale.
Informing	Clarifying tasks and plans, updating, receiving feedback and interpreting.
Evaluating	Feasibility of ideas, performance, enabling self-assessment.

The action-centred leadership model, therefore, does not stand alone; it must be part of an integrated approach to managing and leading. There should be a strong emphasis on applying these principles through training (Table 4.5).

Table 4.5   Adair's leadership checklist

Key functions	Task	Team	Individual
Define objectives	Clarify task Obtain information Identify resources and constraints	Assemble team Give reasons why Define accountability	Involve each person Gain acceptance
Plan and decide	Consider options Establish priorities Plan time	Consult Encourage ideas Agree standards	Listen Assess abilities Delegate Agree targets
Organize	Establish control Brief plan Obtain feedback	Structure Answer questions Prepare and train	Check understanding Counsel Enthuse

Key functions	Task	Team	Individual
Control and support	Maintain standards Report progress Adjust plan if necessary Set personal example	Co-ordinate Maintain external co-operation Relieve tension	Guide and encourage Recognise effort Discipline
Review	Evaluate results against objectives Consider action	Recognise team's Success Learn from setbacks	Appraise performance Identify further training Needs Aid personal growth

2.5.1 Tannenbaum and Schmidts' (1973) leadership continuum

Tannenbaum and Schmidts' (1973) leadership continuum perceives leaders as operating in a variety of ways from a completely authoritarian, autocratic approach (point 1 below) to a more inclusive, consultative, democratic approach (point 7 below). This is a more sophisticated perspective in which the tendency to behave operates in a continuum. The leader will be located at a point on this continuum depending on attributes (including personality) intrinsic to them, forces or characteristics intrinsic to their staff and forces operating in the business environment or a specific situation.

Table 4.6   Tannenbaum and Schmidt's Leadership continuum

Leader makes decision and announces it	Leader 'sells' decision	Leader presents ideas and invites questions	Leader presents intended decision, subject to amendment	Leader presents a problem, gets suggestions, and makes a decision	Leader defines limits and goals and asks the group to make the decision	Leader allows subordinates to act as they wish, within specified limits

Figure 4.4   The continuum of leadership styles

Authoritarian   Democratic
Task orientation   Relationship orientation

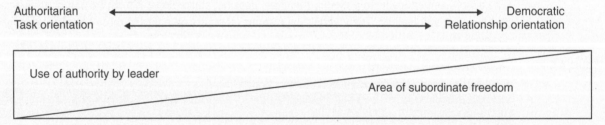

1   The manager decides and announces the decision. The manager reviews options in light of aims, issues, priorities, timescales and so on, then decides the actions and informs the team of the decision. The manager will probably have considered how the team will react, but the team plays no active part in making the decision.

2   The manager decides and then 'sells' the decision to the group. The manager makes the decision as above, and then explains reasons to the team, particularly the positive benefits that the team will enjoy from it.

In doing so, the manager is seen by the team to recognise their importance and to have some concern for the team.

3   The manager presents the decision with background ideas and invites questions.

The manager presents the decision along with some of the background which led to it. The team is invited to ask questions and discuss with the manager the rationale behind the decision, which enables the team to understand and accept or agree with the decision more easily than in 1 and 2 above.

This more participative and involving approach enables the team to appreciate the issues and reasons for the decision, and the implications of all the options. This will have a more motivational approach than 1 or 2 because of the higher level of team involvement and discussion.

4   The manager suggests a provisional decision and invites discussion about it.

The manager discusses and reviews the provisional decision with the team on the basis that the manager will take on board the views and then finally decide.

This enables the team to have some real influence over the shape of the manager's final decision.

This also acknowledges that the team has something to contribute to the decision-making process, which is more involving and therefore motivating than the previous level.

5   The manager presents the situation or problem, gets suggestions and then decides.

The manager presents the situation, and maybe some options, to the team. The team is encouraged and expected to offer ideas and additional options, and discuss implications of each possible course of action. The manager then decides which option to take.

6   The manager explains the situation defines the parameters and asks the team to decide. At this level, the manager has effectively delegated responsibility for the decision to the team, albeit within the manager's stated limits.

The manager may or may not choose to be a part of the team which decides. While this level appears to gives a huge responsibility to the team, the manager can control the risk and outcomes to an extent, according to the constraints that he stipulates.

This level is more motivational than any previous and requires a mature team for any serious situation or problem.

7   The manager allows the team to identify the problem, develop the options and decide on the action, within the manager's authority limits. The team is given responsibility for identifying and analysing the situation or problem; the process for resolving it; developing and assessing options; evaluating implications and then deciding on and implementing a course of action.

2.5.2 The Ashridge Management College model

The Research Unit at Ashridge Management College in the UK distinguished four different management styles, labelled 'Tells', 'Sells', 'Consults' and 'Joins'. Other style models label similar styles as:

- Telling, Selling, Participating and Delegating (Hersey and Blanchard, 1998)
- Telling, Selling, Consulting and Coaching (Tannenbaum and Schmidt, 1973)

Table 4.7   Ashridge Management College – four different managerial styles

Style	Characteristics	Strengths	Weaknesses
Tells (autocratic)	The leader makes all the decisions, and issues instructions which must be obeyed without question.	(1) Quick decisions can be made when speed is required. (2) It is the most efficient type of leadership for highly – programmed routine work.	(1) It does not encourage subordinates to give their opinions when these might be useful. (2) Communication between leader and subordinates will be one-way and the leader will not know until afterwards whether the orders have been properly understood. (3) It does not encourage initiative and commitment from subordinates.
Sells (persuasive)	The leader still makes all the decisions, but believes that subordinates have to be motivated to accept them and carry them out properly.	(1) Employees are made aware of the reasons for decisions. (2) Selling decisions to staff might make them more committed. (3) Staff will have a better idea of what to do when unforeseen events arise in their work because the leader will have explained his intentions.	(1) Communications are still largely one-way. Subordinates might not accept the decisions. (2) It does not encourage initiative and commitment from subordinates.
Consults	The leader confers with subordinates and takes their views into account, but retains the final say.	(1) Employees are involved in decisions before they are made. This encourages motivation through greater interest and involvement. (2) An agreed consensus of opinion can be reached and, for some decisions, this can be an advantage (eg increasing ownership). (3) Employees can contribute their knowledge and experience to help solve more complex problems.	(1) It might take much longer to reach decisions. (2) Subordinates might be too inexperienced to formulate mature opinions and give practical advice. (3) Consultation can too easily turn into a façade, concealing a 'sells' style.
Joins (democratic)	Leader and followers make the decision on the basis of consensus.	(1) It can provide high motivation and commitment from employees. (2) It shares the other advantages of the consultative style (especially where subordinates have expert power).	(1) The authority of the leader might be undermined. (2) Decision making might become a very long process, and clear decisions might become difficult to reach. (3) Subordinates might lack experience.

The Ashridge studies showed a clear preference among subordinates for the 'consults' style of leadership – although managers were most commonly perceived to be exercising a 'tells' or 'sells' style! Team members also had more positive attitudes to their work under leaders who were perceived to be exercising a 'consults' style. The least favourable attitudes to work, however, were not found among team members under a 'tells' style, but

The Chartered Institute of Marketing

among those who were unable to perceive a **consistent** style in their leader. In order words, subordinates are unsettled by a boss who chops and changes between different styles.

2.6 The managerial (or leadership) grid

Blake and Mouton (1964) carried out research into managerial behaviour and observed two basic dimensions of leadership: **concern for production** (or task performance) and **concern for people**.

Along each of these two dimensions, managers could be located at any point on a continuum from very low to very high concern. Blake and Mouton observed that the two concerns did not seem to correlate, positively or negatively: a high concern in one dimension, for example, did not seem to imply a high or low concern in the other dimension. Individual managers could therefore reflect various permutations of task/people concern.

A questionnaire was designed to enable users to analyse and plot the positions of individual respondents on a grid, as a means of analysing individuals' managerial styles and areas of weakness or 'unbalance', for the purposes of management development.

Figure 4.5   Managerial grid

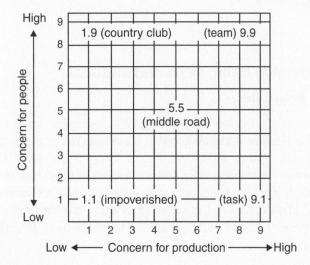

The styles identified on the grid are:

- 1.1 **Impoverished:** the manager exerts (and expects) minimal effort or concern for either staff satisfaction or work targets.

- 1.9 **Country club:** the manager is attentive to staff needs and has developed satisfying relationships and work culture – but with little attention to results. Behaviour is supportive rather than directive.

- 9.1 **Task management:** almost total concentration on achieving results. People's needs are virtually ignored, and work is organised so that human elements interfere to a minimal extent. Behaviour is directive rather than supportive.

- 5.5 **Middle of the road:** adequate performance through balancing the necessity to get work done with maintaining a satisfactory level of team morale. (Alternatively, the manager scores an average of 5.5, as a result of swinging from one extreme to another!)

- 9.9 **Team:** high work accomplishment through 'leading' committed people who identify themselves with organisational goals.

The grid was intended as a tool for management appraisal and development. It recognises that a leader requires a balance between concern for the task and concern for people, and that a high degree of both is possible – and the most effective style of management. It offers a simple and easy-to-use diagnostic tool, showing where the behaviour and assumptions of a manager may exhibit a lack of balance between the dimensions and/or a low degree of concern in either dimension or both.

However, this is a simplified model. For a start, it assumes that 9.9 is the desirable model for effective leadership, while some managerial contexts, this may not be so: a manager may find that a 9.1 approach, for example, is effective in situations of crisis where survival is at stake, or urgent corrective action must be taken to get a project back on track. Moreover, a manager's style of leadership is likely to be influenced by organisational context and culture, technology and wide range of other factors, not just the two dimensions described by the grid.

ACTIVITY 4.3

The following are some statements about a manager's approach to meetings. Which position on Blake and Mouton's Grid do you think each might represent?

(a)   I attend because it is expected. I either go along with the majority position or avoid expressing my views.

(b)   I try to come up with good ideas and push for a decision as soon as I can get a majority behind me. I don't mind stepping on people if it helps a sound decision.

(c)   I like to be able to support what my boss wants and to recognise the merits of individual effort. When conflict arises, I do a good job of restoring harmony.

2.7 Leadership traits, skills and attitudes

Five basic group traits

What makes an effective leader? Most successful leaders can operate in different organisations and this suggests that there are attributes linked to the individual that makes a good leader. Leadership traits has a precise meaning in terms of the ideas presented from psychology, in contrast to the more general usage of this term. What types of characteristics does this include in the context of discussing leadership? McCrae and John (1992) identified five basic groups of traits which could be considered as some of the basic building blocks of personality. In their paper on this subject, they affirm that 'the five-factor model can be profitably used in most applied settings' (1992 p 206). They labelled these five traits (to some extent integrating the ideas of many researchers) as:

- Extraversion
- Agreeableness
- Conscientiousness
- Neuroticism
- Openness.

Generally positive values on all factors are found in leaders, except 'neuroticism', where low levels are desirable (Table 4.8).

2.8 Transactional leadership, transformational leadership

Large changes have been, and will continue to, take place in the work environment with the influence of globalisation, market forces and technologies which in turn affects work force behaviour and expectations. Van Eeden and Cilliers (2008, pp253–255) suggest that changes are taking place in cultural patterns, role definitions, structures, policies, procedures and technologies, and that leadership is central to successful organisational transformation.

They are not alone in contending that the transactional–transformational model of leadership provides a valuable framework for exploring the role of the leader in a changing work environment. Many, they suggest, support the view that transformational leadership provides an ideal of leadership, given contemporary

developments in the global business world including doing business internationally and in multicultural environments.

Table 4.8   Five main personality traits

Factor (trait) category name	Adjectives describing the trait (note that the trait heading embraces a variety of personality attributes which are classified under the heading)
Extraversion	Active, assertive, energetic, enthusiastic, outgoing, sociable, talkative
Agreeableness	Altruistic, appreciative, forgiving, generous, kind, sympathetic, trusting
Conscientiousness	Efficient, organised, planful, reliable, responsible, thorough, thoughtful
Neuroticism	Anxious, emotionally unstable, irritable, moody, self-pitying, tense
Openness to experience	Artistic, curious, imaginative, insightful, original, wide range of interests

(Summarised from McCrae and John, 1992)

Before describing the characteristics of the transformational leader we should consider the characteristics of the contrasting, transactional leader in this view of leadership. In transactional leadership, the leader clarifies what followers need to do as their part of a transaction (successfully complete the task) to receive a reward or avoid punishment (satisfaction of the followers' needs) that is dependent on completion of the transaction (satisfying the leader's needs).

There are two management approaches engaged in by people adopting this leadership style namely active or passive management.

- In the case of **active management by exception**, the leader looks for mistakes, irregularities, exceptions, deviations from standards, complaints, infractions of rules and regulations, and failures, and he or she takes corrective action before or when these occur.

- **Passive management by exception** implies that the leader is reactive and waits to be informed about errors and deviances before taking action.

Transformational leaders, in contrast, move followers beyond their self-interests for the good of the group or organisation. In an ideal form, they achieve a position in which followers respect, admire, and trust the leader and emulate his or her behaviour, assume his or her values and are committed to achieving his or her vision.

The leader shows dedication, a strong sense of purpose and perseverance, and confidence in the purpose and the actions of the group that helps to ensure the success of the group and gives followers a sense of empowerment and ownership. He or she behaves morally and ethically.

In addition, he or she acts as a mentor giving personal attention, listening to others' concerns and providing feedback, advice, support and encouragement. The leader furthermore designs appropriate strategies to develop individual followers to achieve higher levels of motivation, potential and performance providing support and monitoring progress (Van Eeden and Cilliers, 2008, p255).

The transformational leader motivates, inspires and energises staff and ensures that they understand the vision for the future of the organisation. This need not be done in some high-octane, major organisational event but can operate at a much more subtle, low-key and continuous way from talking to individual members of staff, presence at meetings, through to the image that the leader projects for the organisation that motivates employees to deliver that vision.

THE REAL WORLD

The late Steve Jobs of Apple in the United States and Richard Branson of Virgin in the UK are two of the better known examples of the transformational type of leader.

The transactional–transformational leadership framework can be extended to describe teams and group effects as well as how whole organisations differ. People jockey for positions in a transactional group, whereas they share common goals in a transformational group. Rules and regulations dominate the transactional organisation, while adaptability is a characteristic of the transformational organisation.

2.9 The scope of leadership – providing strategic direction

An important role of leadership is providing strategic direction. This is something that really cannot be outsourced and must be controlled closely by the leader. One contrasting perspective in which to view strategic direction is connected with transactional–transformational leadership styles. To some extent, this is also connected to a relative emphasis on efficiency or effectiveness.

Too many leaders operate at the transactional level where they are brought in to 'sort out' the organisation. Most commonly this means a focus on increased efficiency, slashing costs, selling weak performing brands and businesses, getting rid of staff and selling assets. According to Montgomery (2008, p57) 'the challenge [of a leader] is a matter not of unearthing an existing purpose but of forging one'.

So when Lou Gerstner put together strategic direction for IBM, he decided that it would no longer focus on the invention of technology but on its application. Similarly the late Steve Jobs transformed Apple in the late 1990s when its strategy was to focus on high end, differentiated computers even though the market was telling the company (through sales and share price) that this was of decreasing interest. On returning to the company as the CEO, Steve Jobs declared the focus to be as a passionate design company that believed technology would change the world.

2.10 Situational leadership

In their influential situational leadership model, Hersey and Blanchard (1988) focus on the readiness of team members to perform a given task, in terms of both their task ability (experience, knowledge and skills) and willingness (whether they have the confidence, commitment and motivation) to complete the task successfully.

- **High-readiness** (R4) teams are able and willing. They do not need directive or supportive leadership: the most appropriate leadership style may be a joins or 'delegating' (S4) style. An example would be any mature and effectively-functioning marketing team which is capable of getting on with performing, only needing to appeal to the leader for guidance in the event of unforeseen problems or new situations.

- **High-moderate readiness** (R3) teams are able, but unwilling or insecure. They are competent, but require supportive behaviour to build morale: the most appropriate leadership style may be a consults or 'participating' (S3) style. An example might be a team member returning from training to apply newly-learned skills for the first time; or a marketing team going through a period of low morale or resistance to organisational changes.

- **Low-moderate readiness** (R2) teams are willing and confident, but lacking ability. They require both directive and supportive behaviour to improve their task performance without damaging morale: the most appropriate leadership style may be a 'selling' (S2) style. An example might be more experienced members of the marketing team taking on new responsibilities for the first time (eg with the emergence of new communications media).

- **Low-readiness** (R1) teams are lacking ability and motivation/confidence. They require more directive behaviours in order to secure an adequate level of task performance: the most appropriate leadership style may be a 'telling' (S1) style. An example might be where staff are new to the marketing department or to particular technology or procedures.

The model can be depicted as follows.

The Chartered Institute of Marketing

Figure 4.6   The situational leadership model

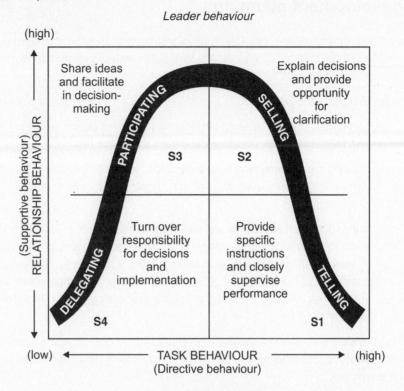

Leader behaviour

(Hersey and Blanchard, 1998)

An effective leader will both adapt his or her style to the current level of readiness of the team *and* help team members to develop maturity or readiness as far as possible (through the process of support and direction that is built into each style).

ACTIVITY 4.4

Identify the leadership style and strategic approach in your organisation. You could focus either on the CEO of the group or where this makes more sense of your business area. To what extent does your leader combine leadership style with an efficient/effective focus?

3 Personal development planning

In order to develop others, individually or as teams, through either management or leadership it is important to consider self-development. Here, we will look at the area of personal development and the creation of Personal Development Plans (PDP).

Pedler, Burgoyne & Boydell (2001) give the following brief definition of self-development.

'Self-development is personal development, with the person taking primary responsibility for his or her own learning, and for choosing the means to achieve this.'

One of the key elements of your assignment will be a 'reflective element', requiring you to reflect on your own performance in given areas of management and leadership, and to plan for learning and improvement.

'If asked to think about how we have learned, most of us may think first of when attempts have been made to teach us. If, on the other hand, we are asked about problems we have solved, we think about difficult situations we have faced and managed to overcome. However, in solving problems, we don't just deal with the immediate difficulty, we **discover a solution which we can use again in some form**, and we may also become better at solving problems generally. Problem solving is, to a large extent, learning'.

The purpose of the reflective element is to enable you to convert your everyday managerial experience and problem-solving into a **learning opportunity**. The following paragraphs offer a framework for doing this in a systematic way.

- In a '**self awareness**' approach to this task, you start by gathering information about your performance (by observation and feedback gathering), and then select specific areas of interest for reflection and self-evaluation.

- In a '**problem-solving**' approach, you start with identified areas of potential weakness/threat (or strength/opportunity), and plan your information-gathering and reflection specifically to investigate them.

Either may be appropriate, depending on your needs.

3.1 Selecting areas for reflection

When deciding what areas of your management performance to reflect, you may focus on:

- **Gathered data**. From your periodic observations, notes and feedback, you identify a pattern of behaviour which does or does not appear to be effective in helping you to achieve your aims as a manager or leader.

- **Critical incidents** in which you have participated: specific incidents which highlight a given behaviour – for example, by illustrating it particularly clearly, or by eliciting particularly positive or negative outcomes.

- **Examination of your goals**. You consider a particular desired outcome or objectives which you are or are not (yet) achieving effectively, and identify the strategies you have been using to pursue it: these may represent potential areas for problem-solving and development.

- **Impressions**. You feel generally satisfied or dissatisfied with your performance in a given area.

Note that the highlighted factors may be positive (indicating a possible strength or opportunity) as well as negative (possible weakness, limitation or threat). Learning opportunities may arise from your strengths (how can you build on them? how can you apply them in a wider range of situations?) as well as from your weaknesses (what do you need to do more effectively?)

The Chartered Institute of Marketing

3.2 Gathering data for reflection

3.2.1 Capturing observation and feedback data

Observations, impressions and intuitions provide valuable data for self-reflection, but in order to make them a durable, flexible and practical source of information, you need to capture and record them. Get into the habit of **making notes** – verbal or visual, paper or electronic – during or shortly after any meeting, discussion or managerial action you are involved in. These will probably not be the kind of notes you usually make (content-based minutes of the discussion, decisions reached, action taken and so on), but notes recording your observations on the following:

- Repeated patterns of behaviour which you notice in your team (or yourself)

- Thoughts or feelings that come up for you in response to others' behaviours or changes in behaviour: how you 'automatically' react to others' behaviour and what happens; how you make a controlled and intentional response to others' behaviour and what happens

- Other people's responses to your 'usual' behaviours and when you experiment with new behaviours

- What happened in the course of critical incidents and interactions

- Feedback from other people about your actions, decisions or performance.

- Such notes will provide the raw material for reflection and self-evaluation. If you rely solely on your memory, you will probably have insufficiently detailed data to go on.

- Get into the habit of collecting and filing data and feedback on your performance in a **Personal Portfolio**. This may include:

- Any completed self-report questionnaires and feedback forms

- The outputs of activities you do as you work through this Study Text, your wider reading and any other training activities

- Copies of reports from performance appraisals or coaching/mentoring and development planning sessions

- Feedback-bearing messages of all kinds (for example, commendation and thank-you letters; complaints; personal or employment references).

3.2.2 Gathering feedback

Other people are one of the most valuable sources of information about your behaviours, decisions and managerial style – because they are 'on the receiving end'. Other people can tell you how you are *perceived* (and important aspect of leadership) and how, your behaviour *affects* them.

Whetten & Cameron (2002, p48) argued that: 'It is almost impossible to increase skill in self-awareness without interacting with and disclosing ourselves to others. Unless one is willing to open up to others, to discuss aspects of the self that seem ambiguous or unknown, little growth can ever occur.'

Identify people whom you trust to give you honest and constructive feedback about your performance in a given area. You may be able to take advantage of existing organisational mechanisms for upward appraisal, coaching or mentoring. Otherwise, you may need to co-opt a trusted colleague and *ask* him or her to observe, evaluate and feedback your performance in a specific area: eg how well you run a team meeting, or what style you use to lead your team in routine (and perhaps also stressful) situations.

3.3 Reflecting on your performance

Reflect on the issues raised by your gathered data in your chosen areas. We have already suggested that there is no 'one best way' to manage, communicate, influence, lead, negotiate and so on: it all depends. It depends on what you want to achieve, on the opportunities and constraints inherent in the situation, and on the skills and objectives of the other parties in the process.

In reflecting on your performance, your focus should not be on whether a behaviour or style is more or less 'right', but on whether it is more or less *effective* in achieving your *objectives.* A behaviour may be a strength or a weakness (or both) depending on what you wish to accomplish. An aggressive leadership style, for example, may support your immediate task goals by allowing you to impose your decisions on other people or quell dissent. It may, however, be counterproductive if your goals are to establish and maintain co-operative working relationships, or to encourage the flow of information for problem-solving and creativity.

There is an infinite number of questions you might usefully ask yourself, but to stimulate your thinking, you might like to consider:

- The **outcomes** you wanted from your behaviour – and those that actually happened

- Your **action tendencies** or patterns of behaviour (how you 'usually' behave or react in a situation) – and perhaps *why* these exist (assumptions, perceptions, past experience, personality factors?)

- Whether you **did anything different** on a particular occasion, and what the results or consequences were

- What you **might do differently**, in order to get a different result

- Any **discrepancies** between feedback from others and your own self-perception or self-evaluation, and what you can learn from them

- What **theoretical models and guidelines** (such as those outlined in this Study Text) might help you to understand what is going on – or what might lead to more effective results.

You may then be able to summarise your **conclusions**: identifying specific behaviours which you perceive to be strengths or limitations in a given context and in light of your goals. This will be the basis of improvement/learning planning.

3.3.1 A Personal Development Journal (PDJ)

A 'journal' is simply a book (or note pad, folder, computer document or whatever) in which you regularly record your experiences and actions – and your reflections on them.

A **PDJ** is a structured approach to recording your experience and reflections, providing you with data which will enable you to learn consciously and intentionally from your experience, and monitor and track your development over time. Pedler *et al* (2006) suggest a PDJ should be stimulated using the following headings:

 The Chartered Institute of Marketing

- **WHAT HAPPENED**: [A brief description of events, with the emphasis on objective facts, including what led up to the situation]

- **MY EMOTIONS**: [Be specific about the emotions you experienced during the event and how they changed during that event]

- **MY THOUGHTS/ IDEAS** [What went through your head during the events]

- **MY TYPICAL BEHAVIOUR** [What you typically do in these sort of situation or similar circumstances.] (Note: These are your typical behaviours, not your actual behaviour in this event.)

- **MY ACTUAL BEHAVIOUR** [What you actually said and did, and how you acted (including verbal and non-verbal behaviours).]

  How did others respond to your behaviours?

- **IMPLICATIONS FOR MY DEVELOPMENT** [What you can learn from analysing the event, and how you might change your behaviour for the future. What behaviour were effective/less effective; and why?] (Note: Try to be as specific as possible about the behaviours you would try to change in future.)

3.4 The experiential learning cycle

Research by David Kolb (1983) and its implications for management (Honey & Mumford, 1992) suggests that effective learning is a cyclical process of experimentation and adjustment, which can be applied in any situation. Experiential learning is a methodology for 'learning by doing'.

- We perform an action or have an experience

- We reflect on the experience, its results and any feedback we may have obtained from other people

- We formulate a hypothesis about what we might be able to do differently next time to get a better results

- We plan an opportunity to test our hypothesis in action

- We perform the action – and so continue the cycle

Figure 4.7   Kolb's learning cycle

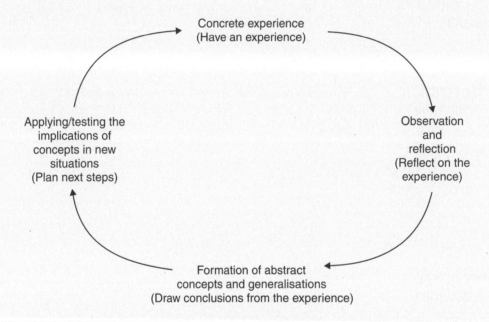

3.5 Competencies and standards that define a good manager

There are many sets of management competencies and organisations sometimes develop their own or use generic management standards. Although the following example is taken from an NHS (UK Nation Health Service) document it could be applied to many different sectors and contexts. These ideas could form the basis of objectives for development within a personal development plan.

As an effective manager, you should be able to:

- Lead a team effectively

- Identify and set objectives

- Communicate clearly

- Manage resources and plan work to achieve maximum benefits

- Make sound decisions in difficult situations

- Know when to seek help and do so when appropriate

- Offer help to those you manage, when they need it

- Demonstrate leadership qualities through your own example

The Chartered
Institute of Marketing

- Manage projects

- Manage change

- Delegate appropriately – to empower others, to improve services and to develop the skills of the people you manage – without giving up your own responsibilities

- Consider and act upon constructive feedback from colleagues.

(General Medical Council, 2006)

4 Teams

4.1 Introduction

Organisations operate within the external marketing environment. They must align themselves with this environment if they are to maintain long-term competitiveness. The complexity of the marketing environment means increasingly that work is undertaken and implemented by teams rather than by individuals.

Teams must work effectively and they too must adapt to the changing requirements of the business environment. This is crucial if marketing strategy is to be implemented fully and effectively.

For this to happen, it requires positive action within the organisation to foster a culture of interdependency and to maximise employee contribution.

Strategic choice theory suggests that the general strategy and direction of change adopted by an organisation is determined by a powerful individual or group and that they design an organisational hierarchy in order to implement it.

> The structure they design is supposed to be largely a self-regulating one in which people are assigned roles and given objectives to achieve that will realise a given strategy.   (Stacey, 2003, p32)

Teams are formed, or exist, to solve organisational problems. They must have clear aims and objectives, comprise an appropriate mix of individuals and be managed to ensure that they make an effective contribution. This does not happen automatically, but requires planning, performance evaluation and strategies to improve the performance of sub-optimal teams when this is diagnosed.

4.2 What are teams?

> **▶ Key term**
>
> A **team** is a small number of people with complementary skills who are committed to a common purpose, performance goals, and approach for which they hold themselves mutually accountable.
>
> Katzenbach and Smith (1994)

We perhaps assume that we all share a common definition of teams. To clarify our thinking on this subject a definition is helpful:

The workplace, or functional, role played by individuals is the basis on which they are recruited, in particular if they are specialists.

Work roles may be defined as:

> The mix of tasks and responsibilities undertaken by individuals or executed within teams.
>
> Belbin (2004)

Management literature is concerned with teams only in as much as this helps us to understand organisational effectiveness. In other words, how effective were organisations in solving problems and implementing their solutions; that is, how effective were they in their work? In a text written after reflection on his definitive work on teams, Belbin (2000) concluded that the balance of emphasis was too uneven. It tended to focus too much on teams and hardly at all on work.

In *Beyond the Team*, Belbin changes his emphasis to focus on the type of work undertaken and how this affects the social arrangements within the organisation for undertaking and completing work. It is useful to remember that the context in which a team operates affects how the team performs and the relationships that develop.

4.2.1 Groups versus teams

Handy (1993) defined a **group** as 'any collection of people who perceive themselves to be a group'. The point of this definition is the distinction it implies between a random collection of individuals (such as a bus stop queue) and a group of individuals (such as a college class) who share a common sense of **identity** and **belonging**, a more or less defined **purpose** or objectives, and some kind of **leadership** to steer them towards those goals.

People are often drawn together into groups by a preference for smaller units where closer relationships can develop; the need to belong and to make a contribution that will be noticed and appreciated; shared space, specialisms, objectives or interests; the attractiveness of a particular group activity or resources; or access to power greater than individuals could wield on their own (one of the reasons for joining a trade union or staff association, say).

(a)   **Informal groups** will invariably be present in any organisation: examples include workplace cliques and networks of people who get together to exchange information, groups of friends who socialise outside work and so on. Such groups have a constantly fluctuating membership and structure.

(b)   **Formal groups** are intentionally and rationally designed to achieve objectives assigned to them by the organisation, for which they are responsible. They are characterised by: membership and leadership appointed and approved by the organisation; compliance of the members with the group's goals and requirements; and structured relationships of authority, responsibility, task allocation and communication.

A high degree of commitment and loyalty is required for people in organisations to operate effectively as teams rather than simply groups. Katzenbach and Smith (1994, pp88–89) make the distinction between groups and teams.

They suggest that a working group (common in bureaucratic, hierarchical structures) linked to formal work roles is based primarily on individual contributions. Performance is assessed by measuring each individual's contribution. There may still be a co-operative attitude in which individuals discuss issues and problems to improve individual work.

Group performance is the sum contribution of individual members; however, team performance is synergistic. The team achieves more than could be achieved with individuals working essentially on their own, even in a co-operative spirit.

The main difference is that teams include mutual accountability, in addition to individual accountability. On other dimensions, the differences between teams and groups tend to be of degree, for example more information sharing, more joint task and target setting and performance review.

Formal groups, or teams, within an organisation may be permanent (eg marketing department) or temporary (one-off project to set up a CRM system). They must have clear goals and tasks and their purpose within the organisation is 'to find solutions to structured problems' (Stacey, 2003, p68).

They may take various forms and can even be autonomous, self-managing and democratic and may even be charged with designing their own approach to a given problem. This is in contrast to the traditional command and control perspective of groups within the organisation operated more along military lines, with edicts from senior management and organisational design focused on reporting and control.

4.3 Benefits of using teams

The basic work units of organisations have traditionally been specialised functional departments. In more recent times, organisations have adopted what Peters and Waterman (1982) called 'chunking': the breaking up of the organisation structure into small, flexible units, or teams. From the organisation's standpoint, teams have a number of advantages.

(a) Teams facilitate the performance of tasks which require the **collective skills**, experience or knowledge of more than one person or discipline.

(b) Teams facilitate the **co-ordination** of the work of different individuals or groups, by bringing them together across organisational boundaries (eg departments and functions) with shared goals and structured communication.

(c) Teams facilitate **interactive communication** and interpersonal relationships, and are particularly well-adapted for:

- **Testing and ratifying decisions**, because they offer multi-source feedback and may make the decision more acceptable, by taking account of a cross-section of stakeholder views. Teams have been shown to produce better evaluated (though fewer) decisions than individuals working separately.

- **Consultation and negotiation**, because they allow an interactive exchange of views and influence

- **Generating ideas**, because of their potential for 'bouncing' ideas off each other and getting multiple inputs

- **Collecting and disseminating information**, because of the multiple networks in which the various members are involved.

(d) Teams can **motivate** their members, since they offer satisfying relationships, mutual encouragement and support, and the opportunity to share work loads and responsibilities. Peters and Waterman (*ibid*) argue that teams enable people to make noticeable individual contributions (which bolsters their self-esteem) *and* at the same time to share responsibility and be part of something bigger than themselves (which bolsters their sense of security).

4.4 Drawbacks to using teams

(a) Teams and team working are very much in fashion, but it is important to recognise their potential drawbacks, limitations and challenges.

(b) Team working is **not suitable for all jobs**: it should be introduced because it leads to better performance, not because people feel better or more secure.

(c) Team processes (especially excessive meetings and seeking consensus) can **delay decision making**: groups make fewer decisions than individuals.

(d) Social relationships might be maintained **at the expense of other aspects of performance** or inter-group conflicts may get in the way of effective collaboration.

(e) Group norms may **restrict or inhibit** individual contribution. Mayo's Hawthorne studies, for example, showed that individuals restrict their output in order not to 'show up' the team by producing more or better work than the team average.

(f) Due to a process called **social facilitation**, performance of simple tasks at which people are relatively confident *improves* in the presence of other people – but performance of new, complex tasks is *hindered* by the presence of an audience. (You may be familiar with this 'flustered' feeling ...).

(g) Groups have been found to take **riskier decisions** than individuals on their own. This may occur due to a number of dynamics.

- **Conformity**: group pressures persuade individuals to agree to decisions, suppressing their questions and 'better judgement'.

- **'Group think'** (Janis, 1972): team consensus and cohesion may prevent consideration of alternatives or constructive criticism. The team becomes blinkered to contradictory information, and feels invincible, leading to ill-considered decisions.

- The **'risky-shift phenomenon'**: if a group is broadly like-minded, discussion will tend to strengthen the prevailing attitude, leading to polarised views (group polarisation). Together with the diffusion of individual responsibility, this can support risky decision making.

- The **Abilene paradox**: group members go along with what they *assume* is the group's intention – leading to a situation where the group does what *none* of its individual members really wants to do.

You should also be aware that while 'team working' is regarded as a positive value in itself, there are such things as ineffective, poorly managed and underperforming teams. Team working involves complex dynamics, roles and relationships and it is not easy to get it right. The important thing is not to have teams – but to have *effective* teams mobilised for *appropriate* applications.

4.5 Creating and developing teams

People obviously implement organisational strategy within the context of organisational structures. In the past, they operated within highly regimented, hierarchical units. As layers have been stripped out of organisational hierarchies, rigid structures and work groups no longer exist.

Flatter organisational structures have resulted in a greater degree of self-management. As structures have become flatter, people are forced to work in fluid, rather than permanent, teams. To understand how strategy may be implemented effectively therefore requires the study of management teams and team management.

4.5.1 Marketing team types and contexts

New teams increasingly cut across traditional functional structures and can upset organisational balance on all key attributes unless they are well managed. Piercy (2002) sees changes required in organisational processes to align the organisation 'to market' and these will result in:

- Changes in organisational hierarchies

- Increasing dependence on high-performing, temporary, multi-functional teams organised around market segments

- Process re-engineering

- Transnational networks of organisations

- Learning organisations

- Increased emphasis on key account management

(Adapted from Piercy, 2002, pp235–236)

Forming a team, or teams, to complete a major task within the organisation may be compared with the external activities of building collaborative networks. Successful internal collaborative networks, just like their external counterparts, are about informal processes based on trust, information sharing, joint decision-making and collective responsibility.

Ever more frequently, requirements for effective market-led implementation require multi-functional teams that operate across conventional internal boundaries and even external boundaries, as networks including suppliers, distributors and customers are required to solve customer-focused problems.

Teams have steadily become more popular in marketing contexts (as in many other business disciplines), because of their potential to improve cross-functional communication and ideas generation. They may include:

- **Quality or service circles** or customer care task forces: cross-functional teams used to discuss quality and improvement issues

- **Brainstorming groups**, brought together to generate new ideas and suggestions, for problem solving, planning or creativity (eg advertising campaign or new product ideas)

- **Training or study groups**: a cost-effective way of training teams, and an effective way of training people specifically in team working, interpersonal and leadership skills

- **Marketing project teams**. These may be set up to handle specific strategic developments (such as market segmentation, brand identity or pricing); tasks relating to particular processes (such as the computerisation of customer relationship management); investigations of procedures or improvement opportunities (such as a marketing audit, or advertising agency selection and operational marketing projects (such as marketing research, event management or product launch).

- **Specialist marketing teams**: permanent teams responsible for functions or tasks, such as market research, marketing planning, media buying, public relations and so on

- **Key account teams:** taking shared responsibility for all aspects of marketing to, and relationship with, a key client or customer segment

- **Cross-functional teams**: whether permanent (in a matrix structure) or temporary (on a project basis), to co-ordinate collaboration on cross-functional processes such as new product development, marketing mix planning, the setting up of operational systems and so on

More generally, it has become common to think of marketing departments and sub-sections of them, as 'teams', in order to emphasise shared goals and contributions, mutual accountability and the need to manage group processes. You might like to think, for example, to what extent your marketing department or section *really* has the attributes and processes of a team, or whether lip service is paid to this idea, purely as a motivational tool.

Extending knowledge
How to transform marketing from its traditional approach to a relatively new approach of organising marketing in order to 'go to market'. See Chapter 5 'Total integration: processes and teams take over from departments' in Piercy, N.F. (2002) *Market-led Strategic Change: A Guide to Transforming the Process of Going to Market*. 3rd edition. Oxford, Butterworth-Heinemann.

4.6 Team diversity and team success

Discussion of success of teams has developed beyond classical roles considered by Belbin to include the impact of diversity within the team on the success of team functioning. Such diversity issues concern both demographic diversity – that is, the degree to which team members vary, for example, in terms of age, gender and ethnicity – and diversity in terms of functional specialism. Pelled *et al*. (1999), on reviewing the literature on diversity in group performance, found that no conclusive influence was evident.

Some studies linked diversity to successful performance while others have linked it to unsuccessful performance. Their own conjecture was to suggest an indirect influence on performance through conflict. They suggested that two types of conflict existed:

1   **Task conflict** – is where group members disagree about task issues, including goals, procedures, key areas in which to focus for decision-making and appropriate choices for action. Factors that tend to reduce task conflict include repetitive, routine tasks as well as the length of time the group has been together.

2   **Emotional conflict** – describes the outcome rather than the causes of conflict in that it focuses on interpersonal clashes, which are characterised by negative attributes such as anger, frustration and so on.

(Pelled *et al*. 1999, p2)

Pelled *et al* concluded that 'task conflict' and its resolution leads to enhanced performance, while emotional conflict tends to diminish performance.

4.7 Team skills, characteristics and roles

Belbin (2004), in his research at Henley, concluded that there were only a few ways that people could contribute to teamwork. The essential contributions comprised the following:

- Co-ordinating the efforts of the team
- Creating ideas
- Motivating and driving the team forward
- Exploring resources
- Evaluating options
- Organising the work
- Following up on detail
- Supporting others
- Providing expertise

Belbin as well as other authors have defined important team roles and assign individuals to these roles based on established personality theories, as illustrated in Table 4.9. Some role names have been amended to fit in more readily with modern approaches to work. Fluid/flexible teams brought together for the life of a task/project result in the term 'Chairman' being replaced by 'Co-ordinator'. Flatter organisational structures rather than rigid hierarchies result in the use of the more appropriate term 'Implementer'. Finally, 'Completer-finisher' has been reduced to 'Completer' to avoid confusion with 'Implementer'.

Please note that Belbin (2004) still employs the original, rather than the amended, terminology (Table 4.9).

Table 4.9   Belbin's team roles

Belbin's named roles	Characteristics	Positive qualities	Allowable weaknesses
Company worker (amended to 'Implementer')	Conservative, dutiful and predictable	Organising ability, common sense in practical work, hard-working and self-disciplined	Lacks flexibility, unresponsive to unproven ideas – tends to stick to the orthodox
Chairman (amended to 'the Co-ordinator')	Calm, self-confident and controlled	Accomplished in encouraging and obtaining contributions from team members without judgement. A strong sense of objectives	No more than ordinary in terms of intellect or creative ability. Tends to take credit for the effort of the team
Shaper	Highly strung, outgoing, dynamic	Has great drive and a readiness to challenge inertia, ineffectiveness, complacency or self-deception	Prone to provocation, irritation and impatience
Plant	Individualistic, serious minded, unorthodox	Possesses 'genius', imagination, intellect and knowledge	Inclined to disregard practical details. Tends to be preoccupied with ideas and has a strong sense of their ownership
Resource investigator	Extroverted, enthusiastic, curious, communicative	Good at developing contacts and exploring opportunities. Possesses an ability to respond to challenge	Liable to lose interest once the initial fascination has passed
Monitor-evaluator	Sober, unemotional and prudent	Judgement, discretion and hard-headedness	Lacks inspiration or the ability to motivate others
Team worker	Socially orientated, rather mild-mannered and sensitive	Possesses an ability to respond to people and situations and to promote team spirit	Indecisive at moments of crisis
Completer-finisher (amended to 'Completer')	Painstaking, orderly, conscientious and anxious	A perfectionist with a capacity to follow through. Delivers on time	A tendency to worry about small things. A reluctance to 'let go' – perhaps a little obsessive

Investigate resources available at Belbin Associates' website.

Belbin's work has spawned a website with this as its focus. Visit Belbin Associates' website at www.belbin.com.

If you have purchased the second edition of Belbin's text (2000), you can determine your own team role online at www.belbin.com.

4.8 Stages in team development (Tuckman)

There is broad support for the assertion that teams go through various stages after formation. As long as any dysfunctional behaviour does not develop, team performance grows over time, however, not at a constant rate.

This is not simply because people, and therefore teams, vary in their effectiveness over time. It is related to a generalisable pattern of development in which performance initially improves at a relatively slow rate as team members get to know each other socially and in terms of the skill set they possess.

As team learning develops about task issues, the project and how to co-operate in achieving its objectives, a phase occurs in which performance increases rapidly. In contrast, towards the end of the life of a project team, the rate of development slows down as diminishing returns set in.

A significant advance in thinking on effective teams was the realisation that this was not a static situation but a dynamic process. Team members interact with one another over time and similarly develop competencies and varying degrees of conflict, both resolved and unresolved.

Consequently, a perspective of teams is required that takes on board this dynamic process. Various theories of team development have been suggested, the most widely discussed and applied is the theory proposed by Tuckman in which he suggests that team performance goes through four stages of group development over time. These he labelled:

- Forming
- Storming
- Norming
- Performing.

Two factors are important in determining, and describing, progression of a team through these stages. These are the resolution of interpersonal relationships and of task activities. In essence, the model by Tuckman describes these two issues, as groups progress through the different stages (Figure 4.8).

Later, Tuckman, working with another colleague, added a fifth stage referred to as 'adjourning' when a team that had been formed for a project was to be disbanded upon completion, during this stage the team works on finishing off the project. The project is disbanded and some emotional baggage will result. This may be highly positive, where group members focus on the success of the team, or it may be negative, due to the loss of friendships and emotional work ties established during the term of the project.

Figure 4.8   Tuckman's four stages of team development

Forming
Everyone in the embryonic team is yet to feel emotionally attached to it. Members tend to feel a certain degree of anxiety as roles and relationships within the team are established. Inevitably they will compare the new team with the former teams they have been members of.

Group members make an initial assessment of interpersonal relationships and norms with the group. The focus on task is to identify what these are, where task boundaries are and the sort of information required to complete the task(s).

Storming
In this phase, people finally understand their function within the team and team relationships settle. It is possible that in this phase, subgroups start to form and the potential for conflict can foment.

Group members begin to know each other. There may be some conflict not only over leadership but also over how the leader will operate. Members of the group struggle to varying degrees for individual autonomy. Individuals may in fact display a lack of commitment to the demands of particular tasks that they do not favour.

Norming
In this stage, group bonding, team spirit and cohesion develop. Their level of commitment to each other, and to the team, increases. People feel sure about their team identify and role. Group 'norms' literally begin to develop to the extent that the cliched phrase 'That is the way we do things around here' becomes appropriate.

As problems over the demands of particular tasks, and task allocation, have been resolved, conflict diminishes and is more likely manifested in greater cohesiveness in group functioning. Task co-operation and mutual support develops.

Performing
The team has fully committed to achieving its goals. They are flexible and collaborate freely and willingly. Now that people feel comfortable with each other and their work role, they can devote a substantial amount of emotional as well as physical energy to the project. This creates a wonderful environment in which creativity can thrive.

This is the most effective in terms of task activity and interpersonal relationships. The latter are established and almost taken for granted, operating in the background. The focus of activity is on completion of task activity.

Extending knowledge

If you have access to journal papers, you may wish to start with the paper Tuckman wrote with a colleague in which he revisited his original work and added an additional stage (Tuckman and Jensen, 1977).

4.8.1 Another stage?

All organisations wish their teams to remain at the 'performing' stage. However, the management writer John Adair, in his book *Effective Teambuilding* (1986), has identified a further stage (dorming) that can come after performing.

This may be regarded as a stage of relative complacency, where people prefer to live on past successes rather than to devote their energies into further innovations and successes. In a sense, team members become institutionalised within their own team and become focused on processes rather than on outcomes.

Each team stage has recognisable characteristics. Sometimes, problems arise during a team stage and other times in the transition from one stage to another.

The Tuckman model is not the only model of team development and it does suffer from some limitations. Perhaps the most important is that not all teams progress through all stages. The model is really an idealised

The Chartered Institute of Marketing

version. With that in mind it still provides a very helpful means of considering team dynamics and progression towards an ideal, highly effective team.

> ▶ **Assessment tip**
>
> When discussing Belbin's team roles and Tuckman's team development stages specific examples should be included to demonstrate how they apply to the context being discussed.

ACTIVITY 4.7

Applying team roles

Consider a team in which you work with all the people in the team. What are your individual roles?

Now answer the following questions:

1. Who establishes team objectives? *mol/teader*
2. Who co-ordinates most of the work? *leader/manager*
3. Who provides most of the creative ideas? *marketing team*
4. Who takes most of the decisions?
5. Who acts as a mediator/peacemaker in times of internal dispute?
6. Who is the main motivator in the team, providing encouragement and support?
7. Who looks after communication?
8. Who is able to provide constructive criticism and is able to do this in a way that is accepted without conflict?
9. Who is good at overcoming difficult issues and situations?
10. Who takes responsibility for controlling and monitoring work?

If most of your answers focus on the leader, then the team is probably at the forming or storming stage. If most of your answers are focused on the team, then your selected team is very likely to have reached the performing stage.

5 Planning teams for effective performance

Belbin (2004, pp 124–125) concludes that team design should be guided by five interlocking principles:

1 Members of a management team can contribute in two ways to the achievement of team objectives. These are high performance in a functional role in drawing on their professional and technical knowledge and performing effectively in their team role. Belbin clarifies that this describes a pattern of behavioural characteristics where the manager interacts with others in the team.

2 Each team needs an optimum balance in both functional and team roles. The ideal blend will depend on the goals and tasks that the team faces.

3 The effectiveness of a team will be promoted by the extent to which members correctly recognise and adjust themselves to the relative strengths within the team. This includes both expertise and ability to engage in specific team roles

4 Personal qualities fit members for some team roles while limiting the likelihood that they will succeed in others.

5 A team can deploy its technical resources to best advantage only when it has the requisite range of team roles to ensure sufficient teamwork.

5.1 Putting a team together

The process of putting a team together must be based on information on the individuals in order to ensure that they fit organisational requirements. Principal sources of information for this include:

- Psychometric tests
- Self-perception questionnaires
- Colleague-completed assessment of 'perceived team role' capability
- Information gained from staff attending in-company training courses

Belbin also cautions us to ensure that recruitment (or internal reshuffling) does not simply recruit more similar people without achieving a balance in team members in terms of the 'team' as well as functional roles that they perform.

With an increase in the number and variety of teams being utilised by organisations, there is an increasing need to understand what in fact makes a team function effectively.

5.2 Recruitment

It will often be necessary to bring new people into the team: to fill an identified skill or competence gap; to replace staff who have left the team; or because the work of the team has expanded, requiring extra people resources. Effective team recruitment is very important. Getting the wrong person can cause problems within the existing group, or the need for extensive training before the desired performance level is achieved.

One common mistake in recruitment is to select people to fit in with the organisation. The perspective taken is often concerned foremost with organisational culture rather than role. The former approach is focused on the status quo while the latter takes account of the need for evolution and development in team performance. One aspect of effective team performance probably includes further empowering team members. This increases work scope.

Recruitment that focuses on the team role that must be filled, taking account of existing skills and roles, is likely to be most successful.

6 Job analysis

Job analysis is 'any systematic procedure by which one describes the way a job is performed, the tasks that constitute a job, anchor the skills and abilities necessary to perform a job' (Friedman and Harvey 1986, p 779). There are various methods that can be used to conduct a job analysis.

This for example includes the job analysis interview and the 'task analysis inventory' approach that involves the use of a structured questionnaire listing a large number of tasks for which respondents identify the frequency of performance as well as the importance of each task in their job.

Job qualifications include the skills and abilities needed to succeed in the job, and these are often derived through job analysis (Table 4.10).

Traits	Knowledge/experience

▪ Integrity
▪ Self motivation
▪ Concern for ethics
▪ Tact
▪ Responsibility
▪ Creativity
▪ Achievement orientation
▪ Ambition
	▪ Experience in handling large accounts of
	    – company operating strengths/weaknesses
	    – company products and/or services
	    – company procedures
	    – customer's company personnel and personalities
	▪ Experience in planning and goal setting of
	    – company personnel and personalities
	    – customer's industry

ACTIVITY 4.8

Job analysis

Find out the approach your organisation takes to job analysis and role definition. Is there a formal approach taken to this as discussed above, including a summary questionnaire that post holders have in the past completed? Alternatively, there may be no formal procedure. In this situation, the identification of the need for a new member of staff is based on an inability to cope with the level of work and a manager, or managers, will quickly agree on a list of characteristics required on an informal basis and advertise this.

Is there or what is the list of traits, knowledge and experience required? Identify the characteristics specified in:

(a)   Sales and marketing for a senior and a junior management position and compare these two posts.

(b)   Another department/specialism with which you frequently work – also including a senior and a junior management position.

THE REAL WORLD

Siemens

Siemens AG is a global electrical and electronics business employing half a million people around the world. A key pillar of the Siemens' business strategy is the way it manages, develops and motivates its employees.

Part of Siemens Vision, Values and Strategy involves a 'path to sustainable value creation' – One Siemens. One of the strands of One Siemens is 'Use the power of Siemens' which includes development of employees. Within this the following is covered:

'We'll continue to leverage our global orientation, size and structure for the benefit of our customers, suppliers and employees. Our outstanding and innovative employees are one of our greatest strengths. The focus areas that will help us use the power of Siemens even more fully are the following:

▪ Encourage lifelong learning and development
▪ Empower our diverse and engaged people worldwide
▪ Stand for integrity'

The elements of these which relate to employee development cover the following details:

▪ Encourage lifelong learning and development

Recognising the outstanding workforce as one of its greatest strengths, Siemens has become the organisation that it is through their expertise, skills and dedication. However, to grow further an identified method is to use continuous learning to enhance the knowledge of employees and their pioneering spirit, initiative and willingness to take on responsibility.

Extending knowledge

See Belbin (2004) for a full discussion on planning an effective team in Chapter 11 'Designing a team' and Ahmed and Rafiq (2002, pp 86–87) on empowerment and recruitment.

7 Sourcing and training teams

7.1 Introduction

Large organisations have human resource management (HRM) departments, and managers can rely upon the existence of clear personnel policies and back-up through the strategic, legal and performance issues related to their HR activity. While this may make recruitment largely the role of the HR function in the largest organisations for many managers there is often little formal support and it is left to them to recruit, select and manage.

Even for managers with HRM support, there is a need to understand the systems and procedures so that they have sufficient understanding to be able to exert control as needed. In this, the relationship with HRM is exactly the same as with any other specialist function.

The recruitment process involves clearly defined stages, and the use of a systematic approach should ensure that you do not overlook anything important and, significantly, will reduce subjective judgement where biases, prejudices and weaknesses can creep in. The law in relation to recruitment and in particular discrimination, is stringent and changes frequently and it is vital that you act within it (and can demonstrate this).

The Chartered Institute of Marketing

7.2 Recruitment

A systematic recruitment process can be depicted as follows.

Figure 4.9   The recruitment process.

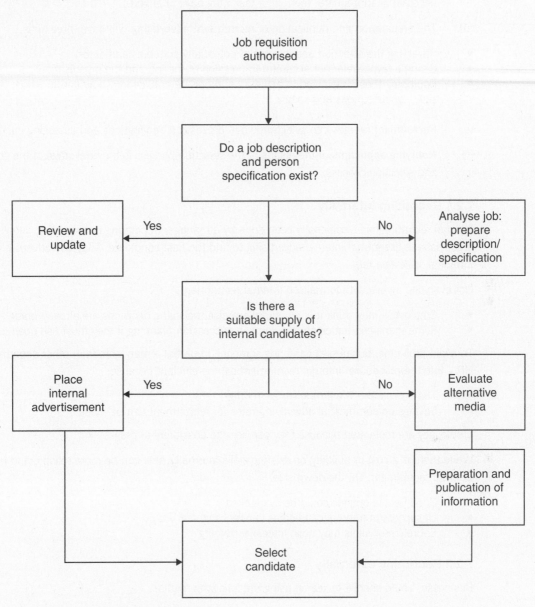

Note that this process is part of a wider whole.

(a)   Detailed **human resource planning** defines what resources the organisation (and marketing department) needs to meet its objectives, and what sources of labour (internal and external) are available. Skill requirements may be met through recruitment – but there may also be plans for *reducing* staff numbers, redeployment, training and development, promotion, retention (to reduce loss of skills through staff turnover) and so on.

(b)   **Job analysis** is a process of analysing the content of jobs, which usually produces two outputs.

- A **job description**: a statement of the component tasks, duties, objectives and standards involved in a job.

- A **person specification**: a reworking of the job description in terms of the kind of person needed to perform the job.

(c) Recruitment as such begins with the **identification of vacancies**, either from the requirements of the human resource plan or by a **job requisition** from a department that has a vacancy or need. (A careful review should be undertaken to ensure that an extra full-time post is justified by the contribution the person is expected to make. It should not be assumed that if a team member leaves, a replacement is necessarily appropriate: the role or task may have changed.)

(d) The preparation and publication of **recruitment advertising** will have three aims.

- Attracting the attention and interest of potentially suitable candidates.
- Giving a favourable (but accurate) impression of the job and the organisation.
- Equipping those interested to make an appropriate application (how and to whom to apply, desired skills, qualifications and so on).

(e) Recruitment merges into **selection** when processing applications and assessing candidates.

(f) **Notifying applicants** of the results of the selection process is the final stage of the combined recruitment and selection process.

7.2.1 Recruiting internally

Internal recruiting has traditionally been done by a manager appointing or promoting people. Some organisations use formal internal advertising to find the best candidate. They will advertise on notice boards, via intranets or newsletters.

Not everyone agrees with formalised internal recruitment:

- Employees may think it is an empty exercise, believing decisions are already made
- Some managers anticipate problems in succession planning if they must use open internal markets

To avoid problems, businesses can bring someone impartial – managers from other departments, someone from HR – into the procedure. Internal recruitment can be efficient because:

- The person and the firm know each other
- Savings on commercial advertising rates for recruitment can be made

Employees are motivated because they can see the possibility of progression.

While there is a cost in building on existing skills internally, this can be more reliable and less expensive than external recruitment. On the down side:

- Good people outside could be overlooked
- Unsuccessful internal candidates can feel slighted
- Entirely new skills may need intensive training

7.2.2 Recruiting externally

Businesses could choose to search using the following media:

- Advertising in papers, magazines or locally
- Employment agencies
- Executive 'headhunters'
- Job centres
- Colleges/universities
- Careers fairs

These are all useful, but there are some disadvantages:

- Companies might be overlooking and frustrating talented internal candidates
- External recruitment can be expensive

The Chartered Institute of Marketing

Advertising and the use of agencies

The concepts of, segmentation, targeting and positioning apply just as much to recruitment as to any other form of advertising. The aim is to design an advert so that only those who have a realistic chance of being successful apply for the position. It is as important for unsuitable candidates to rule themselves out as it is to encourage eligible people to apply. Having a large field of candidates is of little use if many of them would stand little chance of being appointed. If using an agency it is their job is to translate your needs into shortlisted candidates, advertising the post as agreed and necessary.

E-recruitment

E-recruitment is becoming a more important tool in the 'war for talent' environment. Research conducted by DEMOS3 looks at the trends that will shape the recruitment industry for years to come. Recommendations included:

- Companies should align human resources, public relations and marketing, and be clear on core organisational values

- Companies should find ways to connect with the passive job seeker

- Companies should broker and make use of peer-to-peer relationships

- Companies should use Web 2.0 technologies (such as blogs, web-based communities and hosted services including social-networking sites) to build personalised relationships online

Creating relationships with potential employees is important, the key way being through employer brand. In order to maximise a brand's potential to attract the right people, it must express core organisational values and messages and be found in the right places.

Social networking and blogs

A number of organisations have started to make use of recruitment 'blogs' (or online diaries) from employees as part of the information they offer to potential candidates about working for the organisation (eg based on the experiences of graduates on a development scheme). This is a potential way to build relationship with would-be candidates – and to feature different areas of a company and its vacancies.

Advantages of using e-recruitment

E-recruitment has the potential to:

- Speed up the recruitment cycle and streamline administration

- Allow organisations to make use of IT systems to manage vacancies more effectively and co-ordinate recruitment processes

- Reduce recruitment costs

- Reach a wide pool of applicants

- Reach a niche pool of applicants

- Make internal vacancies widely known across multiple sites and separate divisions

- Provide the image of an up-to-date organisation, reinforcing employer branding and giving an indication of organisation culture

- Offer access to vacancies 24 hours a day, seven days a week reaching a global audience

- Be a cost effective way to build a talent bank for future vacancies

- Help handle high volume job applications in a consistent way

- Provide more tailored information to the post and organisation, for example, case histories of the 'day in the life' or self-assessment questionnaire or quiz to assess fit with role

- Be spontaneous for candidates as ease of use means there is the ability for applications to be instantaneous

Disadvantages of using e-recruitment

The disadvantages to using e-recruitment include the potential to:

- Limit the applicant audience as the internet is not the first choice for all job seekers

- Cause applications overload or inappropriate applications if care isn't taken drafting the job profile/specification

- Exclude those who do not want to search for a new job online

- Attract fewer of those unable to fully utilise technology, for example, certain disabled groups

- Give rise to allegations of discrimination, in particular the use of limited keywords in CV search tools

- Make the process impersonal, which may be off-putting for some candidates

- Impact on the 'cultural fit' dimension of recruitment

- 'Turn-off' candidates, particularly if the website is badly designed or technical difficulties are encountered

- Lose out on candidates, especially if your own website is below the search engine ranking of your competitors

- Provide too little or inappropriate information, for example, corporate recruitment guidelines might not be written in a web-friendly style

ACTIVITY 4.9

What are the recruitment methods used in your organisation for:

Marketing jobs?
Sales jobs?
Administrative jobs?

7.3 Applications

After the closing date, a long list of possible candidates can be drawn up. From the long list you can use your personnel specification to compile a shortlist.

It is good practice to respond to all applicants, but some organisations feel they cannot afford it.

Applicants are consumers in the marketplace so it is important to create a favourable impression with everyone who applies for a job – this helps create a good overall impression of the organisation and/or brand regardless of the outcome for the candidate.

7.4 Job description

A job description is the focus of any employee's relationship with the employer. In establishing what the job is, the manager provides the foundation for all the stages of recruitment, selection, training and appraisal that follow. The job description describes the tasks and responsibilities which make up the job. As well as being a prerequisite to the recruitment process, it provides a standard against which the performance and development needs of the post-holder can be assessed. It also enables the department to focus on the characteristics of the post rather than those of the previous occupant. Job descriptions have several standard components, provided in greater detail as needed:

Job title – Accurate titles reflecting the function and level of the job; modest duties should not have grand titles. 'Engineer' should only describe a qualified engineer.

The Chartered
Institute of Marketing

Position – Stating the job title of the person to whom the employee is responsible as well as those who report to the job holder.

Areas of responsibility – Stating the overall purpose of the job; the principal role of the job holder and the expected contribution to achieving objectives.

Main tasks – Identifying the tasks, grouping together related ones. Includes the objective or purpose of each task but not how it is done.

Description of tasks – In short numbered paragraphs, with no more than two sentences per description; gives details of measures of work involved and proportion of time involved for any task; descriptive headings used to group together related tasks.

Special requirements – Equipment, tools, special skills.

Location – of the job and travelling needed.

Special circumstances – Lifting, dangerous or unpleasant conditions, night work, overtime, weekend working.

Challenging aspects of the job – This can be useful in attracting applicants.

What is the overall purpose of the job? – Describe in one sentence, for example, 'to assist the Head of Department in the efficient running of the departmental office'.

What are the main tasks of the job? – Try to use active verbs, for example, 'producing', 'planning', rather than vague terms such as 'deals with', 'handles'.

What are the main responsibilities involved? – 'Responsibilities' define the scope of the job, for example for managing staff, materials, money and so on.

The key result areas of the job and the standards expected – These may include such aspects as the degree of precision required and/or the consequences of error.

With whom does the post-holder work? – These may include other staff, students and so on.

Terms and conditions of the post – Unsocial hours, necessity to work regular overtime and any restrictions on periods during which annual leave can be taken and so on.

Job descriptions can be used for a number of purposes in human resource management.

- In **recruitment**, to set out the demands of the job and what it offers: a useful basis for advertising vacancies, interviewing candidates, assessing candidates against requirements and so on

- In **reward management**: to set pay rates fair for the job

- In **induction**, giving new recruits a clear guide to job requirements

- In **appraisal** and **training/development**, to suggest areas in which job requirements need to be more effectively met

- In **job design**, to indicate where areas of responsibility are ambiguous, or inflexible; where there could be greater challenge or task variety and so on

However, it has been argued (for example, Townsend, 1971) that job descriptions are of limited value, and, at worst, counterproductive. They are able to give an accurate, meaningful description of jobs where the work is largely repetitive and predictable: if a job involves variety, discretion and adaptability (as management and marketing jobs often do), they may be unrealistic and constantly outdated.

Despite the potential problems, the job description provides a basis for drawing up a 'person specification', that is, the skills and experience required to carry out the duties of the job.

7.5 The person specification

Purpose – The person specification forms the basis of the recruitment process from the advertisement through to the final interview stage. It describes the skills, aptitudes and experience needed to do the job and should be based on the job description, rather than a subjective view of the sort of person you would like to see filling the job. Generally, person specifications are laid down under standardised headings.

Qualifications and training:

1   **General education** – It may be more appropriate for applicants to have certain levels of literacy or numeracy rather than academic qualifications. If qualifications are stipulated, equivalent qualifications that would be considered must be included.

2   **Specific training** – For example, vocational certificates, professional qualifications and apprenticeship certificates.

Knowledge – This is knowledge without which the job cannot be done, for example, of computer systems. It should not include knowledge that can be imparted in an induction programme.

Experience – Either directly relevant or similar experience in a different environment might be considered. The type, range and depth of experience should be qualified (e.g. staff supervision). Specifying length of experience is usually unhelpful as some people learn more in a shorter time than others will learn in a longer time.

Skills and abilities – This includes such aspects as the ability to communicate effectively, numeracy, analytical skills, attention to detail and so on. However, these skills must be clearly measurable as part of the selection process.

Special requirements – This should only form part of the specification where it is relevant to the job, for example, a special type of driving licence if fork lift truck driving is to be part of the job, or a need to travel and stay away from home. The required characteristics are then entered against the appropriate heading, and subdivided into essential and desirable categories. The candidate who meets both the essential and desirable criteria will do the job particularly well, but obviously this person may be hard to find. Training and development may be needed in some areas. The person specification should be realistic. Too high an ideal will mean that potentially good candidates are excluded.

THE REAL WORLD

The following advertisement is for a marketing manager working for a market leader in online recruitment.

Advertisement for a marketing manager

This is an opportunity to be part of one of the most highly regarded companies in an exciting and fast-moving industry. We are currently looking for a passionate Marketing Manager with heaps of initiative to oversee all marketing activities and communications. You'll be responsible for devising and implementing the company's annual marketing plan and helping to ensure continued growth in our client, user and subscriber numbers.

The Person

You must have:

- At least 3–4 years of experience in a similar marketing role.

- Extensive experience of planning, buying and monitoring online marketing expenditure, aimed primarily at candidates, including spending time with major search engines.

- Experience of devising and executing trade marketing campaigns to new and existing clients.

- Experience of managing a marketing budget of several hundred thousand pounds.

- Ideal, but not essential, are exposure to and understanding of the (a) accountancy and finance sectors, (b) the online recruitment industry and (c) some exposure to search engine optimization.

The Chartered Institute of Marketing

You must be:

- Enthusiastic, with a hands-on approach to marketing.
- Self motivated and adaptable with a can-do attitude.
- An excellent communicator, with creative, accurate written skills.
- Able to act as part of a wider management team, interfacing with all parts of the business especially sales.

7.5.1 Criteria for a person specification

Rodger's **Seven Point Plan** draws the selector's attention to seven points about the candidate. It is set out, along with another influential classification, the **Five Point Pattern** by Munro Fraser (1978), in the following table.

Table 4.11   Two sets of criteria for person specification

Seven Point Plan	Five Point Pattern
Physical attributes: eg neat appearance, ability to speak clearly	Impact on others: physical attributes, force of personality, interpersonal skills
Attainments: including educational and vocational qualifications	Acquired knowledge and qualifications
General intelligence: IQ, mental agility, verbal dexterity	Innate abilities: numerical/artistic/linguistic aptitudes etc
Special aptitudes: numerical/artistic/ linguistic aptitudes etc	Motivation: what sort of goals drive a person and how much effort goes into achieving them
Interests: demonstrating practical abilities and social competence	Adjustment: emotional stability, tolerance of stress
Disposition: manner (helpful, calm etc)	
Background circumstances: eg family	

The Munro Fraser five-point plan focuses more upon a candidate's career to date as an indicator of future potential while Rodger argued that the requirements fo the job must be described in the same terms as the aptitudes of the people who are to be considered for it (Rodger, 1970).

ACTIVITY 4.10

Using one of the sets of headings in Table 4.11, draw up a person specification for the Media Relations post below.

1.   **Job purpose**

The Media Relations Executive will work in conjunction with the company's senior executives to develop and implement a comprehensive communications strategy. This will require building sound media contacts to ensure positive media coverage for the company's activities.

2.   **Tasks**

(a) Conduct a comprehensive review of media relations and provide a diagnostic report for the Board of Directors.

(b) Develop and implement a company media relations strategy.

(c) Provide a quarterly analysis of media coverage with recommendations to improve coverage.

(d) Arrange and publicise corporate events and host media representatives.

(e) Anticipating and responding to events by issuing press releases, giving professional advice and guidance to other company managers.

(f) Co-ordinate press conferences as necessary.

(g) Provide in-house training on media relations and skills to company staff according to need.

(h) Establish robust relationships with key media representatives.

7.6 The selection process

A systematic approach to selection may be outlined as follows.

Step 1   Deal with responses to job advertisements. This might involve sending application forms or other instructions to candidates, or initial screening of enquiries.

Step 2   Assess each application against key criteria in the job advertisement, job specification and person specification. Critical factors may include age, qualifications, experience or whatever.

Step 3   Sort applications into 'possible', 'unsuitable' and 'marginal. 'Possibles' will then be more closely scrutinised, and a shortlist for interview drawn up. Ideally, this should be done by both an HR specialist and the prospective manager of the successful candidate.

Step 4   Invite candidates for interview.

Step 5   Reinforce interviews with selection testing and other selection techniques, if suitable.

Step 6   Review un-interviewed 'possibles', and 'marginals', and put potential future candidates on hold, or in reserve.

Step 7   Send standard letters to unsuccessful applicants, and inform them simply that they have not been successful. Reserves will be sent a holding letter: 'We will keep your details on file, and should any suitable vacancy arise in future...'.

Step 8   Make a provisional offer to the successful candidate.

7.7 Interviews

In relation to the focus of an interview, there are three principal interview models:

- **Biographical interview** – exploring the candidate's experiences.
- **Behavioural interview** – eliciting information about how applicants have behaved in similar situations.
- **Situational interview** – comprising a series of job-related questions.

Many interviewers (or organisations) prefer to use one technique, but these different models can be useful in different situations and an interview can combine all three aspects.

With regard to the process of interviewing there are, again, various models that can be used, for example, panel interviews.

7.7.1 Types of interview

Individual or one-to-one interviews are commonly used, as they give:

- Direct face-to-face communication, with opportunities for the interviewer to use both verbal and non-verbal cues to assess the candidate
- Rapport between the candidate and the interviewer: each has to give attention solely to the other, and there is potentially a relaxed atmosphere, if the interviewer is willing to establish an informal style
- Flexibility in the direction and follow-up of questions

However, the candidate may also be able to disguise lack of knowledge in a specialist area of which the interviewer knows little. Moreover, a single interviewer's perceptions and judgements may be biased, and this lack of objectivity may go unnoticed and unchecked.

The Chartered
Institute of Marketing

7.7.2 Panel interviews

Panel interviews are designed to overcome such disadvantages. A panel may consist of two or three people who together interview a single candidate: most commonly, an HR specialist and the departmental manager who will have responsibility for the successful candidate. This saves the firm time – and enables better assessment. There is more chance to think about a candidate's responses because the interviewer is more of an observer than a participant. This increases the validity of the assessment. In most one-on-one interviews, the interviewer is often thinking about what question to ask next, rather than listening to a candidate's answer.

Many people dislike this sort of interview and find them an endurance test. To do well candidates need to identify the important figures on the panel and the role of each. See Alec.co.uk.

7.7.3 The interview room

It is important that candidates be made to feel relaxed so that a proper assessment of their suitability for the job can be made. In the case of interview panels, care should be taken to ensure that the candidate is not seated too far away from the interviewers so as to feel isolated, nor so close as to be able to read the interviewers' notes.

7.7.4 Planning the interview

For an interview to succeed, it should be conducted in an orderly, empathetic but efficient manner. It is recommended that interviewers should undertake the following preparation:

- Compare the candidate's application form with the person specification and pick out the points which need investigating further, for example, experience, qualifications, gaps in a career history and inconsistencies.

- Once the interview panel has done this, they should then prepare a plan of how the interview is to be conducted to ensure that nothing is omitted.

- Questions need to be planned. These should be designed to probe the selection criteria of the person specification, namely a candidate's knowledge, ability and experience. Other questions should be aimed at a more general assessment.

- Where a candidate is attending an interview and they have informed you of any disability that they have, which may affect them during the interview process, it is a requirement of the Disability Discrimination Act to carry out 'reasonable' adjustments to ensure they can perform to their maximum potential, for example, if access is a problem for a candidate, the interviews should be held in a room accessible to all.

- Identify key questions pertinent to the job that is asked of all candidates. This ensures that they have been asked equivalent and relevant questions.

- Allocate the subjects to be explored. Each interviewer can cover different areas, for example, work experience and training.

- The candidate should have an opportunity to ask questions and interviewers should be prepared for the more obvious ones, such as hours of work and annual leave.

7.7.5 Objectives for an interview

Interviewers should be clear on the objectives of the interview:

- To find out whether a candidate is suitable for the job advertised

- To find out whether the job and the department/organisation are suitable for a candidate's needs (an aspect which is often overlooked)

- To fairly select the most suitable candidate

7.7.6 Conducting the interview

The interviewer should control the focus of the interview:

- Introduce the members of the panel. Start the interview slowly, to allow the candidate to relax.

- Explain the structure of the interview and what it is trying to achieve.

- Give an overview of the context of and brief background for advertising the job.

- Put the candidate at their ease and begin your questioning by identifying areas that are familiar, for example, his/her present job, before working through to the candidate's thoughts on the job for which he/she has applied.

7.7.7 Finishing the interview

Once the interviewers have obtained all they need from the interview, they should check that the candidate has no further questions and then signify the end of the interview. They should then:

- Tell the candidate when he/she can expect to know the outcome.
- Check the candidate's expenses are covered, if appropriate.
- Thank the candidate for attending the interview and see him/her out.

Key points

- Remove as much stress from the interview as possible.
- Ask open-ended questions.
- Ascertain all relevant facts, and probe ambiguous or vague answers.
- Listen to what the candidate has to say.
- Provide information relevant to the job.
- Provide opportunities for the candidate to ask questions.
- Tell the candidate when they can expect to know the outcome of the interview.

The interview assessment

- When a succession of candidates is seen over a period, it is essential to record accurate views on each immediately after each part of the process.

- Never allow interviewers to rely on memory.

- The interview assessment allows each of your defined categories to be rated and a justification noted. This greatly facilitates the discussions that must take place at the end of the session as the shortlist is constructed or the successful applicant is identified.

- Do not allow any sharing of views about candidates until after individual assessments have been recorded in writing.

7.7.8 Debriefing

Arrange a debriefing to:

- Shortlist or reject candidates.

- Make improvements to the recruitment and selection procedures.

- If possible, provide advice to the unsuccessful candidates – this is good for public relations and is used routinely in the public sector.

The recruitment process at Apple

In marketing, you have the unique opportunity to work on revolutionary products from concept to launch with the best creative minds in the industry. Working with the most creative people in the business on breakthrough products is as satisfying as it is challenging. Our marketing department is comprised of the best and brightest, and we're always looking for stand-out talent to add to our team.

The Marketing division spans a variety of different disciplines including: Developer Relations, Events, Graphic Design, Marketing Communications, Product Marketing, Public Relations, Research and Analysis, Worldwide Markets. Take a look at our website at www.apple.com. Explore the site and get to know our products. If you're a Software Engineer, make sure to visit our Developer site. Interested in Sales? Learn how our customers are using our products in creative ways in the Education, Pro, and Business sections. Make sure you take the time to explore the website, it will tell you a lot of what you need to know about Apple and our customers.

Try our products in person at one of our retail stores or resellers. Listen to music on an iPod. Ask questions of one of the Mac Specialists. When you're at home, download our iTunes software to your Mac or PC and check out the iTunes Music Store. It's important that you familiarize yourself with our products to see what makes Apple unique. Once you're in the interview, relax and be yourself. The interview process is designed for us to make sure that we're a good fit for each other, which means that you should ask questions of us in addition to answering the questions that we ask you. Come prepared to discuss a variety of topics, not just your past experiences and accomplishments. And don't forget, we don't have a dress code, so wear clothes that make you comfortable.

(Adapted from Apple, 2012)

7.7.9 Drawbacks of selection interviews

There is some doubt that an interview is the most appropriate mechanism for assessing candidates' suitability with accuracy, witness:

- First impressions are often lasting impressions; decisions tend to be made early on in the interview.

- Interviewers may prefer candidates who are like themselves, which may lead to discrimination.

- There is a danger of the interviewer only hearing information which supports preconceptions or first impressions.

- Interviewers can get jaded and confused if too many interviews are held in one day – early interviews get forgotten and later ones are less effective.

ACTIVITY 4.11

How have those who have interviewed you performed in their role?
What would you have done differently?
What was good/bad about the best/worst interview you've ever had?

7.7.10 Do's and don'ts for successful selection interviewing:

- Do prepare thoroughly.
- Do check the organisation's policies.
- Do watch for inconsistencies between verbal and non-verbal behaviour.
- Don't make decisions based on a gut reaction.
- Don't break your schedule.
- Don't allow interruptions.
- Don't talk too much.

Working with diversity is an important skill for managers and team members, and they need to have good cultural and interpersonal awareness. The differences amongst individuals and groups should be acknowledged, accepted and valued. Working with people in different countries raises particular issues of cultural awareness.

8 Legal considerations when recruiting

> ▶ **Key term**
>
> **Equal opportunities** is an approach to the management of people at work based on equal access and fair treatment, irrespective of gender, race, ethnicity, age, disability, sexual orientation, religious belief or other differences not directly related to job performance.

For the purposes of The Chartered Institute of Marketing assessment and generally, as marketing manager you are not expected to have a detailed knowledge of employment law. However, you do need to be able to consider the impact of legislation throughout the recruitment process. Let's take a brief survey of the issues.

8.1 Equal opportunities and diversity

Equal opportunity employers seek to redress inequalities (eg of access to jobs, training, promotion, pay or benefits) which are based around differences which have no relevance to work performance. Certain aspects of equal opportunities and diversity, including protection against discrimination and harassment on the basis of sex, race, age and disability, are enshrined in UK and EU law.

Why is equal opportunity and diversity an issue for employers – over and above the humane argument for equity and non-discrimination?

Most organisations have ethical objectives and policies in regard to diversity and equal opportunity, as reflecting principles of decency and fairness.

Equal opportunity and diversity reflects good HR policy, and may help to attract and retain talent: the best people for the job (regardless of race or gender) and those who feel strongly about justice issues.

Equal opportunity and diversity is in most countries a matter of compliance with relevant legislation and Codes of Practice, which are used by Employment Tribunals in arbitrating employee grievances and discrimination claims.

(a) Equal opportunity and diversity widens the recruitment and promotion pool, and aids employee retention, in times of skill shortages (which may exist in certain locations or skill areas, despite high general unemployment).

(b) Equal opportunity and diversity practices contribute to a positive employer brand, and a positive corporate image to consumers (and business partners) who benefit from or support equality principles.

Legal requirements for recruitment do vary in different countries, it is important to recognise these differences if involved in international recruitment and also to reflect local requirements in as assessment if applicable.

9 Evaluating recruitment

To get a clear idea of how efficient your recruitment and selection practices are, you might ask yourself the following questions:

- Can we identify our HR requirements from the marketing plan?
- How fast do we respond to a vacancy or recruitment need?
- How good is our awareness of the internal and external labour market (and do we have access to good advice when we need it)?
- Do we select the right advertising media to reach the market?
- How effective (and cost effective) is our recruitment advertising?

The Chartered Institute of Marketing

- How do our recruits actually perform: do we end up employing the right people?
- Do we retain our new recruits: do they stay with the team and organisation?
- How diverse is our workforce: does it reflect the diversity of the population and customer base, and does it indicate a robust approach to equal opportunity?

Recruitment and selection practices can be reviewed in various ways.

Table 4.12

Review	Comment
Performance indicators	Each stage of the process can be assessed by specific performance indicators: eg the time it takes to process job applications. Data can be collected to check any deviation from standard.
Cost-effectiveness	Eg: number of relevant responses per recruitment ad, or cost of various advertising media per application elicited (or person employed).
Monitoring the workforce	High staff turnover, absenteeism and other problems (particularly among new recruits) may reflect poor recruitment and selection. Lack of workforce diversity may highlight discriminatory practices.
Attitude surveys	The firm can ask its recruits what they thought of the process.
Actual individual job performance	A person's actual performance can be compared with what was expected when (s)he was recruited.

9.1 Improving recruitment and selection procedures

A systematic model has been proposed in this chapter. If it is considered that recruitment and selection procedures need to be improved, attention may be given to matters such as:

- Improvement of **policies and guidelines** for selectors: eg in equal opportunities and diversity and recruit/promote decisions
- Establishment of **systematic procedures** for all stages of the process
- Improved **education and training** of selectors: eg in interviewing skills and testing techniques
- **Auditing of job advertising** content and media, in order to improve the attractiveness and realism of the organisation's offerings and the cost-effectiveness of advertising
- Widening the organisation's **repertoire of selection techniques**, to aim for the highest possible accuracy in predicting job performance and confirming candidate claims
- The possible use of external recruitment and selection **agencies and consultants**.

10 Induction and training

Every organisation should have an induction programme that provides all the information that new employees and others need, and are able to assimilate, without being overwhelming or diverting them from the essential process of integration into a team.

All new employees need some form of introduction to the organisation and the job. A well-planned system of induction provides regular training and/or development sessions. For example, large department stores have a continuing programme of induction with a new course starting every week and special provision for part-time workers.

This leaves individual managers in the position of receiving staff who have at least received training that is specific to their job. Some training, such as health and safety awareness, should be given to all employees.

In larger organisations, line managers may take responsibility for monitoring and encouraging each individual at their place of work and for off-the-job training. However, there may be a specialist training and development section that is usually part of the human resources department.

10.1 Trends in induction

Changing content

- Moving away from being purely about the practicalities of an organisation to discussing culture and values. For example, an online induction and e-learning programme has been developed to introduce the culture for new HR staff in the NHS, and Tesco also uses e-learning for its annual 40,000 new recruits.

- Involving a wide range of personnel in the programme development to ensure that the content continues to match the organisation profile; out-of-date or badly produced material is depressing.

- More awareness of socialisation issues and using induction sessions for cross-function team building.

Procedures

- More written procedures to provide evidence of induction programme, for example, for Investors in People, ISO 9000.

Evaluation

- Holding post-induction reviews, either formally or informally.

- Using statistics (eg on early leavers) to monitor the effectiveness of the induction process.

Insight

Without a good induction new employees get off to a bad start and never really understand the organisation itself or their role in it. This may lead to:

- Poor integration into the team
- Low morale, particularly for the new employee
- Loss of productivity
- Failure to work to their highest potential

In extreme cases, the new employee leaves, either through resignation or dismissal; the results of our most recent recruitment and retention survey showed that 19 per cent of leavers had less than six months' service.

Early leaving results in:

- Additional cost for recruiting a replacement
- Wasted time for the inductor
- Lowering of morale for the remaining staff
- Detriment to the leaver's employment record
- Having to repeat the unproductive learning curve of the leaver
- Damage to the company's reputation

(Chartered Institute of Personnel and Development, 2006)

All new employees should receive an individual induction programme that reflects their specific needs. A typical allocation of induction tasks would be as follows.

- **Line manager/supervisor** – explain the departmental organisation, the requirements of the job, the purpose and operation of any probationary period and the appraisal system.

- **HR** – cover the housekeeping aspects for a new starter (possibly on arrival, certainly on day 1), such as completing employee forms, taking bank details, explaining the induction programme.

- **Safety officer** – explain health and safety issues.

- **Section supervisor or a nominated colleague** – provide an escorted tour of the department and introduce fellow workers; then give day-to-day guidance in local procedures for the first couple of weeks.

- **Senior manager(s) and/or HR** – give an overview of the organisation, its history, products and services, quality system and culture.

- **Training officer (or line manager)** – describe available training services, then help to develop a personalised training plan. Provide details of other sources of information during induction such as the company intranet or interactive learning facilities.

- **Company representatives from trades unions, sports and social clubs etc** – give details of membership and its benefits.

- **Mentor or 'buddy'** – sometimes inductees are allocated a colleague, not their line manager or anyone from personnel, to help speed up the settling-in period.

10.2 The benefits of training and development

- **Improved motivation** – individuals see their skills base extending and their promotion prospects being enhanced.

- **Lower turnover** – opportunities for self-improvement, leads to people staying longer in one employment.

- **Higher levels of performance** – trained and motivated staff are more likely to give of their best, which, in the end, justifies the training budget.

THE REAL WORLD

Polestar Group

The Polestar Group is the United Kingdom's leading commercial printer and the fourth largest in the world. The Group aims to be the most innovative and profitable printers in Europe. This means that its staff need to be trained to use the latest high-tech digital equipment. Polestar's employees experience training at work that includes the following: induction training – training in new ways of working, technology and software multiskilling – employees are trained to do several different interrelated jobs learning management, organisational and leadership skills developing skills through a wide range of personal enhancement programmes.

Skilled print workers are in short supply, and the average age of the workforce is high. Polestar has developed a training programme called 'Printdynamics' which is designed to both attract and retain good workers. It is an interactive CD-Rom and online training package that offers comprehensive coverage of the print industry. It guides the trainee through the different print processes. Ensuring that employees are multi-skilled leads to increased job satisfaction and flexibility. Ongoing training often results in improved productivity by eliminating waste and avoiding delays.

(Print Dynamics, 2012)

---

11 Talent management

▶ **Key term**

Talent management (or **human capital management**) is 'the process of ensuring that the organisation attracts, retains, motivates and develops the talented people it needs' (Armstrong, 2009). It refers to the overall process whereby an organisation systematically attracts skilled, high-quality recruits; integrates new workers into the organisation; systematically performance manages, trains and develops current workers, in order to meet current and future competence requirements; and retains skilled workers within the organisation.

The concept of talent management addresses the flow of 'talent' (skills and abilities) into and through the organisation or team at all levels. It should be included in the human resource planning at the strategic level, and implemented in day-to-day people management processes throughout the firm. As the syllabus guidance emphasises: 'it is important to be mindful that [team design and recruitment] is leading towards building the organisation's capacity and capability, and thus it is essential to ensure that the right level of competency, combined with the right balance of individual talent, is achieved to maximise the organisation's potential to achieve competitive advantage'.

Key talent management processes include (Armstrong, *ibid*):

- Developing the organisation as an 'employer of choice' or 'a great place to work'

- Using selection and recruitment procedures that ensure that good quality people are recruited, who are likely to thrive in the organisation and stay with it for a reasonable length of time

- Designing jobs and developing roles which give people opportunities to apply and grow their skills and provide them with interest and challenge

- Provided talented staff with opportunities for career development and growth

- Developing a positive 'psychological contract' (definition of mutual expectations)

- Recognising those with talent by rewarding excellence, enterprise and achievement

- Succession planning: ensuring that the organisation has suitable people to fill emerging vacancies

- Conducting talent audits to identify individuals with potential

THE REAL WORLD

The Great Place to Work Institute conducts an annual survey identifying the best workplaces in Europe and around the world. The following are the top UK firms in the 2012 survey.

1. Baringa Partners
2. Impact International
3. National Instruments Corporation (UK) Ltd
4. Twining UK & Ireland
5. Net App UK Ltd
6. eBay Companies in the UK
7. UK Fast
8. Brand Learning Partners Ltd
9. Lansons Communications
10. Softcat Limited

You might like to check out www.greatplacetowork.co.uk, and follow up on some of the links to learn more about these best-practice organisations.

(Great Place to Work, 2012)

11.1 Learning style preferences

To best manage and nurture the talent contained within teams it is valuable for managers to recognise that individuals can learn in different ways. Kolb (1983) recognised that people tend to have a preference for a particular phase of the learning cycle, which he identified as a **preferred learning style**.

Honey & Mumford (1992, p5) also noted that 'people vary not just in their learning skills but also in their learning styles. Why otherwise might two people, matched for age, intelligence and need, exposed to the same learning opportunity, react so differently?'

Honey & Mumford (1992) formulated a popular classification of learning styles.

- **Theorists** seek to understand basic principles and models, and to think problems through systematically and logically, before applying their learning. They prefer training to be:

  – Programmed and structured
  – Based on a system, model or theory
  – Designed to allow time for analysis

The Chartered Institute of Marketing

They don't learn well from activities which lack context and theoretical support, involve ambiguity or uncertainty, and require them to act or decide without a basis in principles or concepts.

- **Reflectors** like to stand back and observe and ponder new experiences, preferring to consider all angles and implications, and to analyse all available data, before making any moves. They prefer training to:
  - Allow them to stand back, observe and reflect before acting
  - Allow them to work at their own pace
  - Offer opportunity for painstaking research

They don't learn well from activities which require action without warning or planning, give insufficient data, or impose time pressures (especially if these necessitate short cuts).

- **Activists** involve themselves fully in new experiences – but are easily bored by long-term implementation and consolidation. They prefer training to:
  - Present new experiences/problems and short here-and-now activities
  - Offer excitement, drama, variety and collaboration with other people
  - Allow them to generate ideas without constraints of structure or feasibility (eg brainstorming)
  - Throw them in at the deep end and allow them to 'have a go'

They don't learn well from activities which are passive, require solitary work, involve precise instructions and 'theoretical' concepts, or require attention to detail and follow-up.

- **Pragmatists** are eager to try out ideas, theories and techniques to see if they work in practice. They are down-to-earth: enjoying practical decisions and problem-solving opportunities. They prefer training which:
  - Offers techniques with obvious practical applications and advantages
  - Relates to real problems, with immediate opportunities to implement learning at work
  - Allows practice with coaching/feedback from a credible expert
  - Focuses on practical issues (plans, tips etc).

They don't learn well from activities which are too theoretical or distant from reality, offer no practical guidelines, benefits or rewards, or cannot be implemented due to personal or organisational obstacles.

A knowledge of your own learning styles, and those of your team members, will help you to select learning activities and opportunities that are congruent with preferences and that work to their associated strengths and limitations. Honey & Mumford (1992, p49) suggest two possible strategies.

- **Seek activities which suit the preferred style**: those which *work* for a person.

- **Seek activities which are *not* suited to the preferred style**: those which *stretch* the person. This builds a wider range of learning effectiveness. All four styles are needed to work through the experiential learning cycle: having an experience (Activist); reviewing the experience (Reflector); concluding from the experience (Theorist); and planning the next steps (Pragmatist).

12 Outsourcing jobs and projects

12.1 What is outsourcing?

> ▶ **Key term**
> **Outsourcing** is the current term for the practice of contracting external service providers to undertake activities or functions that the organisation would otherwise perform itself, 'in house'.

To enable an organisation to carry out activities that it doesn't have resources for, or for which others are better equipped to carry out those activities, outsourcing can be used. This can apply to marketing activities and wider organisational activities which impact on marketing. Management of the outsourced activities is a vital element of the manager's role.

Outsourcing is a strategic '**make/do or buy**' or '**boundary of the firm**' 'decision. A firm can perform all its activities in-house, so that the value of the final product or service offered to customers arises almost entirely from its own activity. Increasingly, however, firms seek to reduce or even minimise their in-house activities, buying in products and services from external suppliers or subcontractors, so that they can **focus internal resources** on core, distinctive competences – and reap the benefits of **specialist expertise and economies of scale** available from external suppliers in more 'peripheral' areas.

Thus many firms now **buy in products**, components or assemblies previously produced in-house (often from 'off shore' manufacturers in low labour cost countries), and **outsource a range of support functions** (such as maintenance, catering, warehousing and transport, staff recruitment, training, call centres, data management, 'back-office' administration and so on).

12.2 What can or should be outsourced?

Strategic outsourcing should only be applied to the following.

(a)   **Non-core competencies**. Core competencies are distinctive value-creating skills, capabilities and resources (Hamel & Prahalad, 1994) which: add value in the eyes of the customer; are scarce and difficult for competitors to imitate; and are flexible for future needs. They offer sustainable competitive advantage: for example, by enabling differentiation, or cost leadership, or putting up barriers to competitor entry into an industry. The organisation will therefore need to retain, invest in and develop these competencies, by performing them in-house – or collaborating in partnership with specialist suppliers or service providers.

(b)   Non-core competencies which, **if outsourced**:

- Will benefit from the expertise, cost efficiency or synergy of a specialist supplier

- Will enable the firm to focus on and leverage its core competencies

- Will not disadvantage the organisation with loss of in-house capability, or vulnerability to market risks

- Will enable the firm to exploit technology or other operational capabilities which it lacks (and would find too costly to develop) in-house

- Will represent value for money (due to the supplier's cost/profit structure or economies of scale, or potential for the outsourcer to divest itself of its in-house assets), in relation to the service levels that can be obtained

(c)   Non-core competencies **for which external contractors have the required competence, capability and capacity**.

12.2.1 What jobs or projects might marketing outsource or 'buy in'?

The **marketing function** may choose to outsource a number of jobs and projects to external service providers, including:

- Database development and management, and other information systems tasks (such as record-keeping)

- Call centre operations for customer service and query handling, tele-sales and so on

- Website development and management

- Marketing research projects (market research, customer research, price research, product research)

- Design services (eg for corporate identity, branding and packaging design)

- Advertising services (concept development, campaign realisation, creative origination and production, media buying and scheduling and so on). Most large marketing departments use advertising agencies, whether on a full-service or single-function basis, for on-going advertising work or single campaigns and projects

The Chartered Institute of Marketing

- Other marketing services (which may be provided by a full-service or specialist agency): public relations, direct marketing (direct mail, web marketing), sales promotion, exhibition and event management and so on

- Recruitment, selection or training of marketing staff

- Ancillary functions (probably outsourced by the organisation as a whole): eg catering, car fleet management, security, office/premises management

In addition, marketing should have a role in **make/do or buy decisions at a strategic level**, because of the marketing and branding implications of outsourcing. Marketing will help to:

- Define core competencies (from the perspective of the customer)

- Identify and manage risks of brand or reputational damage arising from association with the contractor

- Ensure that the contractor's service levels, brand positioning and marketing messages are consistent and coherent with those of the organisation

12.3 Benefits and challenges of outsourcing

Table 4.13

Advantages of outsourcing	Disadvantages of outsourcing
Support for downsizing: reduction in staffing, space and facilities costs	Costs of services and relationship/contract management
Enhanced certainty about costs: eg from long-term fixed price service contracts	Loss of in-house knowledge and competencies (which might be required again for future needs)
Long-term partnership contracts encourage planning for the future	Potential reputational damage if service or ethical issues arise with the supply partner
Allows focused investment of managerial, staff and other resources on core/distinctive competencies	Loss of control and difficulties ensuring service standards and coherent/consistent marketing and branding messages
Leverages the specialist expertise, technologies, resources and economies of scale of supply partners, with potential to add more value at less cost than the organisation could achieve itself	Loss of control over confidential information (and possibly also intellectual property: processes, designs etc), particularly if the supplier also serves potential competitors
Flexibility: resources may be scaled up or down depending on demand (without impact on in-house staff and systems)	Ethical, corporate social responsibility and employee relations issues of down sizing and off-shoring
Potential synergy through collaborative supply relationships (eg for co-branding)	Risks of being locked into a long-term, unsatisfactory or incompatible partnership

Recent high-profile examples of outsourcing highlight the risks. British Airways' problems arising from employee strike action at Gate Gourmet, to whom it had outsourced *all* its inflight-catering, illustrate the potential for loss of control, and the risk of problems spreading from the supplier to the outsourcer, with disastrous marketing results.

It should be obvious that marketing managers will not simply be 'saving themselves work' by outsourcing jobs or projects to external suppliers, even at an operational level! There will need to be **rigorous planning and control** effort put into:

- Risk assessment and cost/benefit analysis to ensure the 'buy in' decision is sound

- Selecting and vetting potential suppliers, their financial stability, management, quality/service processes, capabilities and capacities and so on (think about how your organisation goes about selecting an advertising agency, for example)

- Defining requirements, service levels and expectations

BPP
LEARNING MEDIA

4: Management, leadership and establishing teams | **149**

- Drawing up contracts with appropriate controls and protections (best done in consultation with legal or purchasing specialists)

- Developing contact/liaison points and communication, data-sharing and reporting systems

- Developing and maintaining a constructive relationship with the supplier-side customer/account manager

- Contract and performance management: monitoring compliance, conformance and performance on an on-going basis, and pushing for adjustment and improvement where required

- Handling risks, problems, conflicts and disputes constructively as they arise

We discuss outsourcing again in the context of cost management in Chapter 7.

ACTIVITY 4.12

What activities (jobs or projects) does your marketing function outsource to, or 'buy in' from, external service providers? Select one for further analysis.

Who is responsible for managing the relationship and the contract?

What processes or guidelines are in place for managing the relationship and the contract?

Identify two or three key 'points of risk' in the process: how might weaknesses in the process cause the risk of service failure, loss of customer loyalty, poor marketing messages or reputational damage? How could these risks be reduced or managed?

Summary

Teams differ in many ways, including size, purpose, type of work performed, structure, leadership, influence and decision-making ability. It is important to recognise that teamworking is not the best solution in every situation, and teams are not always more effective and efficient than individuals working to solve a problem. However, in many business situations, the ability to work in teams is valuable and teams can accomplish more than individuals who plough their own furrow. Criteria for an effective team were identified. An effective team has cohesion and a common purpose. Recruitment and selection guided by a personnel specification and proper preparation for interviews is of key importance. There are a wide range of selection procedures that can be used depending on the nature of the job and its importance to the organisation.

Recruitment and selection can be expensive but so can appointing the wrong person to a post.

- What is management?

  - Getting things done through other people, but there are many definitions

  - Drucker defined the five main processes of management – setting objectives, organising, motivating, measuring and developing

- Leadership and management

  - Important to recognise the differences
  - There are many models to demonstrate the differences
  - Successful managers know when to manage and when to lead

- Personal development plans

  - Self-development to become a more successful manager is essential, recognising the improvements required through reflection and feedback

- Teams

  - Groups of people with a common purpose and accountability
  - Teams are generally more effective than groups of individuals
  - It is essential to recognise team development stages (Tuckman) and roles (Belbin)

- Team planning

  - Required for effective performance
  - Recruitment and sourcing techniques through appropriate techniques are essential for success

- Legal requirements

  - It is essential to comply with all local legislation when recruiting and working with teams

- Induction and training

  - Induction involves plans to help new team members understand the requirements and integrate with the team

  - Individual development of team members ensures that they perform the required duties

- Talent management

  - When developing team members managers should recognise and work with learning styles of the team members

- Outsourcing jobs and projects

  - Outsourcing can bring many benefits to an organisation but needs to be carefully planned and managed

FURTHER READING

Ahmed, P.K., and Rafiq, M. (2004) *Internal marketing: Tool and concepts for customer focused management.* Butterworth-Heinemann, Oxford.

Belbin, R.M. (2004) *Management Teams: Why they Succeed or Fail.* Oxford, Butterworth-Heinemann.

Boddy, D. (2005) *Management: An Introduction.* Harlow, Pearson Education. Chapter 4, 'The international context of management' and Chapter 15, 'Teams'.

Kotter, J.P. (2001) What Leaders Really Do. *Harvard Business Review – BEST OF HBR Breakthrough Leadership*, December.

Piercy, R.M. (2002) *Market-led Strategic Change: A Guide to Transforming the Process of Going to Market*. Oxford, Butterworth-Heinemann.

Tuckman, B.W. and Jensen, M.C. (1977) Stages in Small-group Development Revisited. *Group and Organisational Studies* 2 (4), pp419–427.

REFERENCES

Adair, J. (2002) *Inspiring Leadership: Learning from Great Leaders*. London, Thorogood.

Ahmed, P.K. and Rafiq, M. (2004) *Internal marketing: Tool and concepts for customer focused management*. Oxford, Butterworth-Heinemann.

Anon (2012) Panel interviews. Alec.co.uk, www.alec.co.uk/interview [Accessed on 14 June 2012]

Apple (2012) www.apple.com [Accessed on 2 June 2012]

Armstrong, M. (2009) *A Handbook of Human Resource Management Practice*. 11th edition. London, Kogan Page.

Bacal, R. (2002) The six deadly sins of team building. The Work 911.com Supersite, http://www.work911.com/articles/teambuidingsins.html [Accessed on 14 June 2012]

Bass, B.M. (1997) Does the transactional–transformational leadership paradigm transcend organisational and national boundaries? *American Psychologist* 52 (2), pp130–139.

Belbin, R.M. (2000) *Beyond the Team*. Oxford, Butterworth-Heinemann.

Belbin, R.M. (2004) *Management Teams: Why they Succeed or Fail*. Oxford, Butterworth-Heinemann.

Blake, R. and Mouton, J. (1964) *The Managerial Grid*. Houston, Gulf Publishing.

Chartered Institute of Personnel and Development (2000) *Recruitment, retention and labour turnover survey 2006*. CIPD, www.cipd.co.uk/surveys [Accessed on 14 June 2012]

CIM (2012) CIM, www.cim.co.uk [Accessed on 20 April 2012]

Drucker, P. (1955) *The Practice of Management*. London, Heinemann.

Fayol, H. (1949) *General and Industrial Management*. London, Pitman.

Friedman, L. and Harvey, R.J. (1986) Can raters with reduced job descriptive information provide accurate position analysis questionnaire (PAQ) ratings? *Personnel Psychology* 39, pp779–789.

General Medical Council (2006) Leadership and management for all doctors. General Medical Council, *http://www.gmc-uk.org/guidance/ethical_guidance/management_for_doctors.asp* [Accessed on 20 April 2012]

Gosling, J. and Mintzberg, H. (2003) The five minds of a manager. *Harvard Business Review* 81 PART 11, pp54 – 63.

Great Place to Work (2012) 2011 UK's 50 Best Workplaces. Great Place to Work, *http://www.greatplacetowork.co.uk/best-workplaces-in -the-UK* [Accessed on 20 June 2012]

Hamel, G. and Prahalad, C.K. (1994) *Competing for the Future*. Boston, Harvard Business School Press.

Handy, C.B. (1993) *Understanding Organisations*. 4th edition. Harmondsworth, Penguin.

 The Chartered Institute of Marketing

Hersey, P. and Blanchard, K.H. (1988) *Management of Organisational Behaviour: Utilising Human Resources*. 5th edition. New Jersey, Prentice Hall.

Honey, P. and Mumford, A. (1992) *The Manual of Learning Styles*. Maidenhead, Peter Honey Publications.

Huczynski, A. and Buchanan, D. (2001) *Organizational Behaviour: An Introductory Text*. 4th edition. Harlow, FT Prentice Hall.

Janis, I.L. (1972) *Victims of Groupthink*. Boston, Houghton Mifflin.

Kanter, R.M. (1992) *When Giants Learn to Dance*. London, International Thomson Business Press.

Katzenbach, J.R. and Smith, D.K. (1994) *The Wisdom of Teams*. New York, McGraw-Hill.

Kolb, D. (1984) *Experiential Learning*. New York, Prentice Hall.

Kotter, J.P. (2001) What leaders really do. *Harvard Business Review – BEST OF HBR Breakthrough Leadership*.

Kouzes, J.M., and Posner, B.Z. (2002) *The Leadership Challenge*. 3rd edition. San Fransisco, Jossey Bass.

McCrae R.R. and John O.P. (1992) An introduction to the five-factor model and its applications. *Journal of Personality* 60 (2), pp175–215.

Mintzberg, H. (1973) *The Nature of Managerial Work*. New York, Harper & Row.

Montgomery, C.A. (2008) Putting leadership back into strategy. *Harvard Business Review,* January.

Pedler, M. *et al* (2004) *A Manager's Guide to Leadership*. Maidenhead, McGraw-Hill.

Pelled, L.H. *et al* (1999) Exploring the Black Box: An Analysis of Work Group Diversity, Conflict and Performance. *Administrative Science Quarterly* 44 (1), pp1–28 March.

Peters, T.J. and Waterman, R.H. (1982) *In Search of Excellence*. New York, Harper Collins.

Piercy, R.M. (2002) *Market-led Strategic Change: A Guide to Transforming the Process of Going to Market*. Oxford, Butterworth-Heinemann.

Print Dynamics (2012) *http://www.printdynamics.co.uk* [Accessed on 20 April 2012]

Sadler, P.J. (1966) *Leadership Style, Confidence in Management and Job Satisfaction*. Hertfordshire, Ashridge Management College.

Siemens (2012) One Siemens. Siemens Global Website. Siemens, www.siemens.com/one-siemens [Accessed on 4 June 2012]

Stacey, R.D. (2003) *Strategic Management and Organizational Dynamics*. Harlow, Prentice-Hall.

Tannenbaum, R. and Schmidt, W.H. (1973) How to choose a leadership pattern: should a manager be democratic or autocratic – or something in between? *Harvard Business Review* 37 (2), pp95–102.

Townsend, R. (1971) *Up the Organisation: how to stop the corporation stifling people and strangling profits*. New York, Michael Joseph.

Tuckman, B.W. and Jensen, M.C. (1977) Stages in Small-group Development Revisited. *Group and Organisational Studies* 2 (4), pp419–427.

Van Eeden, R. and Cilliers, F. (2008) Leadership styles and associated personality traits: Support for the conceptualisation of transactional and transformational leadership. *South African Journal of Psychology* 38 (2), pp253–267.

Whetten, D. and Cameron, K. (2002) *Developing Management Skills*. 5th edition. New Jersey, Prentice Hall.

1   Match the correct columns within the table below.

Demands made on organisations		
Be 'lean and mean'	*but*	Deliberately plan for the future
Be creative and innovative	*but*	Be a good employer
Decentralise to small, simple autonomous units	*but*	Stick to the knitting
Have a sense of urgency	*but*	Centralise to be efficient and integrative

2   What are the four schools of leadership theories?

3   Reorder the following statements on the spectrum so they are correct where task orientated is at one end and relationship orientated is at the other end.

Task orientated						**Relationship orientated**
Leader allows subordinates to act as they wish, within specified limits	Leader defines limits and goals and asks the group to make the decision	Leader presents a problem, gets suggestions, and makes a decision	Leader 'sells' decision	Leader makes decision and announces it	Leader presents ideas and invites questions	Leader presents intended decision, subject to amendment

4   What is action-centred leadership?

5   What is a team?

6   What tests are available to assist selection processes?

7   What does the term 'talent management' refer to?

8   What is the purpose of an induction?

Activity 4.1

Answer will depend on your own research and context

Activity 4.2

Answer will depend on your own research and context

Activity 4.3

(a)   1.1: low task, low people

(b)   9.1: high task, low people

(c)   1.9: high people, low task

Activity 4.4

Answer will depend on your own research and context

Activity 4.5

There are various aspects of work and team roles covered by this site, http://www.belbin.com. A highly informative part of this site is in the category FAQs on Belbin Team Roles and Reports.

Activity 4.6

Belbin uses a 'self-perception inventory' to determine the role of individuals in the team. The original inventory (ie self-assessment based on a variety of questions) is available in the original text. This has, however, been amended and superseded due to several limitations, which have now been discovered. These include, for example:

- Lack of account taken of specialist knowledge, which is particularly critical for people who are in fact specialists.

- No account is taken of false self-perceptions. The latest version now includes a peer/colleague observation/assessment dimension.

Students purchasing their own copy of the second edition of Belbin's text have the opportunity to complete the most up-to-date version of the self-perception inventory, free of charge. You can do this online by visiting the Belbin Associates' website at http://www.belbin.com. However, you must first mail the original card inside the textbook (photocopies not accepted) to register for the free test.

Activity 4.7

Answer will depend on your own research and context

Activity 4.8

Answer will depend on your own research and context

Activity 4.9

Answer will depend on your own research and context

Activity 4.10

Job description for media relations executive

1	Job title	Media Relations Executive
2	Base Location	Head Office
3	Job summary	Development and implementation of a comprehensive communications strategy through building media contacts to ensure positive media coverage.
4	Job content	Typical duties will include:

(a) Conduct a comprehensive review of media relations and provide a diagnostic report for the Board of Directors.

(b) Develop and implement a company media relations strategy.

(c) Provide a quarterly analysis of media coverage with recommendations to improve coverage.

Job description for media relations executive continued

    (d)   Arrange and publicise corporate events and host media representatives.

    (e)   Anticipating and responding to events by issuing press releases, giving professional advice and guidance to other company managers.

    (f)   Co-ordinate press conferences as necessary.

    (g)   Provide in-house training on media relations and skills to company staff according to need.

    (h)   Establish robust relationships with key media representatives.

5	Reporting to:	Marketing Director
6	Experience/Education	Educated to degree level, extensive experience in media relations
7	Training to be provided	Initial on-the-job training.
8	Hours	38 hours per week
9	Personal characteristics required	Organised, friendly manner and enthusiastic.
10	Objectives and appraisal	Comprehensive positive media coverage of organisation
11	Salary	According to experience

Job Description prepared by: Marketing Director

Activity 4.11

Answer will depend on your own research and context

Activity 4.12

Answer will depend on your own research and context

QUICK QUIZ ANSWERS

1

Demands made on organisations		
Be 'lean and mean'	*but*	Be a good employer
Be creative and innovative	*but*	'Stick to the knitting'
Decentralise to small, simple autonomous units	*but*	Centralise to be efficient and integrative
Have a sense of urgency	*but*	Deliberately plan for the future

2   Trait, style, contingency, interpersonal theories.

 The Chartered Institute of Marketing

3

Task orientated						Relationship orientated
Leader makes decision and announces it	Leader 'sells' decision	Leader presents ideas and invites questions	Leader presents intended decision, subject to amendment	Leader presents a problem, gets suggestions, and makes a decision	Leader defines limits and goals and asks the group to make the decision	Leader allows subordinates to act as they wish, within specified limits

4   A scheme of leadership training based on precept and practice in each of eight leadership 'activities' which are applied to task, team and individual: hence, the 'action-centred leadership' model.

5   'A small number of people with *complementary skills* who are committed to a *common purpose,* performance *goals* and *approach* for which they hold themselves *mutually accountable*.

6   Competence, proficiency and psychometric.

7   'The process of ensuring that the organisation attracts, retains, motivates and develops the talented people it needs'.

8
- To help new recruits to find their bearings
- To begin to socialise new recruits into the culture and norms of the team/organisation
- To support recruits in beginning performance
- To identify on-going training and development needs
- To avoid initial problems at the 'induction crisis' stage of the employment life cycle, when frustration, disorientation and disappointment may otherwise cause new recruits to leave the organisation prematurely.

CHAPTER 5

Managing teams

Introduction

Effective team performance involves two complementary processes: the maintenance of the *team* and team working, and the pursuit of *task* functions and objectives. It is important to have a full understanding of the manager's role in maintaining team working and securing task performance.

This chapter looks at a number of key *processes* in team working: the development of teams over time; the emergence of team cohesion or solidarity; group decision making; and group communication and the role the manager plays in these processes. The chapter also explores a number of management and leadership skills for team working. Some of these might appear to be task-focused (such as delegation and empowerment), but they are all to do with the management of *people* rather than time or other resources. Critical to this are the *interpersonal* or people skills, by which a manager or leader can influence the culture, morale and maintenance of the team.

Our outline is intended to be a starting point for your own more detailed study in any areas suggested by assignment tasks – or by your own personal development needs analysis.

Topic list

Performance management and measurement ⓵

Internal marketing ⓶

Characteristics of effective control systems for teams ⓷

Structuring team work ⓸

Motivation theories and performance ⓹

Discrimination ⓺

Interpersonal skills for managers and leaders ⓻

Managing remote teams ⓼

Organisational culture ⓽

2.4	Plan how the work of the team will be undertaken establishing priorities and critical activities required to meet marketing and organisational objectives and with customers in mind:
	■ Performance management and measurement – marketing strategy and individual objectives, communicating standards, techniques to measure performance against objectives and standards
	■ Internal marketing – aligning internal communications with external communications, managing knowledge
2.5	Propose approaches to manage and co-ordinate the work of teams and individuals to create effective working relations including appropriate levels of consultation, taking into account the balance of skills and activities available:
	■ Characteristics of effective teamwork/high-performing teams
	■ Management skills and techniques – communication, motivation, empowerment, involvement, delegation, task allocation, feedback, running effective meetings, listening, assertiveness, group decision making
	■ Assess and apply a range of management theories, eg McGregor's Theory X/Y, Maslow's Hierarchy of Needs, Herzberg's Motivation-Hygiene Theory, McClelland's Motivation Needs Theory, Vroom's Expectancy Theory
	■ Job enrichment/enlargement
	■ Preventing discrimination and valuing diversity – equal opportunities and employment law
	■ Reflect on personal approach to team management and produce a personal development plan
	■ Flexible working practices
2.6	Propose approaches to manage and co-ordinate the work of remote teams to create effective working relations:
	■ Managing international teams, cultural considerations, eg, Hofstede's Cultural Dimensions, Trompenaars' Cross-Cultural Communication
	■ Managing virtual teams – benefits and constraints

1 Performance management and measurement

Marketing implementation is concerned with translating marketing plans into action. The marketing plan is the vehicle for communicating the strategy within the organisation and addresses the issues of 'what' should happen and 'why' it should happen. Implementation is concerned with 'how' the strategy should be carried out, 'who' is to be responsible, 'when' things will take place and 'where' things will happen. Too often in organisations the implementation stage is overlooked and as a result a 'good strategy' can fail. It is important that organisations devote as much time and energy to the implementation of plans as they do to creating marketing strategies. Implementation is planned to be undertaken by ever smaller groups of people in an organisation, down to teams and ultimately individuals.

1.1 Effective and high performing teams

The task of the marketing manager is to build a 'successful' or 'effective' marketing team. You might immediately think of such a team as one which fulfils its task objectives efficiently and effectively, but there is more to it than that. As we saw in Adair's 'action leadership' model (in Chapter 4), team effectiveness – and management – can be measured by three key criteria.

- **Task performance**: fulfilment of task objectives and marketing/organisational goals

- **Team functioning**: maintenance of consistent and constructive team working, managing the demands of team dynamics, roles and processes, and

- **Team member satisfaction**: fulfilment of individual development and relationship needs.

1.2 Assessing the effectiveness of your team

There are a number of factors, both quantitative and qualitative, that may be assessed to decide whether or how far a team is **functioning effectively** – over and above whether it is meeting its work targets. What does an effectively functioning team 'look like'?

- The team has a clear **mission** and **objectives** which are understood and shared by all members.

- The **mix of personalities and skills** is diverse and complimentary. Members respect each others' differences, and appreciate the synergistic effect of diverse individual contributions.

- Each individual is both **supported** and **challenged** to contribute to his or her best ability.

- There is a sense of **identity and belonging** which encourages loyalty and commitment.

- **Information and ideas** are freely gathered and shared for the use of the team.

- **Constructive conflict** – new ideas, challenges to the status quo, constructive criticism and disagreement – is encouraged, as a way of testing and improving group decisions.

- Each member is encouraged to **participate** and have a voice in the team, so that (s)he 'buys in' to its decisions and activities.

- There is **trust and openness**, so that individual and task problems can be safely aired and addressed.

- There are effective mechanisms for maintaining **communication**, both formal (eg team meetings) and informal (networking and socialising).

- The team accepts and supports the designated **leader**, but continues to function well and maintain discipline in the leader's absence, and is able to share leadership roles when required.

You should be able to think of the opposite signs of an ineffectively functioning team. Some of the characteristics of **effective** and **ineffective** teams, as an aid to assessment, may be summarised as follows. Note that some factors cannot be taken as evidence on their own, but may suggest underlying problems: accident rates may be due to poor safety systems, for example – but may also suggest poor morale and lack of focus due to team problems.

▶ **Assessment tip**

The development of teams is a vital management skill, but there is no single method which fits all situations. When answering assignment tasks which relate to team development and motivation it is important to select elements from theories which are most appropriate to the situation being discussed at the time. This could involve a selection of elements which can be applied to demonstrate how they will be effective in the context discussed, with evaluation of the reasoning behind this. Application and evaluation in this way will demonstrate knowledge of the concepts, meeting all areas of the Chartered Institute of Marketing Magic Formula.

Table 5.1   Characteristics of effective and ineffective teams

Factor	Effective team	Ineffective team
Quantifiable		
Labour turnover	Low	High
Accident rates	Low	High
Absenteeism	Low	High
Output and productivity	High	Low
Quality of output	High	Low
Individual targets	Achieved	Not achieved
Stoppages and interruptions to the work flow	Low	High (eg due to disagreement or misunderstanding)
Qualitative		
Commitment to targets and organisational goals	High	Low
Understanding of team's work and why it exists	High	Low
Understanding of individual roles within the team	High	Low
Communication between team members	Free and open	Mistrust
Ideas	Shared for the team's benefit	'Owned' (and hidden) by individuals for their own benefit
Feedback	Constructive criticism	Point scoring, undermining
Problem-solving	Addresses causes	Only looks at symptoms
Interest in work decisions	Active	Passive acceptance
Opinions	Consensus	Imposed solutions
Job satisfaction	High	Low
Motivation/productivity in leader's absence	High	'When the cat's away...'

1.3 High performance teams

Vaill (1989) identified the characteristics of 'high performance' or extraordinary teams, as follows.

- They perform to a high level against defined external benchmarks or standards, and in comparison to their own previous measured performance (ie they continually improve).

- They perform to a level beyond what is assumed to be their potential best (ie they continually exceed expectations).

- They perform to a level that would enable any informed observer to identify them as better than comparable groups (ie they clearly 'shine').

- They achieve results with fewer resources than would be assumed to be necessary (ie they are efficient).

- They embody the best values of the organisation culture and act as role models (or reference groups) for the culture.

The Chartered Institute of Marketing

2 Internal marketing

This is discussed in detail in Chapter 6. Interest here is in making wider connections between internal marketing, strategy, planning and implementation and connecting this with implementation at the level of the individual. In order to be effective with team work and management of teams internal marketing is an essential requirement and skill. The content from Chapter 6 should therefore be applied to the concepts covered in this chapter.

3 Characteristics of effective control systems for teams

In order to develop effective and meaningful control measures to monitor the performance of teams it is essential that the measures are flexible and adhere to the following principles (suggested by Drummond and Ensor, 2001):

- **Involvement** – participants in the control process should be involved in the development of the control measures. If not, there is a danger that staff will fail to take ownership of the measures.

- **Target setting** – objectives should be quantifiable and achievable. These targets should be agreed and communicated in advance.

- **Focus** – recognise the difference between the source and the symptoms of the problem.

- **Effectiveness** – ensure that what is being measured is the right thing: 'what gets measured gets done'.

- **Management by exception** – develop tolerance zones and take corrective action if results fall outside this zone.

- **Action** – effective control systems should promote action rather than just identify problems.

3.1 Elements in team management: Charles Handy's contingency approach

A useful overview of team management was provided by Charles Handy (1993), who took a contingency approach to team effectiveness.

Figure 5.1   A contingency approach to team effectiveness

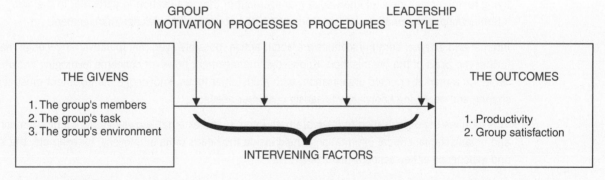

3.1.1 The givens

Some elements of team working may be established by existing arrangements, organisational infrastructure and task structure: they are the raw materials that the manager has to work with.

- There may be an **established team**, providing a mix and balance of skills, competences and personality/role preferences. All these aspects will, as we saw in Chapter 4, shape the personality and functioning of the team.

- The **nature and structure of the task**, as we also saw in Chapter 4, will shape the design and allocation of work for the team, its performance goals and standards, its motivation and culture of work, the type of leadership required (for high-control or high-flexibility, say), the use of technology – and a number of other factors.

- The **environment** includes the physical surroundings and conditions of the team's work, but also the place of the team within overall business processes and structures, the constraint of corporate policies and systems, the influence of organisation culture and so on.

3.1.2 Intervening factors

Intervening factors are the elements which are potentially within the manager's control, and can be manipulated to bring about positive outcomes for and through the team.

- The **motivation** of individuals, and the team as a whole, is a key influence on team effectiveness. The task, and the organisational authority to enforce compliance with task directives, are givens – but motivation is required in order to get team members to comply and perform willingly and to the best of their ability. We will discuss this in detail in Section 5 of this chapter.

- **Processes** describe *how* a team performs its functions and maintains steady and constructive team working: how it establishes ways of operating, how it makes decisions, how it structures communication and so on. We will discuss these kinds of processes in detail in Section 4 of this chapter.

- **Procedures** describe the processes laid down by the organisation and team manager for performing tasks: how things should be done in order to achieve outcomes and targets efficiently and effectively. Procedures often take the form of standardised sequences of tasks, and the instructions, tools and guidelines that will support team members in performing them: how to select a venue for a marketing event; how to co-ordinate a promotional campaign; how to establish marketing budgets; and so on. These aspects will be touched on in Chapter 6.

- **Leadership style** is, in effect, the way in which *all* of the intervening factors are mediated to the team: how they are communicated; how influence is used to secure team member 'buy in' and commitment; and so on. We discussed this aspect in Chapter 4 – but do bear in mind, as you work through this chapter, that team processes may be managed, individuals motivated and managerial skills used *in different ways*, according to the style adopted by the team leader.

3.2 Knowledge management and communications

Market orientation represents the implementation of the marketing concept. Interfunctional co-ordination is an important element of market orientation. Technology developments have resulted in an increased interest in trying to implement ideas of knowledge management in the organisation in particular in the area of interfunctional co-ordination, which is principally the concern of knowledge management.

Internal and external communications are about active, possibly even manipulative, knowledge management to further the goals of the organisation. Knowledge management however concerns leveraging knowledge as an 'asset'. In a market-oriented organisation, with a customer focus, knowledge management must centre on sharing and deploying knowledge to satisfy customer needs.

This requires the organisation to integrate both internal and external knowledge. Much of the most detailed, and organisational critical information is held inside the heads of its employees, for example, the knowledge and experience of key account managers.

Employees commonly withhold knowledge from others and selectively share their knowledge. Part of the problem can also be that they do not know that some of the knowledge that they possess can be useful to others.

Confining this critical knowledge to just one person greatly constrains the extent to which the organisation can serve its customers and be market orientated.

The Chartered Institute of Marketing

Various tools and techniques exist to facilitate knowledge transfer in both formal and informal systems, for example:

- Organisational intranets including marketing information systems. These include data in customer order profiles and product purchases taken from accounting systems.

- Various international organisations have taken this concept much further and include a knowledge repository where staff can search for a wide range of information from product patents, customer product usage, customer profile data to new product idea and customer complaints.

- Regular staff briefings from daily and weekly team meetings to the annual organisational gathering.

- Staff bulletin boards.

- Regular staff social meetings including sports and leisure/arts events.

Through these various devices both tacit and explicit knowledge may be shared for team and organisational benefits in terms of improved performance.

3.3 Characteristics of effective teamwork/high-performing teams

As discussed in Chapter 4, teams go through stages of development and this is normal. What can we do to achieve or maintain a successful team?

First, we must understand the characteristics of high-performing teams. Perhaps ten of the more important include the following (suggested by Wheelan, 1999).

1   Members are clear about, and agree with, team goals.

2   Members are clear about the role they are asked to play, have the ability and skills necessary to accomplish the assigned or chosen task and agree to accept the role.

3   High degree of interdependence exists, as many team tasks require co-operation.

4   The leader's style changes as necessary to meet group needs as they arise. This may be considered in terms of Tuckman's four stages of group development.

5   A very open communication structure (people as well as systems) facilitates the participation and contribution of all members of the team. In addition, team members provide constructive feedback to each other with the focus on individual performance, productivity and effectiveness, and members actually seek this. In addition, they use this to great effect by translating this into improvements on all aspects of their work – that is, productivity and effectiveness.

6   Time is spent initially on planning how decisions are to be made and problems will be solved. That means that time is spent to ensure that there is consensus as to how decisions are to be made – for example, majority voting prior to the occasion when actual decisions must be made.

7   Team solutions and decisions are implemented and they have in place methods by which implementation of decisions are evaluated. This results in rapid detection of poor decisions or indeed poor implementation.

8   Norms of behaviours encourage creative, innovative performance. Unusual behaviour is accepted if this is considered to help individuals to perform at the highest level for the benefit of the team.

9   Suitable structure – as small as is possible to achieve objectives. Subgroups are encouraged and are not seen as threatening; on the contrary, they are considered to be more efficient, especially if part of the team can effectively resolve a problem leaving the rest of the team to resolve other problems.

10 Highly cohesive with co-operative members. Conflict still occurs; however, effective approaches to handling conflict results in their rapid resolution.

(Adapted from Wheelan, 1999)

4 Structuring team work

▶ **Key term**

Job design is the way in which tasks are divided or grouped to form the work responsibilities of a given job, and what decisions are made about specialisation, discretion, autonomy, variety and other job elements.

Success generally requires a degree of order and structure (although there can be exceptions) within the organisation and this can be delivered in part through structured and defined team work.

As we saw from our brief discussion of job in Chapter 3, there are many choices to be made about how work is grouped, structured and allocated as 'jobs' or 'roles' for individuals and teams.

Steiner (1972) suggests there are four basic ways in which groups function.

- **Additive.** All members contribute, but no one member depends on others for their performance. Skills and output are simply pooled.

- **Complementary.** The task can be divided into separate parts and allocated to individuals with the skills needed for each. Members effectively work in parallel.

- **Conjunctive** (or **co-ordination**). There is a high degree of dependence between members' contributions, often in a defined, linear sequence (as in assembly lines and office procedures).

- **Disjunctive** (or **collaboration**). Members contribute different skills and abilities, so that solutions are synergistic, reflecting the optimum contribution of each individual. This particularly suits problem-solving groups.

The nature and structure of the task will therefore dictate to a large extent how work is organised and allocated within a team, together with considerations such as time available (parallel working gets the job done faster than a linear sequence of tasks) and the skills and preferences of the team.

In addition to task structure, which may be flexible (determined according to the demand of particular tasks), there is the question of **job design**: how tasks and responsibilities are packaged together into meaningful, efficient jobs or task sets for individuals.

4.1 Aims of effective job design

Frederick Taylor was an early exponent of systematic job design (sometimes referred to as scientific management). His aims were improved efficiency and control. Jobs were '**micro-designed**': a complex task was broken down into its most basic component parts, which represented the sole 'job' of a worker or group of workers. Jobs were reduced to single, repetitive, detailed motions (as on assembly lines, packaging or quality inspection), which could be quickly mastered and tightly programmed.

The human relations school of management theory, however, associated job design and **job satisfaction**. Workers would not be satisfied as 'small cogs in large wheels', however well rewarded. In an influential model, Hackman & Oldham (1980) identified **core job dimensions** which were thought to contribute to job satisfaction:

- **Skill variety**: the opportunity to exercise different skills and perform different operations, as opposed to micro-specialisation and repetition

- **Task identity**: the integration of operations into a 'whole' task (or meaningful segment of the task), as opposed to task fragmentation

- **Task significance**: the task has a role, purpose, meaning and worth, according to the values of the organisation and the individual

- **Autonomy**: the opportunity to exercise discretion or self-management in areas such as target-setting and work methods
- **Feedback**: the availability of information by which the individual can assess his progress and performance in relation to expectation and targets and the opportunity to give feedback and have a voice in performance improvement

5 Motivation theories and performance

Many studies indicate that teams, and organisations, are successful when people are emotionally engaged and believe in what the team and the organisation is doing. In addition, it is important for them to gain some form of psychological satisfaction for the contribution they make to the organisation, beyond simple monetary benefits.

Table 5.2   Summary of key motivation theories

Herzberg (1965)	Suggested that people are motivated to work in co-operation with others by both extrinsic motivators, such as money, and intrinsic motivators, such as recognition for achievement, responsibility, advancement and personal growth.
Maslow (1948)	Maslow in his hierarchy of needs suggested that when an organisation creates conditions in which people can satisfy their 'self-actualisation' needs (the highest level in his hierarchy of needs) then they are powerfully motivated to work for the good of the team and of the organisation.
Schein (1988)	One of the several authors to consider three categories of relationships. The first two are 'coercive', where individuals only do the bare minimum to evade punishment, and 'utilitarian', where the individual does enough simply to earn the desired level of reward. The final category is a 'normative' form of relationship where individuals value what they are doing for its own sake, as they believe in it. In this situation, the individual's ideology matches that of the organisation and this acts as the highest level of individual motivation for the benefit of the organisation.

5.1 Motivation

One of the best-known theories is McClelland's motivational theory (McClelland, 1953) which is based on three types of motivational needs that are found to varying degrees in all workers and managers.

1   **Achievement motivation**: The person seeks attainment of realistic but challenging goals, and advancement in the job. There is a strong need for feedback about achievement and progress, and a need for a sense of accomplishment.

2   **Authority/power motivation**: The person needs to be influential and effective to make an impact. There is a strong need to lead and for their ideas to prevail. There is also motivation and need towards increasing personal status and prestige.

3   **Affiliation motivation**: The person has a need for friendly relationships and is motivated towards interaction with other people. The affiliation driver produces motivation, and needs to be liked and held in popular regard. These people are team players.

Most people possess and exhibit a combination of these characteristics.

Some people exhibit a strong bias to a particular motivational need, and this affects their behaviour and working/managing style. McClelland felt that people with a strong 'achievement motivation' made the best

leaders although there was a tendency to demand too much of their staff in the belief that they too are highly achievement focused and results driven.

McClelland suggested that for achievement-motivated people:

- Achievement is more important than material or financial reward.

- Achieving the aim or task gives greater personal satisfaction than receiving praise or recognition.

- Financial reward is regarded as a measurement of success, not an end in itself.

- Security is not the prime motivator, nor is status.

- Feedback is essential, because it enables measurement of success, not for reasons of praise or recognition (the implication here is that feedback must be reliable, quantifiable and factual).

- Achievement-motivated people constantly seek improvements and ways of doing things better.

- Achievement-motivated people will logically favour jobs and responsibilities that naturally satisfy their needs, that is, offer flexibility and opportunity to set and achieve goals, for example, sales and business management, and entrepreneurial roles.

Extending knowledge

An interesting and alternative view of motivation which is worth exploring comes from Daniel Pink in the book *Drive: The Surprising Truth About What Motivates Us* – Canongate Books Ltd, 2011.

5.2 McGregor Theory X/Theory Y

In 1960, Douglas McGregor advanced the idea that managers had a major part in motivating staff. He divided managers into two categories:

- Theory X managers who believe that their staff are lazy and will do as little as they can get away with
- Theory Y managers who believe that their people really want to do their best in their work.

Theory X managers believe that staff will do things if they are given explicit instructions and plenty of stick if they do not do what they are supposed to. Theory Y managers believe their people work their best when empowered to make appropriate decisions.

Achievement-motivated people tend towards X-theory style, due to their high task focus.

Theory X assumptions

1   People inherently dislike work.
2   People must be coerced or controlled to do work to achieve objectives.
3   People prefer to be directed.

Theory Y assumptions

1   People view work as being a natural activity.
2   People will exercise self-direction and control towards achieving objectives to which they are committed.
3   People learn to accept and seek responsibility.

Since McGregor, Theory Z has been advanced by William Ouchi (1982). This states that employees crave responsibility and opportunities for growth all the time. It is strongly influenced by Japanese management styles.

Think about jobs you have had. What do you think the assumptions of your boss were?

What impact did those assumptions have on performance and morale?

Can you generalise about organisations you are familiar with? Can you detect patterns of management that reflect either Theory X or Theory Y assumptions?

5.3 Herzberg's motivators and hygiene factors

Herzberg *et al*. (1959) constructed a two-dimensional paradigm of factors affecting people's attitudes about work. He concluded that factors such as company policy, supervision, interpersonal relations, working conditions and salary are hygiene factors rather than motivators.

According to the theory, the absence of hygiene factors can create job dissatisfaction, but their presence does not motivate or create satisfaction. In contrast, motivators are elements that enriched a person's job; he found five factors in particular that were strong determinants of job satisfaction: achievement, recognition, the work itself, responsibility and advancement.

These motivators (satisfiers) were associated with long-term positive effects in job performance while the hygiene factors (dissatisfiers) consistently produced only short-term changes in job attitudes and performance, which quickly fell back to its previous level.

Satisfiers describe a person's relationship with what he or she does, many related to the tasks being performed. Dissatisfiers, on the other hand, have to do with a person's relationship to the context or environment in which he or she performs the job. The satisfiers relate to what a person does while the dissatisfiers relate to the situation in which the person does what he or she does. A manager may not be able to easily influence all the hygiene factors of a person's job, but he or she can have a big influence on many of the motivators.

Motivator factors that increase job satisfaction:

- Achievement
- Recognition
- Work itself
- Responsibility
- Advancement
- Growth

Hygiene factors – absence of 'good' factors can create job dissatisfaction:

- Company policy
- Working conditions
- Salary
- Peer relationships
- Security

(Herzberg, 1965)

5.4 Equity theory

Adams' (1965) equity theory is based on the principle that individuals want a fair balance between the inputs, or what they give to their job, and the outputs, or what they get from it. Employees develop a view of what is fair by comparing their own situation with other people who they regard as 'referents'.

- Typical inputs might be effort, loyalty, hard work, commitment and skill.

- Typical outputs are obvious ones such as pay and expenses and also more intangible ones such as recognition, praise, responsibility, sense of achievement and so on.

If people feel that their inputs outweigh the outputs then they may become demotivated. In this situation, some people switch off and do the minimum that they can, or even become disruptive. Others aim to seek to improve the outputs by making pay claims or looking for other work.

The key aspect of the theory is that extrinsic rewards such as level of pay are neither motivating nor demotivating in themselves. Rather it is how fair we perceive them to be when we compare ourselves with significant others, that is, people who we feel should be paid less than or about the same as ourselves, or people whom we expect to be paid more than us.

If we feel that inputs are fairly and adequately rewarded by outputs (the fairness benchmark being subjectively perceived from market norms and other comparable references), then we are happy in our work and motivated to continue inputting at the same level.

5.5 Maslow's hierarchy of needs

Abraham Maslow (1954) described five innate human needs, and put forward certain propositions about the motivating power of each need.

- An individual's needs can be arranged in a **'hierarchy of relative pre-potency'** (as shown).

- Each level of need is **dominant until satisfied**; only then does the next (higher) level of need become a motivating factor.

- A **need which has been satisfied** no longer motivates an individual's behaviour.

- The need for **self-actualisation** (personal growth and the fulfilment of potential) can rarely be fully or permanently satisfied.

Figure 5.2   The hierarchy of needs (Maslow)

ACTIVITY 5.2

Suggest ways in which rewards or incentives could be offered to team members to satisfy each of the innate needs identified by Maslow.

The Chartered
Institute of Marketing

5.5.1 Evaluating and applying the hierarchy

Maslow's hierarchy is simple and intuitively attractive: you are unlikely to worry about status or respect if you are physically unsafe or about to lose your job. However, it is difficult to use the hierarchy to predict employee behaviour. (Maslow did not intend it to be applied specifically in a work context.)

- The boundaries between the needs are, in practice, indistinct and overlapping: different people emphasise different needs; and the same need may prompt different behaviours in different individuals.

- In some contexts, people are clearly able to suppress even their basic needs for the sake of a perceived 'higher cause' or for the sake of others.

- Maslow's ideas primarily reflected American middle class values and the pursuit of the good life, but these values may not be fundamental universal truths about human psychology.

- The role of pay is problematic, since it arguably acts as a 'stand in' for (or way of obtaining) other rewards.

Nevertheless, the hierarchy is a useful reminder to managers to adopt a contingency approach to team motivation: people may be motivated by different things at different times.

5.6 Vroom's expectancy theory

Expectancy theory is a process theory of motivation, which basically states that the strength of an individual's motivation to do something will depend on the extent to which he expects the results of his efforts to contribute to his needs or goals.

Victor Vroom (1964) worked out a formula by which human motivation could be assessed and measured. He suggested that the strength of an individual's motivation is the product of two factors:

- The strength of his **preference** for a certain outcome. Vroom called this '**valence**': it can be represented as a positive or negative number, or zero – since outcomes may be desired, avoided or regarded with indifference.

- His **expectation** that the outcome will in fact result from a given behaviour. Vroom called this 'subjective probability' or **expectancy**. As a probability, it may be represented by any number between 0 (no chance) and 1 (certainty).

In its simplest form, the expectancy equation may be stated as:

$$F = V \ E$$

where:

F = The force or strength of the individual's motivation to behave in a particular way

V = Valence: the strength of the individual preference for a given outcome or reward and

E = Expectancy: the individual's perception that the behaviour will result in the outcome/reward.

In this equation, the lower the values of valence or expectancy, the less the individual's motivation. A team member may have a high expectation that increased productivity will result in promotion (because of her manager's promises, say), but if she is indifferent or negative towards the idea of promotion (because she dislikes responsibility), she will not be motivated to increase her productivity. Likewise, if promotion is very important to her – but she does not believe higher productivity will get her promoted (because she has been passed over before, perhaps), her motivation will be low.

5.6.1 Evaluating and applying the expectancy model

Expectancy theory can be used to measure the likely strength of a worker's motivation to act in a desired way in response to a range of different rewards, to find the most effective motivational strategy. In particular, it suggests that:

- **Intended results** should be made clear, so that the individual can complete the calculation by knowing what is expected, the reward, and how much effort it will take.

- Immediate and on-going **performance feedback** should be given. Without knowledge of actual results, there is no check that extra effort was justified (or will be justified in future).

- Individuals should be offered **rewards and incentives that they value**: this may require some flexibility (eg a 'cafeteria' approach to rewards and benefits) on the part of the manager.

- If an individual is rewarded for performance tied to **standards**, however, (s)he may set lower standards: the expectancy part of the calculation (likelihood of success and reward) is greater if the standard is lower.

- Managers need to **follow through** with promised rewards for high performance, in order to increase expectancy for future incentives.

5.7 Job enrichment and job enlargement

> ▶ **Key terms**
>
> **Job enlargement** refers to increasing the motivational value of a job through the performance of a greater number and variety of similar level tasks (Lawler, 1969).
>
> **Job enrichment** involves adding tasks, for example, related to planning and controlling work that are typically performed by someone higher up in the organisational hierarchy, for example, a supervisor or a more senior manager (Lawler, 1969).

Motivation theory has had a large influence in job design and in particular in trying to change work roles. The theory being if you can increase work motivation you will get an increase in satisfaction and ultimately in performance.

Two general approaches to this have been popular, namely job enrichment and job enlargement. Job enrichment (getting workers to take on higher level tasks) and job enlargement (greater workers to take part in a greater variety of tasks) have been successful in improving performance and work satisfaction.

See the discussion of related issues in Chapter 4, in the section, 'Job analysis'.

The case study on Siemens is particularly relevant. One word of caution, however, is that a 'one approach fits all' has been found not to be successful. Some workers are happy to do a routine job and or do not want more responsibility. They can even find this to be stressful.

The mechanism by which these are implemented can also affect worker perception and acceptance. Imposition by senior management can be perceived simply as a cost efficient measure and may even be resented. Where worker co-operation is sought they are more likely to buy into the idea and to benefit personally, which can only be good for organisational performance.

5.7.1 Empowerment

> ▶ **Key term**
>
> **Empowerment** is the current term for initiatives designed to give workers (and particularly work teams) more discretion and responsibility for their work, and for supporting and facilitating them in exercising that responsibility.

Empowerment is regarded as an important support for marketing activity, as a tool of '**internal marketing**': enabling staff to use their discretion, judgement, experience and skills to deliver a better quality of service to customers. There are various levels of empowerment, from the ability to make suggestions (low level of involvement) to the latitude to do whatever is necessary to satisfy the customer in a given set of circumstances (high level of involvement and empowerment).

'Empowerment means that the company must create the right culture and climate for employees to operate in. This includes four empowerment criteria: providing employees with **information** about the organisation's performance; providing **rewards** based on the organisation's performance; providing employees with **knowledge** that enables them to understand and contribute to organisational performance; and giving them **power** to take decisions that influence organisational direction and performance'.

(Bowen & Lawler, 1992, cited Peck *et al*, 1999).

The Chartered Institute of Marketing

The changes in organisation structure and culture as a result of empowerment can be shown in the following diagrams.

Figure 5.3   Empowerment and organisational structure

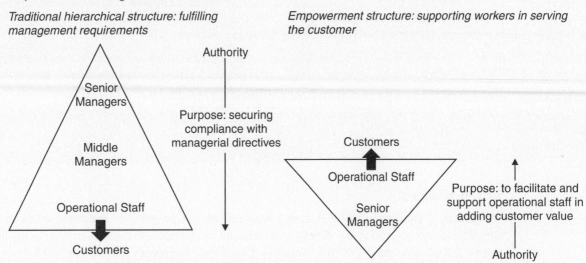

Traditional hierarchical structure: fulfilling management requirements

Empowerment structure: supporting workers in serving the customer

The **argument for empowerment**, in a nutshell, is that by empowering workers (or 'decentralising' control of business units, devolving/delegating responsibility, or removing levels in hierarchies that restrict freedom), not only will the job be done more effectively, but the people who do the job will get more out of it. Advantages claimed for team empowerment include:

- Faster and more flexible response to customers' needs (because staff are better informed and more confident).

- Improved employee job satisfaction, motivation and commitment (because empowerment offers a high degree of challenge, interest, responsibility and trust).

- Improved upward communication (from employees to management), which helps keep the organisation sensitive to stakeholder demands and environmental changes.

- Improved ability to learn and adapt to change (because employees are more flexible in their attitudes and behaviours, and more confident in their coping skills).

Of course, these benefits must be balanced with the increased costs of training, development, reward and retention of empowered employees (they will still expect to be paid for the extra contribution they are making!) – and the risk of their sometimes getting it wrong. There is also an issue of ensuring service consistency, as individual discretion may lead to wide variations (which may be perceived and resented by some customers).

'Virgin Atlantic has long recognised the critical role internal marketing plays in its success. One of the secrets of the airline's success has been enthusiastic empowered, motivated employees. Sir Richard Branson has said: 'I want employees in the airline to feel that it is *they* who can make the difference, and influence what passengers get.'

"We want employees who feel involved and prepared to express dissatisfaction when necessary. In fact, we think that the constructively dissatisfied employee is an asset we should encourage and we need an organisation that allows us to do this – and that encourages employees to take responsibility, since I don't believe it is enough for us simply to give it."

Virgin Atlantic's philosophy has been to stimulate the individual, to encourage staff to take initiatives and to empower them to do so.'
(Christopher *et al*, 2002)

5.7.2 Involvement

The concept of '**employee voice**' embraces 'a whole variety of processes and structures which enable, and sometimes empower employees, directly and indirectly, to contribute to decision-making in the firm' (Boxall & Purcell, 2003). Armstrong (2009) summarises it as 'the say employees have in matters of concern to them in their organisation'. The term has come to embrace a wide range of mechanisms for:

- **Employee involvement:** informing and consulting employees about aspects of decision-making. This is sometimes called 'upward problem-solving': two way communication; the use of staff feedback, suggestion schemes and employee intranet discussion groups; or project teams, which bring staff and management together to solve problems, discuss issues or generate ideas (eg quality circles or customer care task forces).

- **Employee participation:** involving employees (often via their elected representatives) in the decision-making machinery of the organisation. This is sometimes called 'representative participation': collective negotiations and conflict resolution via trade unions, formal consultative meetings with worker representatives, or formal partnership agreements.

Marchington *et al* (2001) argue that paying attention to employee voice offers:

- The ability for individual employees to express dissatisfaction, solve problems within management and preserve working relationships

- The ability for employees collectively to express their needs and wishes in matters that affect them, providing a counterbalance to managerial power

- The ability for employees to contribute to management decisions, allowing the organisation to harness the expertise and commitment of workers to improve quality, productivity and work organisation

The ability for employers and employees to demonstrate their intention to focus on shared goals, mutual interests and co-operative working relations, for the long-term benefit of the organisation and its people.

ACTIVITY 5.3

What aspects of the following situations might be a problem for an effective team meeting? What might you, in the role of facilitator, do about it?

(a) One person suggests a revision to the agenda, a complex issue which the rest of the team is unprepared to discuss, and which two members are likely to feel is 'targeted' at them.

(b) The team has more items on its agenda than it can handle in a simple meeting.

(c) A team member has called ahead to say that she will be unavoidably late for a scheduled project team meeting..

6 Discrimination

In the same way that care has to be taken when recruiting to comply with legislation, management and development also has to meet legal requirements for discrimination. Again, the law varies from country to country so a manager has to be aware of the local legislation

6.1 What the UK law says

There are a number of Acts of Parliament which are relevant to the training and development of staff. The main provisions are the Sex Discrimination Acts of 1975 and 1986, the Race Relations Act 1976, the Race Relations (Amendment) Act 2000 and the Disability Discrimination Act of 1995. These Acts seek to promote equality of opportunity and to ensure that no person is treated less favourably than another person on the grounds of disability, colour, race, nationality, ethnic or national origins, sex or marital status.

The Disability Discrimination Act 1995 gives disabled people the right not to be treated less favourably than others. Special care must be taken in the wording and placing of recruitment advertisements to avoid seeming to prefer one type of person over another.

Since 2005, third-party publishers, for example, newspapers, have been liable for publishing discriminatory advertisements. The Government introduced legislation to combat age discrimination in employment and vocational training. It includes every member of the workforce, young and old.

Employers will have to adopt age positive practices. This means it will no longer be possible to recruit, train, promote or retire people on the basis of age unless it can be objectively justified.

6.2 Discrimination – main forms

The three main forms of discrimination are:

1   **Direct discrimination** – that is where a woman is treated less favourably than a man (or *vice versa*), a married person is treated less favourably than a single person, or someone is treated less favourably on grounds that they are intending to undergo, are undergoing or have undergone a gender reassignment. Direct discrimination can occur where someone is treated less favourably on the grounds of their sexual orientation.

2   **Indirect discrimination** – that is applying a requirement or condition which, although applied equally to all groups, is such that a considerably smaller proportion of a particular racial group, sex or married persons can comply with it and which cannot be shown to be justifiable. Possible examples are unjustifiable age limits which could discriminate against women who have taken time out of employment for child rearing and rules about clothing or uniforms which disproportionately disadvantage a particular racial group. Both types of discrimination are unlawful irrespective of whether there has been any intention to discriminate.

3   **Disability discrimination** – While legislation covering discrimination on grounds of race and sex makes discriminatory conduct unlawful, the Disability Discrimination Act 1995 goes further by requiring employers to make 'reasonable adjustments' to the workplace where that would help to overcome the practical effects of disability. Failure to carry out this legal duty amounts to discrimination unless an employer is able to justify it. People with disabilities who feel that they have been unfairly discriminated against can seek redress through Employment Tribunals.

6.3 Main areas to consider

Some of the main areas which should be considered in terms of discrimination are:

- Sexual orientation
- Religion and belief
- Equal pay

7 Interpersonal skills for managers and leaders

> ▶ **Key term**
>
> **Interpersonal behaviour** is between people. It includes:
>
> - Interaction between people: a two way process such as communication, delegating, negotiating, resolving conflict, persuading, selling, or influencing
> - An individual's behaviour in relationship to other people.

Interpersonal skills are skills in dealing with other people. It is possible to see them as two 'tiers' of skill: the basic elements of interpersonal skill (first-order skills) and the skills which *apply* them in specific interaction styles and contexts (second-order skills).

Such skills are particularly important for team leaders, to support their ability to:

- Understand and manage the roles, relationships, attitudes and perceptions operating in team situations
- Communicate clearly and influence effectively, in order to achieve their aims from a wide range of interpersonal contacts (ideally, allowing other parties to emerge satisfied as well)
- Model constructive interpersonal relationships within the team
- Motivate and build teams: negotiate solutions to problems, manage conflict, conduct interviews, counsel and coach team members, give constructive feedback and so on
- Network effectively within and beyond the organisation, in order to gather information and influence, and mobilise resources, on behalf of the team.

Figure 5.4   Interpersonal skills

Second order skills	
- Persuading/influencing	- Leadership
- Assertiveness	- Managing conflict
- Negotiation	- Counselling
- Team working	- Coaching

First order skills
- Giving and receiving feedback
- Listening and observing
- Questioning
- Communicating clearly
- Understanding and using body language

We will look at some of the key skills mentioned in the syllabus here. Conflict management is dealt with in a late chapter.

7.1 Communication

We will not consider communication skills separately, in detail, as all interpersonal skills (listening, assertiveness, negotiation, feedback giving) are communication skills. However, it may be helpful to use a

The Chartered Institute of Marketing

simple communication process model as a framework for analysing 'critical incident' interactions (to diagnose what went wrong), and for determining areas for improvement and learning.

7.1.1 The communication process

Communication can be depicted as a **'radio signal'** model. The sender encodes a message and transmits it to the receiver who decodes it to 'retrieve' the sender's message. This is a two-way cycle, which can be shown as follows.

Figure 5.5   The communication process

The communication process

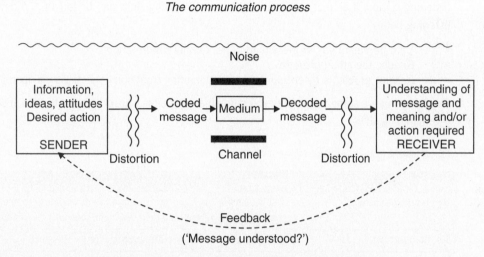

Our diagram raises a number of issues for communication planning and evaluation.

- **Coding and decoding.** The code or 'language' of a message may be verbal (spoken or written) or non-verbal (pictures, diagrams, numbers or body language). The needs and abilities of the target audience must be taken into account: not all codes (eg technical jargon or unlabelled diagrams) will be accessible to others.

- **Media and channels.** The choice of medium (letter, memo, e-mail, report, presentation, telephone call) and channel of delivery (telecom system, notice board, postal system, internet) must be appropriate for the purpose of the communication and its target audience. This may depend on:

    - **Urgency**: the speed of transmission (eg phone or e-mail as opposed to post)

    - **Permanency**: the need for a written record for legal evidence, confirmation of a transaction or future reference

    - **Complexity**: eg the need for graphic illustration to explain concepts

    - **Sensitivity/confidentiality** (eg a private letter)

    - **Ease of dissemination**: wide audience (eg a notice board)

    - **Cost effectiveness** (taking into account all the above)

- **Feedback.** The process by which the sender checks – and recipient signals – that the message has been received and understood. This is a vital skill, as it makes communication a two-way – and much more reliable – process. Feedback may include:

    - Verbal messages ('I'd like to clarify…', 'What does that mean?')
    - Non-verbal cues (eg nodding and making encouraging noises, or looking perplexed)
    - Appropriate action (eg doing as requested by the message)

- **Distortion** is a technical term for processes through which the meaning of a message is lost in the coding or decoding stages. Misunderstandings may arise from technical or ambiguous language, misinterpretation of symbols or tones of voice and so on.

LEARNING MEDIA

- **Noise** is a technical term for interference in the environment of communication which prevents the message getting through clearly. This may be:
    - Physical noise (eg traffic noise when someone is on a mobile phone)
    - Technical noise (eg a bad internet connection)
    - Social noise (eg differences in the personalities, status or education of the parties)
    - Psychological noise (eg anger or prejudice distorting what is heard).

7.1.2 Listening

Listening is about decoding and receiving information and carries much of the burden of communication. Listening is more than just a natural instinct, and listening skills can be taught and developed. **Effective listening** helps:

- Both parties to gather more (and better quality) information
- Reduce the effect of 'noise'
- Resolve problems by encouraging understanding from someone else's viewpoint.

The following are some basic, practical guidelines on being a good listener, to help you evaluate and improve your listening skills.

Table 5.3   Good listening techniques

Guideline	Comment
Be prepared to listen	Put yourself in the right frame of mind (ie a readiness to maintain attention). In meetings, be prepared to grasp the main concepts: familiarise yourself with the agenda.
Maintain interest	Make an effort to analyse the message for its relevance.
Keep an open mind	'Bracket' (put to one side) your own beliefs and prejudices, as they can get in the way of what the other person is actually saying.
Keep an ear open for the main ideas	Learn to distinguish between the 'gist' of the argument and supporting evidence.
Listen critically	Assess what the other person is saying by identifying any assumptions, omissions and biases.
Take notes	Note taking can be distracting at times: give yourself brief reminders – and then re-connect.
Wait before contributing	Don't interrupt (or distract yourself by planning what you will say) while the other person is talking.
Use active listening techniques	'Active listening' means engaging in *dialogue* with the speaker, not just passively soaking up what is said. <ul><li>Give encouraging feedback (nods, 'uh huh's).</li><li>Periodically summarise or 'reflect back' ('You're feeling frustrated by this problem'): a technique which demonstrates empathy and understanding.</li><li>Check understanding ('If I've understood you correctly...', 'Are you saying that....?')</li><li>Ask questions.</li></ul>

7.1.3 Non-verbal communication

We have included non-verbal communication under the heading of listening skills, because – like listening – it involves actively paying attention to the context and process (as well as the content) of communication. Both are used together in face-to-face communication in interviews, discussions, negotiations and team meetings.

Consciously or unconsciously, we send non-verbal messages during every face-to-face encounter. We can use them deliberately to **confirm** our verbal message – for example, by nodding and smiling as we tell someone we are happy to help them – or to **contradict** it, if we want to be ironic or sarcastic (saying 'How interesting!' with a yawn, for example).

More often, however, our body language *contradicts* our verbal message *without* our being aware of it, giving a '**mixed message**' like a team member saying he understands an instruction while looking extremely perplexed. Body language can also '**give away**' messages that we would – for social or business reasons – rather not send, such as lack of interest, hostility or whatever.

Control and use of body language is needed to:

- Provide 'physical' feedback to the sender of a message (eg a nod of understanding)
- Create a desired impression (eg a confident posture)
- Establish a desired atmosphere or conditions (eg a friendly smile)
- Reinforce spoken messages with appropriate indications (eg nodding 'yes')

Reading other people's body language helps a manager to:

- Receive feedback from listeners and modify his or her message accordingly
- Recognise people's real feelings when their words are constrained by formalities
- Recognise existing or potential personal or interpersonal problems in the team
- 'Read' situations in order to modify his or her communication and response strategy

7.2 Assertiveness

Human beings have certain psychological and physical mechanisms which prepare them to 'fight' or 'flee' in response to interpersonal threats or conflicts: by instinct, we fight back (aggression) or give in (passivity). However, we also have a third option: to use rational thinking and language to work our way through a problem in more constructive ways. This is the assertive approach.

According to Back and Back (1999) the differences between assertive, aggressive and passive behaviour can be seen as follows.

Table 5.4   Back and Back's differences between assertive, aggressive and passive behaviour

	Aggressive behaviour	Passive behaviour	Assertive behaviour
Origins	'Fight' reaction to frustration, conflict or threat	'Flight' reaction to frustration, conflict or threat	'Flow' (rational) response to frustration, conflict or threat
Assumptions	I am more important than others	I am less important than others	I am important, but so are others
Main aim	To 'win' or dominate, if necessary at the expense of others	To please, to be liked and accepted, to avoid conflict	To communicate, maintain relationship and get the needs of *both* parties met
Typical behaviours	■ Standing up for your rights in such a way that you violate the rights of others ■ Ignoring or dismissing the needs, wants, feelings or viewpoints of others ■ Expressing your own needs, wants and opinions in inappropriate ways	■ Failing to stand up for your rights, or doing so in such a way that others can easily disregard them ■ Expressing your needs, wants, opinions, feelings and beliefs in apologetic, diffident or self-effacing ways ■ Failing to express honestly your needs, wants, opinions, feelings and beliefs	■ Standing up for your own rights in such a way that you do not violate another person's rights ■ Expressing your needs, wants, opinions, feelings and beliefs in direct, honest and appropriate ways

This is a very important set of distinctions, as being assertive is often misunderstood as being 'aggressive', whereas in fact the two behaviours (and the assumptions underpinning them) are quite different.

7.2.1 Guidelines for assertive behaviour

Assertiveness is a skill that must be learned and practised over time. Some of the key principles of assertive behaviour are as follows.

Table 5.5   Assertive behaviours

Assertive behaviours	Comment
Respect your feelings, but manage them	■ If you are angry or anxious, breathe slowly, control your body language and speak calmly. ■ Don't use exaggerated language to label your feelings (eg 'angry' when you are only 'mildly annoyed'). ■ Keep your messages clear: if you've said 'yes' when you wanted to say 'no', don't start giving 'no' signals (eg sulking).
Say what you want, feel or think: directly, honestly and without games	■ Don't assume that others will know, or work out from vague hints, what it is that you really want. ■ Don't feel the need to justify or apologise: be simple and direct. ■ Don't be pushed into a decision: if you are hesitant about whether to say 'yes' or 'no', say so.
Be persistent	If you don't get a proper response, repeat your statement or request, without raising your voice (the 'broken record' technique). You have the right to be heard – but you must also respect the other person's response.

The Chartered Institute of Marketing

Assertive behaviours	Comment
Focus on the problem, not the person	■ Use 'I' statements expressing how *you* perceive and feel about the other person's behaviour, and focus on specifics (not exaggerated generalities). You are focusing on the problem and its impact on you – not attacking the other person. ■ It would be aggressive to say: 'You're always so inconsiderate: you make me angry.' It would be assertive to say: 'When you're late, I feel annoyed because it suggests to me that you don't care about my time.' This is particularly important in **giving criticism** constructively: describe the undesirable behaviour specifically and objectively; specify the change you want; and end on a positive note.
Acknowledge and encourage other points of view	■ Use 'I' statements to distinguish opinions from facts: 'As I see it…' ■ Show that you understand the other person's point of view, by summarising their argument. ■ Tackle parts of a view that you specifically disagree with, rather than globally rejecting it: 'I agree that it's a problem, but I don't think it's that damaging'. This is particularly important in **receiving criticism** constructively. The assertive response is to encourage specific, objective feedback: 'Can you give me an example? How do you think I could do that better?'
Express willingness to look for joint solutions	Expressions such as 'How can we make this work?' focus attention on **shared goals** (if only the desire to preserve a co-operative working relationship).

Assertiveness training is popularly seen as a prime means of remedying underachievement in women, or of helping women to avoid exploitation at work. It is likely to be a part of a 'Women Into Management' or similar training and education programme. The techniques and insights involved are likely to be of benefit to men as well, but it has been recognised that it is primarily women who are disadvantaged in Western society by the failure to distinguish between assertion and aggression, submission and conflict-avoidance.

7.3 Giving feedback

Team leaders have a key role in giving on-going performance feedback to team members, both informally and formally (as part of a performance management approach).

Feedback may be of two broad types:

■ **Motivational** feedback (praise, encouragement) is given to acknowledge, reward and encourage positive behaviour or performance by the team member. Its aim is to boost the team member's confidence.

■ **Developmental** feedback (constructive criticism, coaching or counselling) is given when an area of the team member's performance requires improvement, helping the individual to identify the problem and plan for change. Its aim is to increase the team member's competence.

7.3.1 Motivational feedback

Praise and recognition should not be underestimated as a reward and incentive: they are highly valued by employees – although they cost the manager nothing to give. Teamworking gurus like Blanchard & Bowles (2001) advocate 'keeping the accent on the positive':

■ Looking for (and rewarding) positive behaviours that reflect the purpose and values of the team
■ 'Catching people doing things right' (or even 'approximately right') instead of wrong
■ Redirecting people towards the goal, when they get things wrong, instead of punishing them
■ Linking all recognition ad rewards back to the team's purpose and goals

7.3.2 Developmental feedback

Some guidelines for giving constructive (developmental) feedback are as follows.

■ Investigate and check your facts before offering criticism: be prepared to coach for improvement

- Choose an appropriate time and place to give feedback; as close as possible after the event being criticised/praised; when the team member will be receptive; and ideally in private, to avoid possible embarrassment

- Clearly explain the positive, development purpose of the feedback

- Start with positives, where possible

- Focus on specific behaviours, actions and results – not generalisations, exaggerations ('you always...') or personality factors: your aim is to facilitate change.

- Gain the team member's cooperation: ask her how effectively she thinks she handled a situation, and invite her to work with you to solve the problem.

- Don't tackle large issues or lots of issues all at once: facilitate 'kaizen' (continuous small-step improvements)

- Close with positive encouragement and support.

7.4 Negotiating

Negotiating is covered in the syllabus in relation to negotiated budgets, but it is also worth mentioning here as a key interpersonal skill for leaders. Negotiation gurus Fisher *et al* (1999), among others, have pointed out that:

> 'Negotiation is a fact of life... Everyone negotiates something every day... A person negotiates with his spouse about where to go for dinner and with his child about when the lights go out. Negotiation is a basic means of getting what you want from others. It is a back-and-forth communication designed to reach an agreement when you and the other side have some interests that are shared and others that are opposed.'

Negotiation may be defined as: a process whereby two parties come together to confer, in a situation in which there is some conflict of interests between them, with a view to concluding a jointly acceptable agreement. Gennard & Judge (2003) describe this process as one of:

- **Purposeful persuasion**: whereby each party tries to persuade the other to accept its case or see its viewpoint.

- **Constructive compromise**: whereby both parties accept the need to move closer to each other's position, identifying the areas of common ground where there is room for concessions to be made.

In this broader sense (beyond the context of commercial or sales negotiations), negotiation can be seen as an interpersonal problem-solving technique, enabling managers to meet their objectives (as far as possible) in a conflict of interests with the team or other stakeholders, without damaging on-going relations between them. A team leader may need to negotiate:

- What objectives will be set and given priority (given the potentially differing needs of stakeholders), particularly in the management of strategic change

- Mutually acceptable terms and conditions of work

- Approaches to conflicts and problems that arise in the course of work: differences of values, expectations, interests, priorities or schedules; competition for scarce resources; and so on.

7.5 Influencing

> ▶ **Key term**
>
> **Influencing** is the process of applying some form of pressure in order to change other people's attitudes or behaviours: to secure their compliance (with requests), obedience (to orders), conformity (to norms or expectations) or commitment (to a shared vision).

Like negotiation, influencing is not mentioned explicitly in the syllabus, but is a key interpersonal skill for leaders (as we saw in our definitions of leadership in Chapter 4).

From your own experience (and other marketing studies), you may be aware that there are many forms of pressure that can be used to change people's minds or gain their co-operation: **persuasive arguments** (whether rational or emotional); **compelling goals or ideas** (as when we talk about 'influential' books or movies); the **desire to emulate** a role model; or the **desire to belong** to a group (and therefore to conform to its ideas and behaviours).

Power can also be applied to direct people's behaviour in various ways, because, as we saw in Chapter 4, it implies the right to do so (as in the case of a manager's positional authority), or the ability to offer (or withhold) something that individuals value enough that they are willing to comply.

7.5.1 Ethical influencing

Most modern writers on influencing recognise that influencing skills are 'dangerous', in that they allow people to manipulate or control others: coercing or tricking them into doing something they don't want to do. Gillen (1999) distinguishes clearly between what he calls 'manipulative' influencing and 'positive' (or ethical) influencing.

- **Manipulative influencing** uses tactics based on dishonest logic or negative emotion (such as fear or guilt). Such an approach seeks to dismiss or override the influencee's beliefs or interests, using tactics such as bullying, false logic, cajoling, bribing and emotional blackmail.

- **Positive influencing** is defined as 'non-manipulative, persuading behaviours that demonstrate that you are treating people openly, honestly and respectfully' – as befits a leader! A positive influencer seeks to understand the influencee's point of view (through questioning and active listening); allows the influencee to feel heard (through empathy); *then* seeks to help the other person to understand the alternative point of view (through clear, assertive communication); and finally invites or leads the influencee to agree (through rapport-building and persuasion).

Manipulative influencing can be effective in gaining agreement or compliance – in the short term. However, it tends to have negative side-effects such as resentment, unhelpfulness, and lack of ownership of what has been agreed. In contrast, positive influencing 'uses openness and honesty which show respect to the other person, and makes it easy for them to appreciate your point of view. If they accept your invitation to agree with you, their commitment is likely to be sustained into the future' (Gillen, 1999, p8).

7.5.2 Skills and techniques of leadership influence

Key skills and techniques for influencing include:

- **Rapport-building**: establishing a positive sense of relationship or connection with another person. 'Influencing is easier if the other person feels comfortable with you; if they feel they can trust you; if they feel you understand them' (Gillen, 1999, p64)

- **Active listening**, to understand the other person's viewpoint and feelings,

- **Using and interpreting body language,** to understand the interpersonal process (rather than merely the content of what is being said)

- **Expressing empathy** with (or understanding of) the other person's viewpoint and feelings

- **Communicating assertively** (as discussed earlier)

Persuasion is the term given to any means of exerting influence over people by means *other* than using authority or power. Persuasion pulls or leads people to change by bringing their beliefs and goals into alignment with those of the leader/influencer.

One key approach to persuasion is **logical argument**, usually supported by relevant and verifiable factual evidence. The demonstration of objectivity or fairness to both sides of an argument or question may also be used to enhance your credibility or 'believability' – since it takes the other party's objections into account. Logical argument is essentially a **facilitative approach**, whereby each step of the argument is clearly explained and linked. 'For someone to be convinced of something, the 'penny has to drop' in their mind. That is, it has to

make sense to *them*. No matter how obvious something is to you, if you want someone's help, co-operation or agreement, it has to be obvious to them.' (*ibid*, p9).

Facilitative techniques include: questions and answers; summarising each section of the argument; asking for feedback (checking understanding); and other forms of **active listening**. Above all, it requires sensitivity and flexibility to respond to signals of resistance, perplexity, readiness to move forward and so on.

A persuasive communication strategy is one which, essentially, appeals to the needs, goals and interests of the person being influenced. Persuasion is a form of motivation: if you can make it look as if aligning themselves with your viewpoint or plans will offer team members something of benefit to them, they will be more amenable to persuasion. This may take the form of positive reinforcement (offering satisfaction of a need or desire, or the solution to a problem) or negative reinforcement (confronting people with the potential negative outcomes of not agreeing or changing).

Extended Knowledge

If you want to focus further on assessing and improving your leadership, interpersonal and influencing skills, we recommend a number of very short, accessible and practical books.

Gillen, T. (2002) *Leadership Skills for Boosting Performance.* London, CIPD.

Gillen, T. (1999) *Agreed: Improve your powers of influence.* London, CIPD.

Bishop, S. (2000) *Develop your assertiveness.* 2nd edition. London, Sunday Times/ Kogan Page.

---

8 Managing remote teams

There has been increasing demand for managerial competence in working with (or within) different cultures in recent decades. Domestic skill shortages have encouraged international recruitment, supported by freedom of labour movement in blocs such as the European Economic Area. There has been a growth in multi-national and global corporations. Meanwhile, Information & Communication Technology (ICT) developments have facilitated virtual organisation and team-working regardless of location.

Marketing managers are increasingly likely to work in organisations that have multinational or multi-ethnic elements; or in another culture (eg via secondment or relocation to an international or regional office); or in 'virtual' teams that include members in other nations.

A number of issues may arise in managing teams whose members are from, or located in, other nations.

- Differences in **educational infrastructure** and opportunities may create wide differences in skills and qualifications, which may need to be harmonised in order to facilitate all-member contribution, and manage differences in expectations

- Differences in **technology infrastructure** between countries may create barriers to effective virtual team working: international offices may need to be supported with hardware or software tools

- **Language** differences may create barriers, where some team members are not equally fluent in the dominant language of the team, organisation or customer base

- **Legal and regulatory** differences (eg on health and safety, quality, intellectual property protection or employment protection) may create issues for people and performance management across national borders

- **Economic differences** between countries in which staff are employed may create issues of equity in team member rewards, in terms of market rates of pay, taxation rates, inflation rates and so on

- **Distance barriers** have been reduced by ICT developments: instant document transmission and data-sharing (via the e-mail and internet), virtual meetings and so on. However, there may still be issues of people working in different time zones and different seasons (eg for seasonal products and marketing campaigns)

- **Socio-cultural differences** are a potential source of divergence in work and management practices, values and assumptions, business etiquette, communication styles – and a wide variety of other factors.

8.1 International culture

Culture plays an important role in intra- and interorganisational communication. Large organisations tend to employ staff from a variety of national backgrounds. Naturally, they bring their own national/cultural approach to communication. Managers need to be aware of, and work with, these cultural differences.

8.1.1 Hofstede's cross-cultural analysis

Doole and Lowe (2004) present a summary of Hofstede's cross-cultural analysis of the influence of national culture on communication within a single global organisation. People from Northern European cultures (including people from English-speaking advanced industrial economies) communicate in a literal sense; that is, what is said, or written, is what is meant, so-called low-context cultures. In contrast are cultures where the context of the message gives meaning to the message. Who said it, how it was said, the context in which the message was delivered, all in combination must be used to decipher the meaning of a message, whether written or spoken, so-called high-context cultures.

Hofstede further researched the role of national culture within the organisation and identified five dimensions which he argued largely accounted for cross-cultural differences in people's belief systems and values. These he termed:

- Uncertainty avoidance
- Masculinity
- Individualism
- Power-distance
- Confucian dynamism

Individualism Versus Collectivism

(Examples: Individualistic = United States, Great Britain; Collectivistic = Pakistan, Taiwan)

Is the individual the basis of society or does society give meaning to the individual? The United States is the best example of a society in which individualistic traits are most pronounced. For example, differences are admired and the cult of individuals prospers most. Perhaps in direct contrast is the Chinese culture, where society's rights and responsibilities are dominant and individual needs are subservient. Here conformity is generally considered the norm.

Masculinity Versus Femininity

(Examples: Masculine = Japan, Italy; Feminine = Denmark, Sweden)

Masculine cultures emphasise 'assertiveness' compared to 'nurture' for feminine cultures. High masculine societies, whether individualistic like United States or collectivist like Japan, provide weaker people with, on average, less support whether from within the organisation or from society at large. People learn to admire the strong and to have a relatively negative view of the weak and dependent.

Power-Distance

(Examples: Low = Denmark, Austria; High = France, India)

Measures the extent to which individuals (society) tolerate an unequal distribution of power in organisations and in society as a whole. In high-power-distance organisations, superiors display their power and exercise it. Subordinates expect this behaviour and feel uncomfortable if they do not personally experience their superiors

displaying their status and power. In high-power-distance cultures, subordinates feel separated from one another: it is not easy to talk with higher-ranking people and real power tends to be concentrated at the top. In low-power-distance societies, members of organisations, and of society, tend to feel equal and relatively close to each other at work. Power is much more likely to be delegated in low-power-distance cultures.

Uncertainty Avoidance

(Examples: Low = Denmark, Sweden; High = Japan, France)

Measures the extent to which people tend to feel threatened by uncertain, ambiguous, risky or undefined situations. In cultures where uncertainty avoidance is high, organisations promote stable careers and produce rules and procedures which staff must follow (and which staff find comforting to follow). Hofstede argues that uncertainty avoidance is about reducing ambiguity and should not be confused with risk avoidance.

Confucian Dynamism

(Examples: Low = United States, Australia; High = China, Japan)

Measures the extent to which conformity according to 'position' is stable and elicits predictable behaviour between individuals. Behavioural attributes that are valued highly include obedience, deference, maintaining the status quo within organisational and social hierarchies and trouble-free social relations. Where you are in an organisational hierarchy predetermines the way you are expected to treat others and in turn the way you should be treated. Behaviour is much more predictable in Confucian cultures that exhibit high levels of Confucian dynamism.

THE REAL WORLD

Lessons From Building International Teams with Staff From Contrasting Cultures – Lenovo and IBM

The huge Chinese computer giant Lenovo's acquisition of the personal computer division of IBM for US$1.75 billion in 2004 was intended to generate huge potential benefits. IBM obviously had a global sales reach and tremendous international management expertise. It had become somewhat of a dinosaur with a highly conservative reputation. In contrast, the Chinese-focused Lenovo was, and is, highly innovative. Almost 10,000 people had to be bound together somehow as a result of this acquisition. For benefits to be realised, a huge team-building management problem had to be overcome. What was this?

The main purpose of the acquisition was for Lenovo to become a world player. To do this, Lenovo managers were required to acquire IBM skills and business culture. However, they first needed to have trust in the IBM staff who were supposed to help them develop.

IBM expats working in China had to operate with an Asian 'relationship' orientation. How could they do this? Spend a lot of informal time with colleagues: for example, outside working hours going 10-pin bowling or eating in restaurants. That would work on trust but to get networks working requires a focus not on the team but on customer needs. This provides a common focus on which co-operative teams are given direction and purpose and a context in which to grow. Collaboration between functional areas allows interfirm networks to develop, including communications networks. Team meetings across the two old organisations, and across areas of functionality, needed to be frequent and this is the context in which problems of managing and coping with change were discussed. This is especially important in Asian countries as such 'collectivistic' orientated societies (in contrast to 'individualistic' cultures) do not cope well with work-role ambiguity.

Contrasting corporate cultures are rooted deeply in the societies in which they are based. People who work in 'western' organisations tend to be highly focused on the job (so called 'task orientation'). This is in contrast to people in 'eastern' organisations, especially Asian organisations, who have the so-called relationship orientation. The focus of the merged organisations needed to develop a 'relationship' orientation for the business to succeed in the long-term, in addition to adopting the international, task orientation.

The problem with using expats from western societies in an Asian context is that they tend to have a task orientation and could ignore the knowledge transfer/training aspects of their work. Senior management must recognise this and ensure that a proportion of expat bonus payments is linked to skills and knowledge transfer to Chinese staff.

The Chartered Institute of Marketing

According to Fallon (2005), Chinese employees have too much faith in the successful operation of international markets and business systems and all too frequently fail to recognise that they themselves must implement and monitor these systems, as well as refine them. Traditional mini-MBA style approaches to training were adopted but found not to work in the Chinese context, without adjustment to the Chinese consensual, rather than western conflict, approach.

In short, the success of the whole enterprise rested on the building of effective multicultural teams where communication was regarded as crucial, as was building trust through socialising in leisure time and through approaches that included IBM staff adopting Chinese-directed approaches to management. Consequently, implementation of strategy was improved considerably. Fallon (2005) concludes that the approach reported has universal lessons for mergers and acquisitions between 'western' and 'eastern' organisations.

(Fallon M, 2005)

8.1.2 Trompenaars' and Hampden-Turner's seven-dimensional model

Trompenaars (1993) and subsequently with Hampden-Turner (1997) follow a functional approach like Hofstede in which the premise is that culture can systematically cause differences in behaviour between people from different countries.

Trompenaars and Hampden-Turner developed the 'seven dimensions of culture model' to analyse cultural differences and this also provides managers with some insight into the complexity of managing international teams. Readers of Hofstede's work will see connections between his work and the ideas of Trompenaars and Hampden-Turner who share a common general perspective. International experience working for Shell informs the authors' practitioner thinking in which they discuss the implications for managing or being managed, working together, building relationships, team working, negotiating and communicating with people from other cultures.

Trompenaars, and Hampden-Turner, explain how reconciling cultural differences will lead to competitive advantage.

Trompenaars's basic premise is that an understanding of the underlying values of different cultures leads to greater respect for diverse ways of operating and to the desire and skills for reconciling cultural differences to achieve business performance. Each one of the seven dimensions is presented below along with a summary definition.

Relationships with other people

1   **Universalism versus particularism**: Cultures with a universalistic tendency emphasis rules and drawing up of detailed contracts, for example, of employment, where particularistic cultures focus on the relationship between people. Here there is consideration of the rules versus relationships. Does the cultural emphasis on living by the rules – respect for law and so on – take precedence over personal relationships or *vice versa*?

2   **Collectivism (communitarianism) versus individualism**: Consideration of groups versus individuals. Cultures, for a variety of reasons, either tend to value self-orientation or group orientation. This can affect the decision-making process and the extent to which authority resides in an individual to make decisions. This can have a profound effect on working practice with widespread consultation favoured by a common orientation culture. There is a danger, for example, that this might be perceived as procrastination by those from an individualistic background. It is this type of understanding that can help support the development of co-operative relationships inside and between organisations where one or both individuals are inexperienced in working with multi-cultural teams.

3   **Neutral versus emotional (affective)**: This reflects the range of emotions that people are able to express openly. This could have a considerable impact upon the way in which products are promoted, and how relationships are established with customers and the organisations in which they operate.

4   **Specific versus diffuse**: Reflects how people will adjust their behaviour in different settings (specific). However, diffuse reflects the consistency of a person's relationships regardless of their situation. This has implications for managing staff, that is 'once the boss, always the boss', as opposed to specific where 'the boss is the boss in work and friend out of work'. This has a number of complexities, particularly for international working relationships.

5   **Achievement versus ascription**: This relates to how status is accorded. Status is achieved via years of experience, service, education and age. In other words, the 'respect your elders' scenario.

Orientation in time and attitude towards the environment

6   **Sequential time versus synchronic time**: This is essentially the difference between a sequence of events or simultaneous events. It is a question of being able to juggle a lot of balls in respect of time or needing to operate in a sequence to differentiate activities. This can indicate a lot about an individual's ability to work individually, within a team, on a self-motivated basis or on a delegated activity basis.

7   **High context and low context**: High-context behaviour will have a form of ritual behaviour in everyday life. Priorities, status and so on will be important. Low context will see little in the way of ritual behaviour and can generally cope with a number of events happening at any one time.
    Fons Trompenaars and Charles Hampden-Turner (2001) interviewed 15,000 managers in 28 countries to explore the cultural differences between what they called universalist societies and particularist societies. In universalist societies, people follow the rules and assume that the standards they support are the correct ones. Further, they believe that society works better if everyone conforms to them. Particularist societies believe that particular circumstances are more important than general rules, and that people's responses depend on circumstances and on the particular people involved. In universalist countries, written contracts are taken seriously. Teams of lawyers are employed to make sure that a contract is correctly drafted, and once signed it must be policed to ensure it is kept. Particularist countries think that the relationship is more important than the contract and that a written contract is not always necessary – the particular people and the particular situation matter more than the universal rules. Different cultures have different ways of coping with life, a different set of responses to the same underlying dilemmas. In Far Eastern cultures, books start 'at the back' and are read from right to left in vertical columns. To Westerners, this seems a reversal of normal practice. Managers need to display cross-cultural competence and reconcile cultural differences. Successful leaders are those who are flexible, sensitive and skilled enough to be able to ride what they call 'the waves of culture'.

THE REAL WORLD

The clash of two cultures?

Inevitably when two organisations work more closely together, in whatever form of business relationship, problems can arise. This can be due to differences in culture, sometimes national, sometimes corporate and sometimes a combination of the two. Culture appeared to be an issue with the merger of German car company Daimler-Benz with the US car maker Chrysler. The German car maker was motivated to merge partly to gain access to a broader product base which could be targeted at the emerging markets. Chrysler found the merger to be appealing, driven by concerns about over-capacity in car industry; they needed a partner to survive.

Potential issues emerged at the negotiation stage that are common in many mergers, eg the name of the new merged business and the location of headquarters, effectively defining the 'nationality' of the company. These appeared to be more deeply significant to the German business, possibly as a business that is seen by some as a company with a very long history that has been intertwined with the State. Daimler Chrysler became a German entity, and this created major morale issues in the US operations of the merged business, even affecting productivity.

Organisational cultural tensions took a long while to resolve. It has been suggested that the two organisations 'did not simply make cars differently, they lived in different worlds' (Badrtalei and Bates, 2007, p310). This was based on a wide variety of differences including executive compensation, provision of first class business travel, formal dress code and decision-making

processes. Differences were even as basic as the policy and practice of wine consumption at lunch time and allowance of smoking in the office. The German business offered executives comparably smaller compensation packages, but allowed more levels of management to travel first class and to have larger expense accounts. They operated in a much more formal work environment, including dress code, and routinely worked late rather than confining this to necessity.

Since the 1998 merger these cultural issues have probably been fundamental to the issues that have affected this 'troubled' business. Operational issues such as closing factories and sacking staff are relatively easier to address compared with more fundamental organisational characteristics that are related to culture.

(Adapted from Badrtalei, J. and Bates, D.L., 2007)

Extended knowledge

Badrtalei J., and Bates, D.L. 'Effect of organisational cultures on merges and acquisitions: the case of Daimler Chrysler' is well worth reading for the substantial detail provided on this merger. As a footnote to the merger, in May 2007 Daimler sold Chrysler to a private equity group.

8.2 Cultural differences in practice

Expressions of the various dimensions and orientations discussed in these models of culture will be very diverse, and specific to particular cultures. However, you should be alert to the possibility of different expectations and norms around practical issues such as:

- The style and formality/casualness of work dress
- Appropriate degrees of formality and deference in different contexts: use of titles, first or last name terms, honorific address (eg variants of 'doctor' are widely used as a courtesy in Europe); deference (to authority, seniority, expertise)
- Social distance or personal space preferred in face-to-face interactions
- The interpretation of body language, gestures, facial expressions and eye contact
- Social behaviours and business etiquette such as bowing, exchange of business cards, greeting styles
- The appropriate balance of task and social communication in business relationships
- The style and pace of decision-making (vote, consensus, autocratic)
- The nature of conflict and the aim and style of conflict management (willingness to challenge, fear of loss of face, reluctance to criticise authority figures)
- The role and status of women in business contexts
- The interpretation of gifts and hospitality as part of business dealings (social facilitation – or bribe?)

These expectations may have to be brought into the open and negotiated as part of a team 'contract': an agreed framework or strategy for how the team will work together.

8.3 Virtual teams

A virtual team is a group of people who are working together, even though they are not all in the same geographical location. Specifically, teams may be distributed for a variety of reasons:

- Organisation-wide projects or initiatives
- Alliances with different organisations, some of which may be in other countries
- Mergers and acquisitions
- Emerging markets in different geographic locations
- The desire of many people and government organisations for telecommuting

- The continuing need for business travel and information and communications technologies available to support this travel

- A need to reduce costs

- A need to reduce time-to-market

8.3.1 Types of Virtual Team

There are essentially four types of virtual team:

1. **Department Virtual Teams** are made up of people who all work for the same department but based in different locations, for example, a team of sales representatives working for the same manager but who spend most of their time out of the office or working from home. The team members have common objectives, work under the same day-to-day management and have a detailed understanding of each other's responsibilities and working conditions.

2. **Company Virtual Teams** comprising people who all work for the same company but within different departments and, most likely, locations. For example, a product development team formed from research and development, design, manufacturing, marketing and customer care divisions. Although the team members have an overriding shared goal – to produce a successful new product – they do not report to the same line of management and have different day-to-day roles and responsibilities. They are unlikely to know one another personally but will be used to working within the same corporate culture and have shared working conditions and hours.

3. **Organisation Virtual Teams** made up of members who do not all work for the same organisation. For example, a marketing team that works in partnership with an external agency responsible for carrying out creative work on their behalf. The team members will most likely have no existing relationship, work under different management and working conditions, have conflicting ideas about what their objectives should be and have no awareness of their colleagues' other responsibilities or big projects.

4. **Multiple Virtual Teams** made up of a mixture of virtual teams. For example, a cross-department team, all based in different locations, that also works with an external supplier based in another country. In addition to the issues highlighted above there will be more complex communication issues that will make it a difficult challenge for members of this team to co-ordinate their thoughts and ideas collectively.

Team members use communication technologies such as e-mail, videoconferencing and telephone more often than face-to-face meetings to communicate with each other. Common reasons for forming virtual teams are to integrate expertise from different locations, to save on travel time and travel costs, and to build relationships, shared understanding and shared identities across workplaces or organisations.

Virtual teams face both the same challenges as traditional teams and some unique ones such as those relating to communication technologies and working at a distance. The dispersion of team members can make it difficult to establish a strong team identity, and it can be more of a challenge for the team members to work towards a common goal. Examples of virtual teams include a team of people working at different geographic sites and a project team whose members telecommute.

It is changes in the nature of teams and not the use of technology that creates new challenges for team managers and members. Most 'virtual' teams operate in multiple modes including having face-to-face meetings when possible.

Managing a virtual team means managing the whole gamut of communication strategies and project management techniques as well as human and social processes in ways that support the team. Knowledge of group dynamics can help managers to understand what happens when people interact using new media.

Managers need to help virtual teams identify roles in the same way required of all teams. Virtual teams may need technical and specialists support in using different media. For all roles, virtual teams need to spend more

time being explicit about mutual expectations for facilitators, managers and members because the patterns of behaviour and dynamics of interaction are unfamiliar.

Virtual teams form and share knowledge on the basis of information pulled from individual members, not a centralised push. One goal is to find ways that support the transformation of individuals' personal knowledge into organisational knowledge. This means designing environments where all the individuals have incentives to share what they know.

Managers of virtual teams can support their teams by:

- Encouraging members to explore questions that matter including questions about how they are working together.

- Supporting the creation of some kind of shared space (the feeling that there is an infrastructure where people are working together).

- Facilitating the co-ordination of the technology, work processes and the formal organisation.

THE REAL WORLD

Virtual teams are having major problems and managing their progress has been a superlative challenge for most. When it comes down to online collaboration, team co-ordination and management, there are so many human-based variables at play, so many critical components to effective information exchange, workflow distribution and knowledge sharing, that delegating technology to take the full responsibility of the solution can only do so much to improve our collaboration and co-operation efficiency. Organisations face the need to analyse and comprehend which are the key obstacles to the successful management of effective online collaborative business networks. Virtual collaboration for networked business teams is a complex and challenging activity in which there are major important components to be accounted for. Virtual business teams **do not** operate like traditional physical teams, as their requirements reflect a whole new way of communicating, working collaboratively, sharing information and mutually supporting other team members.

The new technologies and approaches required to achieve this are completely alien to most of our present organisational culture. And this is why they fail. Co-operative processes are not the automatic results of implementing collaborative, real-time communication technologies, but the result of a carefully designed and systematically maintained virtual team development plan.

(Master New Media, 2012)

Seven things virtual teams can do to work better

1   Have face-to-face meetings with all the members as soon as possible after the team is formed.

2   Find ways of building trust between the team members.

3   Clearly define goals, roles and tasks.

4   Ensure all team members are trained in cultural awareness and interpersonal skills.

5   Encourage informal communication between team members.

6   Set standards for time taken to respond to communications and acceptable times to call those in different time zones.

7   Leaders of virtual teams need to be proactive in building the team, and should anticipate and resolve misunderstandings and conflicts before they are allowed to develop.

Difficult areas for dispersed teams include co-ordination and collaboration, and dealing with conflict and performance problems when team members cannot be observed directly.

9 Organisational culture

An organisation's culture must support it in aligning with the environment if successful strategies are to be pursued. However, as organisations develop and evolve, they tend to progress through a cultural life cycle. Stacey (2003) suggests that cultural evolution goes hand in hand with structural evolution.

Initially, a 'power' culture is appropriate when the organisation is in its infancy. It then becomes more appropriate for a 'role' culture to be implemented to operate a functional structure effectively and finally, as the organisation grows and expands, a divisional structure is used and in this context a 'task' culture is most appropriate.

What are these cultural types? Handy (1981) cited in Stacey (2003, p 65) provides a four-category organisational cultural classification:

1   **Power culture** – with the owner manager/entrepreneur acting with complete authority. Such people are risk takers and tend to see administrative processes and procedures as getting in the way. They are the source of power. They do not emanate from the organisational systems and procedures that legitimise action in larger, long established organisations.

2   **Role culture** – organisations are highly bureaucratic with people specialising on a functional basis. Order, predictability and hierarchy are important. Procedures, rules and regulations for them define the essence of the organisation and adherence to these is the essence of 'good' management.

3   **Task culture** – as the name suggests, these are highly focused on work, whether it is in terms of general work function and/or particular projects with which people are involved.

4   **Person culture** – is where personal goals, satisfaction and interest drive organisational behaviour. This is most commonly manifested in organisations and divisions where technical specialists predominate – for example, engineers, accountants, lawyers and so on. They see their work as a vehicle for personal expression rather than simply getting the job done.

Handy's classification approach is useful when considering most western-style business organisations. However, Burns (1996) suggests that it fails to accommodate Japanese organisations as they contain elements of each extreme. For example, Japanese companies have very tightly defined and highly structured jobs and this is particularly evident at the more junior levels in the organisation. Japanese organisations are very hierarchical and deferential, but in spite of this they exhibit initiative and creativity in problem-solving.

Summary

Teams and individuals implement organisation strategy and marketing plans. Implementation is supported by the classical planning approach through which both the plan, and the individual, is tasked with work activity and finally reviewed, to consider the extent to which objectives have been met. For organisations and teams, the marketing plan may be the subject of review, including staff identified to complete tasks by given dates. The individual's version of this marketing planning review is the annual or more frequent staff appraisal. Internal marketing can be an important device for supporting acceptance of changes in team and individual working practices including changes in terms of job enrichment and/or enlargement.

High-performing teams have, or strive to have, particular characteristics. An important characteristic is that people in these teams are highly motivated. A range of management theories is presented to explain the mechanism by which motivation is understood to work. Based on this thinking the ideas of job enrichment and job enlargement flourished, until people realised that 'one size fits all' did not apply universally, even though frequently, when trying to use motivation theories at the workplace. Another environment in which motivated staff can flourish is where individuals are not subject to intolerance that creates tensions in the workforce, perhaps most commonly in terms of ethnicity and gender. Consequently, diversity and discrimination are discussed.

The Chartered Institute of Marketing

Many teams are now separated geographically. Distance is just one aspect to consider when trying to ensure successful interfunctional co-ordination. Managing virtual teams, as well as their traditional counterparts, to perform is becoming increasingly necessary as well as common. Another major aspect of geographical distance is that team members can often be located in different national cultures, and possibly also be from different organisational cultures, where there has been a takeover or merger. Hofstede and Trompenaars provide helpful theories and dimensions of culture, which may be used to assess problems and issues in managing people from diverse cultures.

CHAPTER ROUNDUP

- High performing teams are measured by task performance, team functioning and member satisfaction to determine the effectiveness and efficiency

- Management of team effectiveness can be through various methods:
    - They should be flexible
    - Charles Handy defines a contingency theory
    - Knowledge management involves leveraging knowledge as an asset

- Structuring team work
    - Job design is how tasks and responsibilities are packaged together

- There are many theories of motivation, the main ones coming from McClelland, McGregor, Herzberg, Adams and Maslow
    - Job enlargement and job enrichment are generally regarded as good motivation tools

- When considering the management and development of teams lack of discrimination is essential, but care has to be taken to ensure local legislation is followed.

- A manager's interpersonal skills affect team effectiveness and are dependent upon:
    - Communication skills, encompassing feedback, negotiation and influence

- Remote teams may require different management, taking into account cultural differences particularly if dealing with international teams

FURTHER READING

Badrtalei, Jeff and Bates, Donald C (2001) Effect of organizational cultures on merges and acquisitions: the case of Daimler Chrysler. *International Journal of Management*, June, Vol24 (2), pp303-317.

Bishop, S. (2002) *Develop your assertiveness*. 2nd edition. London, Sunday Times/Kogan Page.

Gillen, T. (2002) *Leadership Skills for Boosting Performance*. London, CIPD.

Gillen, T. (1999) *Agreed: Improve your powers of influence.* London, CIPD.

Pink, D (2011) *Drive: The Surprising Truth About What Motivates Us*. Edinburgh, Canongate Books Ltd.

REFERENCES

Adair, J. (1984) *The Skills of Leadership*. Aldershot, Gower.

Adams, J.S. (1965). Inequity in social exchange. *In*: Berkowitz, L. (ed.) (1965) *Advances in Experimental Social Psychology*. New York, Academic Press.

Armstrong, M. (2004) *How to Be an Even Better Manager*. 6th edition. London, Kogan Page.

Armstrong, M. (2009) *A Handbook of Human Resource Management Practice*. 11th edition. London, Kogan Page.

Back, K. and Back, K. (1999) *Assertiveness at Work*. 3rd edition. Maidenhead, McGraw,Hill.

The Chartered Institute of Marketing

Badrtalei, J. and Bates, D. C. (2007) Effect of organizational cultures on merges and acquisitions: the case of Daimler Chrysler. *International Journal of Management*, June Vol24 (2), pp303-317.

Bishop, S. (2002) *Develop your assertiveness*. 2nd edition. London, Sunday Times/Kogan Page.

Blanchard, K. and Bowles, S. (2001) *High Five: the magic of working together*. London, Harper Collins Business.

Boddy, D. (2005) *Management: An Introduction*. 3rd edition. Harlow, FT Prentice Hall.

Boxhall, B.F. and Purcell, J. (2003) *Strategy and Human Resource Management*. Basingstoke, Palgrave Macmillan.

Burns, B. (1996). *Managing Change*. London Financial Times Management, pp106–120.

Christopher, M.G., *et al* (2002) *Relationship Marketing: Creating Stakeholder Value*. Oxford, Butterworth Heinemann.

Doole, I. and Lowe, R. (2004) *International Marketing Strategy: Analysis, Development and Implementation*. 4th edition. London, Thomson.

Drucker, P. (1955), *The Practice of Management*. London, Heinemann.

Drummond, G. and Ensor, J. (2001). *Strategic Marketing Planning and Control*. 2nd edition. Oxford, Butterworth-Heinemann.

Fallon, M. (2005) 'What can Lenovo IBM learn from other merged companies? *China Staff, Hong Kong*, February, 11(2): pp4–7.

Fisher, R. *et al* (1999) *Getting to Yes: Negotiating an agreement without giving in*. 2nd edition. London, Random House.

Gennard, J. and Judge, G. (2003) *Employee Relations*. 3rd edition. London, CIPD.

Gillen, T. (1999) *Agreed: Improve your powers of influence*. London, CIPD.

Gillen, T. (2002) *Leadership Skills for Boosting Performance*. London, CIPD.

Goldthorp, J.H. *et al* (1968) *The Affluent Worker: Industrial Attitudes and Behaviour*. Cambridge, Cambridge University Press.

Guirdham, M. (1996) *Interpersonal Skills at Work*. 2nd edition. Harlow, FT Prentice Hall.

Hackman, J.R. and Oldham, G.R. (1980) *Work Re-design*. Reading, MA, Addison Wesley.

Handy, C.B. (1993) *Understanding Organisations*. 4th edition. Harmondsworth, Penguin.

Herzberg, F. (1965) The Motivation to work among Finnish supervisors. *Personnel Psychology* 18(4), pp393–402.

Herzberg, F.W. (1966) *Work and the Nature of Man*. New York, Staples.

Herzberg, F. *et al* (1959) *The Motivation to work*. New York, John Wiley & Sons Inc.

Huczynski, A. and Buchanan, D. (2001) *Organizational Behaviour: An Introductory Text*. 4th edition. Harlow, FT Prentice Hall.

Janis, I.L. (1972) *Victims of Groupthink*. Boston, MA, Houghton Mifflin.

Jobber, D. (2001) *Principles and Practice of Marketing*. 3rd edition. McGraw-Hill, Maidenhead.

Jobber, D. (2007) *Principles and Practice of Marketing*. 5th edition. Maidenhead, McGraw Hill Education.

Katzenbach, J.R. and Smith, D.K. (1993) *The Wisdom of Teams: Creating the High Performance Organisation*. Boston, Harvard Business School.

Kolb, D. (1984) *Experiential Learning*. New York, Prentice Hall.

Lawler, E.E. (1969) Job design and employee motivation. *Personnel Psychology* 22, pp426–435.

Marchington, M. *et al* (2001) *Management Choice and Employee Voice*. London, CIPD.

Maslow, A.H. (1948) Some theoretical consequences of basic needs gratification. *Journal of Personality* 16(4), pp402–416.

Maslow, A. (1954) *Motivation and Personality*. New York, Harper & Row.

Master New Media (2012) http://www.masternewmedia.org [Accessed on 20 April 2012]

McClelland, D.C. (1953) *The Achievement Motive*. New York, Appleton-Century-Crofts.

McClelland, D. (1988) *Human Motivation*. Cambridge, Cambridge University Press.

McGregor, D. (1960) *The Human Side of Enterprise*. New York, McGraw Hill.

Ouchi, W.G. (1982) Theory Z: An Elaboration of Methodology and Findings. *Journal of Contemporary Business* 11(2), 27.

Peters, T.J. and Waterman, R.H. (1982) *In Search of Excellence*. New York, Harper Collins.

Pink, D (2011) *Drive: The Surprising Truth About What Motivates Us*. Edinburgh, Canongate Books Ltd.

Rackham, N. and Morgan, T. (1977) *Behaviour Analysis in Training*. Maidenhead, McGraw Hill.

Schein, E.H. (1985) *Organizational Culture and Leadership: A Dynamic View*. San Francisco, Jossey-Bass.

Schein, E.H. (1999) *The Corporate Culture Survival Guide*. San Francisco, Jossey-Bass Inc.

Stacey, R.D. (2003) *Strategic Management and Organizational Dynamics*. Harlow, Prentice-Hall.

Steiner, I. (1972) *Group Process and Productivity*. New York, Academic Press.

Taylor, F.W. (1911) *Principles of Scientific Management*. New York, Harper.

Trompenaars, F. (1993) *Riding the Waves of Culture: Understanding Cultural Diversity in Business*. London, Economist Books.

Trompenaars, F. and Hampden-Turner, C. (1997) *Riding the Waves of Culture: Understanding Cultural Diversity in Business*. 2nd edition. London, Nicholas Brealey.

Trompenaars, F. and Hampden-Turner, C. (2001). *Building Cross-cultural Competence: How to Create Wealth from Conflicting Values*. Chichester, Wiley.

Tuckman, B.W. (1965) Developmental sequences in small groups. *Psychological Bulletin*, Vol63, pp384–399.

Tuckman, B.W. and Jensen, M.A.C. (1977) Stages of small group development revisited. *Group and Organisational Studies*, Vol2, (4) pp419–427.

Vaill, P. (1989) *Managing as a Performing Art*. San Francisco, Jossey-Bass.

Vroom, V. (1964) *Work & Motivation*. New York, Wiley.

Wheelan, S.A. (1999) *Creating Effective Teams*. Thousand Oaks, Sage Publications.

Whetten, D. and Cameron, K. (2002) *Developing Management Skills*. 5th edition. New Jersey, Prentice Hall.

The Chartered
Institute of Marketing

1   What are the stages of group development in Tuckman's model?

2   What are the features of effective group communication?

3   Match the description with the name:

Name 1 = **Theory Y** / Name 2 = **Theory X**

Description A: _____ is the assumption that the average human being has an inherent dislike of work and will avoid it if (s)he can. People must therefore be coerced, controlled, directed and/or bribed or threatened with punishment in order to get them to expend adequate effort towards the achievement of organisational goals. This is quite acceptable to the worker, who prefers to be directed, wishes to avoid responsibility, has relatively little ambition and wants security above all.

Description B_____ is the assumption that the expenditure of physical and mental effort in work is as natural as play or rest. The average human being does not inherently dislike work, which can be a source of satisfaction. People can exercise self-direction and self-control to achieve objectives to which they are committed. The average human being learns, under proper conditions, not only to accept but to seek responsibility. The capacity to exercise a relatively high degree of imagination, ingenuity and creativity in the solution of organisational problems is widespread.

4   According to Maslow's hierarchy of needs, when does a 'need' cease to motivate?

5   What are the benefits of paying attention to employees?

ACTIVITY DEBRIEFS

Activity 5.1

Answer will depend on your own situation.

Activity 5.2

Self-actualisation: job challenge, task variety, development opportunities.

Activity 5.3

(a)   **Agenda change**. Propose the change to the team, and insist on getting a genuine response. If some members do not want to deal with the item, remind the meeting of the ground rules: consensus is required to put a new item on the agenda. It can be included in the next meeting.

(b)   **Leftover items**. The need here is to prevent frustration and loss of focus. You might assign each member an item and ask them to prepare and distribute information before the next meeting. Alternatively, you might keep a legible list of 'other agenda items', so no-one fears they will be forgotten.

(c)   **Late attendance**. The meeting should start on time, out of respect for the other team members. When the missing member arrives, this would be a good opportunity to summarise the discussion so far. If people are repeatedly late, however, this may need addressing.

1   Forming, storming, norming, performing, dorming and adjourning

2   Features of **effective group communication**, to be modelled, coached and supported by the leader, include:

- **Open, honest communication** – including the ability to deal with conflicts, issues and criticism openly, directly and fairly (without personal animosity or grudge-holding)

- **Task-relevant information sharing** (no withholding on a 'need to know' or 'knowledge is power' basis)

- **All-member participation** in meetings, discussions and decision-making. Equitable participation does not mean that all members will share *equally*, but that all members can get a fair hearing when they have something to say

- **Absence of artificial status barriers**, so that senior and junior members communicate with ease

- **Positive contributions** (giving/seeking information, suggests and opinions; encouraging and affirming others; being appropriately vulnerable; checking understanding; giving constructive feedback; summarising; explaining and so on) *outweigh* negative contributions (attacking, being defensive, difficulty stating, fault finding, interrupting or overriding others) and so on.

3   **Theory X** is the assumption that the average human being has an inherent dislike of work and will avoid it if (s)he can. People must therefore be coerced, controlled, directed and/nor bribed or threatened with punishment in order to get them to expend adequate effort towards the achievement of organisational goals. This is quite acceptable to the worker, who prefers to be directed, wishes to avoid responsibility, has relatively little ambition and wants security above all.

Theory Y is the assumption that the expenditure of physical and mental effort in work is as natural as play or rest. The average human being does not inherently dislike work, which can be a source of satisfaction. People can exercise self-direction and self-control to achieve objectives to which they are committed. The average human being learns, under proper conditions, not only to accept but to seek responsibility. The capacity to exercise a relatively high degree of imagination, ingenuity and creativity in the solution of organisational problems is widespread.

4   When it has been satisfied

5   The ability for individual employees to express dissatisfaction, solve problems within management and preserve working relationships.

The ability for employees collectively to express their needs and wishes in matters that affect them, providing a counterbalance to managerial power.

The ability for employees to contribute to management decisions, allowing the organisation to harness the expertise and commitment of workers to improve quality, productivity and work organisation.

The ability for employers and employees to demonstrate their intention to focus on shared goals, mutual interests and co-operative working relations, for the long-term benefit of the organisation and its people.

CHAPTER 6

Improving team performance

Introduction

Ultimately, we are interested in how to maximise the performance of teams. There are two dimensions to high performance namely:

1. The absence of problematic issues most commonly manifested in conflict.

2. Development in performance, that is, doing things better, rather than the removal of problems.

These are discussed in this chapter.

Topic list

Conflict in organisations	1
Developing the team	2
Managing change in teams	3
Overcoming resistance through internal marketing	4
Performance appraisal	5
Individual performance appraisal	6

2.7	Identify potential areas of team conflict, identifying causes and making recommendations for ways in which to overcome it:
	<ul><li>Sources of conflict – interpersonal, change, organisational, external environment</li><li>Cultural differences</li><li>Assess the impact of conflict both positively and negatively</li><li>Conflict resolution and management</li><li>Change management strategies</li></ul>
2.8	Critically assess levels of performance in order to identify poor performance and reasons for it and recommendations of how to overcome it including consideration of loyalty and motivation programmes:
	<ul><li>Performance management – measuring performance against objectives and standards and providing feedback</li><li>Appraisal and peer review including 360 degree feedback</li><li>Internal marketing – employee motivation and satisfaction, customer orientation and satisfaction, inter-functional co-ordination</li><li>Competency assessment and achievement</li></ul>

1 Conflict in organisations

▶ **Key term**

Conflict is inevitable but it can be minimised, diverted and/or resolved. Workplace conflict can lower morale and productivity, increase staff turnover and employee burnout, and add greatly to sick pay costs. Some conflicts are good and some not so good. Conflict occurs naturally when people interact, and teams, organisations and even individuals can grow as a result of the new ideas and the new ways of thinking that can emerge through conflict.

(Lankard Brown, 1998)

Different people have different ways of dealing with situations but in general, human beings share certain characteristics that are very similar – even across gender, racial and socio-economic lines.

- People tend to like it when people agree with them.
- People tend to not like it when people disagree with them.
- People tend to like other people who agree with them.
- People tend to dislike other people who disagree with them.
- People who are good at resolving conflicts look for some point of agreement and use good people skills to get others to see a different point of view.

Conflict occurs when individuals or groups do not obtain what they need or want and are seeking to look after their own self-interests. Sometimes the individual is not aware of the need and unconsciously starts to act out. Other times, the individual is very aware of what he or she wants and actively works at achieving the goal.

Conflict is destructive when it:

- Takes attention away from other important activities
- Undermines morale or self-concept
- Polarises people and groups, reducing co-operation
- Increases or sharpens difference

The Chartered
Institute of Marketing

Conflict is constructive when it:

- Results in clarification of important problems and issues
- Results in solutions to problems
- Involves people in resolving issues important to them
- Causes authentic communication
- Helps release emotion, anxiety and stress
- Builds co-operation among people through learning more about each other
- Makes people join in resolving the conflict
- Helps individuals develop understanding and skills.

1.1 Causes of conflict

Conflict can occur at many different levels: within an individual (eg over two incompatible goals); between two individuals (inter-personal conflict); between groups or teams (eg because of competition for influence or resources, incompatible goals and schedules, or different cultures); and between different levels in the organisation hierarchy (eg workers and their trade unions versus management, or 'turf wars' between levels of management).

1.1.1 Inter-group conflict

It is possible to identify a number of typical sources of conflict between functions and groups in organisations.

- **Goal incompatibility**. Conflict may be caused by differences in the goals of different groups (or individuals), where these have not been adequately aligned or integrated by management. In some cases, this may be institutionalised: for example, the conflict between trade unions and management.

- **Cultural incompatibility**. Different business functions often differ in style or culture. Different goals, attitudes, job roles, technical jargon and work styles create potential for lack of understanding and frustration. (This effect is often worsened as the size of the organisation increases, and informal cross-functional interaction is reduced.)

- **Interdependence and shared resources**. Conflict is more likely to occur when groups are dependent on each other to achieve their goals, and use shared resources in pursuit of these goals: decisions and actions by each group impacts on the work of the other.

- **Competition for limited or scarce resources**, such as budget, staff or space allocations. The reward system, for example, can cause conflict if rewards or incentives are (or are perceived to be) unfairly distributed.

- **Authority, power and status distribution**. Conflict is often caused by disputes about the boundaries of authority (where these are insufficiently clear) or by attempts by one group to enlarge its authority, prestige or status at the expense of another. (This is often described in terms of warfare: 'encroaching on someone else's territory', or 'empire building'.) There is often conflict between line functions and staff/advisory functions like HR, which may be resisted as 'interfering' by line managers – and may seek to bolster their authority by negative means, such as red-tape and rule enforcement.

- **Change and uncertainty**. Conflict can arise in times of change, where new problems arise. There may be conflicting views as to the need for, or approach to, change. Some units' interests may be affected positively and others' negatively. A temporary power vacuum may arise, causing competition.

- **The external environment** may pose threats, through change, competitive pressure, resource scarcity and so on. Again, there may be competing views as to the required response, or conflict arising as groups attempt to protect their own interests.

1.1.2 Conflict within the marketing team

Similar conflict may arise within a team, due to everyday factors such as the following:

- Disagreement about needs, goals, values, priorities and interests. This will be made worse by lack of direction from the leader as to what the team's purpose, values and goals are.

- Poor communication, creating potential negative assumptions, stereotypes and misunderstandings. The perceived withholding of information may also escalate conflict, as a hostile, competitive or 'political' tactic.

- Competition for scarce resources such as influence, office space, a share of rewards, the manager's recognition/attention and so on.

- Interpersonal issues :'personality clashes', aggression or domination by strong individuals, argumentative or manipulative communication styles – and, at worst, bullying or harassment, unchecked by the team leader.

- 'Hygiene' issues (in the technical sense used by Herzberg): dissatisfaction with the leadership, working conditions or pay, say, which can cause grievance against the organisation (or leader) and/or spill over into interpersonal conflict in the team (eg if some members feel others are being treated better).

1.2 A four-category perspective of team problems

Irwin *et al* (1974) suggest that teams encounter problems whether they are project teams or long-standing operational teams. They highlight four particular categories of problems that can result in conflict and poor performance that are interdependent, namely problems with:

1   Goals

2   Roles

3   Processes

4   Relationships

In their discussion of this topic, there is a sense that these four factors form a type of hierarchy of potential problems starting with the broadest directional issues to the detailed specific aspects of relationships between team members.

This includes team leader–team member relationships and relationships between team members within the team and between teams.

1.2.1 Goal problems

Goals may exist; however, they may be unclear or misunderstood by team members. In the worst situations, goals may be poorly specified and/or may be impossible to measure.

1.2.2 Role problems

Interdependence with the preceding problem is evident on reflection. If there is a lack of clarity about goals, how can there be any clarity about roles for individuals within the team? Once goals, or objectives, have been established, it is possible to clarify individual roles.

This, however, is fraught with many difficulties that are frequently overlooked. To what extent:

- Do individuals understand the boundaries of their roles?

- Do individuals understand the degree of freedom and authority within their roles?

- Does the individual's perception of their role match others' perception? This may lead to, 'Wasn't I supposed to do that' or 'That's my job'. Alternatively, 'I thought you were to do that'.

The Chartered Institute of Marketing

- Inevitably, roles interact or even overlap. An inability to cope effectively with this source of potential confusion or conflict will inevitably lead to sub-optimal team performance.

1.2.3 Process problems

There are many potential process issues. One perspective is to consider the more significant as concerned with:

- Decision-making
- Communications and meetings
- Leadership style

(a) Progress occurs only when decisions are taken. When more than one person is involved this becomes a process issue.

  – Who has the responsibility and ultimately the authority to make decisions?

  – What rights do team members have, especially in relation to the leader, with regard to decision-making?

  – Do all members of the team need to be consulted?

  – Perhaps people outside of the team must be included in some decisions.

(b) How does everyone know that a decision has been made? In other words, how can/will decisions be communicated?

It may be that, due to different roles within the team, and certainly as the team size grows, not every member of a team needs to know the outcome of every decision.

If consideration is not given to this with larger teams then individuals may suffer from information overload. In the more formal setting of meetings, who attends and how are unavoidable absences accommodated?

The team must also have an approach to meeting structure and process.

(c) The leader is in a very different category within the team. Leadership styles may tend towards the autocratic or inclusive. Sometimes the fact that inclusive, participative leadership styles have become more common has led some to place less influence on the role of the leader.

Group development is fundamentally influenced by the style of the leader and this in particular will affect the efficiency of processes. In a 'performing' team the leader is most likely to seek and accept feedback on two aspects of his/her leadership – fundamental style/approach and the impact their role is having on the team.

Team process problems

Analyse a team meeting that you have attended recently in which decisions were arrived at. Answer the following questions, which attempt to assess how many process problems you have.

- How were decisions taken? How many participated in making the decisions? How was disagreement resolved? Did only one person make each of the decisions in effect?

- Were you clear as to who had responsibility for each decision?

- Did everyone have the same amount of information to support their contribution to decision-making? Perhaps each team member had specialist information; however, did those bringing most information to the decision have greater influence?

- Was influence purely on the basis of perceived or actual job role or perhaps on the basis of seniority in the team/organisation?

- How was the meeting structured? Was there a clear agenda? How was timekeeping at the meeting?

- Was there a lot of pointless debate? Was there a feeling that the meeting, perhaps only in places, was going nowhere?

- What role did the 'leader' (however defined) take? To what extent did they let participants exert influence or did the leader use an autocratic approach? Obviously, the leader's approach may vary in the course of the meeting.

How many of the answers to these questions indicated the existence of process problems? If there are many, you must hold a team meeting specifically to address process problems, otherwise you can never become, or remain, a high-performing team.

1.2.4 Relationship problems

Relationship issues may be considered as potentially the lowest level, or most detailed aspect, of potential team problems. They are in fact the most intractable and hardest to resolve as they operate at the most personal level. The other three areas of potential team problems (already discussed) are 'external' to the individual. Individuals are generally not affected fundamentally by changes in any of these. However, relationship problems may be deep-seated. They may arise from a lack of mutual respect or trust in technical competence or judgement.

Unfortunately, 'relationships' may be regarded as an issue when in actual fact the problem is concerned with goals, roles or processes. For example, conflicts between individuals may be due to a failure to clarify goals or roles rather than any personal problem that individuals have with one another.

We understand that teams generally go through various phases, ideally culminating in operating as a 'performing' team. The concept of an evolution of team performance suggests that sub-optimal performance may be different in each phase. The application of the ideas of Irwin *et al* (1974) to the different stages of team development is apparent.

Table 6.1

Goals and priorities	Vital that goals and priorities are established at the *forming* stage. However, the team leader may not have established his/her authority. In addition, often the team must construct their own goals and priorities. At this stage in development, team members may argue forcibly about these issues and it is vital that this is resolved and members come to an agreement on a shared approach or accommodation that they can work with.
Roles	By the time the team gets to the *norming* stage, roles should be established. Prior to this, especially if a new member joins the team, expectations about the non-specified aspects of the role have to be reconciled – an obvious potential source of conflict.
Processes	Meetings can be a very good indicator of performance problems. At the *performing* stage, team members listen actively to one another and exhibit a high degree of collaboration resulting in rapid decision-making. Process issues, especially with regard to meetings and decision-making, will have been determined and members will be open to continuous modification and improvement. However, prior to this stage, for example at the *storming* stage, team members may be prone to talk and not to listen, time management may be poor with meeting time overruns and decision-making may be fairly crude, simply through majority voting.
Relationships	In a *performing* group, there will be a high level of trust and commitment between team members. Effective team functioning will build shared experience and engaging in co-operative behaviour will reinforce relationships and facilitate their development towards a deeper level.

Extended knowledge

Taking action to control sub-standard performance is the focus of the section in Brown (2002) on 'Controlling projects – taking action', pp74–87. Brown, M. (2002) *Project Management in a Week*. 3rd edition. London, Hodder and Stoughton.

1.3 Strategies for dealing with conflict

1   **Unusual non-verbal behaviour** can be an early warning sign of conflict. Ask people to verbalise their feelings wherever possible.

2   **Team development phase** – Use the Tuckman forming, storming, norming, performing model to anticipate conflict. Sometimes conflict is predictable because that is what happens at one particular phase of group development.

3   **Resort to authority** – This means bringing in someone using a legitimate power base (and perhaps other power bases) to lay down the law. This may be necessary if team members are playing destructive roles.

4   **Planning** – Techniques such as task scheduling, timelines and project diaries and meetings may provide an authoritative and neutral way of sequencing tasks to be performed by different individuals or subgroups, thus reducing potential for conflict.

5   **Use communication skills more effectively** – Sometimes it is best to utilise what you know about good communication skills. Try to control destructive role-playing. Acknowledge individuals by praising their input.

- Collaborating: I win, you win
- Compromising: win some/lose some
- Accommodating: I lose/you win
- Competing: I win/you lose
- Avoiding: no winners/no losers

1.4 Conflict handling styles

In an influential conflict management model, Thomas (1976) suggested that individuals' conflict-handling styles can be mapped on two dimensions, according to the **intentions** of the parties involved: *assertiveness* (the extent to which they try to satisfy their own concerns) and *co-operativeness* (the extent to which they try to satisfy the other party's concerns). The five styles identified by this matrix can be shown as follows.

Figure 6.1   Thomas' conflict handling styles

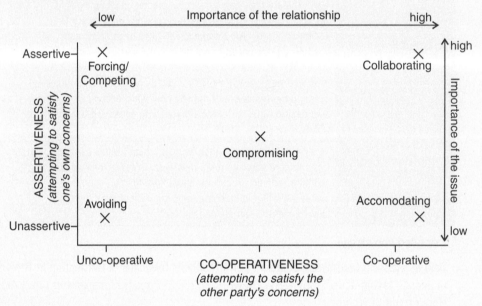

(Whetten and Cameron, 2002, p359)

The five styles can be compared as follows.

1.4.1 Collaborating

Fundamental premise – Teamwork and co-operation help everyone achieve their goals while also maintaining relationships.

Strategic philosophy – Working through differences will lead to creative solutions that will satisfy both the parties' concerns.

When to use:

- When there is a high level of trust.
- When you don't want to have full responsibility.
- When you want others to also have 'ownership' of solutions.
- When the people involved are willing to change their thinking as more information is found and new options are suggested.
- When you need to work through animosity and hard feelings.

Drawbacks:

- Takes lots of time and energy.
- Some may take advantage of other people's trust and openness.

1.4.2 Compromising

Fundamental premise – Winning something while losing a little is OK.

Strategic philosophy – Both ends are placed against the middle in an attempt to serve the 'common good' while ensuring each person can maintain something of their original position.

When to use:

- When people of equal status are equally committed to goals.
- When time can be saved by reaching intermediate settlements on individual parts of complex issues.
- When goals are moderately important.

Drawbacks:

- Important values and long-term objectives can be derailed in the process.
- May not work if initial demands are too great.
- Can create cynicism, especially if there is no commitment to honour the compromise solutions.

1.4.3 Accommodating

Fundamental premise – Working towards a common purpose is more important than any of the peripheral issues.

Strategic philosophy – Appease others by downplaying conflict, thus protecting the relationship.

When to use:

- When the issue is not as important to you as it is to the other person.
- When you know you can't win.
- When it's not the right time.
- When harmony is extremely important.
- When what the parties have in common is much more important than their differences.

Drawbacks:

- One's own ideas don't get attention.
- Credibility and influence can be lost.

1.4.4 Competing

Fundamental premise – Associates 'winning' a conflict with competition.

Strategic philosophy – When goals are extremely important, one must sometimes use power to win.

When to use:

- When you know you are right.
- When you need a quick decision.
- When a strong personality is trying to steamroller you.
- When you need to stand up for your rights.

Drawbacks:

- Can escalate conflict.
- Losers may retaliate.

1.4.5 Avoiding

Fundamental premise – This isn't the right time or place to address this issue.

Strategic philosophy – Avoids conflict by withdrawing, sidestepping or postponing.

When to use:

- When the conflict is small and relationships are at stake.
- When more important issues are pressing and you don't have time to deal with this.
- When you see no chance of getting your concerns met.
- When you are too emotionally involved and others around you can solve the conflict more successfully.
- When more information is needed.

Drawbacks:

- Important decisions may be made by default.
- Postponing sometimes makes matters worse.

(Culbert, 2002)

2 Developing the team

ACTIVITY 6.2

Here is an activity for evaluating your team. Circle the number that is appropriate for your team. What are your priorities for development? You could also ask a trusted colleague to complete a form like this about you so that you can compare your responses with his or her perceptions. If there were large gaps in perception you might want to pursue this further to understand why your perceptions are different.

Rating team development

How do you feel about your team's progress? (Circle rating).

1. Team purpose	I am uncertain	1	2	3	4	5	I am clear
2. Team membership	I am out	1	2	3	4	5	I am in
3. Communications	Very guarded	1	2	3	4	5	Very open
4. Team goals	Set from above	1	2	3	4	5	Emerged through team interaction
5. Use of team member's skills	Poor use	1	2	3	4	5	Good use
6. Support	Little help for individuals	1	2	3	4	5	High level of support for individuals
7. Conflict	Difficult issues are avoided	1	2	3	4	5	Problems are discussed openly and directly
8. Influence on decisions	By few members	1	2	3	4	5	By all members
9. Risk taking	Not encouraged	1	2	3	4	5	Encouraged and supported
10. Working on relationships with others	Little effort	1	2	3	4	5	High level of effort
11. Distribution of leadership	Limited	1	2	3	4	5	Shared
12. Useful feedback	Very little	1	2	3	4	5	Considerable

 The Chartered Institute of Marketing

Serco

Serco recognise that without employees who are qualified, motivated and inspired, they aren't able to maintain a successful business.

On the basis of this they state their commitment to communicating with, supporting, and developing all employees at Serco. The culture at Serco is based on clear values which are monitored to see how well they are put into practice. Serco also maintain contact with customers to ensure they are happy; this is a good way to protect the jobs of employees, and create new ones, whilst making sure they work with customers who enable them to treat their employees with dignity.

Information about the performance of Serco is shared with all staff, with technology investments to improve the communication across national boundaries. An organisation-wide approach to training and development in core values and skills has been established and these programmes are offered worldwide whilst finding ways to equip and encourage staff development.

'At the heart of our approach is our People Strategy. It's designed to ensure we continue to have the people and expertise we need to face today's challenges and those ahead of us. It recognises that a good business depends on good people.'

(Adapted from Serco, 2012)

3 Managing change in teams

3.1 Types and levels of change

For some people in some organisations, change is a positive and energising opportunity to make things better, to innovate and to adapt flexibly to changing customer demands and environmental challenges. For others, it means loss of security, loss of competence – perhaps, loss of livelihood.

The fact is that in today's fast-moving business environment – with its technological innovation, ever-heightening competition and increasingly fickle consumers – **change is inevitable**. The marketing function, for example, has been affected by change in various ways. Think of the emergence of new disciplines like relationship marketing, web marketing and viral marketing; the impact of new technology on products, media and marketing techniques; the globalisation of markets; and constantly changing consumer preferences and trends.

Some authors make a distinction between '**change**' (meaning incremental change) and '**transformation**' (or fundamental, sweeping, discontinuous change). Others use the terminology 'evolutionary' and 'revolutionary' change.

- **Evolutionary change** is a proactive approach, building on the existing situation or status quo, in small steps over a long period of time. This is the basis of business improvement strategies like continuous improvement or Kaizen, for example. Because it requires only realistic, small operational changes, it can be implemented from the 'bottom up', involving team members through suggestion schemes, quality circles and consultation. This makes it a particularly effective approach for building up organisational learning and responsiveness to change (such as shifting patterns of customer demand, sector dynamics and cultural change).

- **Revolutionary change** is often a reactive approach, responding to crisis or the need for a completely new way of doing things. It seeks to throw out the status quo and introduce radical transformation in a relatively short period of time. This is the basis of business improvement strategies such as Business Process Reengineering, for example: because it requires sweeping change across organisational structures and systems, it can only be implemented from the 'top down'. This makes it particularly effective where the status quo has become dysfunctional for organisational survival or growth, or where sudden challenges require a radical response (eg the introduction of a new technology, major competitor initiative or the need for restructuring following a merger).

3.2 The impact of change

Change may affect individuals in different ways: physically (eg different work methods); circumstantially (eg relocations, re-establishing work relationships with a new team); and psychologically (eg the requirement to learn new skills). Change may create feelings of disorientation before new circumstances have been assimilated. Uncertainty may lead to insecurity: especially acute in changes involving work, where there can be very great pressures for continuity and fast acclimatisation.

Individuals and teams often **resist change**, attempting to preserve the existing state of affairs against pressure to alter it. Sources of resistance to change in general may include age and inflexibility, strong needs for security and emotional instability. Sources of resistance to *particular* proposed changes, (eg in location, methods of working or pay structure), may include:

- **Attitudes or beliefs**, perhaps arising from cultural, religious or class influences (for example, resistance to changes in the law on Sunday trading)

- **Loyalty to the team and its norms**, perhaps with an accompanying rejection of other groups, or outsiders (for example, in the case of a relocation so that two departments share office space)

- **Habit, or past norms**. This can be a strong source of clinging to old ways, whether out of security needs, respect for tradition, or the belief that 'you can't teach an old dog new tricks' (for example, resistance to the introduction of new technology)

- **Politics** – in the sense of resisting changes that might weaken the power base of the individual or group or strengthen a rival's position

- The **way** in which any change is put forward and implemented

Not all change is resisted, however, and it is important to realise that the aim of change management is to create a **positive energy and impetus for change**. People's reactions to change depend on the type of change, the reason for change, and the way change is handled. Many people long for change at work, and have a wealth of ideas about how it should be achieved.

3.3 Planning for change

The major problem with implementation of change management strategies is failure to manage change successfully. Many people are resistant to change because they are familiar with the status quo and fear the consequences of change. Marketing managers need to be aware of the internal barriers that exist, and then need to develop strategies to overcome these barriers. In order to facilitate change it is necessary to have an understanding of how change occurs in organisations.

3.3.1 The three-step model

Lewin (1958), cited in Burnes (1996), suggested that in many cases change was very shortlived and after a period of time, group behaviour reverted back to its previous pattern. The idea of the three-step model is that change is regarded as permanent.

The three steps include:

1   Unfreezing the present level
2   Moving to the new level
3   Refreezing the new level

This model recognises that for new behaviour to be accepted, old behaviour has to be discarded.

3.3.2 The phases of planned change model

The three-step model provides a general framework for understanding the process of organisational change. However, it still adopts a rather broad approach and therefore a variety of models of planned change have been developed by a number of writers.

The Chartered Institute of Marketing

For example, Bullock and Battern (1958), cited in Burnes (1996), developed a four-phase model of planned change.

This model explains change in terms of two major dimensions: change phases and change processes. Change phases relates to the stages through which an organisation moves in planned change. Change processes are the means by which an organisation moves from one state to the next:

1   **Exploration stage**: This is the time during which organisations will decide whether to initiate any changes and, if so, allocate resources to the process. *The change processes* may include becoming aware of the need to change and searching for external assistance.

2   **Planning phase**: This involves understanding the organisation's problem. *The change processes* involved may include: searching for information to make the correct diagnosis of the problem, and establishing objectives and gaining support of key decision-makers.

3   **Action phase**: At this stage the changes are implemented. *The change processes* relate to the establishment of arrangements to manage the change process, gain staff support, evaluation of implementation and taking corrective action if necessary.

4   **Integration phase**: This relates to the development of a new status quo. The change processes include reinforcing new behaviour through reward systems, disseminating relevant information and encouraging improvements in all.

This model is useful because it makes a distinction between the phases of change and the methods of facilitating change.

3.3.3 The change process

Burnes (1996) provides a useful framework for analysing the change process. This suggests that the change process consists of three interlinked elements: objectives and outcomes, planning the change and people. This approach acknowledges the multi-dimensional approach to change management that is necessary.

Objectives

It is essential that objectives and outcomes are explicit and open. Burnes (1996) suggests that initially there will be a trigger that prompts the needs for change. From this clarity, agreement must be sought about who has the responsibility and authority to initiate change.

It will then be necessary to identify the assessment team who will clarify the problem/opportunity, investigate possible solutions, provide feedback and then present recommendations. If from this the decision is to go ahead, then it becomes necessary to begin the implementation process.

Planning the change

According to Burnes (1996), this involves six interrelated activities:

1   **Establishing a change management team**.

2   **Management structures** – special structures may be necessary to facilitate the change process.

3   **Activity planning** – constructing a schedule to the change programme.

4   **Commitment planning** – this involves identifying key people whose support is necessary for the successful implementation of change.

5   **Audit and post-audits** – it is essential that progress is carefully monitored to identify whether objectives are being met.

6   **Training** – this may be necessary to provide staff with the new skills they will need or it may involve providing training to help them facilitate change in themselves.

People

This is probably the most overlooked part of the change process. For change programmes to be successful, it is essential that all the people affected are involved and motivated and that their support is gained. This involves creating a willingness to change, involving people and sustaining the momentum:

- **Creating a willingness to change**: Many people will resist change because of the fear of the unknown. It is essential that people are made aware of the need for change and also provided with regular feedback on its progress. In order to create a positive attitude to change, organisations should publicise successful change and the benefits this has brought to employees. It is also essential that the concerns and fears of people should be taken seriously and addressed.

- **Involving people**: In order for people to 'buy into' the change process, they must be able to take ownership of the process rather than having it imposed upon them. This can be achieved through effective communication (two-way) and getting people involved.

- **Sustaining the momentum**: It is difficult to sustain the momentum of change particularly when those involved continue to be faced with the day-to-day pressures of meeting customer needs This can be helped by ensuring that sufficient resources are available, support is given to the 'change agents' and desired behaviour is reinforced through rewards. It is likely that change will result in the need for new skills and competencies and it is essential that staff are adequately trained, mentored, counselled or coached. It is apparent that the change process is a complex blend of objective setting, planning and people.

ACTIVITY 6.3

The change process

Identify a change that has been recently introduced. Evaluate the extent to which the company considered the three elements identified by Burnes (objectives, planning the change and people) when introducing the change. In particular, to what extent did the company acknowledge the importance of 'people'? If people were not involved and motivated, what were the implications of this?

3.4 Why change fails

Up to 80 per cent of change strategies fail. Robbins and Finley (1998) suggest a number of reasons as to why change initiatives fail:

- **It is the wrong idea**: No matter how well implemented, it is not going to succeed because it is inappropriate.

- **It is the right idea but the wrong time**: Maybe too soon after a failed change initiative, too few available resources, lack of top management support.

- **You are doing it for the wrong reasons**: Usually money. For example, companies initiate change as a means of increasing efficiencies and saving money.

- **It lacks authenticity**: Some companies are led to change not because it is inherently necessary but because it is in vogue: that is, everyone else is doing it.

- **Your reality contradicts your change**: For example, a company may announce a flattening of the organisational structure to encourage a more egalitarian culture. However, the reality is far from that – the old practices such as separate dining rooms for managers and workers send out stronger messages that in fact nothing has changed. This often leads to cynicism and distrust in the organisation.

- **You have the wrong leader**: One cannot underplay the role of a strong leader that inspires and motivates staff. It is essential that the leader is compatible with the culture of the company or else this may result in conflict.

- **Change for change's sake**: Senior management initiate change to alleviate the boredom of everyday life. They thrive on creating turmoil and even gain personal satisfaction from this turmoil.

- **People are not prepared or convinced**: In the short term, this suggests the need for training and communication to encourage people to buy into the new ideas. In the long term, it is probably more of an issue of corporate culture.
- **Bad luck**: Contingencies that are not planned for. For example, terrorist attacks, natural disasters, death of a senior manager.
- **There is nothing you can do**: In some cases, there may be nothing anyone can do to stem the rising tide of failure.

ACTIVITY 6.4

Reasons why change fails

Thinking about your company (or one with which you are familiar), identify the change initiatives that have been unsuccessful, and referring to the list above identify why this was the case. What actions could have been taken, if any, to facilitate the change process?

Beer *et al* (1990) suggest that for successful corporate change there are three interrelated factors:

1 **Co-ordination (teamwork)** – within and between departments
2 **Commitment** – high levels are required to ensure co-operation and co-ordination
3 **New competencies** – such as analytical, interpersonal skills are essential

They believe that many company-wide change programmes fail because they do not address all the three factors. Companies can try and avoid the problems associated with pragmatic change by adopting a 'task alignment' perspective, that is, 'by focusing on reorganising employees' roles, responsibilities and relationships to solve specific business problems'. This in turn will shape new attitudes and ideas.

ACTIVITY 6.5

Success of change programmes

Consider at least three changes that have been introduced in your company in the last 12–18 months. How successful have they been? Consider the reasons as to why they succeeded or failed.

3.5 Adapting to change

The development of a culture that embraces change is an essential ingredient of successful implementation. The transition curve can help in understanding how people adapt to change (Figure 6.2).

This model is useful because it illustrates that eventually people will internalise the new status quo (or will have left the organisation). Adapting to change can be a very painful process and the expression of anger and frustration is a natural part of this adaptation. The implication for marketers is that the acceptance of major changes in working practices and responsibilities will take time.

Figure 6.2   Reaction to change

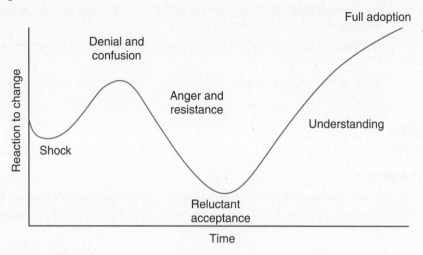

(Adapted from Wilson, 1992).

ACTIVITY 6.6

Managing change

Select one example of change that has been instigated within your organisation. To what extent did the model in Figure 6.2 fit your experiences of this change? How can managers use this model to their advantage?

3.6 Factors critical for success

According to Stewart and Kringas (2003), the success of change programmes depends on a number of factors:

- An appropriate change model
- Effective leadership
- Sufficient resources
- Attention to communication

Table 6.2   Factors contributing to successful implementation

Factor	Comment
Leadership	A strong and effective leader who is able to motivate and build teams is an essential ingredient for successful implementation.
Culture	Culture refers to the shared values and beliefs. If a plan goes against the dominant culture, it is likely the plan will fail, unless support is gained via internal marketing.
Structure	Organisational structures not only denote levels of responsibility but also facilitates communication. Communication is a key aspect of implementation, and organisations must ensure that the structures do not act as barriers to effective communication.
Resources	Appropriate levels of resources should be available – time, money and staff.
Control	Effective controls should be established to measure the progress and success of plans.
Skills	Skills necessary for successful implementation include technical/marketing skills, HRM skills and project management skills.
Strategy	An appropriate and relevant strategy must be communicated to all participants.
Systems	Effective systems should be in place. For example, marketing information systems that generate relevant and timely information.

(Adapted from Drummond and Ensor, 2001, p150)

The Chartered
Institute of Marketing

Drummond *et al* (2007) identify a number of factors that will contribute to the successful implementation of plans and can therefore be applied to implementing change programmes. These are illustrated in Table 6.2.

These factors are embodied in the 7-S model developed by McKinsey & Co., as illustrated in Figure 6.3. This model consists of two categories of factors:

1   **Soft or HRM aspects** – style, staff, shared values and skills
2   **Hard or process aspects** – strategy, structure and systems

Implementation strategies focus all too often on the hard or process aspects and ignore the very real 'soft' aspects that must be addressed if implementation strategies are to succeed.

Figure 6.3   The 7-S model developed by McKinsey & Co.

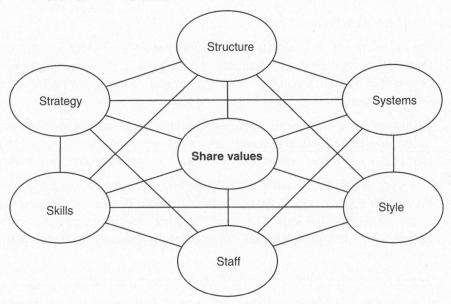

4 Overcoming resistance through internal marketing

Internal marketing can be used to facilitate the change process and overcome resistance to change. This section discusses how this happens.

▶ **Key term**

Internal Marketing (IM) according to Berry (1981), 'The most important contribution the marketing department can make is to be exceptionally clever in getting everyone else in the organisation to practice marketing.'
This is essentially what internal marketing (IM) is concerned with.
It is more of a management philosophy and strategy than a marketing function.

Gronroös (1990) identified two separate but integrated elements of internal marketing: attitude management and communications management. Attitude management is associated with motivating employees to buy into the organisation's goals while communications management involves providing and managing the information that employees need to perform effectively.

Internal marketing can play a key role in the implementation of plans. It is concerned with adopting the principles and practices of external marketing to the internal market. Figure 6.4 illustrates that there are three types of marketing that occur within an organisation.

Figure 6.4   Three types of marketing

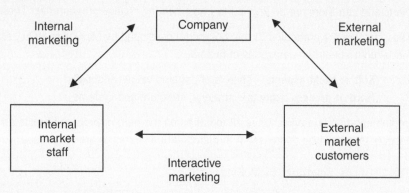

(Adapted from Kotler *et al,* 1999)

The success of external marketing lies in the ability of the organisation to satisfy the needs of the customer. Organisations are dependent on their staff to achieve this, particularly in high customer-contact service businesses. Therefore, successful internal marketing is increasingly being seen as a prerequisite for effective external marketing.

Internal marketing suggests that employees should be treated as internal customers, and marketing plans need to be 'marketed' internally to gain acceptance and to ensure that employees understand the rationale behind the plans, can see how they can contribute to the success of the plan and, importantly, 'buy into' the plan.

This is not an easy task. A survey of employees in British companies with 1,000 people or more, published by the Marketing & Communications Agency (MCA) and MORI, shows the scope of the challenge. The majority of employees said they feel undervalued, uninvolved and lack confidence in their organisation's leaders and vision (Mazur, 2001). Employees who lack motivation and confidence in their organisation are unlikely to buy into new ideas readily.

Internal marketing can play an important role in managing innovation.

There is no single unified definition of what is meant by internal marketing. However, there is general a agreement that internal marketing involves a planned effort to overcome organisational resistance to change and to align, motivate and integrate employees towards the effective implementation of corporate and functional strategies (Ahmed and Rafiq, 1993). It is likely that any change in strategy will require internal marketing to overcome organisational resistance and to help motivate staff.

Ahmed and Rafiq (2002) have undertaken an extensive review of internal marketing and from this they have identified five main elements of internal marketing:

1   **Employee motivation and satisfaction**: Internal marketing acts as a vehicle for staff acquisition, motivation and retention, which in turn leads to increased productivity and external service quality.

2   **Customer orientation and customer satisfaction**: Internal marketing can promote customer-orientated behaviour among staff.

3   **Interfunctional co-ordination and integration**: These are key elements of a market orientation as identified by Narver and Slater (1990). Internal marketing can be used to co-ordinate the efforts of the different functions in an organisation.

4   **Marketing-like approach to the above**: Other tools can be used to achieve the above. However, internal marketing relies on achieving these through the use of marketing principles and tools.

5   **Implementation of specific corporate or functional strategies**: Piercy (2002) suggests that internal marketing plays a crucial role in the implementation of strategic change by ensuring understanding and support for the strategies and also for removing barriers to change.

Ahmed and Rafiq (2002, p11) produced the following definition of internal marketing that encompasses all of the five elements above:

'Internal marketing is a planned effort using a marketing-like approach directed at motivating employees, for implementing and integrating organizational strategies towards customer orientation.'

Extended knowledge

See Chapters 1 and 2 of Ahmed and Rafiq (2002) for a more detailed discussion of what internal marketing is and how it works.

THE REAL WORLD

Internal marketing – not just corporate mantras

It is more commonly accepted that brands and marketing are no longer the sole preserve of marketers. It makes sense that everyone who represents the brand needs to have a very clear idea of the brand and what it stands for. Many organisations, for example BT, Cadbury Schweppes and Unilever, have developed ever more sophisticated internal marketing programmes to ensure that the message gets through to their own staff. Marketers as experts in communicating with external customers need to be responsible for communicating the message internally in conjunction with HR, who can provide advice on internal communication channels and approaches. However, all too many consider they have discharged their internal marketing duties when staff have completed a fairly dull training session that equips them to quote a few organisational mantras.

Internal marketing needs to operate at a much more sophisticated level, educating staff in the negative perceptions customers have of the sector in which they operate. For example, in the car industry, people frequently like the cars but hate the way they are sold, especially the lack of transparency in pricing. In addition, many in the industry still take a macho perspective in their approach to discussing their products that alienates many customers, especially females. Training needs to address this and ensure that the brand remains relevant to potential and existing customers. It is essential that the brand experience is consistent with the brand message.

Ensuring staff understand brand values and corporate history is an important part of the work of the Honda marketing department. Staff even receive a detailed corporate handbook on joining that has been produced by the company's relationship marketing agency. The thinking is that in providing people with a deeper understanding of the brand and its values they will buy into the brand and in turn become very effective brand ambassadors. If staff are going to be responsible for communicating the brand to customers then the more complete their understanding the better.

(Based on, and adapted from, Anonymous, 2006)

4.1 The Internal marketing plan

The internal marketing plan should take the same format as an external marketing plan with objectives, strategy, market segmentation, marketing mix programmes and evaluation.

- Where are we now?
- Where do we want to be? (objective setting)
- How do we get there?
- How do we ensure/ check we have arrived?

4.1.1 Internal market segmentation

Internal markets could be segmented in a number of different ways, such as by job function, role or location. However, these methods may not be the most appropriate. It may be useful to segment according to the extent to which people are likely to accept the proposed change. Jobber (2001) suggests that three different segments can be identified:

1 **Supporters** – likely to gain from the change
2 **Neutrals** – will neither gain nor lose
3 **Opposers** – likely to lose from the change or are traditional opponents

Robbins and Finley (1998) categorise people according to their attitude to change. On one end of the scale, there are those people who not only accept change readily but are also naturally proactive and seek out change. This group of people help to drive organisations forward because they embrace change willingly, as well as initiate it. At the other end of the continuum, there are those people who are largely reactive and resist change. This group of people can be the death of any change initiative. This may be a useful way of segmenting employees. Organisations will have to expend differing amounts of resources and use different strategies for each group.

Christopher *et al* (2002, p 109) suggest an alternative way of segmenting internal customers, according to **how close they are to external customers**:

- **Contactors** have frequent or regular customer contact and are typically heavily involved with conventional marketing activities (eg sales or customer service roles). They need to be well versed in the firm's marketing strategies, and trained, prepared and motivated to service customers on a day-to-day basis in a responsive manner.

- **Modifiers** are not directly involved with conventional marketing activities, but still have frequent contact with customers (eg receptionists, switchboard, the credit department). These people need a clear view of the organisation's marketing strategy and the importance of being responsive to customers' needs.

- **Influencers** are involved with the traditional elements of marketing, but have little or no direct customer contact (eg in product development or market research). Companies must ensure that these people develop a sense of customer responsiveness, as they influence the total value offering to the customer.

- **Isolateds** are support functions that have neither direct customer contact nor marketing input – but whose activities nevertheless affect the organisation's performance (eg purchasing, HR and data processing). Such staff need to be sensitive to the needs of *internal* customers as well as their role in the chain that delivers value to customers. Gummesson (2002) uses the term 'part-time marketers' to describe such employees.

A separate marketing mix can then be developed for each of these segments. It may also be possible to identify influential individuals that are opinion leaders.

ACTIVITY 6.7

- Draw up Christopher *et al*'s internal market segments as a two-dimensional matrix (like the power/interest matrix, say), using the two dimensions mentioned in our explanations.

- List examples of specific departments or job roles in your own organisation that correspond to each segment, building on the examples we have already given.

4.1.2 Internal marketing execution

Successful execution of the internal plan is reliant on three key skills (Jobber, 2001, p 658):

1   **Persuasion** – The ability to develop a persuasive argument and to support words with action.

2   **Negotiation** – It is likely that some negotiations will have to take place so that all parties are happy.

3   **Politics** – Organisations are made up of people, all with their own personal agendas. Therefore, it is essential that the sources of power are identified and used to help implement the plan.

4.1.3 Internal marketing evaluation

In order to evaluate the success of internal marketing programmes, appropriate measures have to be used, such as:

- The extent of support of key players
- Employee satisfaction levels

The Chartered
Institute of Marketing

- Reduced customer complaints
- Higher customer satisfaction scores.

Many companies are now conducting regular surveys to monitor levels of staff motivation, acceptance of the marketing concept and perceptions of the organisation. In addition, it could be argued that if internal marketing is being effective then it should be having an impact on external marketing.

By measuring levels of customer satisfaction and numbers of customer complaints, it may give an indication of the success of internal marketing programmes.

4.1.4 Potential problems

There are a number of potential problems associated with internal marketing. For example:

- Opposers create convincing counter arguments.

- Insufficient time to implement effective internal plans.

- High staff turnover that causes problems in ensuring all staff is involved.

- Low-paid shop (front-line) staff may result in a 'Why should I bother?' attitude.

- Cost – internal marketing programmes can be costly and many organisations are still slow to recognise their importance. Staff training and other solutions can be very expensive and companies have to recognise that there may be diminishing returns on their investment in IM. It is essential that they recognise the optimal level, not necessarily the desired level.

Piercy (2002), Chapter 14, 'Implementing Market Strategies', provides an excellent discussion of internal marketing.

ACTIVITY 6.8

Ahmed and Rafiq (2002) suggest a multi-level model of internal marketing that provides a framework for understanding how implementation of strategy can be created by deploying the internal marketing mix using marketing research, segmentation and positioning. Ahmed and Rafiq (2002) present a case illustration of their multi-level model of internal marketing for Pearl Assurance on pages 47–54. Read the discussion of this model on pages 37–44 and then produce your own model for your own organisation similar to that on page 50.

It is also important to recognise that internal marketing cannot alone solve all employee-related and customer satisfaction problems. In some cases, solutions lie more in ensuring that the right staff are recruited to the right positions in sufficient numbers and that they are adequately trained and motivated.

THE REAL WORLD

Merger of Lloyds Bank and TSB

The merger of Lloyds Bank and TSB could potentially have caused great problems with staff morale. In order to try and manage this momentous change, an internal marketing campaign was carried out by Jack Morton Worldwide. Their task was to unite the 77,000 staff from the two companies and to rebrand the merged company as Lloyds TSB. The campaign consisted of two stages: first, a trial of the jointly branded bank was established in Norwich; and second, an event to present the rationale behind the merger was held in Birmingham.

Many members of staff visited the pilot branch and feedback from this was used to help refine the messages to be used in the internal campaign. Over 4,000 cash machines, 2,300 branches and 40,000 uniforms then had to be rebranded.

It was realised that if the new brand values were to be communicated effectively to external customers, the first need was to communicate these to its employees to ensure they were delivering consistent brand images.

Five thousand members of staff, each representing 15 people, were nominated as 'pathfinders' and attended the live event in Birmingham – 'Your Life. Your Bank'. They were tasked with taking the message back to the branches. The presentation focused on explaining the rationale behind the merger, revealing the new blue and green corporate identity and explaining the new brand values with the objective being to gain staff commitment. The presentation culminated in a live concert by the Corrs, who also provided the music for Lloyds TSB's advertising campaign.

Afterwards the information was cascaded down through the entire organisation. Extensive research was undertaken by an external consultant to evaluate the process. According to the Managing Director of Jack Morton Worldwide, 'The research concluded that the event was a huge success, that it met its objectives and that there was some change in all areas. The staff felt better informed about the changes, the values of the bank and had greater pride in it.'

(Adapted from Benady, 2001)

Extended knowledge

For further discussion of the tools of internal marketing, see Ahmed and Rafiq (2002), Chapter 3. This chapter includes interesting case studies of Sainsbury's and Pearl Assurance.

ACTIVITY 6.9

Internal marketing

To what extent do you think your organisation has embraced the concept of internal marketing?

What impact does this have on its external marketing activities?

How has your company embraced technology (for example, an intranet in an attempt to improve their internal marketing/communications)? How effective is this strategy?

4.2 Employee branding

> ▶ **Key terms**
>
> Minchington (2005) defines your **employer brand** as 'the image of your organisation as a 'great place to work' in the mind of current employees and key stakeholders in the external market (active and passive candidates, clients, customers and other key stakeholders). The art and science of employer branding is therefore concerned with the attraction, engagement and retention of initiatives targeted at enhancing your company's **employer brand**.'
>
> **Employee branding** is an indirect branding effect using company employees to help characterise the company's **employer brand**. In other words, this is a way of helping your brand through good word-of-mouth by the people who work for you.
>
> (Anon, 2011)

Despite many organisations heralding that their employees are their biggest asset, they are often overlooked as a key target audience. Companies have spent millions on building their external brands and developing customer relationship strategies and yet have largely failed to explain to the very people they rely on to deliver the service, the rationale for the strategy and the important role they play.

Even in the most customer-focused companies a minority of staff act as 'brand champions'. Others add no value to the brand because they do not engage with it and the worst-case scenario is when staff actually act as brand saboteurs by actually criticising the company publicly (Simms, 2003). There has been an increased popularity in 'employer branding' where marketers 'attempt to adapt the tools and techniques traditionally used to motivate and engage customers, to secure the engagement and commitment of an internal audience' (Simms, 2003).

Increasingly, organisations are recognising that one of their greatest untapped assets is their own employees and that getting staff to act as brand ambassadors is one of the few things competitors cannot directly copy.

The Chartered Institute of Marketing

Internal marketing is therefore important not only to ensure that staff buy into plans but also to transfer employees themselves into a source of competitive advantage. Internal marketing should be seen as complementary to external marketing. An important goal of an employee branding campaign is similar to that of an external campaign, to create an emotional connection with the company.

There is evidence to suggest that many companies are not in a position to deliver their brand experience because of insufficient internal marketing. Intercommunic 8, an internal communications agency, conducted research with more than 1,000 people in both the private and the public sectors. They found that there was a gap between what is promised to external customers via external communications and what is delivered by staff.

This is particularly of issue as we move further into a service-based economy. The research revealed that 37 per cent of respondents felt that the communication they received was inadequate in helping them to understand what their organisation's values and brand meant. This 'yawning gap' between what is promised and what is delivered has a direct effect on a customer's relationship with that brand. The research revealed that the value of internal communication in improving company performance is best implemented by the retail sector (Anon, 2003).

Unfortunately, in most companies, internal marketing is done badly, if at all. Most managers realise there is a need to keep staff informed of the company's strategy; however, few appreciate the importance of convincing them of the brand's uniqueness. Employees can enhance a brand's reputation with external customers and when employees also believe in the brand, customers are more likely to experience the brand in the way that the company has intended.

Extended knowledge

For further discussion of how to empower staff, read Chapter 5 of Ahmed and Rafiq (2002).

THE REAL WORLD

Employee branding

B&Q

An employer brand manager has been employed ('great place to work manager') to cut across HR and Marketing divisions. A distinct culture has evolved over the last 30 years that is built on its employees being brand ambassadors. Staff are used in all B&Q advertising and they have a well-known strategy of appointing over-50s. Each morning an 'Energize' session is held to encourage staff to work together and express their opinions about the store. At the centre of its business are five core values; a down-to-earth approach, respect for people, being customer-driven, being positive and striving to do better. These are the values that it wants its employees to work towards. Ensuring brand consistency is a huge challenge due to the size of the business and the geographical distance of its employees – around 22, 000 in 286 stores.

Carlsberg-Tetley

Marketing and corporate communications are responsible for the 'education and engagement of staff in the brands' at Carlsberg-Tetley. Consumers are particularly interested in their product range and it is therefore essential that the 2500 employees are well informed and act as brand ambassadors by communicating the right messages. Staff are regarded as a key target audience and have the opportunity to improve their knowledge and skills through an 'innovative and interactive' marketing-led training programme. 'Brand days' are held prior to the launch of new/revitalized brands, where staff are given the opportunity to sample the products and enter competitions. Staff have the opportunity to see and discuss advertising campaigns and participate in internal promotions linked into key rugby or football sponsorships.

(Adapted from Simms, 2003).

Extended knowledge

There is an interesting and extremely relevant discussion of internal marketing by Colin Mitchell in the *Harvard Business Review* (January 2002), pp 99–105. This article outlines key principles of internal marketing and provides many relevant examples.

Ahmed and Rafiq (2002), Chapter 4 provides a comprehensive discussion of the relationship between HRM and internal marketing.

4.3 Internal marketing communications (IMC)

The boundary between external and internal stakeholders is not as clear as one may first think, and may be should not even be considered as a boundary. For example, there has been an increasing trend towards more flexible working practices, such as part-time workers, temporary staff, consultants and so on, and these people spread themselves across organisational borders.

In addition, stakeholders may assume multiple roles in relation to the organisation, such as employee, customer, financial stakeholder and so on. For example, an employee of Bradford & Bingley Building Society may also have a savings account or mortgage with them and, in addition, may also be a shareholder.

This has major implications for the way in which organisations communicate with their various stakeholders. It is therefore essential that internal and external communications are compatible and communicate the same messages, because internal stakeholders will also be exposed to external communications.

4.3.1 Role of internal marketing communications

Internal marketing communications is a key aspect of internal marketing and plays an important role in facilitating change. According to Fill (1999), internal marketing communications has several roles.

DRIP factors (Differentiate products and services, Remind and reassure customers and potential customers, Inform and Persuade targets to think and act in a particular way):

1   To provide information
2   To be persuasive
3   To reassure/remind
4   To differentiate employees/groups

Transactional:

1   To co-ordinate actions
2   To promote the efficient use of resources
3   To direct developments

Affiliation:

1   To provide identification
2   To motivate personnel
3   To promote and co-ordinate activities of non-members

This demonstrates the important role that internal marketing communications can play in helping to facilitate change management. However, internal communications cannot be viewed in isolation and must be viewed in relation to all external communication.

> ▶ **Assessment tip**
>
> When answering questions relating to internal marketing avoid generically discussing supporters, opposers and neutrals for the changes, instead considering the specific people or groups of people who would have views in relation to the changes and what those views would be. This will enable the proposed internal marketing to be specifically tailored to the situation of these groups such that the terminology for the internal marketing mix does not have to rely on the four or seven Ps which, if also presented generically, are unlikely to gain many marks.

The Chartered
Institute of Marketing

5 Performance appraisal

This is concerned with trying to maximise the performance of staff either individually or in teams. Performance appraisal focuses on the control and development of staff through the setting of objectives and the review of their performance. Areas of strengths and weaknesses may be identified and training needs developed to overcome the weaknesses. Many organisations implement an annual appraisal scheme for staff to review progress and establish objectives for the next year. Effective appraisals call for managers to have good people skills and the process should be seen as a positive and constructive experience. Three key skills are necessary:

- Reviewing performance
- Giving feedback
- Counselling

5.1 Marketing strategy and team objectives

One of the key principles of performance management is that it clarifies, translates and cascades **corporate goals** 'down' into divisional, department, team and individual goals. The performance goals of marketing teams, and individual marketers, need to be **integrated** or **aligned** with those of the marketing function and the organisation as a whole.

- **Vertical alignment** is about ensuring that the goal of every activity contributes towards the overall or higher objectives of the business. Corporate plans and objectives should 'cascade down' to the strategic plans of business units and functions, which should in turn influence the objectives set for teams and individuals. Conversely, individuals and teams in marketing should formulate performance goals which *support* the marketing strategy, which in turn should be formulated to support corporate strategic plans. So, for example, an organisation with a vision for innovation may set objectives for new product development. These will flow down to marketing objectives for adding value through market research, relationship development, market penetration, corporate brand positioning and so on.

- **Horizontal alignment** is about ensuring that the plans of every unit in an organisation are co-ordinated or dovetailed, so that they work effectively together. So, for example, marketing plans must be co-ordinated with the requirements of production (operations planning), the availability of resources (eg through HR and financial planning) and so on – just as marketing messages delivered from units across the organisation must be integrated to present a consistent, coherent face to the world.

Taylor argues that the process of mapping unit plans onto each other, and onto corporate strategy, has a range of advantages.

- Apart from giving a cohesive view, it helps prevent duplication of effort and resources, encourages everyone to help each other and gives each team a view and feeling of corporate impact – tying everyone's role to the bigger picture. This is hugely motivating for people and teams at every level.'

- 'In addition to improved planning and understanding by all involved in the vision and journey, such contentious issues as ownership, prioritisation and delivery can be more fully explored and explained.'

- 'Adopting this method also leads to improved measurement of your value. It will only be possible to list each and every activity as it is matched to a business justification, rather than being done for its own sake.'

5.2 Establishing priorities, objectives and standards

Prioritisation involves identifying **key results** (objectives which *must* be achieved if the department or section is to fulfil its aims) and **key tasks** (those things that *must* be done on time and to the required standard if the key results are to be achieved). These may be established using various broad approaches.

5.2.1 Role profiling

Role analysis may be carried out to develop a role profile or definition, as a framework for performance management at the individual level. Role analysis defines:

- The **purpose** of the role: what the role holder is expected to do or contribute (in the light of the objectives of the team and department as a whole)

- The **key result areas** or main accountabilities of the role, which define the main output areas for which objectives and performance standards can be agreed

- The **key competencies** of the role: what the role holder has to do in order to perform the role effectively. This may take the form of a separate competence profile, providing the basis for competence assessment and improvement planning.

Armstrong (2009) suggests that information on objectives and priorities can be obtained by asking:

- What do you think are the most important things you do?
- What do you believe you are expected to achieve in each of these areas?
- How will you – or anyone else – know whether or not you have achieved them?

5.2.2 Performance agreements or contracts

Performance agreements may be formulated in collaboration with individuals and teams, to define and agree objectives, standards and expectations of performance. The points to be agreed may cover:

- Objectives, targets and standards of performance to be achieved

- Performance measures and indicators: criteria that will be used to assess how far the objectives, targets and standards have been achieved

- Competence assessment methods (where used): what competences will be required to deliver the expected results, what competence definitions will be used, what evidence of competence will be gathered and so on

- Operational requirements for performance: procedures and standards for health and safety, security (of premises and data) or budgetary control

- Values or principles to be upheld: diversity, ethical codes, and the core values of the organisation (eg quality, customer service, team working and so on).

5.2.3 Individual objectives

Individual objective setting supports not only integration, but motivation and learning. People need to know exactly what their objectives are in order to: plan and direct their effort towards the objectives; monitor their performance against objectives and adjust (or learn) where required; experience the reward of achievement once objectives have been reached; feel that their tasks have meaning and purpose; experience the motivation of a challenge; and avoid the *de*-motivation of vague, unrealistic or unattainable tasks.

Objectives or **goals** describe something that has to be accomplished: a point to aim for. They may be expressed as:

- **Tasks** or projects to be completed (by specified dates and to achieve defined results or deliverables).

- **Targets**: quantified results to be attained – in terms of productivity (output or throughput), sales volume/value, levels of service, cost reduction, learning attainments and so on. Targets may be set for **performance**/output or **improvement** (eg reducing costs or errors).

- **Standing objectives** or **performance standards**: definitions of what competent or 'up to standard' performance consists of. These may be quantified (eg in terms of speed of response or level of output) or qualitative (eg in terms of flexibility, creativity or customer satisfaction). Standing objectives often remain in place unchanged from one review period to the next: that is, they apply more or less continuously (unless the nature or context of the key task changes). One common example is the speed with which telephones are answered in customer service units.

The Chartered Institute of Marketing

- **Developmental goals**: how an individual can improve his or her own performance, skills and competence attainment.

Most authors agree that objectives should be 'SMART':

- **Specific:** stated in clear, detailed terms: precisely what the desired outcomes or deliverables are

- **Measurable**: susceptible to monitoring, review and measurement (ideally in quantitative terms) so that you know when or how far progress/success has been attained

- **Attainable**: target outcomes and standards, and the contexts and timescales within which they must be attained, must be realistically achievable, using the capacities, capabilities, readiness and resources available. (We might also add '**Ambitious**': stretching or challenging, in order to motivate development, learning and improvement.)

- **Relevant**: supportive of the strategic objectives of the unit and the business as a whole: leading somewhere meaningful

- **Time-framed**: agreed target timescales and deadlines for completion (or review) must be included in the objective: it is not open ended.

5.2.4 Individual performance measures

The setting of **performance measures** (often called Key Performance Indicators or KPIs) is closely linked with the setting of objectives. Objectives define what is to be achieved: performance measures define how stakeholders will *know* whether or how far it has been achieved, as the basis for performance monitoring and feedback.

The idea of 'SMART' objectives reminds us that performance measures must be results-focused, objective and measurable. However, in order to be motivational, the results must be within the individual's direct control – otherwise they will be measured on something they have no control over, which is very frustrating! As the balanced scorecard (which we will look at in more detail in a later chapter) suggests, performance measures may address a wide range of indicators or metrics:

- **Finance:** eg economic value added, cost reductions, rates of return on investment

- **Productivity**: eg number of new accounts, throughput of work

- **Time**: speed of response or task turn-round, achievement of deadlines, lead times for campaign development

- **Response**: internal and external customer satisfaction, enquiry/response/recall rates for marketing campaigns

- **Results**: standard/qualification attainment, changes in internal stakeholder behaviour (eg improved customer focus), changes in external stakeholder behaviour (eg increased sales, order value or customer retention), completion of projects, innovations suggested/adopted

- **Technology leverage**: adoption of new media and technology, transaction costs saved through technology

- **Relationships**: partnership development (eg collaborative promotions); agency relationships; customer retention

- **Ethics and corporate social responsibility:** diversity and equal opportunity; compliance with codes of ethics, law and regulation; stakeholder awareness of CSR initiatives.

ACTIVITY 6.10

A senior sales executive has a job which involves: 'building the firm's sales' and maintaining 'a high degree of satisfaction with the company's products and services'. The firm buys sports equipment, running machines and so on, which it sells to gyms and individuals. The firm also charges fees to service the equipment. Service contracts are the sales executive's responsibility, and he has to manage that side of the business.

Here are some possible performance indicators to assess the sales executive's performance in the role. What do you think of them? Are they any good?

(a) Number of new customers gained per period

(b) Value of revenue from existing customers per period

(c) Renewal of service contracts

(d) Record of customer complaints about poor quality products

(e) Regular customer satisfaction survey

5.3 Communicating the objectives and standards

A wide range of methods is available for communicating performance objectives and standards (standing objectives) to team members. Some will be collaboratively set and agreed and built into individual and team performance agreements. Others may be communicated via:

■ The departmental procedures manual, policy documents and notices (or their electronic equivalents on the department intranet)

■ Team briefings and periodic performance or project review meetings

■ Statements of project deliverables, milestones and targets in project plans and review meetings

■ Individual performance appraisals and periodic performance reviews

■ Role and competence definitions, used as the basis of performance planning

■ Problem-solving meetings such as disciplinary proceedings and employee counselling, at which objectives and standards are re-emphasised as improvement targets

■ Training, coaching and mentoring sessions, in which objectives and standards are re-emphasised as learning objectives

■ Customer charters and service level agreements (statements of the services and service levels to be delivered to internal and external clients)

■ Informal, motivational 'reminders' from the team leader in the course of performance: spoken or emailed re-statement and encouragement, posters in the work space and so on.

5.4 Performance monitoring and measurement

We have stressed that individual performance management is an on-going process of monitoring, measuring and reviewing performance – *not* just a once-a-year formal performance appraisal (which is nevertheless necessary, and is discussed in the following section of this chapter in detail).

Team leaders must take advantage of a range of formal and informal opportunities to monitor, measure and review performance, including:

■ **Observation** of individuals at work, both formal (by agreement) and informal (by 'walking around'), giving the leader a chance to observe the processes and approaches of work, not just its results. This may be helpful for complex, creative and relational jobs such as marketing and management, which depend more on *how* things are done than on task outputs.

■ **Work sampling**: periodically assessing sample task outputs (eg marketing communications or designs produced, reports, budgets, personal work plans and so on) to check that they are up to standard or specification.

■ **Results reporting**: the leader should monitor reports on progress and results, to check that milestones are being met and desired results achieved. Many operational reports are made on an 'exception' basis: that is, only when there is a deviation from the plan or standard, in order to alert the manager to the need for problem solving. However, this represents only negative feedback (requiring corrective action), rather than positive feedback (requiring reinforcing and celebration). Managers should sample a range of reports in order to 'catch people doing something right'.

- **Team feedback and review meetings**. Regular team meetings should be used to check in with progress and results, and gather information about potential problems, resource needs and so on. More formal interim reviews may be conducted: say, twice yearly, or at the end of a project stage, or on completion of a 'milestone' in a project or development plan (eg at the end of a training programme).

- **Feedback mechanisms**. Formal feedback on progress and results may be gathered from key stakeholders, for consideration in interim, stage or special reviews: eg internal or external customer satisfaction at the end of a project or project stage; attainment, proficiency or learning assessments obtained from a trainer at the end of a training programme; or feedback provided by a third-party assessor at the close of a certification programme or assessment for an award, say.

- In addition, there should be a continual flow of **informal feedback** which should be monitored: customer complaints or evaluations, commendations, comments from other managers and so on.

- **Discussion with individuals**. The manager may take a coaching or facilitating role in relation to the team, as part of his or her leadership style, and may therefore have the opportunity to sit down with individuals periodically to discuss how they think they are progressing or performing, and what they need to help them perform better.

6 Individual performance appraisal

The general purpose of any staff appraisal system is to improve the efficiency of the organisation by ensuring that the individuals within it are performing to the best of their ability and developing their potential for improvement and added contribution. Within this overall objective, appraisals have several specific purposes. You should remember from Chapter 3 that they are designed with the following in mind:

- To review **performance**: to plan and follow up training and development programmes, to solve performance problems and to set targets for future performance

- To review **potential**: to predict the level and type of work an individual will be capable of in future, and plan learning and development activities to fulfil this potential

- To enhance **motivation** by providing more systematic performance feedback

- To review **rewards**: measuring the extent to which an employee is deserving of performance-related bonuses or pay increases

You may wonder if formal appraisal systems are necessary to achieve these aims: managers gather performance evaluations, and give feedback, on an on-going basis. However, a formal system ensures that managers make the effort to form a coherent, complete and objective picture of team members' performance (not just random impressions based on their more noticeable successes and failures). It also ensures that managers give adequate feedback, in a positive context of systematic learning, improvement and development planning.

6.1 Multi-source feedback

An individual's immediate manager may not be the only or best person to give feedback on his or her performance. In recent years, other stakeholders have been involved in appraisal reporting.

6.1.1 Self appraisal

Individuals may carry out their own self-evaluation as a major input into the appraisal process. There are a number of advantages to such an approach: saving managerial time; utilising the individual's insights into his/her own performance issues; and engaging the individual in the process, with greater likelihood of commitment to improvement targets. On the other hand, people are not always the best judges of their own performance, and may deliberately over- (or under-) estimate their performance in order to gain approval or reward (or to conform to team norms).

Many schemes, however, combine self-appraisal with other sources of feedback.

6.1.2 Peer appraisal or rating

An individual may be assessed by workmates or colleagues. This also has advantages: getting feedback from team members who have experienced and observed the individual in action; removing a direct link to reward/promotion planning, and removing a potential cause of negative attitudes to the process; and solving performance problems within the context of the work team.

However, peer appraisal requires sensitivity and skill if it is not to cause interpersonal hostility and team conflict – or avoid development feedback altogether, in favour of maintaining working relationships and solidarity. It is often reserved for professionally qualified staff.

6.1.3 Customer appraisal

In some companies, the appraisal process includes feedback from customers, both internal and external. At Rank Xerox, for example, 30 percent of a manager's annual bonus is conditional upon satisfactory levels of customer feedback. Customers may be the best judges of the service level and added value provided by team members.

6.1.4 Upward appraisal

A notable modern trend, adopted in the UK by companies such as BP and British Airways, is upward appraisal, whereby managers are rated by their team members: the followers appraise the leader. This has a number of advantages.

- Subordinates tend to know their superior (particularly in the area of leadership skills) better than anyone

- As multiple subordinates rate each manager, ratings may be more reliable: instead of the potential bias of a single rating, multiple ratings offer a representative view

- Subordinates' ratings may have more impact because it is more unusual to receive upward feedback from subordinates

A major problem with upward feedback is fear of reprisals and vindictiveness: ratings may be made anonymously, but then there is little accountability for their accuracy and truthfulness.

Some bosses in strong positions might refuse to act, even if a consensus of staff suggested that they should change their ways.

6.2 360-degree feedback

The focus, and emphasis, here is on teams; however, the preceding discussion reminds us that it will always be necessary to include the role and performance of the individual in planning and evaluation of team performance.

An increasingly popular technique, now commonly in use across a wide range of businesses, is 360-degree feedback. This is an approach to performance appraisal that captures a wide range of views on the performance of an individual and in addition requires the completion of a self-assessment. As people work in teams, and with a wide range of colleagues, including people outside the organisation, it makes sense to include all sources of contact. Consequently, this process obtains inputs from peers, subordinates, managers, customers, suppliers and support staff. 360-degree appraisal can be viewed as an amalgamation of all elements of the multi-source feedback mentioned above.

The intrinsic merits of 360-degree feedback are not in doubt; rather there is an increasing amount of evidence to suggest that the process by which it is implemented has created a barrier to the successful exploitation of this technique. Too often the purpose of the feedback is not identified so that feedback is aimless and not connected to job function, or to organisational goals and strategies.

To yield most benefits, participants require training and ideally the allocation of a trained mentor. Trust needs to be developed and it must be made clear whether the feedback is going to be used for personal and professional development or for performance evaluation. Rogers, Rogers and Metlay (2002), cited by Carson

(2006), found that organisations using the technique to foster a 'development culture' resulted in higher performance individuals and teams throughout the organisation.

This was because individual performance is enhanced and the process fosters the development of a more functionally integrated organisation (Carson, 2006).

Extended knowledge

McGregor, J. and Kripalani, M. (2007) The Employee is Always Right; at India's HCL Technologies, workers get to grade the boss, and everybody can see the ratings. November (4059), pp80.

Carson, M. (20060 Saying it like it isn't: The pros and cons of 360-degree feedback. *Business Horizons*, 49, pp395–402.

Rogers, E. *et al* (2002) Improving the payoff from 360-degree feedback. *Human Resource Planning* 25 (3), pp44–55.

6.3 Improving the team's performance, including plans to improve motivation, commitment and loyalty

> ▶ **Key term**
>
> The aim of **team development** is considered by Moxon (1994) to: help people who work together to function more effectively in teams and to assist the team itself to work more effectively as a whole.

Two general approaches to this may be considered. One is continuous, ongoing development of team performance on a daily and weekly basis. The other is to instigate specific team-development events. In addition, this section will be concluded with a discussion of the positive and negative approaches used to incentivise desirable team behaviour, that is, through rewards and discipline (punishment).

Both 'on-going' and 'specific' approaches require some form of review or assessment of the current situation before recommending further action. The general problem-finding approach of goals, roles, processes, and relationships provides one suitable approach to improve team performance through team building and development.

Team cohesion

Co-operative groups have been shown to be more effective than competitive groups, where individuals focused on their own contributions rather than the group's shared performance. Team cohesion or solidarity is broadly regarded as desirable in order to create committed, co-operative working, mutual loyalty and accountability, and open information sharing – all of which may help to maximise the potential synergy of team working *and* individual satisfaction.

However, you should be aware that it is possible for groups to become *too* cohesive. Problems may arise in very close-knit groups because:

- The **group's energies** may be focused on its own maintenance and relationships, instead of on the task. Handy (1993) argued that: 'ultra cohesive groups can be dangerous because in the organisational context the group must serve the organisation, not itself'.

- The group may be **suspicious or dismissive of outsiders**, and may reject any contradictory information or criticism they supply; the group will be blinkered and stick to its own views, no matter what; cohesive groups often get the impression that they are infallible: they can't be wrong – and therefore can't learn from their mistakes.

- The group may **squash any dissent** or opinions that might rock the boat. Close-knit groups tend to preserve a consensus – falsely, if required – and to take risky decisions, because they have suppressed alternative facts and viewpoints.

Janis (1972) identified this as groupthink: 'the psychological drive for consensus at any cost, that suppresses dissent and appraisal of alternatives in cohesive decision-making groups'.

Since by definition a group suffering from groupthink is highly resistant to criticism, recognition of failure and unpalatable information, it is not easy to break such a group out of its vicious circle. The leader must challenge and encourage the group to:

- Actively seek outside ideas and feedback
- Welcome self-criticism and dissent within the group, and
- Deliberately evaluate conflicting evidence and opinions, looking for useful learning.

Group decision-making

Decision-making is a key team process, because:

- Pooling skills, information and ideas from different individuals (or functions, specialisms and levels in the organisation) may increase the **quality of the decision.**

- Participation in the decision-making process makes the decision **acceptable to the group**, whether because it represents a compromise or consensus of their views, or merely because they have been consulted and given a sense of influencing the decision.

Team decisions may be arrived at in various ways.

- **Imposition** or application of authority by the leader. This may be most appropriate where the speed or 'rightness' of the decision are more important than team agreement. The manager may involve the team in areas such as problem definition and the formulation of alternative solutions, but will take the final decision herself.

- **Majority rule**: by vote, or the leader's 'getting a sense' of the view supported by the majority of team members. This may be most appropriate where the acceptance of the group is the most important factor, rather than the 'rightness' of the decision.

- **Consensus**: a process by which a range of potentially divergent views is examined and persuasive arguments used until there is broad agreement among all members. This takes longer, but is often more effective at the implementation stage, since all members of the group are able to 'own' the decision.

In less effectively functioning teams, this may be negative process, where decisions are taken without input from team members; by a minority (eg a dominant clique within the team); by default (eg if the leader has abdicated responsibility for decision-making); or not at all (eg the issue is left open until events or higher authority make the decision for the team).

As we mentioned in Chapter 5, group decision-making tends to take longer (especially through consensus-seeking), but decisions are often better evaluated and more representative (owing to the input of different viewpoints) and therefore implemented with more commitment. Perhaps the key tasks of the manager are to:

- **Elicit and utilise team members' views, knowledge and expertise**, without abdicating responsibility for the final decision – but without giving the impression that contribution is a waste of time, or that participation is not genuine

- Encourage **progressively less leader-centred decision-making**, as the group matures (as suggested by the situational leadership model discussed in Chapter 4)

- Providing **information, coaching and other forms of facilitation and support** for group decision-making

- **Avoid the 'risky-shift' phenomenon**, whereby groups tend to take greater risks than the same individuals would on their own. There should be rigorous insistence on hearing divergent viewpoints and evaluating options.

Team communication

Effectively functioning groups tend to move from a leader-centred, leader-initiated pattern of communication to one where interaction is multi-directional or 'all-channel': any member can communicate directly with any other member. Cliques and isolated individuals become included within this web of interaction over time, facilitating the involvement and contribution of every-member.

The Chartered Institute of Marketing

Features of **effective group communication**, to be modelled, coached and supported by the leader, include:

- **Open, honest communication** – including the ability to deal with conflicts, issues and criticism openly, directly and fairly (without personal animosity or grudge-holding)

- **Task-relevant information sharing** (no withholding on a 'need to know' or 'knowledge is power' basis)

- **All-member participation** in meetings, discussions and decision-making. Equitable participation does not mean that all members will share *equally*, but that all members can get a fair hearing when they have something to say

- **Absence of artificial status barriers**, so that senior and junior members communicate with ease

- **Positive contributions** (giving/seeking information, suggests and opinions; encouraging and affirming others; being appropriately vulnerable; checking understanding; giving constructive feedback; summarising; explaining and so on) *outweigh* negative contributions (attacking; being defensive; difficulty stating; fault finding; interrupting; overriding others).

Rackham & Morgan (1977) suggest the technique of **contribution profiling**: analysing the number of contributions of different (positive and negative) types made by each member of a team during a meeting or discussion, to identify dysfunctional behaviours which can be fed back to the individual for adjustment, or countered in communication situations by positive leadership intervention.

Team communication tools

You should be aware of a wide range of tools for communicating within and between teams in your own organisation. These may include:

- Internal mail systems, carrying messages, letters and memoranda, forms and reports

- E-mail and other forms of electronic communication and data-sharing (eg shared database access)

- The telephone (including mobile phones and their email and SMS messaging capabilities)

- Team meetings, briefings and discussions, whether routine (eg a weekly sales or project team meeting) or required by particular tasks or events

- Individual interviews and discussions

- Electronic equivalents of meetings and discussions eg via teleconferences, video-conferences, web casts and 'virtual' meetings from linked computers

- General 'management by walking around': informal contacts and information sharing in the course of daily activity.

6.4 Team meetings

Teams spend a large proportion of their working week in meetings, particularly with the rise of project working. Meetings are both a major cost to organisations, and a major context for decision-making, interpersonal influencing and team collaboration.

Poorly managed meetings can, however, be non-productive or even counter-productive. If meetings are a significant cost, they need to be efficiently utilised – but poorly managed meetings are a waste of time. If meetings are where most decisions are made, they need to facilitate quality decisions – but some group dynamics (as we have seen) result in poor or risky decision-making. If meetings are where teams mainly 'touch base' with each other, they need to facilitate integrative collaboration – but they are often perceived as a waste of time.

Regular team meetings have particular purposes, over and above problem-solving and decision-making on any particular work-related issue.

- They provide an opportunity to review team working processes and appraise (formally or informally) how well they are working. Team members may raise problems of co-ordination or communication, for example.

- They reinforce the team's sense of itself as a team, drawing them together to focus on their shared goals.

- They allow for goal reinforcement, progress feedback and information sharing, to ensure that team members are 'on the same page' with their efforts – especially if they do not directly work together (eg in remote or virtual project teams).

- They allow for all-member involvement and development in team decision-making and information sharing processes. (Discussion leading and research/presentation roles might be rotated, for example, to facilitate this.)

- They allow for informal communication, which is important for working relations, ideas generation and information-sharing. This can be built in at the beginning and end of meeting time.

6.4.1 Managing meetings effectively

Whatever the purpose and level of formality of a given meeting, its effectiveness will broadly depend on the following.

- There is usually a discussion **leader**, chair, or at least an organiser, who guides the proceedings of the meeting and aims to maintain order.

- There is often a **sequence of business** or at least a list of items to be covered: topics of discussion or decisions to be reached. It is not essential to formalise this point with an **agenda**, but meetings usually do have one.

- The purpose of the meeting is achieved by reaching some **decision or expression of opinion** at the end of the discussion. In some circumstances this may lead to taking a vote to determine what is the majority view. In other circumstances, the discussion may just be **summarised** by the leader and written confirmation of the decisions reached provided later for perusal by the various parties.

Whetten and Cameron (2011) suggest that the attributes of effective meetings can be classified as five Ps.

Table 6.3   Summarised from Whetten and Cameron: the five Ps of effective meetings

Purpose	Meetings should only be convened when there is a defined and adequate reason for doing so; when the cost of meeting is less than the potential benefits; and when face-to-face meeting is more effective than an e-mail or phone call.
Participants	Meetings can fail because they are too small (insufficient participation) or too large (insufficient information or representation).
	Meetings require a balance of skills and competencies – like any team: there may need to be problem identifiers, problem solvers, resource controllers and decision authorisers, for example, in a project meeting.
	Key roles and responsibilities in a meeting will include:
	- A leader (in formal meetings, called a meeting chair) or facilitator.
	Responsible for ensuring that: the meeting follows the agenda; discussion is conducted in a way that permits equitable participation by all members and decisions are reached in appropriate ways.
	- A scribe (in formal meetings, called a secretary)
	Responsible for taking notes of what is discussed and agreed, what actions will be taken and by what deadlines. Team meetings may or may not require formal minutes, but it will help if someone is concentrating on recording the proceedings.
Planning	It will be necessary to make arrangements for meeting space, seating layout, equipment and so on.
	Notice of the meeting (announcement of and invitation to the meeting): timing and location should be planned to facilitate attendance by those who need to be there.
	Agenda: a clear list of the items of business to be discussed at the meeting, ideally circulated in advance to allow preparation. A well-drafted agenda will indicate the meeting's priorities, both in the sequence of the items (so that the meeting focuses its 'best' time on the most important or difficult items) and by allotting target times for the discussion of each item.
Process	The interpersonal and decision-making processes of the meeting, and the facilitator's efforts to ensure participants contribute appropriately.
	Formal meetings have particular rules and conventions covering matters such as how proposals are put

	forward, how debate is to be managed, how decisions are to be reached (eg by vote) and how resolutions are recorded.
	Informal meetings also require structure and leadership, but these will generally come from the facilitator (see below).
Perspective	Meetings should be reviewed to evaluate their effectiveness, and decide what can be improved next time.

6.4.2 Leading team meetings

Effective facilitation of a team meeting involves the following.

- Ensuring that all members have the information they require to contribute meaningfully

- Ensuring that all members are able to contribute equitably (eg by encouraging less communicative members, and controlling more dominant members)

- Keeping the discussion 'on track' with the agenda or matter in hand. (Potentially useful but not immediately relevant contributions should be tabled for inclusion at the next meeting.)

- Managing any conflict that emerges in the course of the meeting

- Ensuring that agreed decisions are accurately recorded in the notes or minutes of the meeting, ideally with clearly defined responsibility for action

- Following up on decisions and action points from previous meetings, to ensure that agreed action has been taken

---

ACTIVITY 6.11

What aspects of the following situations might be a problem for an effective team meeting? What might you, in the role of facilitator, do about it?

(a) One person suggests a revision to the agenda, a complex issue which the rest of the team is unprepared to discuss, and which two members are likely to feel is 'targeted' at them.

(b) The team has more items on its agenda than it can handle in a simple meeting.

(c) A team member has called ahead to say that she will be unavoidably late for a scheduled project team meeting.

6.5 Ongoing development

Moxon (1994) suggests that team development involves (Figure 6.5):

- Regular meetings to establish and review processes, procedures and objectives. Effectiveness will decline if this is not undertaken.

- Sessions specifically on addressing issues. Strengths and the causes of successes are examined rather than simply focusing on weaknesses and their causes. The focus is on workable solutions.

- Ongoing emphasis on encouraging open and honest discussion rather than superficial politeness. This requires the creation of a sense of security within the team where team members feel able to take risks and share their deeper and true feelings.

- A commitment to personal change and development and to improve team performance. Change will be detailed in action plans and these will also be subject to review.

- Frequent time away from the job, especially in the early stages of team formation, in support of team development.

- Openness of the leader to receive feedback from the team on leadership style and effectiveness.

- Development of interpersonal skills, especially with regard to processes (eg meetings) and relationships. This normally should take place as a team.

Figure 6.5   An approach to team development

Diagnosis	Data collection
	One-to-one interviews – provides very detailed contextual information, although very time consuming and relies on an open and frank discussion with the manager
	Questionnaires – quick, less threatening than an interview and allows easy and rapid analysis
	Provides suitable information in order to arrive at a diagnosis of the problem(s)
Design and planning	Session design can be tailored to the particular problems that must be overcome Define objectives Broad design Exercise selection Administration (of session facilities and equipment) Pre-work (by the team before they attend the session)
Running the sessions	Introduction
	Discussion
	Action plans
	Summary and agreement
Follow-up	Write-up outcomes Review progress Future dates

(Adapted from Moxon, 1994)

6.5.1 Team reward

Team reward aims to reinforce behaviour which leads to effective teamwork. It encourages group endeavour rather than individual performance. Most team reward systems emphasise team pay rather than non-financial rewards. However, teams may respond to all types of reward from pay, bonuses and public recognition. An advantage is that team pay can encourage co-operative work and behaviour, and develop self-managed and directed teams.

Team pay works best if teams stand alone with agreed targets and are composed of people whose work is interdependent. For it to work well, everybody must understand and accept the targets and the reward must be linked clearly to effort and achievement.

Teams may be able to plan and implement their own improvement programmes if they receive feedback and meet regularly to discuss performance. Team reward is a way for organisations to demonstrate that they value teams and individuals who perform well, and that high levels of performance are important. The quality of teamwork depends on:

- Culture
- Structure and operating processes
- Values
- Performance management
- Management style
- Employee development programmes.

However, there may be times when it is not enough to incentivise the team to adopt the desired behaviours. Where a team fails to perform disciplinary measures may be required.

The Chartered Institute of Marketing

6.5.2 Discipline

A disciplinary interview can be thought of as having three stages:

1   **Establishing the gap**: Future performance is the main concern, so any discussion about present behaviour should be focused on changes that are needed for the future and how to achieve them. It is important to be specific about concerns and to provide evidence or examples of how there is a gap between present behaviour and what is required.

2   **Exploring the reasons for a gap**: It is important to allow the person subject to a disciplinary interview to explain the circumstances and to put forward their point of view about the gap. This may uncover problems or issues of which the manager is unaware but will need to be dealt with in some way, for example, suggesting that they seek advice and guidance or specialist help in sought.

3   **Eliminating the gap**: There will need to be agreement to a plan of action that may involve training. Arrangements for keeping the situation under review will need to be agreed, and the people involved should be aware of how and when their performance is going to be monitored. The aim is to help facilitate an improvement in performance.

THE REAL WORLD

Putting it altogether

A highly successful, and growing, air conditioning repair business in the USA achieves its success through teamwork in an industry where many work in isolation. Its success is due to a close and detailed consideration of all aspects of team development and performance. This is a highly thriving business, permanently operating near or at full capacity, obtaining new business based on personal recommendations. It is understandable that customers are highly satisfied when the business sets impressive customer guarantees. This includes refunds of $500 if installation is not achieved on time, $500 refund on property protection and also $500 guaranteeing client respect.

The business obviously expects its people to deliver on these promises and the means by which it achieves this is through operating high-quality teams. How do they do this in a business where many technicians work on customers' sites individually or in pairs? The principal approach is to maintain constant communication and offer high levels of training. Everyone meets up first thing in the morning to foster a team spirit and this encourages a co-operative, supportive working 'mindset' where technicians are comfortable ringing each other for support and advice. Buddy work practices are operated, fostering on-the-job training by more experienced colleagues in the organisation, in addition to around three weeks' equivalent of off-site, paid training each year for every member of staff. Retention and recruitment policies attract and keep the best people, while marketing activity is geared towards levelling the peaks and troughs of work inherent in this seasonally influenced industry.

This is not only crucial for work flow but also for staff morale. Employee burnout can be a problem in a service business: someone has to cover the anti-social hours of a 24–7 service guarantee policy, which the business uses as one aspect of its competitive advantage. People do volunteer to support each other when there is a big job that needs more than one or two people to sort out. Such 'goodwill' among employees results from fostering a team mindset of co-operative, supportive behaviour. The company reciprocates by ensuring employees working a long day during the busy season are compensated by a reduced workload on the next day. Performance-linked bonuses, company social get-togethers and daily manager–staff face-to-face contact takes place, especially during peak periods, to see how they are coping.

Recognising difficulties of obtaining high calibre staff, the business, as it continues to grow, uses word-of-mouth referrals from its own workers to attract new staff. This allows them to be ahead of the competition when it comes to recruitment. High levels of team performance lead to satisfied customers who keep coming back. The individual elements of this success hardly amount to rocket science. However putting it all together is another matter, judging by the numbers of organisations who manage to do it successfully.

(Based on Anon, 2008)

Assess your team on each of the criteria presented in Figure 6.6. Read the brief comment supporting the single-word description before assessing your team on the scale of 1 to 9 as shown.

Extended knowledge

Belbin (2004) Chapter 13: Where are we now, and Stacey (2002) Chapter 4, especially Sections 4.5 to 4.8 inclusive.

Figure 6.6   Assess the effectiveness of your team

Assess your team on each of these criteria [circle your selection]		
Group objectives Well understood and accepted by all team members. These are reviewed frequently.	1 2 3 4 5 6 7 8 9	We are unclear about our objectives and there is frequent lengthy discussion on our priorities when we have achieved the latest working objective.
Atmosphere Informal and comfortable with everyone at their ease. People are involved and even excited in their work.	1 2 3 4 5 6 7 8 9	There is a high degree of tension. The majority of people are overloaded or have insufficient work to do at times.
Communication We are very good at communicating and highly focused on the task. We are sensitive to the views of one another and listen in a non-judgemental way.	1 2 3 4 5 6 7 8 9	Communication appears to suffer from a few people dominating the conversation. We frequently go off the subject during meetings. It seems that we do not listen attentively to each other.
Conflict resolution We handle conflict, such as exists, very well. People are prepared to disagree and these are debated openly rather than shouted down. The minority who sometimes do not agree with a decision accept the disagreement graciously.	1 2 3 4 5 6 7 8 9	People become highly charged during disagreements or seem not to let conflict arise, either through the role of the chairperson or because there is a concern about being perceived as negative. We tend to use majority voting and it seems the more dominant group members get their way.
Decision-making This is consensual. Team members feel able to raise disagreements. However, we are good at laying bare the basis for disagreement, especially where this is due to subjective weighting of influencing factors.	1 2 3 4 5 6 7 8 9	Decisions seem to be taken far too quickly without sufficient debate or consultation. The leader tends to dominate leaving many uncommitted to the final decision.
Criticism Very open but certainly not personal. We find criticism to be well considered and delivered sensitively. Team members usually take it on board without feeling a loss of status.	1 2 3 4 5 6 7 8 9	It seems that we try and score points off each other. There is a certain pleasure by some in criticising others and this creates a certain degree of tension.
Expression of personal feeling Uninhibited and people do not seem to want to follow a personal agenda.	1 2 3 4 5 6 7 8 9	We are never usually clear about people's personal feelings. There is a reluctance to expose our personal feelings to group scrutiny because of the potential risk that this engenders.
Leadership The leader is not overly concerned with exercising and demonstrating authority. In fact, at times, group members appear to take on group leadership. We seem to be more concerned with completing the work rather the display of power.	1 2 3 4 5 6 7 8 9	It is obvious who the team leader is. Frequently, we may discuss an issue and then the leader makes the final decision, even though the case for the decision is not apparent and perhaps many of us have argued against that particular decision.
Achievement of tasks We operate with clear, mutually agreed action plans. We regularly review performance against these plans and indeed, the plans themselves. Team members are highly committed to achieving the action plans.	1 2 3 4 5 6 7 8 9	We don't tend to know who is to do what and by when. We seldom review performance against plans or indeed the plans themselves. When people are given particular tasks, these are often ambiguous. We are not good at following up who has done what.
Review of team processes We are in control of our own processes. These are reviewed to see if they can be done better, from decision-making to the way we run meetings and allocate tasks. We assess whether process issues are causing a reduction in the effectiveness of the team.	1 2 3 4 5 6 7 8 9	We do not really discuss team process issues and review these. Some team members like to talk about our failings in private, or outside team meetings when only a few members of the team are present, but for some reason they do not raise these issues in team meetings.

(Adapted from Moxon, 1994)

Summary

Team conflict is a fairly difficult issue to understand and address. That is because its cause may not simply arise from the participants in the conflict but in the context in which workers find themselves working. For example, the goals, roles and processes with which people must comply may be the original source. Once identified, there are various strategies that may be adopted to resolve conflicts. This involves the individual and the team in change and managers, and the organisation, in the management and implementation of change programmes. An understanding of the change process, and the possible reactions to change, provides a valuable insight into how change may be implemented successfully. Training and development may be part of the solution to successful change. This is perhaps one of the more important outcomes of the ongoing process of performance evaluation and review of individuals and teams, of which 360-degree feedback is an example that is particularly effective in a team context.

A helpful perspective to frame our thinking on improving team and organisational performance is market orientation. By being more market orientated, teams and organisations are likely to be more successful and also, consequently, to suffer from less conflict. Approaches to achieving greater market orientation revolve around better performance focused on the customer in which high levels of interfirm co-ordination exists. An important vehicle in support of this is internal marketing, which aligns individual and team work to organisational requirements. If successful, increased loyalty and emotional involvement with the brand can be achieved. This in turn will result in increased employee satisfaction, loyalty and motivation both for ongoing programmes and 'one off' campaigns.

- Conflict in organisations

    - Conflict can be both constructive and destructive
    - Conflict sources need to be recognised, whether within marketing or elsewhere

- Team problems can come from four areas (Irwin)

    - Goals
    - Roles
    - Processes
    - Relationships

- Team development and communication help overcome conflict

- Change is inevitable but it can be evolutionary or revolutionary

- Change has to be managed, simple but effective model is Lewin three step model

- Internal marketing

    - Covers attitude management and communications management – taking place between the organisation and the internal staff

    - Take the same format as external marketing plans

    - Employer branding relies on successful employee branding through internal marketing

- Internal marketing communications has many roles, including DRIP (differentiate, remind, inform, persuade)

- Marketing strategy has to be integrated and aligned with wider organisation objectives and individual objectives

    - Objectives need to be communicated and monitored

- Individual feedback can take many forms, culminating in 360-degree feedback

FURTHER READING

Ahmed, P.K. and Rafiq, M. (1993) The scope of internal marketing: Defining the boundary between marketing and human resource management. *Journal of Marketing Management* 9, pp219–232.

Boddy, D. (2002) *Management: An Introduction*. Harlow, Pearson Education (Chapter 13, 'Motivation' and Chapter 15, 'Teams').

Brown, M. (2002) *Project Management in a Week*. 3rd edition. London, Hodder and Stoughton.

McGregor, J. and Kripalani, M. (2007) The Employee is Always Right; at India's HCL Technologies, workers get to grade the boss, and everybody can see the ratings. November (4059), p80.

Rogers, E. *et al* (2002) Improving the payoff from 360-degree feedback. *Human Resource Planning* 25 (3), pp44–55.

The Chartered
Institute of Marketing

Adair, J. (1986) *Effective Teambuilding*. Basingstoke, Gower.

Adair, J. (2002) *Inspiring Leadership: Learning from Great Leaders*. London, Thorogood.

Ahmed, P.K. and Rafiq, M. (1993) The scope of internal marketing: Defining the boundary between marketing and human resource management. *Journal of Marketing Management* 9, pp219–232.

Ahmed, P.K. and Rafiq, M. (2002) *Internal Marketing Tools and Concepts for Customer-Focused Management*. Oxford, Butterworth-Heinemann.

Anonymous (2006) [Feature] Case Study – Marketing Capability: blend for flexibility. *Brand Strategy*, July 17 2006, p30.

Anonymous (2008) Focus – Best Contractor To Work For: Classic Air's One Hour Grows As A Team. *Air Conditioning, Heating and Refrigeration News*. Jan 21, pp40–42.

Anonymous (2011) Employee Branding. ADSAINT, http://adsaint.com/columns/bravenewadworld/employee-branding/ [Accessed on 8 March, 2012]

Armstrong, M. (2009) *A Handbook of Human Resource Management Practice*. 11th edition. London, Kogan Page.

Beer, M. *et al* (1990) Why change programs don't produce change. *Harvard Business Review*. November–December.

Belbin, R.M. (2000) *Beyond the Team*. Oxford, Butterworth-Heinemann.

Belbin, R.M. (2004) *Management Teams: Why they Succeed or Fail*. Oxford, Butterworth-Heinemann.

Benady, D. (2001) The inside story. *Marketing Week*. 30–31 6 September.

Berry, L.L. (1981) The employee as customer. *Journal of Retail Banking*. 25–28 3 March.

Brown, M. (2002) *Project Management in a Week*. 3rd edition. London, Hodder and Stoughton.

Burnes, B. (1996) Managing Change. *Financial Times Management*. London 106–120.

Carson, M. (2006) Saying it like it isn't: The pros and cons of 360-degree feedback. *Business Horizons* 49, 395–402.

Christopher M. *et al* (2002) *Relationship Marketing: Creating Stakeholder Value*. Oxford, Elsevier Butterworth-Heinemann.

Culbert, H. (2002) Conflict management strategies and styles: Improving group dynamics, *http://home.snu.edu/* [Accessed on 15 June 2012]

Davidson, H., (2002) The Committed Enterprise: How to Make Vision and Values Work. Butterworth-Heinemann, Oxford.

Drummond, G. *et al* (2007) *Strategic Marketing Planning and Control*. 3rd edition. Oxford, Butterworth-Heinemann.

Egan, G. (1975), *The Skilled Helper: a problem-management approach to helping*. 5th edition. Pacific Grove, CA, Brooks/Cole.

Fill, C. (1999) *Marketing Communications Contexts, Contents and Strategies*. Harlow, Prentice Hall.

George, V. R. and Grönroos, C. (1989) Developing customer conscious employees at every level – internal marketing. *In:* Congram and Friedman (eds) *Handbook of Services Marketing*. New York, AMACOM.

Gronroos, C. (1990) *Service Management and Marketing*. Massachusetts, Lexington Books.

Gummesson, E. (2002) *Total Relationship Marketing*. Oxford, Elsevier Butterworth-Heinemann.

Hamblin, A. C. (1972) Controlling the Training Process. *Management Learning,* Vol3, No2 pp92-97.

Handy, C.B. (1993) *Understanding Organisations*. 4th edition. Harmondsworth, Penguin

Huczynski, A and Buchanan, D. (2001) *Organizational Behaviour: An Introductory Text*. 4th edition. Harlow, Essex , FT Prentice Hall.

Irwin, I.M. *et al* (1974) *Task Orientated Team Development*. New York, McGraw-Hill.

Janis, I.L. (1972) *Victims of Groupthink*. Boston, Houghton Mifflin.

Jobber, D. (2007) *Principles and Practice of Marketing.* 5th edition. McGraw Hill Education, Maidenhead.

Johnson G. *et al* (2005) *Exploring Corporate Strategy: Text and Cases*. 7th edition. Harlow, Essex, Pearson Education.

Kotler, P. *et al* (1999) *Principles of Marketing: European Edition.* 2nd edition. Harlow, Financial Times/Prentice Hall.

Kotler, P. (2002), *Marketing Management.* 11th edition. US Imports and PHIPES.

Kramer R. *et al*. (1997) *Human Resource Management in Australia*. 3rd edition. Melbourne, Addison Wesley Longman.

Lankard Brown, B. (1998) *Conflict Management*. ERIC Clearinghouse on Adult, Career, and Vocational Education, Center on Education and Training for Employment, College of Education, the Ohio State University, Columbus, OH.

Lockett, J. (1992) *Effective Performance Management*. London, Kogan Page.

Maier, N. R. F. (1966) *The Appraisal Interview: objectives, methods and skills*. London , John Wiley & Sons.

Mazur, L. (2001) Acquisition activity is on a high, but in most cases the deal fails to deliver. *Marketing* 26 8 February.

McGregor, J. and Kripalani, M. (2007) The Employee is Always Right; at India's HCL Technologies, workers get to grade the boss, and everybody can see the ratings. November (4059), p80.

Minchington, B (2010) *Employer Brand Leadership – A Global Perspective*. Collective Learning Australia.

Mitchell, Colin (2002). *Harvard Business Review*, Jan, Vol80 Issue 1, pp99-105.

Moxon, P. (1994) *Building a Better Team: A Handbook for Managers and Facilitators*. Aldershot, Gower.

Narver, J.C. and Slater, S.F. (1990) The Effect of a Market Orientation on Business Profitability. *Journal of Marketing*. October 54 (4), pp20–35.

Pedler M. *et al* (2004) *A Manager's Guide to Leadership*. Maidenhead, McGraw Hill.

Piercy, R.M. (2002) *Market-led Strategic Change: A Guide to Transforming the Process of Going to Market*. Oxford, Butterworth-Heinemann.

Profex (2007) *Leading and Influencing in Purchasing*. 2nd edition. Maidenhead, Profex Publishing.

Rackham, N. and Morgan, T. (1977) *Behaviour Analysis in Training*. Maidenhead, McGraw Hill.

Robbins, H. and Finley, M. (1998) *Why Change Doesn't Work*. London, Orion Business Book.

Rogers, E. *et al* (2002). Improving the payoff from 360-degree feedback. *Human Resource Planning*. 25(3), pp44–55.

Serco (2012) About us: People. Serco, www.serco.com/about/people/index.asp [Accessed on 15 June 2012]

The Chartered Institute of Marketing

Simms, J. (2003) HR or Marketing: Who gets staff on side? *Marketing,* 23–24 July.

Stacey, R.D. (2003) *Strategic Management and Organizational Dynamics*. Harlow, Prentice-Hall.

Stewart, J.and Kringas, P. (2003) Change management – Strategy and values in six agencies from the Australian public service. *Public Administration Review* 63 (6) November/December.

Thomas, K. W. (1976) Conflict and conflict management. *In:* Dunnette M. D. (ed)] *Handbook of Industrial and Organisational Psychology*.Chicago, Rand McNally. pp889–935.

Varey, R. J. (2002), *Marketing Communications: Principles & Practice*. Abingdon, Oxon, Routledge.

Wilson, D. (1992) *A Strategy of Change: Concepts and Controversies in the Management of Change*. Thompson Learning, England.

Whetten, D. and Cameron, S. (2011) *Developing Management Skills*. 5th edition. New Jersey, Prentice Hall.

QUICK QUIZ

1   Where does conflict in groups often stem from?

2   How can cross cultural competence be enhanced within managers?

3   How can change impact individuals?

4   What stage process does Kurt Lewin advocate using when trying to make a positive and maintained change?

5   Why is internal marketing relevant to HR?

ACTIVITY DEBRIEFS

Activity 6.1

This will depend on the specifics of the meeting attended

Activity 6.2

The answer to this depends upon the circumstances of the team considered

Activity 6.3

This will depend upon the change implemented and the situation of the organisation

Activity 6.4

The response to this will depend upon the change initiatives and the context

Activity 6.5

As above

Activity 6.6

As above

Activity 6.7

Involvement with customers		Involvement with marketing	
		Low	High
	Low	**Isolateds**	**Influencers**
	High	**Modifiers**	**Contactors**

Specific departments will depend upon the context of the organisation

Activity 6.8

This will depend upon the structure and culture of the organisation considered

Activity 6.9

The response to this will be related to the organisation concerned

Activity 6.10

(a)   This depends upon whether the new customers include service contracts and the profitability of the customers

(b)   A very relevant measure, particularly if related to profit

(c)   A good measure which should be a KPI

(d)   An important measure but could be misleading if complaints are encouraged as the number may increase regardless of performance

(e)   Good to conduct

Activity 6.11

(a)   Could cause team unrest, could recommend it be covered at a later date when all can be prepared for it

(b)   The meeting will either over-run or not all items will be covered adequately, a revised agenda with an additional meeting could be proposed or ideas for some items considered away from the meeting if possible

(c)   This team member will miss out on some agenda items, suggest rearranging the agenda to ensure the member is present for the most important items

Activity 6.12

This will depend upon the team members considered

1.
   - Goal incompatibility
   - Cultural incompatibility
   - Interdependence and shared resources
   - Competition for limited or scarce resources
   - Authority, power and status distribution
   - Change and uncertainty
   - The external environment

2.
   - Encouraging diversified work experience in international or multi-cultural settings
   - Undertaking training exercises (reading, language learning, cultural briefings)
   - Networking with managers from other cultures and using them as consultants
   - Seeking to learn through all cross-cultural interactions.

3. Change may affect individuals in ways: physically (eg different work methods); circumstantially (eg relocations, re-establishing work relationships with a new team); and psychologically (eg the requirement to learn new skills). Change may create feelings of disorientation before new circumstances have been assimilated. Uncertainty may lead to insecurity: especially acute in changes involving work, where there can be very great pressures for continuity and fast acclimatisation.

4. Unfreeze, change then refreeze

5. Positive employees will provide a better overall customer experience and help to instil quality.

Section 2:

Senior Examiner's comments

The assessment for Section 2 requires you to consider the inputs to team management both from the current team and through the development of a team to enable change and development of marketing activities. A key area in this section is the justification for resources required and consideration of the impact and interdependence of marketing on other areas of the organisation.

In the assessment, you will be required to demonstrate your capability to manage teams of marketers, assessing team and individual performance while providing appropriate recommendations to make improvements. Assessments may require you to reflect on your own management style and consider ways in which you can develop yourself, possibly through a personal development plan.

The assignment produced should include plans that illustrate the current situation, justifies proposals for how teams should be managed and the measures that can be used to ensure this happens to produce improvements in all aspects of team and organisational performance. Practical examples of best practice should be used where appropriate and contextually justified. Where priorities for actions are requested, it will be important that you use an appropriate framework for justification of your choice, rather than providing a simple numbered list.

Links between areas of the unit that should be considered include handling conflict and legal considerations of HR activity. Innovative and appropriate solutions to problems associated with team management will be rewarded.

For the assessment tasks related to Section 2, activities for team management should be linked to the infrastructure described for Section 1, building on the recommendations made.

Section 3: Operational finances for marketing

This section of the text is focused on ensuring that the marketing function achieves its objectives within budget. It explores costing, budgeting approaches, cost management and financial measurement so that you will be able to make recommendations to improve marketing performance based on financial analysis.

A detailed section on budgeting and its role in the management and control of marketing performance is embedded in this section – we are not expecting you to be a qualified accountant to use it, rather just to have an understanding of the process with the ability to communicate successfully with an organisation's finance department. Importantly, it shows you how to apply the budgeting process within an organisational context and examine the costs associated with marketing activities. This will allow you to determine information sources that could be used to gather the necessary information to determine the costs. Finally, it will help you to prepare appropriate budgets, identify causes of budget variances and make recommendations to improve performance against budget, including a cost benefit analysis of marketing activities that considers both qualitative and quantitative measurement.

CHAPTER 7

Budgeting for marketing

Introduction

Increasingly, it is a common practice for the objectives of marketing to be expressed in wider business terms. In addition to the traditional targets of increasing turnover, building loyalty and raising awareness, marketers are being charged with goals that include revenue generation, cash flow and shareholder value. With the emphasis on accountability – to investors, customers and clients, suppliers, staff, the local community, government, the public at large – marketing needs more than ever to be a performance-driven unit.

Topic list

The manager's role	1
The purpose of budgeting	2
Setting the marketing budget	3
Other considerations	4
Information sources	5

3.1	Assess the different requirements of managing the finances of the marketing function and associated marketing activities:
	■ The manager's role – control, managing information, cross-functional communication
	■ The purpose of budgeting – planning, co-ordination of activities, motivation, control, relationship to management of the marketing team
	■ Budget considerations – fixed, semi-fixed, variable and semi-variable costs
3.2	Critically evaluate the different approaches to setting the marketing and communications budget and associated marketing activities:
	■ Top-down budgets, bottom-up budgets
	■ The financial approach to setting budget – the budgeting process, percentage of sales/profit, competitive parity, affordable method
	■ The marketing approach – the planning and control process, objective and task approach, Share of Voice, cost-volume-profit
	■ Forecasting, financial analysis, balanced scorecard, resourcing
3.3	Evaluate the different information sources required to determine the marketing budget for marketing operations and activities:
	■ Data, information, intelligence and knowledge
	■ Internal data sources – sales figures, headcount, outsourcing costs, consultant costs, electronic point of sale (EPOS) system, MkIS external data sources including exchange rates variances arising from international trading

1 The manager's role

> ▶ **Key term**
>
> **Manager's role:** Managers are responsible for using the organisation's scarce resources efficiently to help the organisation achieve its objectives.

Manager's role: A great deal of research and thinking has been applied to the nature of management. There are many theories used to explain the relationship between a manager and the things that are managed. These in turn depend upon different explanatory models of organisations themselves. One way, for example, of capturing the diverse roles of a manger is through the following mnemonic:

- **C**ommunicating
- **O**rganising
- **M**atching
- **M**onitoring
- **A**cting
- **N**egotiating
- **D**ecision-making
- **E**nergising
- **R**eporting

This list could certainly be expanded, but it illustrates the wide scope of activities that fall within a manager's remit. In this section, we are going to focus on control and managing information, and how these contribute to the budgeting process and managing the finances of the marketing function.

1.1 Control

Control is required because unpredictable events occur and actual performance differs from the plan. For example, a powerful new competitor may enter the market. Control systems allow managers to identify deviations from plan and to do something about them.

Robert Anthony (1965) provided a definition of management control that is recognised as a classic and remains valid today. Anthony defined management control as 'the process by which managers assure that resources are obtained and used effectively and efficiently in the accomplishment of the organisation's objectives'.

As Anthony's reference to the organisation's objectives demonstrates, planning is linked very closely with control.

(a) It is necessary to verify whether or not the plan has worked or is working, and whether the objectives of the plan have been/are being achieved. This is where control becomes part of the planning process.

(b) Actual results and performance are therefore compared to the plan. If there are deviations, weaknesses or errors, control measures will be taken – which involves adjusting or setting further plans for ongoing action. Therefore, planning becomes part of the control process.

Figure 7.1   Basic control cycle

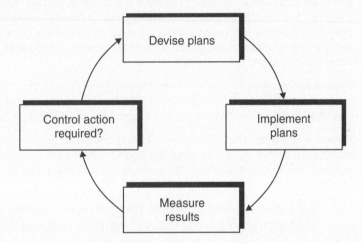

An important aspect of both planning and control activity is the **budget**, which we cover in detail in the next section.

Marketing decisions often depend upon others and must be considered in the context of broader strategy and background information, such as competitor activity, market research, availability of alternative and complementary goods, existing organisational profile, whether the organisation is a price giver or a price taker, whether it is customer led or product led and so on.

It is likely that the manager will have to take into account a large volume of information, both qualitative and quantitative, and decide which is relevant to the decision in hand. Effective decision-making also relies on recognising those factors over which it is possible to exercise control – operational finance falls into an area that can be controlled.

Decisions are based on past experience with a desire to influence the future. It is important to understand (although obvious) that we cannot influence the past. Energies should be expended on those things that can be changed. At the same time, we must recognise that the future is inherently uncertain, the past being only a

guide to what may happen. While this may sometimes result in indecision, we should also regard the lack of decisive action as being a decision in itself.

There is a wide range of decision-making tools (decision trees, the Pareto effect, force field analysis and so on), including cost-benefit analysis that we shall explore in detail later. While useful, these can never make the decision for you.

The manager carries the responsibility for exercising due judgement and taking an informed decision. Decision-making goes hand in hand with risk taking. A risk-based approach seeks to identify and measure potential risks as part of the process of deciding upon a suitable course of action. There is nothing wrong with taking a calculated risk. What is inexcusable is taking an uncalculated one, namely one that fails to take into account the relevant information available.

1.2 Managing information

A marketing manager has to exercise control over a range of factors – people, budgets, time and so on. In order to manage any of these components, it is first necessary to manage information.

There is an important sequence to the process of managing information.

- **Objectives**: It is necessary to start with a clear statement of your objectives. What are you trying to achieve? This may include the high-level objectives of the marketing function, such as maximising sales, as well as specific objectives relating to particular issues, such as fixing a problem with the organisation's website.

- **Decisions to be made**: In order to achieve the stated objectives, what decisions must be taken? Typically, these will centre on the marketing mix. If making a decision about price, for example, the marketing manager will want to know what will happen if the price is altered. As decision-making is about trying to influence the future, a lot of the information required may be in the form of forecasting. What would happen if we do this?

- **Type of information**: Having identified the decisions needed to achieve the desired objectives, it becomes a little easier to specify the information required to support the decision. Both qualitative and quantitative data can underpin decisions, and often a combination is required.

- **Format and timing**: The importance of format and timing is often overlooked, resulting in a series of requests for *ad hoc* reports because the original information supplied did not help address the problem in hand. This can be frustrating, time-consuming and expensive as well as derailing the decision-making process.

  - If the volume of sales is required, then this must be decided in advance. If an analysis by geographical region is essential, this must also be agreed.

  - If the value of sales is to be included, this too should be part of the information supplied.

  However, there is little to be gained from unnecessary detail that may simply complicate the decision-making process. Just because the information can be split by age, gender and any number of other customer characteristics, there is no guarantee that this is relevant to the decision in question.

- **Accuracy/reliability**: Sometimes a close estimate is sufficient and in other situations detailed accuracy may be required. The level of accuracy may relate to the significance of the decision. Where there is a large spend, a long-term impact on the organisation or something as sensitive as potential redundancies then a high degree of accuracy is essential.

- **Application**: Having collected the information, the most important requirement is that it is actually used to inform the decision-making rather than simply stored away.

Information can be drawn from readily available internal sources (such as customer databases, financial records and other reports), from external marketing intelligence (including formal and informal sources of data on competitors and the sector) and from active market research in specific areas of interest.

The Chartered Institute of Marketing

In Section 5 we will see more specifically how the management of information may be used in support of preparing the marketing and communications budget in order to make a persuasive bid for resources. We will also examine the use of marketing intelligence systems (MkIS) (in Section 5.3) as a mechanism for aiding management information.

1.3 Cross functional communication

Given the imperative for marketing managers to operate in concert with other divisions, cross functional communication is a high priority. It is not just a matter of having good relationships with counterparts in finance, production, human resources, research and development, logistics and so on. It is a way of doing business.

Maintaining effective cross functional communications will help the marketing manager maximise their personal impact as well as the overall impact of the marketing function. It will also help prepare for bids and negotiations around financial resources. Dialogue is always an opportunity for advocacy to promote the needs and interests of the marketing function.

At the same time, members of other departments should naturally be regarded as internal customers and so there should be an expectation of delivering excellent customer service. Mutual support and greater organisational effectiveness can be achieved with collaborative (rather than competitive) efforts that are maintained through interdepartmental communication. There is an interdependency that exists between organisational functions.

When marketing managers understand the important business drivers that are the primary concerns of their peers as well as the obstacles they face, there is a much better chance that departmental plans will be synchronised and high-level strategy will be effected. It is very useful to develop cross functional communication plans to sit alongside strategies for external communications.

ACTIVITY 7.1

How does your marketing function pro-actively support cross-organisational communication, especially in relation to marketing finances? Is it effective and what more could be done to improve it?

2 The purpose of budgeting

> ▶ Key term
> A **budget** is a statement of desired performance expressed in financial terms.

For our purposes in this section, a **budget** is a **quantified plan of action** for a forthcoming accounting period. A budget is a plan of what the organisation is aiming to achieve and what it has set as a target.

Budgeting is so central to the processes of planning, delivery, monitoring and control that it should be considered to belong to the same continuous cycle of management.

However, the term 'budget' is often used in a variety of ways. When talking about 'the budget', some people may be referring to any of the following.

Table 7.1

Aspect	Comment
Forecast	A budget may be used to forecast expected performance. Forecasting helps managers consider the future. Given conditions of rapid change and uncertainty, however, this function will only be helpful over short periods of time. Budgets or forecasts need to be updated or recast often.
Means of allocating resources	Budgets can be used to decide what resources are needed and how much should be given to each area of the organisation. Budgets often set ceilings on spending, for example on project teams.
Yardstick	Budgets are often used as a yardstick against which to compare actual performance. The budget provides a means of indicating where and when control action may be necessary (and possibly where some managers or employees are open to censure for achieving poor results).

2.1 Planning

It is often simply the process of joint planning that creates a much higher degree of understanding and co-ordination. The resulting plan may be of less value than the benefits gained of working through the various budgetary stages together.

The formal nature of budgeting determines a careful examination of strategies, priorities, assumptions, contingencies, risks, opportunities and so on, and as a joint activity, it should lead to an enhanced appreciation of issues across the organisation.

2.2 Co-ordination

As a marketing budget cannot be properly designed and implemented in isolation from other functional plans, the budgeting process is an effective way of ensuring that organisational activity is appropriately co-ordinated.

Innovations in research and development, production, logistics, routine operations and strategic direction should dovetail neatly into marketing activity – promotional initiatives, product launches, public relations events, internal and external communications, consultation, feedback, advocacy, and so on.

The timing of such activity is often critical and must coincide with the related activity in other departments. Examples of co-ordination may include:

- Increased production and stockpiling ahead of a new marketing campaign
- Changes to inventory and in-store signage to coincide with a price promotion
- Staff training and development to disseminate news of a major update of website information
- Amendments to invoice handling and processing as new trade and cash discounts are introduced.

Budgeting should ensure a higher degree of joined-up thinking and prevent the more selfish indulgences of individual managers pursuing their own objectives. One of the principles of budgeting is that the scarce resource of finance will be applied to the areas where there is the greatest likelihood of maximising the return. Clearly, this is not done to the detriment of essential activity and must be undertaken with a long-term perspective. It will also attempt to sequence cash inflows and outflows as efficiently as possible to minimise liquidity problems and the costs associated with borrowing.

2.3 Motivation

The level of co-ordination achieved across the organisation is also required within functions. For this reason, it is useful to involve staff in the budgeting process, where this is practicable. Greater awareness of thinking behind the numbers is likely to add to a sense of collective responsibility and a desire to hit or exceed targets.

Awareness alone may be sufficient to motivate staff and managers. Recognition for higher performance may also act as an incentive and may be given in the form of an announcement and public praise, time off or bonuses. There are always dangers with implementing such schemes and care must be taken not to aggravate or demotivate others, or shift the focus on to targets while ignoring other objectives.

The Chartered Institute of Marketing

2.4 Control

A budget provides a ready set of metrics by which to gauge and evaluate performance. Unless they are produced by simply guessing income or expenditure based on previous years with an allowance for growth or inflation, budgets have to be derived from a series of assumptions about activity.

The process of budgeting requires a level of thinking and analysis that naturally leads to a better appreciation of critical areas of performance. Control can be more readily achieved by reacting to warning signs as activity falls short of targets. Variance from planned or expected performance will pinpoint where investigation and possible remedial action are required.

2.5 Budgeting and management

It should be clear from what has already been said that budgeting is very closely integrated with the business of management. Planning, control, decision-making, action, monitoring and motivation may all be linked through the budgeting cycle.

Budgets and the budgeting process are also great opportunities for communication. They provide a ready-made message for staff at all levels about priorities, challenges and expectations. The scope for co-ordination, control and motivation is greatly weakened if the key points are not widely disseminated. Communication, as we have already seen, is one of the components of management responsibility, none more so than for marketing managers.

So as not to overstate the case, it should be remembered that managers may exercise managerial control over people and resources without reference to any budget. Other 'softer' targets are equally appropriate for the purposes of monitoring performance.

An example of this would be adopting a triple bottom line (economic, ethical, environmental or profit, people, planet) – managers are also rightly concerned with corporate social responsibility. However, the budget should still form a spine that runs down the middle of operational and strategic plans. An organisation that fails economically is then unable to invest in sustainable resources, reduce its carbon footprint and provide aid to the local and global communities.

THE REAL WORLD

The case for effective budgeting

With the economy on the ropes, companies need some kind of lifeline. One overlooked strategy is to go back to basics: overhaul fundamentals like financial planning, budgeting and forecasting.

Companies require their financial plans to clearly represent their strategic objectives. Budgeting encompasses all the details for costs and sales across a company. Managers are then able to forecast a number of 'what-if' scenarios based on recent actual performance.

A shrinking economy is reason enough to get a handle on budgets, says William Soward, chief executive of Adaptive Planning. 'If there ever was a good time to manage budgets, it's now'.

Effective budgeting has a big impact on performance. Companies with best-in-class budget processes improved their profitability by 17% over the last 24 months, according to a survey from tech research firm Aberdeen Group. Aberdeen's survey found that best-in-class companies consistently tighten up their internal processes for planning, budgeting and forecasting. They shorten the times between budget cycles and they finalise budgets before the new fiscal year begins.

Aberdeen's survey also found these companies use specialist budgeting software (rather than spreadsheets) to manage their budgets. Spreadsheets are vulnerable to manual errors, whereas budgeting software usually extracts numbers directly from the nominal ledger. That reduces data-entry errors and reduces the likelihood of 'garbage in, garbage out'.

2.6 Budget considerations

2.6.1 Cost analysis

There are particular benefits to the marketing department to be gained from the process of budgeting. It requires a focus on measures other than the more traditional but harder to quantify values of customer loyalty, brand profile and corporate image.

In order to make a persuasive case to the senior team, and in particular the chief finance officer and CEO, it will be necessary to show how marketing activity contributes to cash flow and earnings per share. It is important to consider marketing's net contribution as a profit centre rather than just a cost centre. Campaigns should be appraised in terms of their return on investment (ROI) and payback.

This focus on costs requires a way of analysing and differentiating between various groups of expenditure items. A common way of doing this is by considering cost behaviour.

■ **Fixed costs** are those that remain the same regardless of the level of activity (including no activity at all), at least in the short and medium term. Fixed costs include overheads such as light and heat, salaries, business rates, the lease of vehicles, rent, security and depreciation. Irrespective of the volume of production or the level of sales, such costs remain effectively fixed. In the longer term, they may increase as operations grow or costs rise, or they may be manipulated by altering other aspects of activity through reorganisation, relocation, downsizing and so on (see Figure 7.2).

Figure 7.2   Fixed cost behaviour

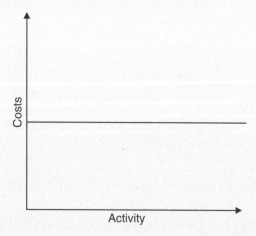

■ **Semi fixed (or step) costs** are those that remain fixed up to a given volume of activity and then suddenly step up to another level. An example of this is warehousing costs for holding stock. The cost of maintaining a storage unit – including security and other overheads – remains fixed until that unit becomes full and another is required, causing the costs to rise dramatically and then to remain fixed until the second unit is full, and so on (see Figure 7.3).

The Chartered Institute of Marketing

Figure 7.3   Semi fixed cost behaviour

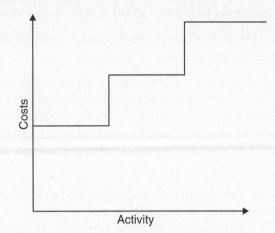

- **Variable costs** vary directly with the activity and are zero if the activity is nil. In a production context this would include all the costs of raw materials used in the manufacture of each item as well as wages, assuming this is incurred on a piece rate basis. For a marketing campaign this might include postage costs for mailouts to customers (see Figure 7.4).

Figure 7.4   Variable cost behaviour

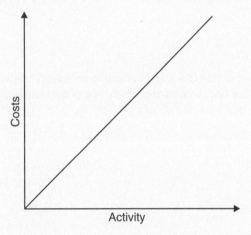

- **Semi-variable costs** vary with activity but do not fall to zero. The cost of sales staff would fit this profile if they enjoy a fixed salary with commission earned on top according to the quantity of items sold (see Figure 7.5).

Figure 7.5   Semi-variable cost behaviour

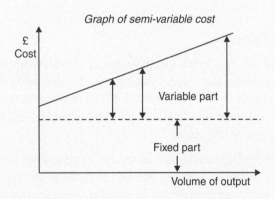

A sketch graph of a semi-variable cost would look like this.

Knowledge of cost behaviour is important to help identify the impact of costs of a particular strategy. It may help to set the parameters for planned activity as the manager strives to keep costs within budgetary levels.

As an example, if there is no budget for expanding into larger premises for holding surplus stock, then a different approach to inventory control is required.

Understanding cost behaviour also helps the manager to remain focused on those that are the relevant costs to a particular decision. If within the timescale of the proposed decision a given cost remains fixed, then its value is of no relevance to the decision-making process For example, if choosing between two options for stimulating additional sales in the short term, such as a mail out versus a telephone campaign, the fixed costs associated with the salaries of the marketing team are irrelevant since these will be incurred regardless of the option selected.

Having established the importance of budgeting to the role of the marketing manager, we now turn our attention towards the process of setting the budget.

Additional terms which are used when analysing costs are marginal costs and absorption costs:

The **marginal cost** is the change in total cost arising from the production of one extra unit.

Absorption Costing is a costing method which includes all the costs associated with manufacturing a particular product. Absorption costing takes the directly attributable costs of manufacturing the product such as materials and labour used in production and adds a share of the general costs such as heating or lighting.

ACTIVITY 7.2

The following costs have all arisen as part of a direct marketing campaign in which customers were contacted by the marketing team through various channels. For each cost decide which type of cost behaviour it is likely to most closely resemble.

- Telephone
- Postage
- Design and printing
- Salaries
- Agency costs
- Consultancy
- Office overheads

3 Setting the marketing budget

3.1 Introduction

Companies often ask 'how much should we spend on marketing?'. Although the average spend in the sector or actual spend by competitors may be useful guides, the answer to 'how much' is that it depends, and ultimately the marketing budget should be determined by the organisational objectives. It is easy to create a mismatch between marketing spend and what is appropriate (either too much or too little) by not building a budget that relates to the organisation's goals.

A number of different approaches are commonly adopted when setting marketing and communications budgets. The choice may depend on historical accident or personal preference, but it is important to be aware of the significance of each method in stressing particular dimensions. A mature organisation may use a combination of different approaches simultaneously to develop a more rounded picture.

The Chartered Institute of Marketing

3.2 Creating the budget

One simple way of comparing and contrasting different approaches to producing a budget is by considering at what level of detail the process begins. Where the process starts by setting a target or a limit on overall spend first and then breaks this down into discrete tasks, this is a *top-down approach.*

Top-down methods include using a percentage of profit or sales as an initial guide for the marketing budget.

Similarly, setting parity with competitors' marketing spend as a target for marketing expenditure or starting with an assessment of how much the organisation can afford (usually based on what is left after everything else has been accounted for) are also top-down methods.

Consideration of the share of voice may also be used to inform a top-down approach, commencing with a target for gaining a particular share of the available advertising (roughly equivalent to market share) and developing the budget in more detail.

Conversely, when budgets are built up from adding together the detailed planned activity this is known as a **bottom-up approach**. This includes an objective and task method where the goals of marketing are translated into actions and each of these are costed.

A planning and control approach is similar, involving working out what it would cost to create and maintain markets that serve the objectives of the organisation. Share of voice considerations may also be used to inform a bottom-up approach, starting with the objective of controlling a minimum percentage of the available media and then identifying and costing the individual tasks needed to achieve it.

Top-down methods include:

- Percentage of sales/profit
- Competitive parity
- Affordable method
- Consideration of share of voice

Bottom-up methods include:

- Objective and task
- Planning and control
- Consideration of cost-volume-profit (CVP)
- Consideration of share of voice

3.2.1 Top-down

Top-down budgeting starts by assessing the costs of higher order tasks first. This is then used to set the parameters for the subsequent evaluation of more detailed activity. For example, the marketing budget may be defined by a number of major headings such as:

- New product launch
- Customer website upgrade
- Planned PR event
- Main catalogue print run

The higher level headings may be individual campaigns or projects as above. Alternatively, the headings may be analysed by types of expenditure such as:

- Agency costs
- Printing and distribution costs
- Staff costs
- Broadcast media costs

From these total amounts, the budget is then broken down into more detailed activity, determining how much is to be spent on the sub-components of each of these headings within the overall limits given.

Clearly, a top-down approach relies upon the experience and judgement of the manager who determines the higher level budgetary limits in the first place. There needs to be an appropriate rationale for doing this.

Sometimes, it is by *historical budgeting,* that is, by starting with previous budgetary limits or actual spend as a guide. These are reviewed and adjusted accordingly (perhaps by a simple percentage increase but more commonly by an adjustment that takes changed circumstances of the internal and external environment into account).

3.2.2 Bottom-up

Bottom-up budgeting works in the opposite direction from a top-down approach. Typically, the detailed stages of individual projects are identified and costed from which the higher level is then constructed. Costs are estimated based on likely staff hours, materials and other consumables required. Estimates may always be challenged and cheaper sources sought, although usually at the expense of quality or speed.

Unlike historical budgeting, *zero-based budgeting* may be used whereby the budget must be recreated from scratch. Each figure must be justified rather than simply relying on the past as a reason for repeating the same spend. However, it is also more time consuming to complete.

In comparison with top-down budgeting, the bottom-up approach has the advantage that it is based on a more detailed, and therefore a more accurate, analysis of the component costs. It is also common to involve more people in the planning process, hence drawing upon their expertise where it counts as well as buying in their commitment.

However, there is a danger that these individual items can be over-inflated as the manager (consciously or not) builds in margins for unexpected expenses, wastage or delays, resulting in an overall exaggeration of the resources required. Psychologically, there is a temptation to ask for more than is needed believing you are unlikely to get all of it.

This can then lead to inefficiencies as there is no imperative to work within as tight a budget as possible. In comparison, the top-down approach imposes limits at the outset within which the manager must find ways of maximising the benefits of the allocated expenditure. On the other hand, there is no direct relationship between the objectives of the organisation and the limit set on the budget.

Table 7.2

Top-down budgets – advantages	
Simplicity and speed	The process can be relatively simple and quick, with figures simply imposed from above.
Authority	Those making the budget have the authority to do so – their figures won't be overruled.
Aware of bigger picture	Senior management aren't focused on one particular area of the business to the detriment of others – they are aware of the bigger picture and therefore perhaps best placed to decide relative priorities.

Table 7.3

Top-down budgets – disadvantages	
May be arbitrary	Senior management may set spending levels simply on the amount they feel the organisation can afford. There may be little analysis of what actually is required if organisational goals are to be achieved.
May cause resentment	Managers often feel they don't have sufficient funds to meet their targets. This can cause resentment and reduce motivation.
Short-term focus	If senior management bonuses are based on annual results (they usually are), the temptation may be to produce a budget that delivers results in the short-term but neglects investment.
Inefficient and divisive	As top management fixes the total budget, lower level managers must compete directly for funds. This does not promote co-operation and can result in a less than optimal allocation of funds.
May be worked-around	Creative accounting may be used to move costs from one area to another. This may happen with any budgeting method, but is more likely if managers feel their actions are justified because the budget is unreasonable.

The Chartered Institute of Marketing

Table 7.4

Bottom-up – advantages	
Empowering / motivation	Involving supervisors and employees in the process recognises their knowledge. If employees are expected to take responsibility for ensuring their roles are performed well, they need the resources to do so.
Encourages acceptance and ownership	Assuming the figures passed up aren't altered too much, employees are more likely to accept the budget and to try to remain within it.

Table 7.5

Bottom-up – disadvantages	
Time consuming	Employees may be distracted from their day-to-day tasks by the budget process. Bottom up budgets also tend to go through more reviews and amendments. This process of negotiation takes time.
Funds may not be available	The figures passed up for approval may simply be unrealistic and unaffordable. Then, significant alteration downwards of the budget figures by senior management can cause resentment.
Narrow focus	Employees are unlikely to be aware of competing priorities elsewhere in the organisation.

A hybrid or combination of these two approaches is the 'goals down, plans up' approach. This involves top management setting overall goals and lower-level employees devising plans and budgets to achieve those goals. This approach is often used in the formulation of marketing communications budgets.

3.3 The financial approach

The financial approach tends to emphasise a top-down model although not exclusively, and it may be on an historical or zero-base, as referred to above. Total marketing spend is often determined at the outset and then broken down into more discrete activity. However, there are good reasons why this is a popular way of doing things (especially amongst CFOs). As we have seen, budgeting is a process by which the scare resource of finance is apportioned out to different functions and activities with a view to maximising the return. This is why marketing managers need to be able express their intended outcomes in terms that indicate a direct contribution to the bottom line, such as:

- Increase to sales
- Positive cash inflows
- Returns on investment
- Growth in customer value

With this kind of analysis, they will have the makings of a very powerful case for the desired resources.

3.3.1 The budgeting process

Although there are variations in the relative importance attached to each stage, we can describe a typical budgeting process as being a cycle, normally an annual one that has many if not all of the stages shown in Figure 7.6.

Figure 7.6   The budgeting process

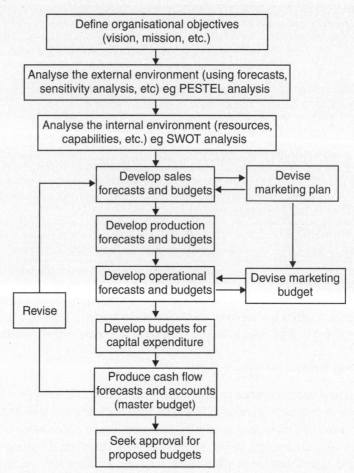

When using a process such as this it is important to ensure that it is applied appropriately to the context of the organisation and the budget being prepared – this is suitable for the complete marketing budget for example, but not all stages may be necessary for individual elements or discreet marketing activities.

There is a natural sequence to the various portions of the budget. The sales forecasts and budgets should come first, allied very closely to the marketing plan, and everything else is designed to support the achievement of these targets. It is usual that it is an iterative process, such that when the master budget is produced it becomes clear that revisions are required. This may be repeated several times until the total planned income and expenditure is in line with guiding assumptions and expectations.

3.3.2 Percentage of Sales/Profit

One of the most common top-down methods for setting an appropriate limit on marketing spend is by taking a given percentage of sales or profit, either actual or forecast. This allows for comparisons from year to year as well as with other organisations (especially competitors). As a percentage of sales, marketing spend varies quite widely from less than 1% to 10 or 15% and sometimes more.

It appears that organisations selling consumer packaged goods are likely to spend the most on marketing. For the launch of new products this may be as high as 50%, falling to between 8 to 10% thereafter. Retail stores typically spend between 4 and 6%[1].

According to same report, the average spend in advertising as a percentage of gross sales for a selection of different business sectors is given in Table 7.6.

Counsellors to America's Small Business[2] (SCORE) and The United States Small Business Administration[3] (USSBA) indicate the normal range is between 2 and 10% of sales but for B2C, retail and pharmaceuticals it

can exceed 20%. The overall average for all sectors is 6%. The scale of marketing spend also varies with the size of organisations, with larger companies spending a smaller percentage of revenue, falling to as low as 2 to 3% for the very largest, as indicated by Table 7.7.

One of the disadvantages of setting marketing budgets as a percentage of sales or profit is that it indicates a cut in marketing when sales or profits are falling, whereas the received wisdom is that this is precisely when an organisation needs to redouble its efforts to attract attention for itself and its goods and services to protect or gain market share.

Table 7.6   2012 ratio of advertising spend to sales industry sector — US data (Schoenfeld & Associates)

Business sector	Percentage advertising spend of gross sales
Grocery stores	1.3
Apparel	2.9
Soft drinks	2.9
Lawn/garden	4.0
Education	5.0
Computers	5.1
TV, radio and electronics	5.3
Catalogue mail order	5.7
Retail stores	5.8
Investment advice	8.6
Cosmetics	10.4
Confectionery	10.6
Memberships	11.0
Toys	14.2
Cleaning supplies	14.5

Table 7.7   Typical marketing budgets related to the size of organisations, based on US data

Turnover	Marketing budget (%)
US $5 million	7–8
US $5–10 million	6–7
US $10–50 million	5–6
US $50–100 million	4–5
US $100 million	2–3

3.3.3 Competitive parity

Matching competitors' spend on marketing is another approach commonly taken, if the information is available. However, this ignores the fact that organisations have different priorities, means of operating, structures, product portfolios and so on.

The comparison may be helpful but it should not be taken too far. Large organisations naturally have large resources at their disposal with which smaller organisations compete at their peril. The ability to focus on distinctive features and the unique selling points is probably more important than absolute spend in a given market.

This approach has several disadvantages.

- It assumes that the competitor has made good budgeting decisions or arrived at a 'correct' level of spending, which may not be the case. Competitive parity may be a case of the blind leading the blind!

- It is reactive and lacks direction. It does not take account of specific marketing objectives or opportunities. There may be an opportunity to build market share by additional expenditure, say, or to harvest profits from a declining product by reducing expenditure.

- Like affordability, competitive parity may create pressure to 'spend up' to competitor levels, when the organisation doesn't need to do so – or when, if given the incentive, it could find opportunities to achieve the same marketing effect for less.

- It may also create pressure to 'spend down' to competitor levels, reducing the organisation's ability to exploit opportunities to grow sales and profits by higher-level communications expenditure.

3.3.4 Affordable method

Another top-down approach, particularly common for smaller enterprises, is to work out what is needed for the rest of the business for operational costs and planned capital projects and to apportion what is left (or some of it) to marketing.

Although financially prudent, it creates an uncertain base for marketing to plan its activities over a period of several years. Marketing budgets must be based on a realistic assessment of what the function can achieve in any given period of time. Promotion is a long-term investment. There are no quick fixes. Because translating marketing spend into bottom line performance takes time and care, there needs to be a commitment to marketing that is sustained even in times of less favourable conditions.

Maintaining a profile is what will help the organisation survive in the long term. Many marketing initiatives take time to have an impact. Customers need to hear the key messages several times (and maybe in several media) before it creates sufficient interest that can be converted into a sale. Prudently, marketing budgets should not put all their eggs into one basket, favouring a multi-channel, multi-media approach instead.

A marketing initiative should commonly include a mix of media relations, promotion and advertising, together with a budget that supports this – this can be difficult to achieve successfully with the limitation the affordable method brings. With marketing budgets, there can be a case made for is it affordable to not spend the money – without the marketing promotion there may be no income generated and therefore the organisation becomes unsustainable.

ACTIVITY 7.3

Do you know what your nearest rivals or other similar organisations spend on advertising? How much does this influence the limits set on your own budget?

3.4 The marketing approach

The marketing approach tends to favour a bottom-up model (although not exclusively) by linking planned spending directly to the function's strategic objectives. Marketing budgets are often supported by an operational plan following the usual kinds of headings (objective, outcomes, milestones, action, by whom, by when and so on) with an additional column for required spending.

Each tactical marketing decision can be analysed according to the spend needed for advertising, market research, promotions, PR events, mailout, or another activity, with a planned date in the business calendar. This may also be analysed to indicate the relevant product, segment, region and channel of distribution the planned tactical initiative aims to address.

The following approaches vary in the ways they set and define the objectives in the first place from which the budget is then built. In some cases (such as the share of voice approach), an appreciation of marketing may be used either to inform a top-down or a bottom-up approach.

3.4.1 Planning and Control

When deriving the tactical activities from which the costs are then summarised, a planning and control approach seeks to establish and perpetuate positive contacts with key markets in support of organisational goals. It begins by analysing the intended market and identifying strategies for achieving the level of expansion, penetration, growth or diversification to gain and sustain control over it. Plans are then costed from which the budget is built.

The plans must be closely monitored and additional action taken where necessary to keep control of the market. Although similar to other bottom-up approaches such as objective and task (see below), the specific focus on control ensures a very tight grip on what is happening in the market in response to the activity undertaken and the ability to respond to changes in a timely manner.

This may be given in the form of a diagram as shown in Figure 7.7.

It may be necessary to adjust the action plan to deal with adverse variances in performance. As a result, the budget may also need to be flexed. However, it would be impractical to operate a totally flexible budget as it would no longer serve the purpose of controlling spending. Therefore, if actions need to be altered in order to address new circumstances, the marketing manager will either work within the existing total budget or be required to seek additional resources through a further process of bidding and negotiation.

Figure 7.7 Planning and control approach to budgeting

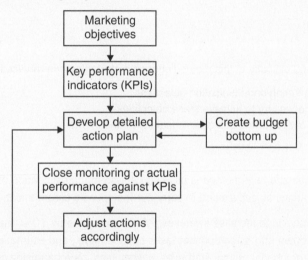

The performance indicators or KPIs may reflect different factors, such as:

- Total market share or share of market segments
- Reported levels of customer satisfaction
- Number of direct responses to advertisements
- Volume or value of sales
- Competitor performance
- Distribution of customers
- Responsiveness to promotional campaigns
- Distributor support

- Gross ratings points (ie number of impressions or the number of times target audiences receive key messages)

3.4.2 Objective and task

The objective and task method is probably the one which is most logical and appropriate to the complex situation found in planning marketing communications programmes.

The method is based on **three main steps**.

Figure 7.8   Objective and task method

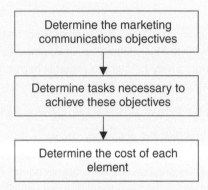

This approach is simple to understand and uses carefully considered and linked objectives and tasks. It is necessary to be realistic about the objectives and accurate in the costing of the tasks. This is an extremely difficult process in reality because of the large number of unknowns.

ACTIVITY 7.4

To demonstrate the logic and difficulty of this method choose a marketing communications problem with which you are familiar.

- Define the precise marketing communication objectives.
- Determine the tasks necessary to achieve these objectives.
- Cost out the problem both in terms of the individual tasks and in total.

The objective and task method is based on a systematic calculation of the expenditure required to fulfil communications objectives and to carry out the specific communications tasks planned to achieve them.

If the objective is to increase awareness of a brand name by 10%, the planned communication campaign will be broken down into its component tasks and elements, and estimated (or known) costs will be allocated to each (eg promotional media, staff time, agency fees, merchandising costs and so on).

The total estimated cost of all such campaigns (perhaps with an added contingency sum for emergencies and opportunities) will comprise the communications budget.

Advantages of the objective and task method

- It is relatively scientific and systematic, and can be based fairly closely on known costs (eg media rate cards and known discount rates, agreed agency fees, quoted print costs and so on).

- It can be performed for each communications activity, at a detailed level, building up to the total communications budget.

- It focuses managerial attention on objectives, tasks, opportunities and the effects of expenditure on outcomes (return on communications investment).

- It can be readily justified to internal and external stakeholders, as a sound and results-focused method.

The Chartered
Institute of Marketing

Although it will not necessarily produce perfect results, the objective and task method will lead to disciplined thinking and provide an excellent communication and decision device.

Disadvantages of the objective and task method

- The amount of effort and activity required to achieve communications objectives is difficult to estimate (particularly if objectives are long-range or qualitative in nature).

- Contingency sums are required to take account of unforeseen tasks (such as crisis communication or countering competitor campaigns).

- The method may reduce the funds available to take advantage of opportunities (such as newly available communication media or reduced-cost media space).

3.4.3 Share of voice

Share of voice refers to the share of available advertising for a particular market, or the number of marketing messages in the primary marketing area. Roughly speaking, for established brands (especially fast moving consumer goods) share of voice corresponds to share of market, although this rule of thumb requires very careful application.

To maintain your market share, you probably need a slightly larger share of voice – up to 25% more. So, if your product or service enjoys a 10% share of the market, to maintain this position the marketing budget should be sufficient for about 12.5% of the share of voice.

Share of voice is not just about spend and crucially the budget must be focused to gain the biggest impact for the resources available. Having used this concept to gauge the size of total spend (although for a specific product within a particular market), this can be used as the start of a top-down approach to building the budget. Alternatively, having decided that the ambition is to control a certain share of the available media, the budget could also be built bottom-up by identifying and costing tasks that need to be undertaken to achieve the desired share.

The following matrix (Schroer, 1990) shows how different spending strategies are appropriate depending on your competitors' share of voice and your own share of market.

Figure 7.9   SOV/SOM matrix

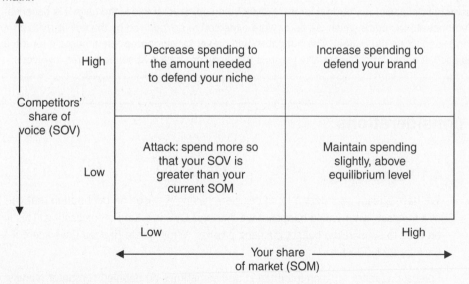

Note that careful monitoring of the fortunes of competitors is needed: if you know that a competitor is spending large sums on restructuring, then they may not be in a position to retaliate to a sudden advertising burst by your company.

3.4.4 Cost-Volume-Profit

We shall be examining CVP analysis in more detail in a later chapter. At this stage, it is important to note that knowledge of the relationships between volumes of sales, costs and incomes is vital to compiling a budget. CVP can be used to model a range of different scenarios to demonstrate what would happen if:

- Unit prices are increased or decreased

- The volume of units sold increases or decreases

- The fixed costs associated with a particular product or service (including marketing and promotion) rise or fall

- The variable costs of producing a product or service (including the cost of bring it to market) rise or fall

This tool can then be used by marketing managers to put together a budget and help set performance indicators. Therefore, it may inform some of the Key Performance Indicators (KPIs) for a planning and control approach to the budget. It is a very simple model (and can be criticised for being over-simplistic) and perhaps only has applications across a narrow range of activity where costs and revenues conform to approximate straight lines.

Nevertheless, it does focus on key factors (costs and incomes) and aids the forecasting, budgeting and decision-making process. It shows very readily the relationship between revenue, costs and profits, and helps inform the decisions about pricing.

ACTIVITY 7.5

It is a common practice to use a number of different approaches to setting the budget. Which of the different approaches described above are part of the way the marketing budget is built in an organisation you are familiar with? Of those that aren't used, are there any that would have a useful application to complement current practice?

▶ **Assessment tip**

Many assignment briefs ask for a budget for the activity being covered. If this is the case it is essential that the budget includes figures to demonstrate the costs which will be or were expected to be incurred by the activity with an explanation and justification for the method used to set the budget. The budget should be set for an appropriate timescale for the activity and should be realistic, it is accepted that for confidentiality reasons they may not be the absolute figures involved.

---

4 Other considerations

4.1 Forecasting

We have already seen that a lot of decision-making is based on information that can be presented in the form of a forecast: what would happen if we did this? CVP is a kind of forecasting. This kind of approach can readily be used to support the budget planning process. What would happen if we spent a further £10,000 here or cut back by £25,000 here?

Forecasting relies on good information and sometimes on detailed computer models. Ultimately, however, it requires experience, judgement and a good dose of gut instinct. The marketing manager will need to make decisions where the timing is critical, such as:

- When to make an investment
- When to launch a new product

The Chartered Institute of Marketing

- When to retire an old one
- When to hold a PR event
- When to make a major announcement

The budget, as a central component to the plan, will be tied into such deadlines. Knowing the likely pattern of demand for a given product or service is critical for planning other fundamental activities such as:

- Co-ordinating changes to the customer website to ensure the correct sequence of information is available at all times

- Managing the availability of staff with the appropriate skills to support promotions, dealing with enquiries, providing after sales service and so on

- Engineering the appropriate promotional mix at any period

- Scheduling the levels of production required at key points in the year

- Working with suppliers and distributors to ease the pressure points on the supply chain

Macro forecasting will provide information of the market as a whole whereas micro forecasting includes a more detailed level by focusing on individual products and services within segments and niches. It is likely that a combination of these will prove useful in compiling evidence to support the proposed budget.

4.2 Financial analysis

There are many different ways that accountants and finance directors assess the value of a project, either proposed or historical. It is not necessary here to learn the detailed workings of the various models and undertake lengthy calculations, but it is important to recognise the ways in which marketing proposals may be scrutinised and interrogated. We will be looking in more detail at cost-benefit analysis later.

Financial analysis of marketing initiatives may focus on their impact on the following aspects of performance:

- Increase in sales
- Increase in profits
- Return on investment
- Payback
- Discounted cash flow
- Break-even analysis

Although the marketing manager may be inclined to focus on the impact certain initiatives will have on brand awareness, customer loyalty, market profile, share of voice and so on, this needs to be supported by an awareness of the financial implications.

The first, and perhaps most obvious, hoped-for result will be an **increase in sales**. This could be measured in numbers of units sold but perhaps more usefully in value. As part of a proposal, this can only be estimated and targets can be set for a rise in revenue.

To monitor performance, it will be possible to compare actual results with previous years for the same period. Ideally, the marketing manager would like to be able to attribute sales to particular initiatives, and while this may be achieved by asking customers at the point of sale what prompted their purchase or by tracking promotional voucher numbers, the nature of marketing often makes it hard to see any direct and immediate connections between activity and sales – hence Lord Leverhulme's famous quote – that half the money he spends as advertising is wasted – the question is, which half.

Increased sales revenue is only one part of the intended outcome. If the costs involved in making the sale outstrip the additional cash inflow, it would be necessary to consider whether it was worth it.

There is often a good case to be made for securing an initial sale at no profit or even a loss, as a loss leader, to raise awareness, penetrate new markets, gain market share over competitors and encourage repeat purchasing.

In the long term, however, it will be an **increase in profits** rather than simply sales that will determine the success of marketing. Even if losses are expected, measurement is still vital to check that they remain within budget.

Sometimes, the return on the outlay is expressed as a percentage of the initial investment. ROI is expressed by the following formula:

$$ROI - earnings/investment \times 100\%$$

The higher the ROI the more attractive the investment. This figure may be compared with the cost of borrowing the capital (from investors, from the bank) or with the return that may be gained from alternative activity. The return would have to exceed these in order to be an appropriate use of scarce funds.

Payback looks at the additional revenues generated by an initiative and calculates how long it will take to recover the initial investment. For example, if a £100,000 spend on a particular marketing initiative this year can be expected to generate an additional £30,000 net income per year, it will not be until the fourth year that the investment has been 'paid back'.

Discounted cash flow techniques take a more sophisticated approach to payback by also taking into account the decreasing benefit of future incomes. In essence, future cash flows are worth less than present ones since we would rather have the money today than next year in five years' time. This is related to the cost of borrowing and the opportunities for alternative investments that may pay back less quickly but give greater value overall (when discounted to present values).

Finally, **break-even analysis** (much the same as CVP) is another common technique discussed in Chapter 8, that attempts to match incomes, costs and profits. Identifying the level of sales needed at different prices is a useful way of appraising a marketing proposal.

Such models have various strengths and shortcomings. In general, they tend to focus on different features and are best used in combination. No analysis can make the decision for you but they are part of the picture that will help inform such decisions.

4.3 Balanced scorecard

The balanced scorecard is a popular technique for strategic planning and management designed to keep the attention focused on what is important. It was developed by Kaplan and Norton at the Harvard Business School and provides a ready framework within which to monitor high-level goals. As such, it has the potential to be applied to a wide number of areas of management, including the marketing plan and budget.

The scorecard is 'balanced' because rather than providing solely financial measures, it aims to cover and link a broader range of key indicators. Financial measures suffer from being historical and only tell part of the story that managers need to know if they are making decisions about the future direction of their organisation. The process followed to create and monitor the scorecard forces senior manages to clarify their vision and think carefully about their priorities. It includes both internal and external dimensions and drives the organisation towards continuous improvement. It comprises four quadrants:

- **Learning and growth**: This is an internal perspective and focuses on the development of individuals and the organisation as a whole.

- **Business processes**: This is also an internal perspective that considers how well the organisation is running.

- **Customers**: This provides an outward looking view of the needs and wishes of the organisation's customers, and will be of particular interest to the marketing manager.

- **Financial performance**: Although not the sole focus, profitability and liquidity remain a central concern.

The scorecard contains a range of metrics within each quadrant that are kept under regular review. This approach provides a wealth of understanding and data that can be used to monitor KPIs that form part of the budget as well as provide a focus for setting priorities within future plans.

If applied properly, a balanced scorecard should lead to improvements in customer satisfaction, financial performance, operational processes, and employee effectiveness and performance.

We shall be revisiting the balanced scorecard model as part of our considerations of cost-benefit analysis in Chapter 8.

4.4 Resourcing

In a general sense, resourcing is concerned with the practicalities of delivery, especially with who is going to carry out the planned activities. Consideration of staffing needs to underpin the marketing plan and budget. Although in practice many marketing budgets do not include staffing costs they should always be considered, especially where changes are proposed.

The marketing manager must consider the level, complexity, volume and required expertise of tasks to assess the staffing needs. Options include:

- Full- and part-time permanent members of the team
- Secondment from other teams
- Fixed-term contracts
- Agency staff
- Outsourcing
- Consultancy

Bidding for extra staff or changes to the composition of the marketing team will be part of the budgetary process requiring analysis and supporting information. There is a balance to be made on the basis of costs, flexibility, expertise, control and risk. Decisions about staffing naturally form part of the budgeting process. Bids for staff costs will form part of the overall proposal.

Resourcing is also used as a term to refer to a particular way of supplementing the marketing budget by enabling the manager to draw upon expertise not readily available within their own team. The process involves engaging staff for a fixed-term as an alternative to permanent additions to the team and so increasing headcount or undertaking lengthy retraining and upskilling programmes.

It is particularly useful where specific specialisms are needed for projects, assignments and campaigns for a limited time period, and can also address seasonal variations in the demand for staffing.

Resourcing is not the same as contracting, which usually implies a commitment for a specified time period, but may be very open-ended. The services of a resourcing agency enable the marketing manager to seek out critical expertise and engage individuals for the duration of a given project. In fact, the individuals used in this way remain employed by the agency throughout the engagement while being based within the marketing manager's team.

Initiatives for which resourcing may be used include:

- Market research
- Marketing audit
- PR event
- Short campaign
- Website development
- Product launch

There are clear advantages with such an approach. It provides great flexibility and rapidly delivers sought after talents for short or medium term initiatives. This fits the demand within the marketing function to instigate a tight series of events, campaign and particular activities, either as one-offs or as part of a cyclical programme. It also enables the best use to be made of the permanent marketing team members rather than deploying them in contexts to which they are not best suited.

Analyse a marketing team in terms of how activity is resourced. What are the costs associated with full-time, part-time, agency, consultancy and other staff costs?

5 Information sources

5.1 Types of information

> ▶ **Key term**
>
> **Information** is required for informed decision making. The **marketing budget** will require information from inside the organisation (eg what products and services will be produced) and from outside the organisation (eg what are competitors doing?, what will our campaign cost?).

Regardless of the approach taken to formulating the marketing budget, it is imperative that it is based upon a broad range of reliable and relevant data. CFOs and CEOs are more likely to be persuaded of the need to increase spend on advertising, for example, if the case is supported convincingly by clearly documented information. It is part of the job of the person preparing and proposing the budget to ensure that the assumptions and predictions stand up to scrutiny. Although there is always the need to exercise a certain amount of professional judgement, this only comes after the available evidence has been duly considered.

Terminology

The following definitions are relevant when discussing information sources and requirements.

Table 7.8

Term	Meaning
Data	Raw facts, for example a customer list.
Information	Data that has been arranged or processed in some way to add meaning. For example a customer list in order based on sales value.
Intelligence	Information that is suitable for a particular purpose, for example reducing risk.
Knowledge	Information within people's minds.
Tacit knowledge	Expertise held by people within the organisation that has not been formally documented.
Explicit knowledge	Knowledge that the company knows that it has, for example facts, transactions and events stored in information systems.
Knowledge management	The process of collecting, storing and using the knowledge held within an organisation.
Environmental scanning	The process of gathering external information, which is available from a wide range of sources.

5.1.1 Data, Information, intelligence and knowledge

Although we tend to use the words interchangeably, we should be careful to distinguish between raw data, information, intelligence and knowledge.

Data is the simplest form of information such as numbers, words and pictures, but lacking any context. On its own, it does not tell us anything beyond the simple fact that it states. Individual pieces of a jigsaw are not very revealing.

The Chartered
Institute of Marketing

When collected together, however, data starts to have meaning and so becomes **information**. The fuller picture emerges as the pieces are assembled.

Intelligence is a particular way of using this information, of manipulating and applying it.

Intelligence can then be seen to provide us with useful **knowledge** that has explanatory power and helps us to understand.

These are not absolute hard and fast definitions, and there are many shades of grey between one term and the next. The important thing to recognise is that data in the form of numbers, pictures, graphs and mere facts needs to be analysed and interpreted, understood in context, connected with other information and applied to a particular issue before we can really begin to say that we have knowledge.

Data might include the volumes of units sold as a series of numbers

Information might include other pieces of data about sales, production and profits that fit together into a broader picture about what is happening

Intelligence might include the patterns inherent in these figures following analysis, revealing percentage changes

Knowledge might include an appreciation of seasonal variations and underlying trends that explains the patterns revealed

A manager relies on information that is accurate, timely, in the appropriate format, comprehensive for the purpose in hand but not unnecessarily detailed. Based on a clear identification of the data required, information systems need to be devised to deliver this in a manner that is not overly time consuming or expensive.

Collecting data as a task in addition to ordinary operational procedures can become a significant burden if care is not taken to develop systems efficiently. Good information systems are able to take the required information at the appropriate point as part of routine activity. For example, if it is important to the organisation to count the number of visitors to one of its stores, the best time to do this is at the moment of entry, rather than trying to derive it later from other information. Automated collection of data could be used. Alternatively, customers could be asked to sign in, take a ticket or in some other way register their arrival.

Data mining is a term used to describe the techniques for identifying multiple sources, gathering them and extracting useful and relevant information. The greater the variety of sources used, the more useful data mining is in building up a picture of the internal or external environment in which the organisation is operating.

With tremendous advances in information technology used to capture and store data, managers have access to vast arrays. Users can 'drill down' from higher to lower level data to reveal the detail needed. **Data warehousing** refers to the management of collecting, storing and retrieving data from one or more databases, often with the added capability of linking several data sets.

In analysing information either by using software or manually, managers are looking for patterns. In particular, the following may be revealing:

- **Classes** – repeated patterns, such as purchasing habits, that can be used at the basis for predicting similar trends in similar customers in future

- **Clusters** – uneven distribution of data that falls naturally into groupings around events, times, geographical regions and customer characteristics that helps to identify the existence of a recognisable market segment

- **Associations** – relationships that may be uncovered between apparently unrelated data

- **Sequences** – sequential patterns that show the development of customer and/or behaviour and demand enable organisations to provide a changing marketing mix to suit progressive conditions

Such patterns may be exploited to improve efficiency, maximise sales and revenues, and elevate customer satisfaction. Armed with the right data, marketing managers are empowered to take control over the marketing

mix, monitoring the effectiveness of decisions made and making adjustments in response to changes in internal and external factors.

5.2 Internal and external data sources

Technology enables vast amounts of data to be available to marketing managers. This can be liberating and empowering but may also have the opposite effect. Rapidly increasing process speeds and memory space create huge opportunities for analysis and calculation. Advanced data mining techniques may reveal thousands of unexpected correlations between various fields.

However, just because the information can be gathered and retrieved does not guarantee that it will be of any use. Managers might find that their time is diverted regarding detailed data that fails to produce any real intelligence pertinent to the issue under consideration.

THE REAL WORLD

Data mining

A grocery chain in the United States used data mining software to assess the buying habits of its customers. Quite unexpectedly, they found that when men were buying disposable children's nappies they commonly bought beer at the same time. This was noticeable on Thursdays and even more so on Saturdays. As a result of this discovery, the grocery chain made various changes to its stores, including relocating beer so that it could be found next to the nappies and ensuring that beer was sold at full price on Thursdays.

(DSS Resources, 2012)

Marketing audits are certainly aided by the use of technology and the capability that enables continuous auditing.

Data is routinely collected, very often in electronic form, from transactional processing such as sales, purchasing, wages and salaries and stock keeping. Other forms of data are also held, such as predictive data in the form of forecasts, as well as external data relating to economic trends, competitor performance and market behaviour. It is also possible to hold data about data (meta data) that helps the user find their way around databases and extract what they require.

5.2.1 Sales figures

The best model we have for predicting the future is generally the past. There is normally a wealth of data relating to actual performance that can be analysed and used to help support a budgeting proposal. The point was made above that when information systems are designed, it is important to be clear about what is going to be needed. The volume, mix and value of sales figures can be analysed by a wide range of characteristics, including:

- Customer characteristics (gender, age, lifestyle, income, class, occupation, etc)
- Spending per customer
- Geographical location
- Timing and date
- Buying behaviour (patterns of purchasing)

In order to make sense of this data, it is necessary to understand more clearly what is going on. Statistical tools such as time series analysis help to see the patterns underneath the data and then enable managers to make forecasts. In patterns of data that occur over a period of time, there are three separate causes of variation:

1   Random fluctuations
2   Cyclical or seasonal variations
3   Underlying trends

The Chartered Institute of Marketing

If we made a simple numerical comparison between one month and the next, we are likely to get a false impression of performance. It is first necessary to identify and separate out the random fluctuations that occur in order to reveal the seasonal patterns that are repeated within the course of a single year or across several years.

Seasonal variations arise due to changes in weather, public holidays and culturally determined behaviour. Religious festivals, cold weather, patterns of unemployment and the school calendar all impact on sales to a greater or lesser extent, depending upon the particular sector. Only then is it possible to distinguish the underlying trends.

Having done this, firstly one has a much clearer appreciation of the data and secondly forecasts and predictions can be made.

5.2.2 Headcount

Headcount is a measure of the number of employees, and may be broken down by full-time and part-time. It is most likely that staffing costs (including the on-costs of health care, national insurance and pension contributions) are the single largest item in the budget.

It is commonly argued that staffs are the most valuable asset (as well as being the most expensive), and so it is important to give headcount a high level of scrutiny when reviewing past performance and preparing future budgets.

We have already examined resourcing options, including more flexible and cost-effective means of securing specialist skills for short periods of time. The composition of the permanent membership of the marketing team is critical to the success of any initiative and deserving of special attention.

Some of the data available on staff will relate to their performance. For sales staff, for example, it will be easy to assess the relative effectiveness of each member of the team. For others, it may be more difficult.

Such data might be used simply as a means of control and possibly as grounds for dismissal, but it is just as important to learn from the patterns of staff performance as it is from sales data. Careful analysis may reveal a range of highly significant relationships that may be used to reinforce marketing plans, including:

- The relative strengths of individuals
- The importance of timing as a component of high performance
- The impact of training
- Cyclical patterns of behaviour related to personal development and motivation
- The effectiveness of feedback and bonus schemes
- The ratio of productivity to salaries and wages

Headcount may also be used to compare the size of the marketing team with other teams within the organisation as well as with competitor and rival firms. It is a very rough measure but may be useful as an indicator of effective power and capability.

There are difficulties in counting part-time and fixed-term staff, and practice varies (sometimes within the same organisation). Headcount may simply be the numbers of bodies employed or there may be a more sophisticated attempt to reflect the number of full-time equivalents. As with all data, headcount must be used judiciously.

5.2.3 Outsourcing costs

Outsourcing (or subcontracting) costs arise when an organisation employs another to undertake some or all of the roles of an entire function, rather than having an in-house facility. This may occur in any number of areas and is fairly common in areas such as:

- Internal auditing
- Payroll
- Information technology support
- Human resources
- Accounting

It requires a strategic decision to outsource rather than develop or maintain your own capability (as discussed in Chapter 4). The basis for such a decision may be purely economic but there are other advantages to be gained, including greater flexibility, choice, access to expertise and operational effectiveness as well as freeing managers up to focus on areas of greater priority (such as production, selling and marketing communications).

Outsourcing some or all of the marketing function is a consideration that many organisations make. It is likely that portions of it, such as advertising, are already outsourced through the use of agencies.

There is great appeal in seeking to benefit from the expertise of specialists in market research, PR, campaign management, product launches, website development and maintenance, customer engagement, direct mail management and market analysis. When outsourcing, control of the data associated with items outsourced is essential.

Potential benefits of outsourcing are:

- Reduction in overall costs
- Improved quality of service
- Opportunity for better deployment of own staff
- Greater predictability of costs
- Better access to talent and expertise
- Enhanced scope for innovation and change
- Greater speed to market
- Transfer of operational risk to subcontractor

Outsourcing is not an option that should be entered into lightly. Extensive research and modelling would be needed to support any bid that proposed a move towards moving key functions out of the organisation.

5.2.4 Consultant costs

Similar points may be made in relation to consultant costs, although it is much easier to enter into short-term arrangements. In preparing marketing plans and budgets, it is important to consider the staffing of each planned activity and identify where consultants may be needed to supplement the skills and expertise of the marketing team.

Such costs must be researched and included with an appropriate rationale. The historical costs of consultants used may be an important internal source of information on which to base the prediction for future expenditure.

5.2.5 Electronic Point of Sale (EPOS) System

EPOS data capture through an EPOS system can provide a wealth of useful material with which a marketing manager can develop information to support a budgeting proposal. Used principally to manage inventory and minimise the time taken to move products from warehouse and distribution centres to retail outlets, the system can also be used to gather information about a customer's purchasing habits, which in turn may be applied by targeting future promotions. Supermarket loyalty cards are regarded by customers as rewards for repeat purchasing but for the retailer they provide a substantial bank of serviceable data.

Similarly, cookies that record items purchased as well as those previously viewed can be matched to databases of typical customer behaviour and used in e-commerce to make recommendations to the grateful customer. 'Previous buyers of this product also bought the following'.

EPOS data may take many forms and may be used to track any of the following:

- Customer buying habits, including a typical 'basket of goods'
- Impact of promotions on buying patterns
- Stock movements, including time spent on shelves
- Market share of individual products, brands and lines
- Distribution of products

5.3 Marketing Information Systems (MkIS)

> ▶ **Key term**
>
> The **marketing information system** (MkIS) is 'the framework for the day-to-day management and structuring of information gathered regularly from sources both inside and outside an organisation' (Dibb *et al*, 2001).
>
> A marketing information system consists of people, equipment and procedures to gather, sort, analyse, evaluate, and distribute needed, timely and accurate information to marketing decision makers.

Marketing information or intelligence systems (usually abbreviated to MkIS to distinguish it from more general Management Information Systems) is a term used to refer to the processes, equipment and people involved in gathering, analysing and disseminating information to marketing decision makers. It can be a useful tool for supporting a large number of management tasks including information gathering, analysis, evaluation, planning, decision-making, control and budgeting.

As with any such system, there is a balance to be had between the amount of data collected, accuracy, cost and speed. It is always possible to gather more data, in more detail and more quickly but this comes at a price (see Figure 7.10).

Marketing intelligence systems vary in terms of the sources and types of information they hold, the complexity of the system and the ways in which users can access the available data. However, despite these differences, marketing research usually plays a central role, providing valuable information about the market and how its responds to various initiatives (see Figure 7.11).

The information works on the basis that raw data is provided from a number of sources, both internal and external. This requires market research and market intelligence.

Figure 7.10   The competing pressures on information gathering

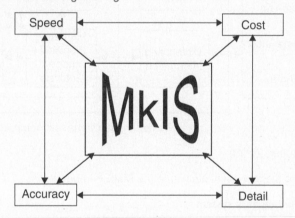

Figure 7.11   Role of MkIS

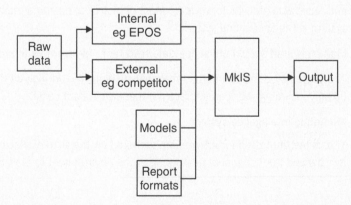

The system also needs a number of models. These are prepared programmes that shape the data into useful information on the basis of certain theories and assumptions about the way markets behave. Finally, in order to access the information, there should be a series of defined reports (standard and *ad hoc*) that allows the data to be viewed and presented in a user-friendly format.

A wide range of information is systematically gathered for marketing purposes. Some examples include:

- Prices
- Advertising expenditure
- Sales
- Competitor activity
- Distribution costs
- Stock levels
- Attributes of potential promotional/supply chain partners
- Buyer behaviour (and the social trends affecting it)
- PESTLE (Political, Economic, Socio-cultural, Technological, Legal and Environmental) factors
- Internal audit (and/or SWOT analysis) of the organisation's marketing capabilities

Often, unless it is carefully organised and all stakeholders know where they can access it, the value of the information is lost. Marketing information systems provide a way of centralising the information contained within an organisation and facilitating knowledge through it's careful usage.

Figure 7.12   The marketing information system

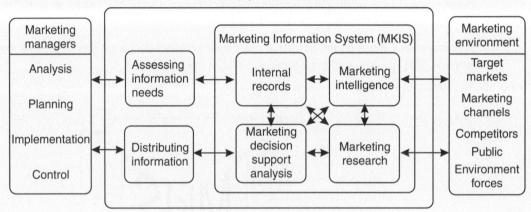

The marketing information system

(Based on Kotler, 2008)

Let us look at the four elements within the MkIS in more detail.

- **Internal records system**

    Internal records includes reports of orders, sales figures, headcount, consultancy costs, accounts payable and receivable etc which provide a store of historical customer data. One aspect of the internal records system is the accounting system.

    Marketing staff should utilise the data held here, for example to monitor customer profitability.

    The payroll systems and human resource systems should include details of factors such as headcount (ideally including headcount forecasts) that will impact costs.

- **Marketing intelligence system**

    This is the term used for information gathered on the market place by managers on a day-to-day basis. It is derived from continual monitoring of the environment to alert managers to new trends.

- **Marketing decision support system**

  Firms can use statistical analysis within this level of the system including regression and correlation analysis, sales forecasting, time series analysis, product design and site selection models.

- **Marketing research system**

  Marketing research aids management decision making by providing specified information in time for it to be of value.

  In addition, data is also drawn in from the external environment.

- **External data sources**

  The MkIS is linked to external sources, perhaps via an internet link or simply by individuals gathering information from external sources and feeding it into the system. The internet can be a fast, efficient way to search for and access data that may be required for budget setting (for example, competitor activity, advertising agency rate cards).

ACTIVITY 7.7

How is marketing intelligence assembled within an organisation you are familiar with? If you can, itemise all of the internal and external sources of data that are collected. How much of this is used to inform planning and decision-making?

5.4 Exchange rates variances arising from international trading

If international trade forms a part of current or projected business, then the budget should reflect the costs associated with currency exchange and overseas purchasing and selling. Given the uncertainty of exchange rates, it may be prudent to factor in a number of contingencies should they become less favourable. A combination of historical data analysis and forecasting will be needed. Clearly, the volume of funds subjected to exchange rate variations will affect the scale of the potential impact on the bottom line. The timing of the changes – whether just before or just after a transaction – will also be significant.

- The manager's role – the mnemonic COMMANDER can be used to cover the roles of the manager

- Control is required because of unpredictable events and variations in performance

  - Information has to be managed, using a variety of tools, in order to deliver control
  - Cross functional communication is a high priority

- Budgets are quantified plans of action related to accounting periods – covering aims and targets

  - Budgets require forecasts of the future
  - Knowledge of all costs is required for budgets – fixed, variable and those in between

- Many methods exist for setting budgets, primarily divided into a financial approach or a marketing approach

  - Objective and task is generally considered most appropriate for marketing

- Information sources needs to be evaluated for their suitability for budgeting

  - Both internal and external data should be used
  - Marketing information systems help with gathering and utilisation of data

FURTHER READING

Collier, P. (2008) *Accounting for Managers*. 2nd edition. Chichester, John Wiley & Sons.

REFERENCES

[1]Source: Schoenfeld & Associates, 2006, quoted in, amongst others, http://www.saibooks.com/adv-ind-sector-ratios.html [Accessed on 13 June 2012]

[2]http://www.score.org

[3]SBA.gov (2012) http://www.sba.gov [Accessed on 15 June 2012]

Anthony, R. N. (1965) *Planning and Control Systems: A Framework for Analysis*. Boston, Harvard Business School Press.

Bonasia, J. (2009) The case for shorter budget turnarounds. Investors.com, http://news.investors.com/article/473636/200904091720/the-case-for-shorter-budget-turnarounds-.htm?p=full [Accessed on 21 June 2012]

Buckley, A. and McKenna, E. (1972) Budgetary Control and Business Behaviour. *Accounting and Business Research* (Spring 1972), pp137-150.

Collier, P. (2008) *Accounting for Managers*. 2nd edition. Chichester, John Wiley & Sons.

Dibb, S. *et al* (2001) *Marketing Concepts and Strategies*. 4th European edition. New York, Houghton Mifflin.

DSS Resources (2012) DSS News. DSS Resources, http://www.dssresources.com/newsletters/66.php [Accessed on 21 June 2012]

Hucyznski, A. and Buchanan, D. (2003) *Organisational Behaviour: An Introductory Text*. London, Prentice Hall.

Kotler, P. (2008) *Marketing Management: Analysis, Planning, Implementation and Control*. 13th edition. London, Prentice Hall.

Schroer, J. (1990) Ad Spending: Growing Market Share. *Harvard Business Review* January/February 1990, pp44–48.

QUICK QUIZ

1   *Choose the appropriate words from those highlighted.*

A **forecast/budget** is an **estimate/guarantee** of what is **likely to occur in the future/has happened in the past**.

A **forecast/budget** is a **quantified plan/unquantified plan/guess** of what the organisation is aiming to **achieve/spend**.

2   The basic principle of cost behaviour is that as the level of activity rises, costs will usually fall. True/false?

3   Costs are assumed to be either fixed, variable or semi-variable within the normal or relevant range of output. True/false?

4   What name is given to the approach to budgeting that involves budgets being set by senior management and passed down the organisation?

5   The approach to budgeting that relies to a significant extent on the actions of competitors is known as:

A   Share of voice
B   Affordability
C   Objective and task
D   Competitive parity

6   The approach to budgeting considered the most logical is:

A   Share of voice
B   Affordability
C   Objective and task
D   Competitive parity

7   What is the main advantage of affordability as an approach to setting the marketing communications budget?

8   What is the main advantage of competitive parity as an approach to setting the marketing communications budget?

9   Briefly explain the main disadvantage of the percentage of sales approach to budget setting.

10   Briefly explain the main disadvantage of the objective and task approach to budget setting.

ACTIVITY DEBRIEFS

Activity 7.1

Answer will depend on your own situation

Activity 7.2

- Variable
- Variable
- Semi-fixed
- Fixed
- Semi-fixed
- Semi-fixed
- Fixed

Activity 7.3

Answer will depend on your own situation

Activity 7.4

Answer will depend upon the communications problem considered

Activity 7.5

Answer will depend on the situation considered

Activity 7.6

Answer will depend on the situation considered

Activity 7.7

Answer will depend on the situation considered

QUICK QUIZ ANSWERS

1   A **forecast** is an **estimate** of what is **likely to occur in the future**.

   A **budget** is a **quantified plan** of what the organisation is aiming to achieve (in financial terms).

2   False. They will rise.

3   True

4   Top-down budgeting.

5   D. Competitive parity is dependent upon the actions of competitors.

6   C. The objective and task method is probably the one which is most logical (and the method most appropriate to the complex situation found in planning marketing communications programmes).

7   Affordability is a realistic approach as it takes account of resource availability.

8   Competitive parity ensures matching of competitor activity so may help preserve market share.

9   Percentage of sales doesn't take account of marketing objectives and opportunities. Effective promotion causes sales. The strict implementation of the percentage of sales method means a reduction in sales leads to a reduction in promotion. It could be that increased promotion would reverse the decline in sales.

10   The main disadvantage of objective and task budget-setting is the time, effort and difficulty involved in estimating the costs of tasks, particularly unforeseen contingencies.

The Chartered
Institute of Marketing

CHAPTER 8

Justifying and managing marketing finances

Introduction

Marketing has to compete with other organisational functions and demands for funds (or budget). To compete effectively, marketing managers must be able to explain the benefits the marketing spend they are requesting will bring (in financial terms). This isn't possible unless the marketing manager has financial awareness to be able to present a justified case to the finance department.

While in the past marketers may have left the numbers to the accountants for credibility this is no longer possible. The marketing budget is the marketing manager's budget. Through understanding it, taking ownership of it and learning how to negotiate effectively to grow it, marketing managers have a far better chance of securing the resources needed to do an effective marketing job for the organisation. This element of the syllabus gives the ability to do this along with other aspects of cost management and measuring effectiveness such as ratio analysis, activity based costing and the use of key performance indicators based on critical success factors.

When looking at numbers or ratios, it is important to use awareness of the operating environment and of general business issues to enable reasonable conclusions to be drawn.

Topic list

Negotiating marketing budgets	1
Cost benefit analysis of marketing	2
Cost control, cost improvement	3
Managing costs in marketing	4
Business process re-engineering	5

3.4	Negotiate delegated budgets with colleagues and agree provisional budgets:
	▪ Preparing a budget bid/business case to obtain priority budget for marketing activities ▪ Negotiation tactics for bidding internally for budget to senior management
3.5	Undertake cost benefit analysis of marketing activities establishing priorities and best value approaches to operations:
	▪ The balanced scorecard – learning and growth perspective, business process perspective, customer perspective, financial perspective
	▪ Value chain analysis
	▪ Cost control, cost improvement
	▪ Cost-volume-profit analysis
	▪ Break-even analysis
	▪ Sensitivity analysis
3.6	Establish effective cost management processes for marketing operations to ensure that costs are managed effectively to achieve viability in the long term:
	▪ Variance analysis – sales variance, cost variance ▪ Cost control ▪ Activity-based costing ▪ Business process re-engineering

1 Negotiating marketing budgets

There is a difference between simply preparing the budget and making a case for it. There is a skill to organising and presenting information in such a way that it has maximum impact by focusing the attention of the reader on the most important and telling items.

The process of bidding for financial resources varies considerably between organisations, and the manager must conform to the specific requirements set.

1.1 Preparing a budgeting bid/business case

Before preparing a budgeting bid, it is important for the manager to ensure that they are following the criteria set. The formality of such arrangements will depend on the size and nature of the organisation. Sometimes, the submission is purely made in writing, but it is more usual for the manager to make a presentation to a senior panel and be available to explain and justify the proposals.

It is common to have a preset *pro forma* that dictates the layout and composition, with main headings and analysis required. The budget is often divided between:

▪ Operational budget
▪ Capital budget

The operational portion covers all of the routine activities that form part of and support day-to-day trading. This will be further divided between income and expenditure. There may be further subdivisions according to product, service, location, time period or other means of distinguishing different aspects of business appropriate to the organisation.

There may be a requirement to show each major project and initiative separately.

The operational budget is sometimes split between base budget (which is simply a projection of continued activity at present rates with corresponding income and expenditure) and growth (which as the name suggests includes activity additional to previous years).

Table 8.1 Sample extract of a proposed budget and the variance with current year's forecast actual outturn

Ref	Description	Actual 2010/11 £	Actual 2011/12 £	Forecast 2012/13 £	Budget 2012/13 £	Variance £
001	Advertising	11,234	11,488	11,833	12,030	(197)
002	Printing and stationery	802	1,109	1,201	1,458	(257)
003	Postage	209	315	432	587	(155)
004	PR	2,806	1,321	2,571	3,265	(694)
005	Training	5,204	2,836	1,242	3,566	(2,324)

The capital budget covers one-off items of investment that sit outside of normal operations. Such items would include the acquisition or disposal of fixed assets (such as machinery, motor vehicles, computer equipment and office furniture) and the refurbishment of or extensions to premises.

Items of expenditure that are deemed to have financial benefit that lasts for more than one year are regarded as capital items, and so it may be decided that a major upgrade to the MkIS or developments to the customer website are to be included in this section of the budget.

It is common that, as next year's budget is being prepared, the current year is still in progress, and so it is necessary to use forecast figures to estimate the most likely outturn for the current year. As the current year is usually incomplete as next year's budget is being prepared, forecast figures will be used instead to estimate the most recent levels of activity. An example of an extract from a budget is given above in Table 8.1.

In this case, a marketing budget for the financial year 2012/13 has been prepared. Each cost item has a code number for ease of dialogue and for cross referencing purposes. The historical data for the past two years is available as is the latest estimate for current year. The variance in the final column is a measure of the difference between the forecast outcomes for the current year and the proposed budget for next year. Numbers in brackets indicate adverse variances.

In this example this means that the expenditure is set to be greater than the most recent turn out. This kind of budget may be supplemented with a notes column in which explanations can be given as to why training, for example, is set to rise by nearly 200%.

A total proposed figure for the year is useful, but sometimes it is necessary to profile this planned expenditure over the year by quarterly predictions or even monthly. This requires more work in the preparation but once undertaken it provides a very useful set of figures against which to monitor actual performance (we will examine budget variances in more detail in Chapter 9 later).

Table 8.2 Sample extract of a proposed budget with projections per quarter

ref	Description	Q1 £	Q2 £	Q3 £	Q4 £	Total £
001	Advertising	2,955	3,020	3,288	2,767	12,030

Using the same figures as above, the advertising spend has been estimated for each of the four quarters of the budget year in Table 8.2.

This could be built up to form a cash flow projection for the year.

In support of the numerical information, the marketing manager should provide explanatory notes and supplementary data, much of which has already been discussed in previous sections. This may include:

- High level aims and objectives and an explanation of how these support strategic targets

- A review of previous years' activity with an explanation of major variances between planned and actual outcomes

- A marketing audit and an analysis of the internal and external environments (using SWOT, PESTEL, Porter's five forces and so on)

- An operational plan for the coming year detailing activities and events, linked to targeted income and expenditure

- Extracts of market research and intelligence in support of key assumptions

- Break-even analysis and other diagrams, graphs, charts and illustrations

- Sensitivity analysis modelling the effect of positive and negative variations in forecast variables

These elements go beyond the process of budgeting itself and overlap significantly with other matters, most significantly strategic and operational planning and analysis. It should come as no surprise, however, that they are linked so closely.

1.2 Negotiation tactics

If the organisation requires more than a paper-based submission, then it is likely that budget setting will require some form of negotiation. The term 'negotiation' implies a process of dialogue and debate through which two or more parties seek an agreement. It is not confined to the world of work and most people are engaged in a degree of negotiation every day.

Of course in an organisational context, the aims of the two parties (here the marketing manager and representatives of the senior management team) ostensibly are the same. However, there may well be disagreement about priorities and the most effective way of achieving goals.

A number of separate stages may be identified in the negotiation process through which the marketing manager hopes to secure a workable budget. These are illustrated by Figure 8.1.

Figure 8.1   The process of negotiation

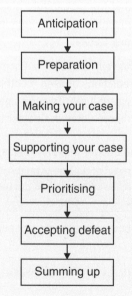

There are a number of other important factors in a successful negotiation.

Preparation

Key to negotiation are the initial stages of anticipation and preparation. The marketing manager should familiarise themselves with the requirements of the process, ensure they meet with the expected deadlines and comply with documentation and so on. It is also vital to attempt to anticipate the possible objections and requests for further information.

To be ready with the necessary detail is very impressive and also shortens what might otherwise be a protracted business. The marketing manager should know what the corporate objectives are and have a realistic appreciation of the parameters of what is acceptable and what is not. It can be helpful to know what the absolute minimum required for the marketing department is to perform the marketing activities to contribute effectively to the organisation.

Take control

In order to make the case as clearly as possible, it may be appropriate to produce a visual presentation. Certainly some kind of summary can be very effective. It is necessary to decide in advance what the key points are that need to be stressed at the outset before you get into the detailed discussions of particular expense headings and various adverse variances. This is about taking control of the situation. Otherwise, the negotiations may quickly become derailed by discussions that prevent you from making your key points.

Supporting the case is all about the preparation you have done previously, having examples, statistics and arguments that you can draw upon if you are challenged. Linked to this is a recognition that you may not be able to win all of your battles.

Naturally, managers make more demands on financial resources than can feasibly be met in any given budgetary cycle, and so in creating the master budget, the finance director is required to make some judicious pruning from the initial proposals. Knowing this, it is worth having in mind which of your initiatives you are prepared to concede and which are central to you overall strategy.

It is important to negotiate professionally and with confidence, but not with arrogance. Aim as high as you feel is credible, other parties may bring this down but it is always easier to go down than to gain.

Remain reluctantly flexible! Ensure your preparation included establishing clear concise benefits the organisation will obtain from the marketing budget you are requesting. Unless you are work for a very large corporate, reasons such as 'improved brand awareness' are unlikely to be sufficient! Quantifiable benefits, in monetary terms, are more likely to succeed in securing the budget you require.

Consider consequences

If cuts to the budget bid you have submitted are proposed, point out the **consequences** of the cuts. For example, if the organisation has a target to grow sales in the London area by 10%, but you have been asked to reduce radio advertising spend with London radio stations, ensure senior management is aware that this reduction will make the sales increase unlikely.

Emphasise priorities

Remain positive, and know your priorities. The budgeting process can be frustrating. Just when you think a figure has been agreed you may find an edict is issued that 'all budget figures must be cut by 15%' - an example of top-down, affordability budgeting discussed earlier.

The whole process is based on the premise that from a series of proposals, some will be taken up and accepted while others, no matter how good they may seem to the marketing manager, may be shelved or rejected outright. Recognising when the point has been reached beyond which it is not worth arguing is a further key stage in the negotiation process.

Concluding

The final stage of summing up is often lost and so it remains unclear what has been accepted and what has been rejected. The marketing manager proposing their budget can take the initiative at the end of the process to itemise what they believe has been agreed so that a record is made. Further action may be required at this point and some matters may remain undecided. There may need to be several cycles of negotiation before the budget is finalised.

The style that an individual adopts through the process of negotiation may have real impact on the outcome. Whether someone is combative or more passive in their bidding might depend upon their personal proclivities, but care should be taken to be mindful of the expectations placed upon them in the negotiations.

If one is expected to act and talk tough, then it becomes a necessary way of behaving. The same is true if the organisation demands a more gentle and reasoned approach. Above all, a calculated stance that demonstrates political nous will always be advantageous.

1.3 Delegated and provisional budgets

1.3.1 Delegated budgets

> ▶ Key term
>
> A **delegated budget** is one that the ultimate budget holder passes-on (delegates) responsibility for.

This is relevant from **two points of view**.

- The marketing budget is delegated to the **Marketing Director** from above (for example, from the managing director). Responsibility for the marketing spend has been delegated to the Marketing Director, but ultimate responsibility for all aspects of the organisation's performance remains with the Managing Director.

- The Marketing Director may also delegate budget to others, for example part of the marketing staff costs budget may be delegated to the **Marketing Manager**.

Typically, budget requests are passed to senior management annually. Heads of divisions pass this information to departments and sections, who complete and aggregate the relevant parts of the budget, and pass them back up the ladder.

Along with the formal budget request comes supporting information, such as: the percent of wage increases estimated for the year and potential project priorities. As the budget requests are passed up the organisation, they are reviewed against organisational goals and adjusted.

1.3.2 Provisional budgets

Organisations that favour a **participative** approach foster dialog and compromise between management levels. A typical iterative approach starts with top management setting a budget framework for each year of a strategic plan. This framework then directs the selection of new projects and serves as a guideline for managers as they prepare their budgets.

Detailed project budgets are aggregated into provisional functional unit or departmental budgets and finally, into a provisional organisational budget that top management reviews and, usually, modifies.

Depending upon the top management approach, departmental and project managers may then be asked to modify their respective budgets. The process may undergo several iterations until the budget is finally agreed.

This process is based on input from all levels of management and should help ensure coordination between the different budgets (functional versus project and long- term versus short- and mid-term).

The Chartered
Institute of Marketing

What experiences have you had of negotiation? Did you formally prepare for it or did you rely chiefly on gut instinct? In readying yourself for negotiation in the future, what are you likely to do differently? Do you think it is the best way to arrive at the most appropriate budget for your department?

2 Cost benefit analysis of marketing

> **Key term**
>
> **Cost-benefit analysis** (or CBA) is a technique used to determine the feasibility of an activity, project, decision or plan by quantifying its costs and benefits.

Cost benefit analysis is a general approach of adding up the benefits, taking away the costs and seeing whether what is left is worth the original investment in time and resources, including the opportunity cost of doing something else instead.

This is not always as easy to do as it sounds. Not all costs and benefits arise in one go and often accrue over time, possibly over many years. Techniques such as payback analysis and discounted cash flow technique attempt to group all of these costs and benefits together in order to make an overall appraisal. This carries the health warning that future cash inflows and outflows are harder to predict the further ahead in time they are set to occur.

In simple models of cost benefit, only the financial items are included. In more sophisticated models other, less tangible, factors are taken into account, including social and environmental costs and benefits. In this section, we will be examining a range of techniques that help managers understand the relationships between performance, costs and revenues and so evaluate the overall value of marketing initiatives.

The simplest form of cost benefit analysis simply lists all of the costs and all of the benefits. This makes the assumption that is possible to assign a financial value to costs and benefits.

Imagine, for example, that an organisation wishes to appraise a proposal for investing in a new customer database. The marketing manager could begin to assess its value by identifying and analysing all the relevant items. Often the costs are easier to quantify than the benefits.

2.1 Example: proposal for investing in a new customer database

Costs

■ Initial purchase of commercial off the shelf software	£65,000
■ Annual licence	£4,000 pa
■ Customisation of software to meet specific organisational needs	£18,000
■ Additional annual support licence	£1,300 pa
■ Staff training and development	£2,800
■ Upgrade of hardware	£8,480
■ Installation	£1,700
■ Testing	£820
■ Data transfer	£3,400

Total cost: £105,500 in the first year, £5,300 in each following year.

Benefits

- Shorter processing time of membership applications (calculated as a percentage of data input staff time)
  £4,500 pa

- Savings from reductions in system down time (calculated from emergency call out charges)   £800 pa

- Improvements to targeted marketing, reductions in mailout costs and increases in sales   £31,200 pa

- Disposal of old equipment less costs of disposal   £22,000

Total benefits: £58,500 in the first year, £36,500 in each following year.

In this case, it would not be until the third year that the project had recovered the initial outlay and ongoing additional costs.

An analysis such as this, however, does not take into account the intangible benefits which may be derived from the activity. These do need to be included within the benefit analysis.

Some examples of benefits of marketing activity which are intangible and difficult to value:

- Greater customer satisfaction and loyalty, arising from brand awareness

- Improved staff morale and staff retention from working in a well-known, reputable company

- Willingness of other organisations to do business with us due to our reputation

- Benefits accruing from gaining competitive advantage

- The fact that so many of the benefits of marketing activities are intangible means that it is difficult to construct a meaningful cost-benefit analysis

There are three possible approaches to dealing with this problem.

Table 8.3   Putting a value on intangible benefits

Approach	Comment
Calculate a value for the benefits	We could estimate the worth of each of the intangible benefits and allocate an appropriate cash value.
	The problem with this approach is that realistically it is nothing more than guesswork.
Ignore the 'too intangible' benefits	Allocate a value to those intangible benefits we are able to estimate a realistic value for and ignore other intangible benefits.
	This approach will significantly undervalue marketing activities.
Adopt a qualitative approach	Find a reasonable non-financial way of stating intangible benefits. For example, customer brand-recognition ratings could be established through questionnaires, market share could be used to assess competitive advantage.
	The problems with this approach are:
	• Determining appropriate measures
	• Isolating the effect of the specific activity from other factors

2.2 The balanced scorecard

We have already considered how budgeting and the balanced scorecard may be connected in setting and monitoring KPIs and feeding back performance into future budgetary limits (see previous chapter). In this section, we examine more specifically how the technique may be applied to appraising activity within marketing.

The first thing to appreciate is that all four quadrants of the balanced scorecard apply as much to marketing as to any other area of the organisation as shown in Table 8.4.

The Chartered Institute of Marketing

It is common to specify that such targets should conform to the SMART acronym in order to facilitate taking remedial action and make improvements, where SMART stands for:

- Specific, so that it is clear what the expectation is
- Measurable, so that it can be readily monitored
- Achievable, so as to motivate and inspire action rather than describe an unattainable aspiration
- Resourced[1], so that those charged with delivery have the tools to do the job
- Timely, so that there are built in deadlines that prevent constant backsliding and deferral.

One of the principles of the balanced scorecard is that it is designed to drive improvements, so when targets have been achieved new targets should be set as this will facilitate further improvements.

Similarly, if it transpires that the unworkable targets have been set (because circumstances have changed or the original analysis was incomplete), these too should be changed since there is no value in chasing impossible goals.

Table 8.4   Shows how each quadrant of the balance scorecard relates specifically to the marketing context

Quadrant of the balanced scorecard	Application to a marketing context
Customers	This quadrant is very much core to the marketing function as it attempts to define and measure the effectiveness of the organisation from the customer's perspective. Appropriate measures that may be used include: - measures of customer satisfaction - rate of new product acceptance - the conversion ratio from enquiry to sale - market share - customer retention rates - delivery performance measures (numbers of orders fulfilled correctly and on time) - quality performance measures (such as sales returns)
Business processes	There are processes within the marketing function that need to be monitored to ensure that they are both effective and efficient. Measures used to monitor these could include: - simple count of tasks completed (phone calls made, letters sent, catalogues dispatched, events held, etc.) - percentage of activities carried out within service level guidelines (such as complaints and enquiries responded to within time) - efficiency gains in time and cost for key activities (printing costs, stock turnover rate)
Learning and growth	The skills and expertise within the marketing function should be kept under review to ensure it constantly matches the demands being placed upon it. The picture should be broad enough to take into account outsourcing, agency and other resourcing options. Measures used may include: - headcount - staff turnover rates - measures of staff satisfaction - compliance with HR requirements for induction and appraisal - targets for personal and professional development
Financial performance	Marketing activity should be evaluated on financial indicators. Appropriate financial metrics for monitoring marketing via the balanced scorecard may include: - increases in sales and profits - net cash flows - return on capital employed - return on investment - average purchase per customer - the customer lifetime value - the average cost of securing custom

2.3 Value chain analysis

Value chain analysis is a process first described by Michael Porter in his 1988 best seller Competitive Advantage: Creating and Sustaining Superior Performance. In his model, the value chain consists of a series of activities through which products or services pass and gain value. In fact, they gain more value than the sum of all the individual activities put together.

The value added is not the same as the cost of the activity, and in fact a commercial enterprise could not survive if the processes involved in the value chain cost more than the added value for which customers are prepared to pay – value can be added through reduced costs which can then be passed on to customers through lower prices.

There are five distinct kinds of value-adding or primary activities in the value chain:

1   **Inbound logistics**, referring to the activities in bringing and preparing materials and resources to production (handling, warehousing, shipping)

2   **Operations**, referring to production activities (machining, assembly, testing, packaging)

3   **Outbound logistics**, referring to the activities of taking the goods to market (processing orders, warehousing, transportation, distribution)

4   **Marketing and sales**, including building brand value, advertising and promotion

5   **Service**, such as installation and after-sales service

There are also capabilities that an organisation requires to carry out the primary activities, which Porter called support activities:

- Firm infrastructure
- Human resource management
- Technology development
- Procurement

See Figure 8.2.

Figure 8.2   Porter's value chain analysis.

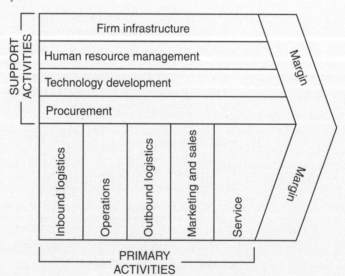

The usefulness of the value chain analysis is to enable organisations to focus on and identify those features that create competitive advantage. Each of the five types of primary activities is critical. Being able to compete by offering a better or faster distribution process, or superior after-sales service, for example, may prove to be the distinctive benefit that is decisive in gaining market share over competitors.

As part of a cost analysis and control approach, the value chain model provides a gen[...] down different kinds of activities and support mechanisms that can [...] provides a means for determining linkages between different parts of [...] have an impact on later activities.

The value chain of any organisation links upstream and downstream i[...] contributing to a complex value system. All of this analysis can be put [...] outsourcing or resourcing.

The ultimate **value** an organisation creates is measured by the amount [...] products and services above the cost of carrying out value activities.

- **Customers 'purchase' value**, which they measure by comparing an [...] with similar offerings by competitors.

- **An organisation 'creates' value** by carrying out its activities either m[...] organisations, or by combining them in such a way as to provide a u[...] We continue this point in the activity below.

ACTIVITY 8.2

Outline five different ways in which a restaurant can 'create' value.

2.4 The value chain and competitive advantage

According to Porter (1985), an organisation can develop sustainable competitive advantage by following one of two strategies.

- **Low-cost strategy**. Essentially this is a strategy of cost leadership, which involves achieving a lower cost than competitors via, for example, economies of scale and tight cost control. Hyundai (in cars) and Timex (wrist watches) are examples of organisations that have followed such a strategy.

- **Differentiation strategy**. This involves creating something that customers perceive as being unique via brand loyalty, superior customer service, product design and features, technology and so on. Mercedes Benz (in cars) and Rolex (wrist watches) are examples of organisations that have followed such a strategy.

An organisation's ability to develop and sustain **cost leadership** or **product differentiation** as a means of **competitive advantage**, depends on how well it manages its own value chain relative to competitors.

Competitive advantage is gained either from providing better customer value for equivalent cost or equivalent customer value for lower cost. Value chain analysis can be used to determine the activities within an organisation's value chain that could be improved by either lowering costs or enhancing value.

2.4.1 Cost management and the value chain

Shank and Govindarajan (1992) explained how the value chain framework can be used with a view to lowering costs and enhancing value.

They suggest a three-step approach.

Step 1   Build up the industry's **value chain** to determine the activities in the chain and to allocate operating costs, revenues and assets to individual value activities.

Step 2   Establish the **cost drivers** of the costs of each value activity.

BPP
LEARNING MEDIA

Develop sustainable **competitive advantage**, by **controlling these drivers better** than competitors. For each value activity, sustainable competitive advantage can be developed by reducing costs while maintaining value (sales) and/or increasing value (sales) while maintaining costs.

3 Cost control, cost improvement

It is worth reminding ourselves that the central purpose of budgeting – indeed one of the core functions of management itself – is to control costs with a view to maximising performance.

Marketing should be regarded as an investment in the future of the organisation, but the control of costs is as important here as it is anywhere else.

For effective control, it needs to be embedded within normal operating procedures. Cost information should be collected at regular interval and compared with the budget forecast.

Cost control and cost improvement depend largely upon a continual awareness and reappraisal of activity. It is not enough to repeat doing things in a certain because that is how they have always been done. Suppliers should be reassessed regularly and compared with others.

The process of tendering and re-tendering may be time-consuming but if handled carefully should be part of a designed approach to improving costs and should ensure that the organisation always gets the best available deal.

Similarly, the marketing manager should revisit the question of outsourcing versus doing everything in-house. Joint ventures, sponsorships, alliances and strategic partnerships may provide alternative ways of sharing costs and risks while ensuring a better outcome for the investment.

3.1 Cost-volume-Profit and break-even analysis

We have already seen how cost-volume-profit analysis (CVP) may form part of the process of compiling information in support of a budget. As volumes of sales increase so do incomes and costs. Total costs (comprising both fixed and variable costs) will behave like semi-variable costs overall. That is, they will not fall to zero as overheads (rent, rates, light and heat and so on) will be incurred even if sales are zero. They will also rise as sales increase, hopefully at a lower rate than sales income so that at some point the income and total costs lines cross. This point is at the break-even point, where total income is equal to total costs. Any increases in sales above this point means an excess of income over costs so that a profit will be made. Any drop in sales below this point means an excess of expenses over income so that a loss will be made. The steeper the total income line in comparison with the total costs line, the more sensitive the system is to making profits and losses. A small change in sales results in a more rapid increase or decrease in profit or loss (Figure 8.3).

Figure 8.3   Cost-volume-profit (or break-even) graph

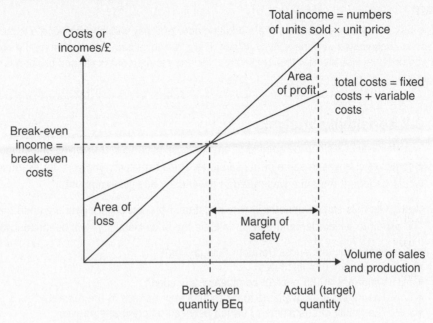

A formula can be derived for the break-even quantity, BEq, as follows:

$$\text{BEq} = \text{Fixed costs/Contribution per unit}$$

where Contribution per unit = selling price per unit – variable cost per unit

Contribution is fundamental to CVP analysis, and essential for marketers to understand as part of the pricing process.

For example, if a campaign is analysed such that its fixed costs (such as salaries and brochure design) total £15,000, the variable costs per sale (printing and postage) are £12 (based on an assumption of how many brochures need to be sent to different people before one is converted into a sale) and each sale has a net worth of £15, then we would need to make 5,000 sales to break even (fixed costs £15,000, total variable costs 5,000 × 12 = £60,000, so total costs = £75,000, while total net sales are 5,000 × 15 = £75,000 as well).

We can also calculate profit or loss as being the difference between revenue and costs at any given volume of sales, as follows:

$$\text{Profit (or loss)} = \text{total revenue} - \text{total costs}$$

$$= \text{volume} \times \text{selling price per unit} - (\text{fixed costs} + (\text{volume} \times \text{variable cost per unit}))$$

Profit is zero at break-even point as this is where total revenue equals total costs. We can use the model to experiment with changes to price or costs or volumes of units sold. This will yield a sensitivity analysis, revealing how quickly profits will fall in response to changes in one or more of the variables.

This strategy is important as we are unable to forecast conditions with perfect precision. Therefore, it is common to take several estimates to define the upper and lower limits of expectations. The margin of safety is the distance between the break-even quantity and the anticipated volume. The larger this margin, the less likelihood that small variations will cause the graph to move into a loss.

3.2 Sensitivity analysis

Sensitivity analysis can be applied to any forecast or budget. It involves modelling the effect on other costs and incomes of changes in some of the variables. Price sensitivity analysis, for example, can be used to see what would happen if the price was raised or lowered by any given amount.

Costs, volumes and revenues will vary in different proportions, depending upon their particular relationships. The extent to which demand rises or falls (ie the price elasticity) will be influenced by

- Stochastic influences (random fluctuations)
- Availability of substitutes
- Variations in the price of complementary goods
- The information available to customers about prices in the market
- The ability of customers to switch between different alternatives
- The strength of brand loyalty

What sensitivity analysis enables marketing managers to do is to consider different scenarios and identify the sources of variability in costs and revenues. Those factors that are the most critical then become subject to closer scrutiny and demand extra levels of control. MkIS is likely to be used to support such analysis. Other bespoke software also provides more sophisticated tools with greater ease of manipulation.

ACTIVITY 8.3

Consider an activity that is part of the responsibility of the marketing function involving costs and revenues. Analyse the data and construct a CVP (or break-even) graph. Use the graph to model the result of changes in the variables.

4 Managing costs in marketing

> **Key term**
>
> **Cost management** is a wide, general concept. Any activity intended to ensure expenditure is monitored and achieves value can be considered a cost management activity.

As we have already seen, control in general and controlling costs in particular are central to the role of the marketing manager, as for any manager. Planned activity needs to be effectively costed. Budgets and other types of forecasts provide a useful guide for expected results, covering not just predicted revenues and expenditure but also the anticipated volumes on which those predictions were made.

Once the actual results begin to emerge (often through monthly management accounts), it is possible to compare these with the budget and so identify and analyse any differences. A detailed understanding of what has caused any variances enables the marketing manager to control costs more effectively and re-engineer processes in a more efficient manner to ensure long-term efficiency gains.

The Chartered Institute of Marketing

4.1 Cost control

The intended result from budget setting and monitoring is to control costs. Control implies something active and dynamic. Any process that requires managers to do more than submit last year's budget proposal creates a need to review and rethink the way things are normally done.

We have already reviewed options that may be considered, such as outsourcing, flexible resourcing arrangements, strategic alliances and joint ventures as well as asking suppliers to retender on a regular basis to test their offer against the market. Using monthly management accounts and information systems, it is imperative that costs are monitored as they occur.

While it is not possible to control something after the event, the most recent results you can access will provide the best possible guide to what action is needed.

We should note once again the distinction between controllable and uncontrollable costs. The direct costs are more immediately controllable. For marketing, this might include part-time wages, printing and postage. However, where something benefits more than one product or activity, such as advertising costs, it is less controllable in that it would be hard to influence the costs with immediate action.

Fixed costs generally are not controllable in the short term. Office overheads, salaries and warehousing fall into this category. Operational decision-making therefore focuses on controllable costs.

4.2 Activity-based costing

> ▶ **Key term**
>
> **Activity-based costing** is an approach to cost management that relates costs to the factors that cause or 'drive' them to be incurred and to change. These factors are called **cost drivers**.

In discussing cost variance, we noted the difficulties of attributing overheads to individual products or services. It is relatively easy to calculate the cost of the labour and raw materials for each unit, but the further away from the process the costs arise, the more difficult it becomes.

Machine costs may be apportioned on the basis of the number of hours a product requires of machining, but remote overheads such as administration and marketing seem to have no direct relationship with numbers of units produced. The danger of using an arbitrary basis for absorption is that it does nothing to help with cost control.

However, allowing functions within an organisation to operate as cost centres rather than profit centres makes it impossible to determine their contribution to the bottom line.

Activity-based costing (ABC) attempts to draw in as much of the overheads to individual's units or production (or separable items of service provided) in order to improve accountability, manage costs more effectively and produce greater profitability.

It reveals more clearly the extent to which one product or service may be subsidising another and hence provides a better basis for decision-making. In essence, ABC seeks to move away from arbitrary percentage-based absorption costing to a closer causal basis on which to attribute costs.

There are several stages to such a process. First of all, the organisation is subdivided into identifiable costs centres appropriate to their activity. For a manufacturer, for example, this may include:

- Machining
- Assembly
- Finishing
- Canteen
- Administration
- Marketing
- Logistics

Then, costs that clearly belong to an individual centre are allocated accordingly. Costs that are unique to a cost centre are easily attributable (such as wages of staff). Some costs will need to be apportioned because they are shared between more than one cost centre. A manager, for example, may supervise two departments and so their salary needs to be split.

The difficulties arise in attributing indirect costs (overheads). When apportioning costs, a suitable basis is needed. In the case of salary, the number of hours spent in each division would be appropriate. Relative floor space may be used to split rent, rates, light and heat.

ABC uses the principle that whatever activity is the *cost driver* should bear the cost. In traditional manufacturing concerns, this was usually based on the volume of production but such an assumption is no longer reflective of many structures and practices. Other more appropriate bases of apportionment need to be used (Table 8.5).

Table 8.5   Possible bases for apportionment of overheads

Overhead	Possible basis for apportionment between cost centres
Light and heat	Floor area
Maintenance	Machine hours
Depreciation	Capital value of equipment held
Telephone	Numbers of staff in administrative roles
HR consultant	Headcount
Business rates	Floor area

Cost drivers may be distinguished between structural costs drivers (linked to organisational goals and purpose) and executional costs drivers (linked to operational activity). There will inevitably be some costs that are not easily attributable to specific activity and ultimately are regarded as general overheads that apply to the whole organisation (such as the CEO's salary).

Activity-based costing can have direct relevance for the marketing manager. For one thing, some form of ABC is an essential prerequisite for value chain analysis because to identify added value one needs to know the costs associated with each link in the chain. Better knowledge of where costs arise will also facilitate a better marketing mix.

ABC analysis can also be applied directly to the question of how much it costs to acquire and retain customers. By identifying services customers receive and the costs associated with each service, it is then possible to work out how much cost is attributable to each user of those services, even to each actual paying customer.

4.3 Customer profitability analysis

▶ **Key term**

Customer profitability analysis (CPA) assigns revenues and costs to customers or groups of customers with the aim of focusing effort and resources towards more profitable customers.

Many costs are driven by customers (delivery costs, discounts, marketing costs, after-sales service and so on), but traditional absorption costing systems do not account for this. Organisations may be trading with certain customers at a loss but may not realise it because costs are not analysed in a way that reveals the true situation.

ABC can be used in conjunction with customer profitability analysis (CPA) to determine more accurately the profit earned by servicing particular customers.

Customer profitability analysis involves an analysis of the income and costs associated with specific customers or customer groups.

The use of activity based costing in a marketing context should enable you to establish how much it costs you to acquire and retain each of your customers. This depends initially upon identification of the cost drivers for customer attraction and retention. Many of these costs may be outside the marketing department, for example customer retention may be influenced by customer service.

4.3.1 Example: Customer profitability analysis

Assume you are a marketing manager for the credit card division of a large bank. You are running a campaign to existing customers to sign them up for a new credit card. As you begin your campaign, you suspect the following:

- Only 40% of your bank's customers are profitable
- You don't know who those profitable customers are

Your goal is to market to this 40%

How can you identify the profitable customers?

Under traditional cost accounting, you can establish what resources your company allocated to staff all customer interactions, but you are unable to establish what individual customer interactions cost. Under ABC, each customer activity (related to identified cost-drivers) is recorded and attributed its actual cost. This makes it possible to establish the total cost for each customer. Combining this with the revenue each account brings in gives a profit (or loss) figure for each customer.

ABC and CPA requires close partnership between the accounting and marketing functions, including information systems (for example, both should work from the same customer database).

Marketing should also partner with the production function to ensure that the products you are about to do a promotion on are actually available, or to help decide which products to promote, based on inventory levels. The most creative campaigns in the world are doomed from the start if they are not built using relevant information from inside the company.

4.3.2 ABC, CPA and service businesses

Many service businesses have **characteristics** similar to those required for the successful application of ABC.

- A highly competitive market
- Diversity of products, processes and customers
- Significant overhead costs not easily assigned to individual types of service
- Demands on resources such as customer services which are not directly proportional to volume

If this approach were to be used in a hotel, for example, attempts could be made to identify the activities required to support each guest by category and the cost drivers of these activities. The cost of a one-night stay midweek by a businessman could then be distinguished from the cost of a one-night stay by a teenager at the weekend. Such information could prove invaluable for CPA.

ABC, used with CPA, can assist with **decision making** in a number of ways.

- Provides accurate and reliable cost information
- Establishes a long-run product cost
- Provides data which can be used to evaluate different ways of delivering business.

It is therefore particularly suited to the following types of decision.

- Pricing
- Promoting or discontinuing products or parts of the business
- Redesigning products and developing new products or new ways to do business

BPP
LEARNING MEDIA

5 Business process re-engineering

One of the ways of responding to adverse variances or unacceptable increases in costs is to take a fundamental look at business processes in the context of organisational objectives with a view to minimising expenditure. The aim of business process re-engineering (BPR) is to boost efficiency (get things done more cheaply) as well as effectiveness (get things done better).

Business processes often develop organically over long periods of time out of inventiveness born of necessity and soon become embedded through custom and habit. There is no guarantee that they suit the particular requirements of the organisation.

BPR seeks a radical reappraisal with the business' strategic objectives in mind. Information technology and advanced network and communication systems provide unprecedented opportunities for doing things in a fundamentally different way rather than simply adding ICT to support existing processes.

Figure 8.4   Business process re-engineering cycle

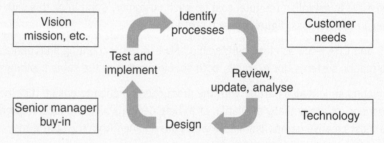

BPR is conceived as a cyclical process, illustrated by Figure 8.4.

The BPR cycle:

- BPR begins is with a **reconsideration** of the strategic vision, mission, tactics and aims of the organisation to ensure that these meet with its aspirations as well as the needs and interests of its customers or clients.

- Each process involved in delivering goods and services to its customers is broken down into its constituent parts such as resources, location, activities, costs and information requirements.

- Redesign of the processes, sometimes eliminating altogether, to maximise effectiveness (quality, speed, value added) and minimise costs. For example, changing the way that invoices are processed may seem small but can lead to a real impact in overall performance.

- The process of analysis has to be carried out at the detailed level as well as at the higher order level to ensure that not only are sub-processes operating well, but that a holistic view is taken of each major process and that these too are designed as well as they can be. ICT is utilised in its capacity to offer new ways of working and collaboration. Wireless communication, networking, home-working, decision-making tools, shared databases, expert systems and continuous auditing could be applied to shift routines in a profound way.

For BPR to work and to have a lasting impact, recognising the importance of business processes has to remain part of the culture of the organisation. It is one of the quadrants of the balanced scorecard because it is widely regarded as critical to business success. The cyclical diagram highlights the significance of maintaining a process of review, improvement and implementation. Even while implementing new and improved processes, existing ones should be under review for further enhancement.

5.1 Principles of BPR

The *Harvard Business Review* published an article by Michael Hammer in 1990 that presented **seven principles of BPR**.

1 Processes should be designed to achieve a desired outcome rather than focusing on existing tasks.

2 Personnel who use the output from a process should perform the process. For example, a company could set up a database of approved suppliers; this would allow personnel who actually require supplies to order them themselves, perhaps using online technology, thereby eliminating the need for a separate purchasing function.

3 Information processing should be included in the work which produces the information. This eliminates the differentiation between information gathering and information processing.

4 Geographically-dispersed resources should be treated as if they are centralised. This allows the benefits of centralisation to be obtained, for example, economies of scale through central negotiation of supply contracts, without losing the benefits of decentralisation, such as flexibility and responsiveness.

5 Parallel activities should be linked rather than integrated. This would involve, for example, co-ordination between teams working on different aspects of a single process.

6 'Doers' should be allowed to be self-managing. The traditional distinction between workers and managers can be abolished: decision aids such as expert systems can be provided where they are required.

7 Information should be captured once at source. Electronic distribution of information makes this possible.

5.2 Re-engineered processes

A re-engineered process has certain **characteristics**.

- Often several jobs are combined into one
- Workers often make decisions
- The steps in the process are performed in a logical order
- Work is performed where it makes most sense
- Checks and controls may be reduced, and quality 'built-in'
- One manager provides a single point of contact
- The advantages of centralised and decentralised operations are combined

BPR has been criticised for following the goal of efficiency and effectiveness by implementing new technology while forgetting the impact on individuals. Quite often the process has led to (or perhaps been an excuse for) reorganisation and redundancies.

However, while this may be a consequence as an organisation strives for improvements, it would require an imbalanced view to ignore the importance of individuals in delivering processes. Sometimes, a labour intensive approach is the most appropriate.

When implementing change, it is always necessary to anticipate resistance and ensure that hearts and minds are won over. Another criticism is that expectations are often too high that following the PBR philosophy will result in immediate and dramatic improvements to the bottom line.

Given the need to frame business processes within strategic objectives coupled with an ongoing cycle of review, BPR cannot be implemented successfully without support from senior management. However, when entered into sensibly with a long-term commitment, it can provide useful insights into potential improvements and savings and add to an organisation's competitiveness.

The Leeds City Council undertook a Business Process Reengineering (BPR) project. Among the areas it looked at were:

Recruitment

The BPR Team identified £3m of projected savings over five years – £2m of which were purely on advertising costs by designing a more efficient way for advertising roles. It also took the 'average time to recruit' figure from 110 days to just 12.

Transforming the Housing Advice Centre

This project took a 'service in crisis' and transformed the experience for customers, involving and developing the staff and laying a solid foundation for closer partnerships between a raft of different agencies dealing with different aspects of homelessness.

The whole team benefited from the experience. [The analysts] spent a lot of time with the staff, and they really appreciated the fact that, stuck away in an old building, people were finally paying them attention. People had come in before and made promises but disappeared, whereas [the analysts] saw it through to the end, and everybody has seen the results.

(Leeds City Council, 2012)

ACTIVITY 8.4

Are any of the routine operations in the marketing function of an organisation you know well formally set out and recorded? Analyse one such process in detail. Ask yourself whether each stage in the process is as effective and as efficient as it can be. What role could technology play in boosting these? Can you quantify (in time or money saved, errors reduced and so on) the scale of the potential improvements?

CHAPTER ROUNDUP

- Budgets are often divided between operational and capital costs – the routine activities (operational) and one off items (capital).

- In many cases budgets have to be negotiated to make the best use of resources which are limited in any organisation – preparation for negotiation and specific negotiation skills are required.

- Cost benefit analysis – looks at the costs of an activity along with the benefits – quantitative and intangible which the activity are expected to bring
  - A CBA helps to justify a budget
  - Tools such as the balanced scorecard and Porter's value chain also help to justify budgets

- Cost-Volume-Profit and break even analysis are important elements of the budget process to demonstrate the returns likely and help with pricing decisions

- Variances from budgets should always be investigated to improve future budgets and to evaluate performance against plan- for marketing, sales and cost variances are the most relevant

- Business process re-engineering – a cyclical process to understand, improve, implement and analyse the processes within the organisation to help control costs

FURTHER READING

Collier, P. (2008) *Accounting for Managers*. 2nd edition. Chichester, John Wiley & Sons.

REFERENCES

[1] Often the R of SMART is given as Realistic, but this is very similar to Achievable, and so Resourced is offered as an important and more helpful alternative.

Collier, P. (2008) *Accounting for Managers*. 2nd edition. Chichester, John Wiley & Sons.

Dibb, S. *et al* (2001) *Marketing Concepts and Strategies*. 4th European edition. New York, Houghton Mifflin.

Drucker, P. (1954) *The Practice of Management*. New York, Harper & Row.

Emmanuel, C. *et al* (1990) *Accounting for Management Control*. 2nd edition. London, Chapman Hall.

Hammer, M. (1990) Reengineering Work: Don't Automate, Obliterate. *Harvard Business Review* Vol.68(4), pp111-118.

Hammer, M. and Champy, J. (1993) *Reengineering the Corporation*. London, Nicholas Brealey Publishing.

Hucyznski, A. and Buchanan, D. (2003) *Organisational Behaviour: An Introductory Text*. London, Prentice Hall.

Kaplan, R.S. and Norton, D. P. (1996) *The Balanced Scorecard: Translating Strategy into Action*. Boston, Harvard Business School Press.

Kotler, P. (2008) *Marketing Management: Analysis, Planning, Implementation and Control*. 13th edition. London, Prentice Hall.

Leeds City Council (2012) Corporate ICT Services. Leeds City Council, www.leeds.gov.uk. [Accessed on 23 April 2012]

Porter, M. (1985) *Competitive Advantage: Creating and Sustaining Superior Performance*. New York, The Free Press.

Rockart, J. (1979) Chief Executives Define Their Own Information Needs. *Harvard Business Review*. Vol 57, (1) pp81–93.

Schroer, J. (1990) Ad Spending: Growing Market Share. *Harvard Business Review* January/February 1990. pp44-48.

Shank, J. K. and Govindarajan V. (1992) Strategic cost management: The value chain perspective. *Journal of Management Accounting Research* (4), pp179-197.

QUICK QUIZ

1   The three steps of a control process, in order, are:

   A   Measure and evaluate actual performance; Set standards or targets; Take corrective action.
   B   Take corrective action; Set standards or targets; Measure and evaluate actual performance.
   C   Set standards or targets; Measure and evaluate actual performance; Take corrective action.
   D   Set standards or targets; Take corrective action; Measure and evaluate actual performance.

2   The difference between planned, budgeted, or standard cost and the actual cost incurred is referred to as a:

   A   Standard
   B   Driver
   C   Ratio
   D   Variance

3   The main purpose of a cost-benefit analysis is to:

   A   Attempt to reduce the cost of an activity
   B   Establish the breakeven point
   C   Establish suitable key performance indicators
   D   Compare costs with benefits to establish the value of an activity or a decision

4   Which one of the following is **not** a valid approach to dealing with intangible benefits of marketing activity?

   A   Reduce associated costs by an estimated value of the benefits
   B   Attempt to calculate a value for the benefits
   C   Ignore the 'too intangible' benefits
   D   Adopt a qualitative approach

5   Contribution per unit is the difference between selling price per unit and variable costs per unit. True/False?

6   If contribution per unit is £5 and fixed costs are £2,500, what is the breakeven point (in units)?

7   Sensitivity analysis aims to:

     A   Ensure marketing material doesn't cause offence

     B   Identify the variables most likely to significantly influence results

     C   Ensure all marketing staff feel valued

     D   Calculate an exact value for intangible benefits

8   What are the four perspectives of a balanced scorecard?

9   Which one of the following is **not** a primary activity in Porter's value chain?

     A   Operations

     B   Marketing and sales

     C   Human resource management

     D   Inbound logistics

10   Which one of the following is **not** a word associated with business process re-engineering?

     A   Radical

     B   Dramatic

     C   Fundamental

     D   Gradual

ACTIVITY DEBRIEFS

Activity 8.1

This will depend upon previous negotiation experiences

Activity 8.2

Possible suggestions include:

- Speed of service
- Quality of food and drink
- Attentive service
- Innovative food
- Special price offers
- Flexible menus

Activity 8.3

This is dependant upon the activity considered

Activity 8.4

This will depend upon the operations carried out by the organisation

1   C   Set standards or targets; Measure and evaluate actual performance; Take corrective action.

2   D   The difference between planned, budgeted, or standard cost and the actual cost incurred is referred to as a variance.

3   D   The main purpose of a cost-benefit analysis is to compare costs with benefits to establish the value of an activity or a decision.

4   A   The three valid approaches to dealing with intangible benefits are shown in options B, C and D.

5   True. Contribution per unit is the difference between selling price per unit and variable costs per unit.

6   500 units (500 units × £5 = £2,500)

7   B   Sensitivity analysis aims to identify the variables most likely to significantly influence results.

8   Customer; financial; internal business; innovation and learning

9   C   Human resource management is a support activity in Porter's value chain.

10   D   Gradual is not a word associated with business process re-engineering.

CHAPTER 9

Variance and monitoring

Introduction

Despite the best efforts when setting budgets they are rarely accurate over the life time of the budget period, therefore it is a requirement to identify and analyse budget variances (that is, results that differ from budget).

Standards of performance and the sources of internal data which can be used to provide the evidence for the variances and forecasts are an important area for marketing managers to understand. These syllabus sections cover this, helping to inform plans to improve performance through cost reductions and marketing activities.

Topic list

Budget variance	1
Evaluating performance of marketing operations	2
Internal sources of data	3
Plans to improve performance	4

3.7	Assess budget variances, identify causes and recommend corrective actions where appropriate:
	■ Internal variance – organisational, impact of marketing strategy, internal constraints, product portfolio, international exchange rates
	■ External variance – the macro environment, customers, competitors, partners, suppliers, external stakeholders
	■ Reconciling variances
3.8	Establish systems to monitor, evaluate and report on the financial performance of marketing operations and associated activities against the delegated budget:
	■ Stated standards of performance, KPIs, qualitative and quantitative standards
	■ Internal sources of data – operating statements, expenditure, profit forecasts, cash flow statements, MIS, MkIS
	■ Actual versus forecast
	■ Plans to improve performance – cost reduction, marketing activities

1 Budget variance

> ▶ **Key term**
>
> **Variance analysis** involves comparing actual results against budgeted or expected figures to evaluate performance and as a basis for managerial action

In practice, there is nearly always a degree of variance between budget and actual results. The budget, after all, is the best-guess forecast, and circumstances are unlikely to run exactly according to plan. We have seen that costs may be controllable or uncontrollable and this applies to variances as well. Variances may arise due to internal or external factors, and it is much more difficult to exercise control over the latter. Nevertheless, controllable or not, variances need to be identified and understood.

Budget variances, whether internal or external, can be grouped under four main headings.

1   Profit variance, where incomes and/or expenses differ from forecast resulting in higher or lower profits.

2   Volume variance, where levels of activity (especially sales or production) are greater or lower than expected.

3   Efficiency (or utilisation) variance, where the usage made of resources to generate activity (staff hours, raw materials, etc) is more or less efficient than planned.

4   Rate variance, where the unit cost or price differs from plan.

Often, they occur in combination as variances in one area impact on others.

The Chartered Institute of Marketing

1.1 Variance analysis

Variance analysis A variance is simply a difference. In the context of budgeting and cost control, the term refers to differences between the planned results (from budgets and forecasts) and actual performance. In its most basic form, variance analysis identifies and expresses the absolute difference as shown in Table 9.1).

A favourable variance (F) is one that is better than expected, namely higher income or lower costs. In Table 9.1, sales income is higher than the budget and the variance is favourable, this is commonly shown as a positive number. An adverse variance (A) is one that is worse than expected, namely lower income or higher costs. In Table 8.5, say the advertising budget is overspent and hence is an adverse or negative variance, this is usually shown in brackets and sometimes referred to as unfavourable.

Variance is sometimes expressed as a percentage of the planned figure, so using the figures in Table 9.1, sales is showing a 17% favourable (or positive) variance and advertising a 29% adverse (or negative) variance.

However, variance analysis really becomes useful when we attempt to break down the difference to understand more clearly what has occurred. This analysis is the first step towards tighter budgetary control.

Table 9.1   Extract of actual results compared with budget and resulting variances

Budget heading	Budget for the year to date £	Actual for the year to date £	Variance £	Adverse (A) or Favourable (F) £
Sales income	11,240	13,182	1,942	F
Advertising costs	2,420	3,111	(691)	A

Rather than making a direct comparison between actual performance and the original budget, variance analysis recognises that actual activity levels (production and sales volumes) will differ from the master budget, and so naturally you would expect revenues and expenditure to be different also.

Before we compare results, we need to do so on a common footing and so the master budget is **flexed**. That is to say, we re-scope the budget on the new assumption of actual activity levels. What would the budget have been if we had expected this level of production or sales? We then compare actual revenues and costs with this flexed budget. This will become clearer by looking at sales and cost variances separately.

1.2 Sales variance

There are two main reasons why the actual sales income may differ from the forecast:

1   Differences in **sales volume**

2   Differences in **sales price**

Sales variance analysis separates out these two components.

In the figures quoted earlier in Table 8.5, imagine that the budget had been prepared on the following basis:

Budgeted sales volume: 2,810 units
Budgeted sales price per unit: £4
Hence, budgeted sales income: £11,240

Let us suppose that analysis of the actual results reveals the following:

Actual sales volume: 3,380 units
Actual sales price per unit: £3.90
Hence, actual sales income: £13,182

When we re-scope the budget, we do so on the basis of actual levels of activity. If we had planned to sell 3,380 units (instead of 2,810) what would the budgeted income have been? The answer is 3,380 at the planned selling price of £4, namely £13,520. This is the flexed budget income.

We are now in a position to separate out two variances from the overall variance, namely:

1   Sales price variance
2   Sales quantity variance

Sales price variance is the variance due to unexpected differences in the selling price and is found by taking the difference between the actual and the planned price and multiplying by the actual number of units sold. In our example:

$$\text{Sales price variance} = (3.90 \times 4.00) \times 3{,}380 = £338 \text{ (A)}$$

It is adverse because we sold each item for 10p less than budgeted. Overall, the actual income (£13,182) is £338 less than the flexed budget income (£13,520).

Sales quantity variance is the variance due to unexpected differences in the volume of sales and is found by taking the difference between the actual and the planned quantity and multiplying by the planned price. In our example:

$$\text{Sales quantity variance} = (3{,}380 - 2{,}810) \times £4.00 = £2{,}280 \text{ (F)}$$

It is favourable because we sold more items than we planned to.

If we add the variances together (treating adverse variances as negative) we find:

Table 9.2

Sales price variance	£338 (A)
Sales quantity variance	£2,280 (F)
Total sales variance	£1,942 (F)

In other words, the total variance that we calculated originally (£1,942) is shown to be a combination of an adverse variance (because we sold products more cheaply than planned), and a positive variance (because we sold more products than we planned). Overall, the additional sales more than compensated for the drop in price.

There are other important elements to the analysis not covered here. In particular, we are interested not just in sales but in profit, and so a consideration of margins is equally significant. The positive sales variance is only an overall benefit if it results in a positive profit variance.

1.3 Cost variance

As we have seen, it is quite easy to measure the total variance of a cost associated with marketing against the budget. Using the figures in Table 9.1, advertising costs were £691 greater than planned.

When considered in conjunction with the favourable sales variance, especially the favourable sales quantity variance, we might be able to identify a causal connection. Certainly, the marketing manager might feel justified in explaining the overspend in such terms.

However, it is harder to carry out the same kind of analysis that we did for sales by attempting to break down the difference between budget and actual into volume and price. There are different approaches that can be made.

The Chartered Institute of Marketing

A common method in the case of production is to **absorb** overheads, such as marketing, into a standard unit cost. This is done on the basis of planned costs for the year being divided in some fashion between the individual units of production, so that we can say the cost of a unit is equal to:

- The direct costs of one unit (materials, labour), *plus*
- A proportion of factory overheads (light, heat, maintenance, depreciation), *plus*
- A proportion of other overheads (administration, accountancy, marketing).

Variance analysis on production costs can then be performed in a similar way to sales variance, namely by flexing the budget to consider what the planned costs would have been had they been based on actual units of production.

We can then analyse the variance on the basis of number of units produced and the costs per unit (overheads and variable). Similar analysis can be done for organisations that provide a service rather than produce products.

This analysis can be unsatisfactory for the marketing manager as it is based on the necessarily arbitrary assumption about how much marketing cost goes into producing one unit, when in fact there is no simple correlation that can be made across the organisation to all products. We spend £100,000 on marketing and make 10,000 units in the factory. On a simple absorption costing basis, each unit carries a £10 cost for marketing. When comparing this standard costing with actual results, the variance of most interest to the marketing manager (overhead variance) simply tells us that marketing was more or less than expected.

Therefore, a more useful approach is to set standard costs for marketing based on an analysis of the sector and past results.

For example, we may employ telesales staff on a part-time basis and we know how many days we want over the year. We can set standards in terms of how many calls would be expected to be made per day from which a given value of sales would be generated. We can then compare actual performance with the standard model, flex the budget and separate out the different variances. Let us illustrate this with an example.

1.3.1 Example

Suppose the budget was prepared on the assumption that the marketing manager would employ 20 days of telesales staff at a daily charge of £220 (ie £4,400). However, the actual costs were £3,900 and this is shown in Table 9.3.

Table 9.3   Extract of a budget variance report

Budget heading	Budget for the year £	Actual for the year £	Variance £	Adverse (A) or Favourable (F) £
Telesales	4,400	3,900	500	F

In the budget, the following standards for telesales were specified:

Cost per day,	£220
Planned number of days over the year,	20
Number of calls per day,	50
Average sales generated per day,	£900

Analysis of the results reveals the following:

Actual cost,	£3,900
Actual days used,	25
Number of calls per day,	45
Average sales generated per day,	£765

The actual daily charge therefore has been £156 (ie £3,900/25).

$$\text{The variance in telesales days} = (\text{actual days used} - \text{planned days used})$$
$$\times \text{planned rate}$$
$$(25 - 20) \times £220$$
$$= 5 \times £220$$
$$= £1,100\,(A)$$

This is an adverse variance as the marketing team used more days than planned.

$$\text{The variance in telesales costs} = (\text{actual rate} - \text{planned rate})$$
$$\times \text{actual days used}$$
$$((3900 / 25) - 220) \times 25$$
$$= £64 \times 25$$
$$= £1,600\,(F)$$

This is a favourable variance as the cost per day is less than planned.

If we add the variances together (treating adverse variances as negative) we find:

Table 9.4

Telesales days variance	1,100 (A)
Telesales costs variance	1,600 (F)
Total telesales variance	£500 (F)

Overall, we have a positive variance of £500. However, when we examine the effectiveness of the telesales we notice that they have made fewer calls per day than planned and have generated fewer sales per day. Even when calculated as average sales generated per call, we find that the plan is £900/50 = £18, while actual performance was £765/45 = £17. So, the telesales staff made fewer calls per day and generated lower sales per call.

This analysis would make clear that although a saving had been made in the overall budget, the results achieved from the spend were disappointing. It seems likely that the telesales staff employed were cheaper because they were less experienced or simply less capable.

This analysis has been carried out to illustrate the importance of revealing a fuller picture than simply the numerical differences between planned and actual spend. Similar analysis could be conducted on variances in advertising, warehousing, mailouts, distribution and so on, depending on the ability to identify a number of different dimensions by which to measure units of input and/or units of output against standard rates.

With this kind of analysis, management is in a better position to understand and therefore controls costs and make cost improvements. It may also reveal that there was something wrong with the budgeting process in the first place or that conditions have changed that have undermined the initial assumptions.

This is still useful as it deepens the understanding of cost behaviour and helps to separate out the controllable and uncontrollable costs.

There are other types of variance which we will study below.

1.4 Internal variance

Internal budget variances normally arise through actions directly under the control of the organisation. These include the decisions it makes about purchasing, staffing, business processes and the promotional mix.

The Chartered Institute of Marketing

1.4.1 Organisational

Internal variances may be analysed according to variances in profit, volume, efficiency and rate.

Internal profit variances

These will occur when the value of sales or of costs varies from the original budget. The other internal variances described in the chapter will impact on profit or it may simply be that the budget was based on false assumptions, and items on the operating statement are different from forecast.

The result is that incomes and costs vary from the original forecast and so impact on profit. Such variances have nothing to do with changes in the external environment but arise through internal decisions.

Internal volume variances

These arise when levels of production or levels of sales differ from planned volumes due to organisational factors rather than features of the market or the economy. A manufacturer may produce more units than had been planned due to higher than expected levels of activity, such as more hours worked in the factory or a larger team of sales operatives employed in the field.

Alternatively, the organisation may shift a smaller volume of goods to its customers due to changes in its process for warehousing and distribution. The introduction (or failure) of technology may also be a factor. Variances in efficiency often result in volume variances. In addition, one-off events may also arise, causing unexpected shut downs and interruptions to production and sales.

Internal efficiency variances

These occur when the organisation is able to derive greater or lesser productivity or sales from its units of input. Staff work rate, machine output rate, time taken for goods to move through particular stages of production and the effectiveness of sales operatives may all contribute to such variances.

Internal rate variances

These will occur when the organisation decides to change its rates of pay or policies on overtime. Alternatively, it may seek new suppliers and accept a different rate on the grounds of the quality or level of service provided. For example, it may pay more for a superior product or else actively seek a cheaper but inferior alternative.

All these variances are within the control of the organisation and to some extent should not be unexpected as they spring from actions taken or from an internal change of circumstance. Nevertheless, they may indicate the need for remedial action. For example, if work rates have fallen there may be a need to review aspects of training, performance management or employee reward schemes.

If changes to systems have had an unexpected impact on the efficiency or effectiveness of processes, it may be necessary to think again (as would be the case with a cyclical approach to business process re-engineering (BPR) – see Chapter 8). With the decision to pay less for raw materials and accept a reduction in quality should come the readiness to accept adverse variances in other areas, as more material may be wasted or more finished products rejected as faulty.

1.4.2 Impact of marketing strategy

Analysts sometimes refer to the net marketing contribution, that is, the impact that marketing has on the organisation, as measured by a combination of sales volume, price and product mix. In other words, it is the difference between net profits as a result of marketing. It is hard to measure unless we are able to attribute sales and income streams to particular marketing activity, and that is the challenge to the marketing director.

The change in net marketing contribution is sometimes expressed as the sum of the volume variance, price variance and product mix variance.

The marketing plan should contain an element of flexibility to enable the marketing manager to respond to variances as they emerge. Within the advertising budget, for example, there could be an amount set aside as a contingency for disappointing sales.

Variances require careful interpretation and it is unlikely that there will be any quick fixes. However, all aspects of the marketing mix may be adjusted if adverse internal budget variances indicate that it is not working as expected.

The KPIs set by the marketing function are a showcase of the intended impact of the marketing strategy. Performance against anticipated financial targets for sales, profit, share premium, return on investment and others will be indicated by the monthly management accounts, and internal budget variances are likely to have a direct effect on them. Additional spend on advertising to alleviate shortfalls in sales will impact on costs and create a variance with the budget unless the amount had been set aside as part of the original plan.

1.4.3 Internal constraints

Although, in general, it is easier to exert control over internal variances than external ones, a number of internal constraints may also impede action. These may include the following.

- **Authorisation levels and internal controls**: Additional spend or the ability to move amounts from one budget heading to another may require approval from a more senior manager and may in some cases be prevented altogether. This is a necessary part of budgetary control, but to enable a marketing manager to respond rapidly to adverse variances a degree of flexibility and trust is required.

- **Resistance to change**: There is always a natural tendency to resist innovation as it can be disruptive and unsettling, even if budget variances indicate that change is necessary. Keeping others informed and involved in the process are useful strategies for countering this resistance.

- **Time**: In responding to budget variances, the marketing manager is already at a disadvantage as the information is based on past activity. Even if a decision is taken rapidly, there will be some delay before it has an impact on performance. This is why it is vital to monitor actual performance against targets very closely on a regular basis. An unfavourable trend over six months may be very hard to redress over the remainder of the year.

- **Resources**: Resources (money, staff hours, equipment and other resources) are usually in limited supply. Taking action to address adverse variances means diverting resources away from planned activity. Care should be taken not to simply create a problem somewhere else.

- **Indecision**: In the midst of an emerging problem, it is not always clear what to do. Adverse variances may be interpreted as the start of a worrying trend or just a blip that will somehow go away. Not knowing what is going to happen next may result in indecisiveness. In our earlier discussions of the role of the manager (Chapters 1 and 8), we noted the importance of decision-making. Not taking a decision is a kind of action unless it is a firm decision to do nothing for the time being it may undermine the effectiveness of management. Managers need to take control over controllable variances.

1.4.4 Product portfolio

The product portfolio, if properly managed, will have a built-in resistance to adverse budget variances. Knowing that the future is inherently uncertain, there is good sense in spreading the risk. The greater the uncertainty the greater the need to invest in a mixed portfolio, selling, as it were, a mix of ice creams and umbrellas to survive in any environment. Market intelligence plays a vital role in this. The following strategies may be used to offset the impact of possible adverse variances:

- Monitoring the market and competitor activity closely

- Applying marketing intelligence in strategic planning

- Understanding the market and customers or clients

- Soliciting continuous customer feedback

- Segmenting the market on the basis of appropriate characteristics and targeting products or services accordingly

The Chartered Institute of Marketing

- Staying mindful of product life cycles and the need to vary the promotional mix at different stages
- Maintaining an active research and development function to keep the product portfolio refreshed and exciting

1.4.5 Marketing communications

There is no one uniform method of deciding what to spend on marketing communications. This is not so surprising. The following are some of the **considerations that can affect the amount of expenditure**.

- What variety of marketing communications is to be used?
- What tasks are to be undertaken?
- How competitive is the market place?
- How well known is the organisation?
- Are there any special requirements?

Costs to be budgeted

- Air time and broadcast media
- Space and printed media
- Production costs
- Staff salaries
- Overheads and expenses

Marketing communication budgets may be very substantial and have a major effect on profitability (depending upon the organisation and the industry they are in). The effectiveness of this spend may be difficult to measure. It is possible is to use normal budgetary control techniques in marketing expenditure, and to review its effectiveness regularly, even if this is only by means of informed judgement.

Figure 9.1   Controlling budget expenditure and measuring effectiveness to understand variances

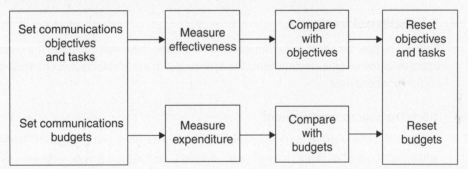

Media evaluation

Launched in 2007, the marketing effectiveness evaluation tool, Marketing Mix Optimisation (MMO), from *Dunnhumby* is designed to help sales and marketing directors, finance directors and chief executives understand the effectiveness of marketing activity.

Based on the actual shopping behaviour of about 13m households (roughly half the population), MMO offers what the firm claims is 'unrivalled statistical robustness'.

Because it uses individual transaction data taken straight from the till, the system produces granular information, down to the level of hourly sales.

The shopper data comes from Tesco, which is such a significant magazine and newspaper retailer that the MMO tool can cross-reference shopper behaviour with their press consumption. But Dunnhumby can also quantify the effect of TV and outdoor advertising, for example, by analysing the behaviour of customers who have been exposed to such campaigns. The tool also tracks relations between pricing and sales.

Martin Hayward, director of strategy and futures at Dunnhumby, said at the launch of the tool: 'This is the beginning of a new wave of analysis that is possible as a result of getting better data. It should spell the end of marketers having to allocate budgets based on the analysis of tiny groups.'

It also ushers in a new era of accountability and transparency for marketers and their agencies, who are under pressure to measure return on investment in marketing activities in the short term.

(Adapted from Simms, 2007)

1.5 External variance

External budget variances arise through actions outside the direct control of the organisation. These include changes in the external environment, the economic climate, demographic changes, new legislation and competitor behaviour.

1.5.1 The macro environment

Budgets and forecasts are framed on the basis of assumptions and guesswork. These will include attempts to anticipate levels of demand, interest rates, inflation, competitor activity, economic viability of suppliers, the price of fuel and international exchange rates.

The organisation has little direct control over such factors and yet its performance could be significantly affected by them. A risk-based approach takes account of the likelihood and impact of things not going as expected, so that suitable contingencies can be put in place.

Even though the costs may be inherently uncontrollable, the variances still need to be investigated and understood to determine whether the planned (or unplanned) remedial actions need to be implemented.

Potential variances arising in the macro environment can be modelled following a PESTEL assessment, as illustrated in the Table 9.5.

Clearly, individual organisations would need to decide for themselves the relevant sources of external variances that could impact on them. The potential external budget variances arising from activity by a range of stakeholders and the possible contingencies that may be used by the marketing manager to offset them is illustrated in Table 9.6.

Itemise all of the internal and external causes of variance that impact on your own marketing budget. Do you have metrics to measure them? How do you control these causes of variances?

Table 9.5   Potential source of budget variances from the external variance

Aspect of the external environment	Potential source of budget variance
Political	■ Strikes in protest of the government action cause delays in production and distribution
Economic	■ New import and export tariffs add to the costs of materials and reduce the competitiveness of sales overseas
	■ The collapse of key organisations results in a supply failure
	■ Increases in fuel prices add to the costs of distribution
	■ Falls in unemployment make specialist staff harder to find and more expensive to engage
Social	■ Changes in fashion renders product or service less desirable and so demand drops
	■ Customer demands for environmentally friendly policies add to the cost of operations
	■ A flu epidemic results in a fall in productivity due to absence of staff
Technological	■ Advances in technology makes it easier for competitors to copy product, eroding its perceived added value and reducing demand
	■ A new computer virus has the potential to destroy customer databases and requires an expensive solution
Environmental	■ Shortages of raw materials such as timber add to production cost
	■ Severe weather causes disruptions to operations and an inability to fulfil client orders on time
Legal	■ New health and safety requirements add to the costs of production
	■ New employment legislation adds to the cost of labour

1.6 Reconciling variances

To reconcile is to bring into agreement. In the case of budget variances, it is not possible to amend actual results so that they agree with the budget for individual items (unless there has been an accounting error), but it may be possible to make changes elsewhere.

What is required is to explain them financially and to seek ways of recovering the position, where possible. We have already described the processes for identifying the cause of variances. It should be possible to account for the difference by detailing what has occurred in comparison with the assumptions in the budget.

Table 9.6   Possible budget variances arising from activities by stakeholders and possible contingencies for mitigating their impact

Stakeholder group	Possible source of external budget variance	Possible contingencies
Customers	Demand for the organisation's product or service changes due to changes in ■ Lifestyle ■ Disposable income ■ Fashion/taste ■ Availability of complementary goods ■ Availability of substitutes	■ Continually refresh the product portfolio ■ Anticipate changes in market conditions (using MkIS) and adjust promotional mix ■ Launch new products as old ones reach end of product life cycle ■ Find new and innovative ways to communicate brand value
Competitors	Demand for competitors' products or services increase due to changes in their ■ Price ■ Distribution ■ Promotion ■ Features ■ Perceived brand value	■ Change own promotional mix ■ Increase share of voice ■ Appeal to customer loyalty through direct marketing
Competitors	Demand for competitors' products or services increase due to changes in their ■ Price ■ Distribution ■ Promotion ■ Features ■ Perceived brand value	■ Change own promotional mix ■ Increase share of voice ■ Appeal to customer loyalty through direct marketing
Suppliers	■ Suppliers may fail to fulfil contracts due to financial failure or may raise prices, causing volume and rate variances	■ Maintain a database of alternative suppliers that are able to satisfy resourcing requirements
External stakeholders	Investors may seek higher returns or withdraw funding altogether, causing liquidity problems and possible fall in share value	■ Communicate strength of financial position to market to bolster confidence and draw upon reserves or alternative sources of finance
Trade unions, the public, the Government	■ Trade unions may encourage industrial action, causing disruption to activity and volume variances ■ Members of the public may take legal action, causing increased costs and profitability variances ■ Government may pass new legislation requiring expensive compliance, causing profitability variances	■ Maintain a contingency fund in the budget for industrial action, legal claims and compliance issues

For example, suppose that the budgeted spend on telesales for the year to date was £2,100 and the accounts reveal an adverse variance of £300. A possible attempt at reconciliation might be produced as follows:

Budgeted telesales = 14 days @ £150 = £2,100

Actual spend = 16 days @ £150 = £2,400

Reason for additional spend: response rates for telesales campaign were lower than expected requiring additional activity to generate target level of sales.

Plans to recover budgetary position: £300 of planned expenditure in PR event has been saved by scaling back the guest list.

In this case, the adverse profit variance of £300 has now been addressed by reducing expenditure in another area.

1.6.1 International exchange rates

International exchange rates were covered earlier; they are relevant however, for organisations trading internationally as they can affect both selling prices and costs so variances from plans need to be recorded.

▶ **Assessment tip**

When reconciling variances quantified figures should always be used with totals included. It is also important to evaluate the variances to consider what actions could have been taken to reduce them (if desirable) and what lessons can be learned and applied to future plans and budgets.

---

2 Evaluating performance of marketing operations

There is a much quoted saying in management circles: if you can't measure it, you can't manage it. This probably overstates the case for having metrics, but it serves to highlight the need for defining your expectations and gauging your successes accordingly and is the direct counter to the much quoted words of Lord Leverhulme (Half the money I spend on advertising is wasted and the problem is I don't know which half!).

2.1 Critical success factors (CSFs) and key performance indicators (KPIs)

The use of **critical success factors (CSFs)** can help to determine the information requirements of an organisation.

2.1.1 Critical success factors (CSFs)

▶ **Key term**

A **critical success factor** is an element of organisational activity that is key or central to the organisation's future success.

Stated in a slightly different way, **critical success factors** are a small number of key **operational areas** vital to the success of an organisation. CSFs are **measured by key performance indicators** (KPI) – which are explained later in this section.

The philosophy behind this approach is that managers should focus on a small number of objectives, and information systems should be focused on providing information to enable managers to monitor these objectives.

Two separate types of critical success factor can be identified.

- **Monitoring** CSFs are important for maintaining business. A monitoring CSF is used to keep abreast of existing activities and operations.

- **Building** CSFs are important for expanding business. A building CSF helps to measure the progress of new initiatives and is more likely to be relevant at senior executive level.

Data sources for CSFs

In general terms Rockart (1979) identifies **four general sources** of CSFs.

- The **industry** that the business is in.

- The **company** itself and its situation within the industry.

- The **environment**, for example consumer trends, the economy, and political factors of the country in which the company operates.

- Areas of corporate activity which currently represent a **cause of concern**, for example, low customer satisfaction ratings.

More specifically, possible internal and external data sources for CSFs include the following.

- **Customer service department**. This department will maintain details of complaints, refunds, customer enquiries and satisfaction ratings.

- **Customers**. If such information isn't routinely collected, a survey of customers should be undertaken to identify (or confirm) areas where satisfaction is high or low.

- **Competitors**. Competitors' operations, pricing structures and publicity should be closely monitored.

- **Accounting system**. The **profitability** of various aspects of the operation is probably a key factor in any review of CSFs.

- **Consultants**. A specialist consultancy might be able to perform a detailed review of the system in order to identify ways of satisfying CSFs.

Determining CSFs

One approach to determining the factors which are critical to success in performing a function or making a decision is as follows.

Step 1   List the organisation's corporate objectives and goals.

Step 2   Determine which factors are critical for accomplishing the objectives.

Step 3   Determine a small number of key performance indicators for each factor.

Table 9.7   Example CSFs which cover both financial and non-financial criteria

Sphere of activity	Critical factors
Marketing	Sales volume
	Market share
	Gross margins
Production	Capacity utilisation
	Quality standards
Logistics	Capacity utilisation
	Level of service

Table 9.8   Example CSFs which relate to specific elements of the marketing mix

Activity	CSF
New product development	Trial rate
	Repurchase rate
Sales programmes	Contribution by region, salesperson
	Controllable margin as percentage of sales
	Number of new accounts
	Travel costs
Advertising programmes	Awareness levels
	Attribute ratings
	Cost levels
Pricing programmes	Price relative to industry average

Activity	CSF
	Price elasticity of demand
Distribution programmes	Number of distributors carrying the product

In Chapter 8 the use of the balanced scorecard was discussed as part of the model for monitoring and control and we identified a series of potential SMART targets that could be used for marketing. These are quantitative measures, in that they can be expressed in numerical form. Some of these may be formally expressed and promoted to internal or external customers in the form of a service level agreement. It is common, for example, to have standards relating to the speed with which queries and complaints will be addressed. Customers know that if they send an email or a letter they can expect a reply within so many working days. Some organisations report to their customers the actual performance against such standards.

2.1.2 Key performance indicators (KPIs)

> **Key term**
>
> **Key performance indicators** are measures that help an organisation determine if it is reaching its performance targets and operational goals. KPIs can be financial and non-financial.

Standards such as those which are communicated to customers can be added to other key performance indicators (KPIs) for gauging the effectiveness of the marketing function. Actual performance can be compared with budget or KPIs as well as with previous years and benchmarks for the sector.

The CMO Council – an US-based peer group of Chief Marketing Officers – has produced a classification of marketing metrics, arranging them under four headings:

1. Business acquisition and demand generation (such as market share)
2. Product innovation and acceptance (such as product adoption rates and customer churn)
3. Corporate image and brand identity (including brand value and customer retention)
4. Corporate vision and leadership (eg share of voice)[1]

The following table takes a series of measures of performance and suggests possible quantitative measures that a marketing manager may use (Table 9.9).

Table 9.9   Possible metrics for marketing

Measure	Possible standard or KPI
Customer satisfaction	85% of customers who respond to a quarterly online survey report that they are pleased or very pleased with the service they received
Rate of new product acceptance	New product is amongst the top ten best sellers by volume in the market within two years of launch
Conversion ratio from enquiry to sale	15% of logged enquiries are converted into a sale within six months
Market share	Market share of product × increases by 5% within six months from a baseline of 32%
Customer retention	88% of customers make a repeat purchase within 12 months
Delivery performance	97% of orders received are fulfilled correctly (no errors) and on time (within 14 days of order being received)
Quality performance	No more than 5% of sales by value are returned by the customer as unsatisfactory
Customer liaison	New catalogue to be dispatched to 100% of customers on the database within three months of publication
Customer complaints	98% of customer complaints are responded to within five working days or fewer
Increases in sales	Sales volumes of product × increase to 1,550 per month within the year from a baseline of 1,230 per month

Measure	Possible standard or KPI
Sponsorships	Income from sponsorships to exceed £150,000 over the year
Return on investment	Growth in profit on sales of product × to exceed 12.5% of the product launch costs
Average purchase per customer	Average annual purchase per customer to increase by 4% from £328
Retention cost per customer	Average retention cost (customer service, invoicing, promotion and so on) per customer falls to below £80 by end of July

In setting targets, it is vital to be sensitive to the needs of the organisation, the product, the market, the suppliers and the customers. For example, it may be inappropriate to set an across-the-board target that sales of all products will grow by 5%.

We know about product life cycles and question mark products (from your earlier studies at the Boston Matrix model). A certain amount of sensitivity and good sense are required.

Qualitative standards are harder to specify and monitor as they are by definition not readily quantifiable. Nevertheless, they can provide valuable insights into the effectiveness of the marketing function. Customer feedback, for example, will reveal important first hand experiences of dealing with the organisation and using the product or service. It is not possible (or appropriate) to respond to every criticism or suggestion but customers are often the best source of innovative ideas.

That is why it is common to maintain consumer panels of one kind or another. It is also worth trying to spot unsolicited feedback, either made directly to the organisation or else appearing elsewhere in blogs, newsletters, articles, reports and so on. Being able to employ someone to scan the media looking for stories may seem like a luxury but it is surprising what this may turn up.

Being qualitative does not mean that you cannot have targets or metrics. Marketing managers should leave room in their KPIs that reflect the wow factor of their products, the personal impact felt by customers of their advertising and the level of desirability attached to the brand.

Table 9.10   Marketing metrics arranged by strategic priorities

Priority for organisation and/or particular product	Appropriate metrics may include:
Penetrating new markets	Speed to market
	Share of voice
	The number of value of strategic alliances
	Rate of new product acceptance
	Conversion ratio from enquiry to sale
Growing market share	Number of customers
	Number of new leads generated
	Share of voice
	Share of distribution
	Increase in sales volume
	Conversion ratio from enquiry to sale
Retaining existing customers	Customer loyalty measured by retention or churn rates
	Customer satisfaction rate
	Customer lifetime value
Growing market value	Price/share premium
	Increase in profits
	Increase in share value

The Chartered Institute of Marketing

An organisation has an objective to fill orders quickly and effectively from stock held, but also not to hold excessive amounts of stock. This has been quantified in the form of a goal, 'to ensure that 95% of orders for goods can be satisfied directly from stock, while minimising total stockholding costs and stock levels'.

Three critical success factors in this situation have been identified as:

- Supplier performance (as if suppliers fill our orders quickly we can hold less stock ourselves)

- Stock records reliability (as we need to be able to rely on stock figures to trigger reorders at the appropriate time)

- Accurate demand forecasting (to enable us to order an appropriate amount of stock in advance)

These CSFs are shown in the table below.

Table 9.11

CSF	KPI
Supplier performance	
Stock records reliability	
Accurate demand forecasting	

Required

Complete the table by identifying appropriate KPIs.

ACTIVITY 9.3

Review the range of metrics used in your marketing function. Are they appropriate for the strategic priorities you are trying to achieve? What changes could be made to provide you with a better dashboard of measures?

3 Internal sources of data

In all cases, care must be taken to ensure that the data required to support the KPI can be readily found. Collecting statistics can be time consuming and expensive and may get in the way of routine operations. It is better to think of innovative ways to exploit the data that is routinely collected and stored.

From previous discussions, we have already noted that most organisations have at their disposal a wealth of internal sources of data, none more so the general Management Information System (MIS) and the Marketing Intelligence System (MkIS).

The **operating statement** fulfils the same role as the trading and profit and loss account (or income statement). It provides details of all incomes earned and expenditure incurred for a given period of time. It is produced annually for the purpose of reporting the results of the year's trading, but more usefully for managers it is common to have internal reports on a quarterly or monthly basis. It is important to distinguish the operating statement from the cash flow statement.

The operating statement is based on the accruals (or matching) principle that aims to match incomes and expenses to the period in which they arise, regardless of when money changes hands. Many sales are made on a credit basis, and for the purpose of the operating statement they are recorded at the point of sale rather than at the moment of payment. The same is true of purchases and other costs. Operating statements often contain details of previous years' performance and budgeted figures at the same point in time (year to date) for comparison.

Expenditure forms part of the operating statement. The ways in which the items are analysed and grouped together will depend entirely upon the needs of the organisation.

Profit forecasts go beyond the actual performance to date and extrapolate figures to the end of the year on the basis that current levels of activity will be sustained. They provide a useful guide about likely outturns and may provide early indication of whether it is going to be a good year or not.

Cash-flow statements show the movement of funds in and out of the business (or segments of it). While the operating statement measures profitability, the cash-flow statement shows liquidity (the availability of funds). Organisations generally need both, at least in the long term.

Management information systems refer to any structured collection, storage and reporting system of operational data specific to the organisation. This may included related or stand alone databases for details on personnel, customers and finances. **Marketing information systems**, as discussed in Chapter 8, take raw data from a range of sources and combine it with some means of analysis based on various models and assumptions. Output is provided in the form of standard or *ad hoc* reports.

A summary of the usefulness of data available from internal sources is shown in Table 9.12.

Table 9.12   Internal information sources to support potential KPIs

Information source	Available data	May be used to support the following KPIs
Operating statement	Actual sales, expenditure and profits for the year to date (may also include historic and budget figures for comparison)	Growth in sales (year to date) Growth in profitability (year to date) Share premium Return on investment (year to date) Average purchase per customer
Expenditure	Actual expenditure for the year to date (may also include historic and budget figures for comparison)	Retention cost per customer
Profit forecasts	Projected figures for income and expenditure to the year end	Return on investment (year end) Growth in profitability (year end)
Cash flow statements	Cash inflows and outflows and net position, usually on a monthly basis	Debtor payment period Creditor payment period Net cash flows
MIS	Personnel records Financial records Customer records	Headcount Customer retention Customer complaints Customer profile
MkIS	Internal data plus market intelligence and competitor analysis	Share of voice Share of market Market share Market penetration

The Chartered Institute of Marketing

3.1 Actual versus forecast

Forecasts, budgets, metrics, targets and KPIs are devised to help control performance through timely decision-making. It is essential that actual results are monitored in comparison with these, and, as we have seen, this is the basis of variance analysis. The outcome of this scrutiny will lead to developing plans for improvements, which is the final section of this chapter.

4 Plans to improve performance

4.1 Cost reduction and marketing activities

The purpose of control and of setting performance targets is to make improvements. Let us suppose that the marketing manager has followed the steps described elsewhere in this and the previous chapter, has produced a budget and supported it with a detailed operational plan and a series of bespoke performance indicators which are routinely monitored. What are the processes needed to respond to variances and prepare a plan for corrective action? This is summarised in Figure 9.2.

First of all, data should always be checked, especially when the variance is unexpected or significant. It is possible that the method of collecting and reporting the figures has failed somehow and something has ended up in the wrong box.

Figure 9.2   Using variances to improve performance.

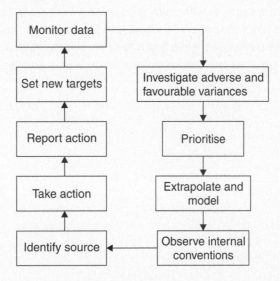

Assuming the data proves to be correct, the marketing manager should be interested in investigating both favourable and adverse variances. It is a common fault to miss the good news and thereby fail to repeat successes.

Depending on the pressures of time and the number of variances under review, it is helpful to prioritise them in some fashion. Uncontrollable items relating to the external environment are still worthy of consideration, even though they cannot be addressed directly, as other mitigating actions may be needed elsewhere to minimise the impact. At the very least, they need to be understood for what they are, rather than making the assumption that it is outside of direct control.

Things to watch out for that may affect the urgency with which a variance is addressed include:

- Unexpected variances – before seeing the variance report, the manager will have a feel for actual performance, and so unexpected variances are more startling and potentially the cause of greatest concern

- Large variances

- Variances that have been occurring for a period of time, especially those that may be increasing over time (it is getting worse more quickly)

- Costs that impact on the value chain

- Completely unbudgeted items – something that is not just different in value from what was expected but not anticipated in the first place

We have seen that internal financial reports may include a column for variance which may be expressed in absolute terms or as a percentage. It is also useful to extrapolate year to date figures to show what will happen if the trend continues (as is shown in profit forecasts, for example). Organisations have their own internal rules for responding to performance reports. They may have preset limits for allowable variances, particularly for budgetary overspends, before formal action is required, in the form of a resubmission for further funds or at least an account of what has occurred and what remedial action is being taken.

Identifying the source of the variance may be difficult. Variance analysis (splitting the total difference between different dimensions such as efficiency, rate and volume) will help isolate the problem, although further detective work is likely. Sometimes, an apparent overspend is simply a timing issue, as the agency invoice was received earlier than expected, say, and will rectify itself over the rest of the year. Here the marketing relies upon their knowledge and expertise in being able to drill down into the problem.

Once it is identified and explained, it is time to consider what action is appropriate. This is where it is useful to understand whether it is a controllable item. It may also be necessary to query the original budget assumptions – perhaps we simply got it wrong, forgot to include the annual renewal fee or something similar.

To make improvements, as with much good management behaviour, it is advisable to involve the members of the team. The closer the owner of the cost is to the cost driver activity, the more chance is that they will be able to exercise control over it in a timely fashion. This is not always true, of course, because sometimes the problem only becomes apparent when information is amalgamated and the overall pattern emerges.

The Chartered Institute of Marketing

CHAPTER ROUNDUP

- Budget variances always exist in practice and can be grouped under four headings – profit, volume, efficiency and rate variance

  - The sum of the volume, price and product mix variances can be called the net marketing contribution

  - Variances occur through uncontrollable external factors – principally from the macro environment

- Setting and communicating standards of performance through critical success factors and key performance indicators are vital to the success of organisations

- When using KPIs data to measure the actual performance has to be available through data available internally

- Continuous improvement (Kaizen) in performance terms is required to reduce costs and improve value created

FURTHER READING

Collier, P. (2008) *Accounting for Managers*. 2nd edition. Chichester, John Wiley & Sons.

REFERENCES

[1]See http://www.cmocouncil.org [Accessed on 15 June 2012]

Rockart, J.F. (1979) Chief executives define their own data needs. *Harvard Business Review*, Mar/Apr79, Vol 57 (2) pp81-93.

Simms, J. (2007) Dunnhumby's media evaluation tool threatens the long view. Marketing, www.marketingmagazine.co.uk [Accessed on 21 June 2012]

QUICK QUIZ

1   The difference between planned, budgeted, or standard cost and the actual cost incurred is referred to as a:

A   Standard
B   Driver
C   Ratio
D   Variance

2   Outline three internal constraints which could impede budget actions

3   Critical success factors and key performance indicators are the same thing.

True
False

Activity 9.1

This will depend upon the context of the organisation; for the external influences it will be dependant upon the environmental set of the organisation.

Activity 9.2

KPIs are likely to be based on measures for the following

Table 9.13

CSF	KPI
Supplier performance	Average order lead time
Stock records reliability	Number of discrepancies found
Accurate demand forecasting	Difference between forecast and actual demand

Activity 9.3

This will depend upon the metrics used in the organisation

QUICK QUIZ ANSWERS

1   D   The difference between planned, budgeted, or standard cost and the actual cost incurred is referred to as a variance.

2   Possible responses are:

- Authorisation levels and internal controls
- Resistance to change
- Time
- Resources
- Indecision

3   False. Critical success factors are a small number of key operational areas vital to the success of an organisation. Key performance indicators measure progress in these areas (so a KPI may indicate how an organisation is performing in an important area or towards a key goal such as a CSF).

The Chartered Institute of Marketing

Section 3:

Senior Examiner's comments

For Section 3, the assessment will require you to make and justify financially sound activities. You are not expected to produce financial accountancy figures, although you may need to use these to produce appropriate management accounting data to include in budgets and variance analysis.

Overall, the assessment for this section requires you to consider the financial implications of the structural and team issues proposed and recommended for Sections 1 and 2. The approaches to budget setting and sources of information available will need to be considered along with appropriate models for measuring the approaches currently used and proposed.

The process by which the operational finances for marketing are determined, justified, negotiated and measured are more appropriate than the actual figures provided, although figures should be appropriate for the context of the organisation considered. A thorough consideration of the costs involved in marketing activities should enable appropriate budgets to be set and justified through cost benefit analysis.

Marketing managers need to be comfortable dealing with quantitative data, financial or otherwise, in addition to qualitative data. The elements of the integrative assessment for this section will require this to be demonstrated through the evaluation and use of appropriate financial concepts.

Within tasks for Section 3, you should be discussing budgets and other financial considerations of the infrastructure and team developments proposed for Sections 1 and 2.

Index

Index

The Chartered Institute of Marketing

The Chartered
Institute of Marketing

The Chartered
Institute of Marketing

The Chartered
Institute of Marketing

Review form

Please help us to ensure that the CIM learning materials we produce remain as accurate and user-friendly as possible. We cannot promise to answer every submission we receive, but we do promise that it will be read and taken into account when we update this Study Text.

Name: _____   Address: _____

_____

_____

1. How have you used this Text?
(Tick one box only)

☐ Self study (book only)

☐ On a course: college_____

☐ Other _____

3. Why did you decide to purchase this Text?
(Tick one box only)

☐ Have used companion Assessment workbook

☐ Have used BPP Texts in the past

☐ Recommendation by friend/colleague

☐ Recommendation by a lecturer at college

☐ Saw advertising in journals

☐ Saw information on BPP website

☐ Other _____

2. During the past six months do you recall seeing/receiving any of the following?
(Tick as many boxes as are relevant)

☐ Our advertisement in *The Marketer*

☐ Our brochure with a letter through the post

☐ Our website www.bpp.com

4. Which (if any) aspects of our advertising do you find useful?
(Tick as many boxes as are relevant)

☐ Prices and publication dates of new editions

☐ Information on product content

☐ Facility to order books off-the-page

☐ None of the above

5. Have you used the companion Assessment Workbook?   Yes ☐   No ☐

6. Have you used the companion Passcards?   Yes ☐   No ☐

7. Your ratings, comments and suggestions would be appreciated on the following areas.

	Very useful	Useful	Not useful
Introductory section (How to use this text, study checklist, etc)	☐	☐	☐
Chapter introductions	☐	☐	☐
Syllabus learning outcomes	☐	☐	☐
Activities	☐	☐	☐
The Real World examples	☐	☐	☐
Quick quizzes	☐		
Quality of explanations			
Index	☐	☐	☐
Structure and presentation	☐	☐	☐

	Excellent	Good	Adequate	Poor
Overall opinion of this Text	☐	☐	☐	☐

8. Do you intend to continue using BPP CIM products?   ☐ Yes   ☐ No

On the reverse of this page is space for you to write your comments about our Study Text. We welcome your feedback.

Please return to: CIM Publishing Manager, BPP Learning Media, FREEPOST, London, W12 8BR.

Managing Marketing

TELL US WHAT YOU THINK

Please note any further comments and suggestions/errors below. For example, was the text accurate, readable, concise, user-friendly and comprehensive?

yes   When you say **"yes"** it means you **agree** to something.
When you say "no" it means you do not agree.
Will you come to my party? You must tell me **yes** or no.
If you say **yes,** I know you will come.

yet   Bill will be here but he has not **yet** come.
Bill will be here but he has not come **up to now.**

It did not rain but there is **yet** a chance of rain.
It did not rain but there is **still** a chance of rain.

Don't eat your dessert **yet.**
Don't eat your dessert **this soon.**

you   Does this pencil belong to **you?**
You are the person I am speaking to.

Mother said, "All of **you** must act nicely."
Mother said, "**Everyone** must act nicely."

young   Mary is too **young** to drink tea.
Mary is **not old** enough to drink tea.
Mary is **young** now but she will grow old.

your   Is that **your** dog?
Does that dog **belong to you?**

you're   **You're** a very pretty girl.
You are a very pretty girl.

Z

Z z

zebra

A **zebra** is an animal that lives in Africa.
A **zebra** has dark and white stripes on its body.
The **zebra** looks like a small striped horse.

zero

Zero means **nothing.**
The teacher put a **zero** on Bill's paper.
All of Bill's answers were wrong.

Father said, "It's almost **zero** outside."
Father said, "It's **very, very cold** outside."

This is a **zero: 0.**

zone

A city is divided into different parts. We call
each part a **zone.**
Sometimes we stand in a **safety zone.**
A **safety zone** is a **place marked off for people to stand.**

*zoo

People catch wild animals and put them in the **zoo.**
We go to the **zoo** to see the animals.